CANADIAN COMMUNICATION THOUGHT: TEN FOUNDATIONAL WRITERS

Canada has a rich heritage of communication thought. For the first time Robert E. Babe assembles in one volume much of this knowledge by introducing and examining the ideas of ten foundational scholars writing in the English language: Graham Spry, Harold Innis, John Grierson, Dallas Smythe, C.B. Macpherson, Irene Spry, George Grant, Gertrude Robinson, Northrop Frye, and Marshall McLuhan. The author presents a survey of their contribution to the field, relates their writings to their biographies and to the Canadian physical and cultural environment, and compares their work to that of foundational American communication scholars. He finds that there is indeed a mode of theorizing that is 'quintessentially Canadian.' Compared with the work of foundational American writers, for instance, the Canadian literature is significantly more dialectical, ontological, holistic, and critical; it emphasizes to a much greater extent the impact of communication on social change; and it is more concerned with mediation and the formation and sustenance of culture and community. The Canadian writers are also much more engaged than their American counterparts with the question of power in communication – with what can generally be regarded as matters of political economy.

Canadian Communication Thought argues that the wisdom of these ten experts is invaluable for understanding important issues of our day, such as globalization, rapid technological change, the erosion of privacy, the diminution of public space, the commodification of information and culture, and the waning of democracy.

ROBERT E. BABE teaches in the Department of Communication, University of Ottawa.

CANADIAN COMMUNICATION THOUGHT

Ten Foundational Writers

Robert E. Babe

UNIVERSITY OF TORONTO PRESS
Toronto Buffalo London

© University of Toronto Press 2000
Toronto Buffalo London
Printed in the U.S.A.

Reprinted 2014

ISBN 0-8020-4098-5 (cloth)
ISBN 0-8020-7949-0 (paper)

Printed on acid-free paper

Canadian Cataloguing in Publication Data

Babe, Robert E., 1943–
  Canadian communication thought : ten foundational writers

  Includes bibliographical reference and index.
  ISBN 0-8020-4098-5 (bound)
  ISBN 0-8020-7949-0 (pbk.)

  1. Communication – Philosophy.   2. Communication –
  Canada.   3. Communication specialists – Canada –
  Biography.   I. Title.

  P92.5.A1B32 2000   302.23′092′271   C00-930165-8

University of Toronto Press acknowledges the financial assistance to its
publishing program of the Canada Council for the Arts and the Ontario
Arts Council.

University of Toronto Press acknowledges the financial support for its
publishing activities of the Government of Canada through the Book
Publishing Industry Development Program (BPIDP).

For Jane Babe, my life's partner;
to Harry M. Trebing, one of the three;
and to Gary Hauch, precious friend.

CONTENTS

ACKNOWLEDGMENTS

During my graduate studies at Michigan State University, I learned from Professor Harry Trebing, renowned public utilities economist and now professor emeritus, that economists can specialize in communication. For many years I followed in Professor Trebing's footsteps, applying economic modes of analysis to communication sectors. Although today my concern is more that of applying communicatory modes of analysis to a broad range of subjects – even to economics – this, too, would have been impossible without Professor Trebing's seminal instruction. With the late Walter Adams and Warren J. Samuels, Harry Trebing is one of the three to whom I remain, as always, indebted and grateful.

Two written pieces in particular germinated this book. First is James Carey's masterful article 'Harold Adams Innis and Marshall McLuhan' (1967). I can remember well the pure joy I experienced years ago reading this essay, which seemed so very true! Also I must acknowledge Arthur Kroker's monograph *Technology and the Canadian Mind: Innis/ McLuhan/Grant* (1984), where I first encountered the Canadian dialectic on technology. In this book I have selected, among others, the three figures profiled by Kroker.

Several people did me the immense courtesy of commenting on at least portions of previous drafts and/or providing me with insights and materials. Gratitude is extended to David A. Babe, Sandra Braman, Hilary Horan, Edward Comor, Frank Cunningham, Gary Evans, Heather Menzies, Vincent Mosco, David Staines, Dwayne Winseck, Margaret Williams, and James Winter. I also thank Gary Evans, the late Irene Spry, the late Kay Macpherson, Art Ferri, and Gertrude Robinson for formal interviews.

Gratitude is expressed also to the University of Ottawa for a six-month leave of absence, during which portions of this manuscript were prepared, and to the fine students in communication at the University of Ottawa who read previous drafts as part of their course materials.

Thanks, too, to my family – for understanding why Christmas vacations were not vacations for me; for nodding understandingly at my penchant for rising in the wee hours; for accommodating me by conversing on Canadian communication thought; and, most of all, for simply being there.

As always any and all deficiencies are those of the author alone.

CANADIAN COMMUNICATION THOUGHT

1

INTRODUCTION

This is a beauty
of dissonance,
this resonance of stony strand …
This is the beauty
of strength
broken by strength
and still strong.
– *The Lonely Land,* A.J.M. Smith

GOALS OF THIS BOOK

Canada has a rich heritage of communication thought. It is time to put much of this erudition together, to see where we stand.

This book has essentially four goals. First, it seeks to introduce and convey the communication thought of ten foundational theorists writing in the English language: Graham Spry, Harold Innis, John Grierson, Dallas Smythe, C.B. Macpherson, Irene Spry, George Grant, Gertrude Robinson, Northrop Frye, and Marshall McLuhan. The reasons for selecting these ten are provided below.

Second, this book relates these writers' communication thought to their biographies. If, as Paulo Freire has suggested, a profuse capacity to communicate characterizes humanness,[1] it is to be expected that an author's communication thought will relate profoundly to his or her biography.

Part of a writer's personal history, of course, is the geographic region where he or she grew up and the location or locations in which the writing was undertaken. Not all the theorists considered here were born or raised in Canada, but all lived in this country during the period in which they were engaged in their mature writings. The third goal of this book, then, is to relate and compare the thought of these ten theorists to discern whether there exists a mode of communication inquiry that might be termed 'quintessentially Canadian,' at least as far as foundational theorizing in the English language is concerned. Finally, the book comments on and critiques the writers' communication thought – 'critiques,' however, less in the sense of levelling criticism, and more with a view to pursuing questions arising from their work, and in particular judging the relevance of their thought to Canada in the new millennium.

MAPPING THE FIELD OF COMMUNICATION STUDY

Canadian communication thought is but a small part of a much larger field of study dating back at least to the early Greeks. Aristotle, for example, analysed rhetoric, the art of pleasing and persuading through speech. Today's interdisciplinary study of communication, likewise, as it engages writers worldwide, deals with skills and techniques of communicating. But it also entails much more. For communication is related intrinsically to culture, to community, and to power. To communicate is *to carry over* a thought, sentiment, perception, theory, order, belief, outlook – or, more generally, *a message* – from one or more persons to another or others. To communicate is *to make common*,[2] either across space or through time. Indeed, these terms – 'space' and 'time' – figure prominently in and help configure the communication literature.

Time and Space
According to U.S. humanities scholar James W. Carey, the space–time distinction is crucial: on the one hand, to conceive communication primarily as the transmittal of messages over space (what Carey calls the 'transmission view') is, in his opinion, to concentrate unduly on the *intent* of message senders and/or on the *effects* of messages on recipients. This approach, in other words, minimizes the role or capacity of communication to form and maintain relationships among groups of people and obscures the capacity of communication to provide continuity for both collective and individual life. Concentrating on the temporal dimension of communication, on the other hand, what Carey

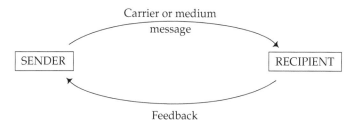

Figure 1.1 Communicating System: Transmission Model

calls 'a ritual view,' links communication with sharing, participation, association, culture, and the 'possession of a common faith.'[3] Let us look more closely at these dichotomous ways of conceiving communication, and as well at controversies within each of these schools concerning their proper scope.

Space: The Transmission View
The transmission view is represented by a *communicating system*, as illustrated in figure 1.1. This view of the communication process was given expression notably by Harold Lasswell in 1948, when he proposed that the essential questions communication researchers must address are:

Who
Says What
In Which Channel
To Whom
With What Effect?[4]

Lasswell's verbal formulation of the scope of the communication studies discipline soon gave rise to Shannon and Weaver's famous diagrammatic model (see figure 1.2).

For communication to take place over space, according to the transmission view, there must be, first, a *sender or information source,* and also a message *recipient* at a different location, that is, a *destination*. These two rather obvious requirements, however, actually serve to limit the domain of communication studies for some. A town clock, for example, being inanimate, is not a 'sender' in the usual sense; neither does there need to be a single, identifiable person responsible for its

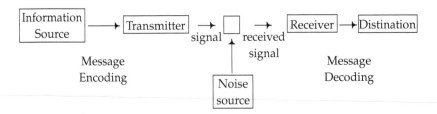

Figure 1.2 Shannon and Weaver Transmission Model

presence. Therefore, some analysts would not consider observing the time as 'communication.' On the other hand, people glancing at the clock certainly are informed; they receive a message (or messages). Further, the clock did not manufacture itself or set itself in place; that is, there must be a human agent or agents who can properly be designated the 'sender.' Theorists taking a more holistic view, therefore, might surmise that the clock was manufactured and positioned with a certain intention by some organization, perhaps (speaking metaphorically) by an economic/political system, making the organization or system, at least figuratively, the sender. Lewis Mumford, for one, was renowned for attributing great communicatory power to clocks, arguing that the Industrial Revolution would have been impossible without them. Mechanical clocks, according to Mumford, synchronize human activity and alter our very conception of time, giving rise to and helping to sustain a mindset concerned with exact measurement.[5]

Communication also entails the encoding of a message or messages (what Shannon and Weaver term a 'signal') onto a *carrier* or *medium*. This means that the carrier, or mode of transmission, is shaped or patterned in some recognizable way. For the electric telegraph, a pattern of dots and dashes is imposed upon an electric current. Likewise, human speech entails the patterning of air through condensations and rarefactions that auditors interpret as 'sound.' Writing entails enscribing patterns onto paper or some other medium by pen and ink, chisel, knife, and so on. Some carriers exist in nature – air and sunlight being examples – and humans fabricate others from materials available to them – paper, clay tablets, telegraph and telephone lines, and so forth. As was the case with message senders, however, so too with media: just what constitutes a medium of communication is subject to some contention. Many of our artefacts, for instance, clothing, housing, food, hair styles (and clocks!), *mediate* human relations, that is, they 'go between' and 'join' communicators, and thereby help structure people's interactions. On the one hand, a police officer's uniform is a message in and of itself; but since that message is ever present as the parties communicate, it constitutes as well an environment or context for their entire conversation, permeating or shaping their interaction, meaning that it can also be thought of as *mediating* their communication. Language, too, is considered by some to be a medium of communication, since, like other media such as paper, it is virtually infinite in its potential for being shaped into specific messages. Moreover, it can also be argued that language constitutes a part of the symbolic environment that, like the physical environment, provides context for (and hence affects the meaning of) all human interaction.

This expansive notion of media and mediation was adopted particularly by Marshall McLuhan, who defined media as any and all extensions of the human mind or body:[6] wheels extend or amplify feet, for example, while clothing and housing extend the skin and the body's heat-control mechanisms. Extensions of the person come between and link people, and hence *mediate* and help shape human interaction. McLuhan further defined a *message* as any 'change of scale or pace or pattern that [a medium] introduces into human affairs.'[7] In other words, different media (different extensions) have different consequences.

Other theorists, however, take a much narrower view, regarding language, for example, not as a medium but as a 'code,' since selections from language still need to be embossed on a physical carrier for purposes of storage or transmission. Different researchers, then, draw different boundaries about what they consider to be communication media. In this book, as McLuhan does, we recognize and deal with expansive conceptions of media and mediation.

For communication, a carrier must be *encoded* (that is, shaped or patterned) with a message at its origin, and *decoded* (interpreted) at the point of reception. Some researchers consider communication to be 'successful' only if the receiving party understands (decodes) the message in the way it was intended by the sender;[8] others, however, presume that there can seldom be an exact correspondence between intention and interpretation, and investigate how and why people of different cultures, subcultures, or backgrounds decode or 'read' messages differently. Some suggest that interpretation is a site of struggle or tension that entails either resistance or acceptance, autonomy or subordination.[9] *Messages* consist of assemblages of *signs* that denote or connote meaning. People sharing a code will be cognizant of the same meanings, by and large, for these signs. Signs may, however, have multiple meanings, and recipients may be cognizant of more than one code. A goal of scientific communication, unlike that, say, of poetry, is to reduce ambiguity – to maintain a coding system of 'one word one meaning.'[10] Moreover, messages may not always be consciously perceived or understood; nonetheless, they may still have consequences for recipients, and this too is subject to communication theorizing.

Finally, all communication occurs within a *context* or contexts. 'Context' in this sense can comprise the physical, emotional, and mental circumstances in which messages are formed, transmitted, or interpreted, including the socio-economic–political circumstances, the mental or emotional state of the sender or recipient, and the history of communication between or among them. Again, much room is open as to how narrowly or broadly researchers define and consider context in analysing communication. In accordance with the previous discussion, moreover, context can also be construed as mediation or milieu. Much depends upon the level of analysis chosen by the researcher.

While virtually all scholars addressing communication recognize that all the aforementioned components must be present and in interaction for communication to take place, different researchers afford different emphases. Some focus on the interplay between senders and recipients; others emphasize how a medium or carrier shapes or biases messages; still others insist that the communicating system must be studied as a whole and in context.

Another important consideration differentiating communication scholars concerns the principle of causation. Some consider causation to be unidirectional; others see it as bidirectional; and still others propose that people possess an ultimate freedom. Researchers intent on discerning 'effects' of messages will tend, for example, to presume that causation flows unidirectionally from a message to a recipient, whereas analysts positing an 'active reader' maintain that recipients in their freedom (or, alternatively, as a result of their particular cultural conditioning) ascribe particular meanings to messages.

Perhaps enough has been said to indicate that substantial, indeed profound, differences in approaches to the study of communication exist, even within a 'transmission view.'

Time: Ritual, Cultural, Evolutionary Views[11]
For writers emphasizing the temporal dimension of communication, the 'communication system' of figure 1.1 is far too static. *Symbolic inter-*

actionists such as Herbert Blumer, R.S. Perinbanayagam, and George Herbert Mead maintain that communication is ongoing, that message senders and recipients have histories which shape their thought patterns, languages, modes of perception, and patterns of message construction. We are all born into ongoing systems of signification (i.e., cultures) in which objects (i.e., 'signs') have designated (that is, culturally agreed upon) meanings. We acquire these meanings as we grow up and live in the culture. The emphasis here, then, is not so much on components of the 'communicating system' interacting, such as was the case with the transmission view, but rather *upon the system itself,* which is ongoing, evolving, and which, in a sense, produces or reproduces its components, including message senders, recipients, and the media used for its own perpetuation and evolution.[12]

Considered broadly, theorists stressing the temporal dimension of communication adhere to one or other of two schools of thought. Some, such as Carey and, at times, Northrop Frye, accentuate the *continuity* that communication can bring: the past speaks to, and in a sense controls, the present. Others such as R.S. Perinbanayagam, George Herbert Mead, and, more generally, postmodernist writers emphasize the dynamic, evolutionary thrust of communication. Signs today do not necessarily mean what they did yesterday; a sign in one temporal context can mean something radically different from what it meant previously. Perinbanayagam argues that, since people can think only with signs, even the self (the 'I') is an assemblage of signs (a 'maxisign'), which is in flux according to the particular components (such as a person's possessions) that make it up at any given moment. Perinbanayagam writes: 'All signs are constituted by earlier signs. An infinite regress is involved here; all the signs that are being used now are begot [*sic*] by earlier signs, which were begot by still earlier signs … The *I* has no origin as such in the body or brain or gene of the individual, but is part of a semiotic chain in which there is a constant emergence.'[13]

From 'constant emergence' it is but a short step to the postmodernist contention that meaning is elusive. British communication scholar Frank Webster, for instance, characterized postmodernism as rejecting the belief that 'reality' exists beyond symbolic representations since (postmodernists maintain) the meaning of all signs changes according to context, which is itself continuously in flux.[14] Marshall McLuhan is sometimes regarded as a forerunner of postmodernism for the very reason that he insisted that the meaning of artefacts ('figures') depends upon their context ('ground').

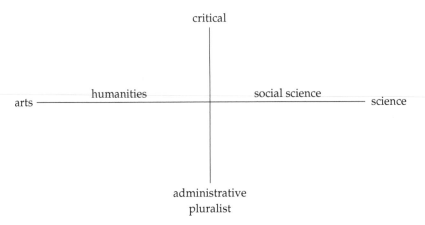

Figure 1.3 Four-Fold Typology of Communication Studies

In any event, for scholars affording serious attention to time as an element of the communication process, a message 'sender' is not a self-sustaining site of message formulation, as is so often implied by the 'transmission view.' Rather, the 'self' is produced by and evolves in accordance with a much grander field of communicative interaction.

FOURFOLD CLASSIFICATION

An alternative to the space–time taxonomy for understanding the scope of and approaches to communication studies is depicted in figure 1.3. Here it is proposed that theories of communication can be distinguished on the bases both of the ontology/epistemology that the theory embodies and the political/economic orientation of the theorist. In figure 1.3, one axis represents a continuum between *Arts* and *Sciences*, with *Humanities* and *Social Sciences* forming intermediate regions. The other axis distinguishes *Critical* from *Administrative* and *Pluralist* thought. Four quadrants, therefore, signify main variants of communication thought and research.

Arts and Science
Epistemology and Ontology
Arts/humanities scholars differ from social science/scientific researchers in epistemological and ontological premises.[15] *Epistemology* con-

cerns the nature of knowledge – how we come to know, and how we can be assured of what we know. One major epistemological divide concerns *universalism versus particularism*.

For example, in setting forth a 'staples'– or resource-based theory of Canadian economic development, Harold Innis was reacting against the purported universality of economic 'laws'; for Innis, social-scientific knowledge is particular to a time or place because people facing different material conditions interpret phenomena differently and act differently.[16] At a fundamentally different level of analysis, political philosopher George Grant likewise maintained that scientific and social-scientific knowledge is inherently particularistic; for Grant, such knowledge is always concerned with only some part or aspect of life. However, philosophic knowledge, by contrast, Grant opined, is universalistic since it pertains to 'the whole of human existence.'[17]

A second hoary epistemological issue concerns *mentalism versus empiricism*. Adherents to mentalism claim that the mind imaginatively or logically constructs knowledge. Empiricists, on the other hand, maintain that external reality *imposes* knowledge upon the perceiver. Sometimes this duality, or dialectic, is referred to as 'subjectivity/ objectivity' or as 'social constructionism versus (in Frye's phrase) "the truth of correspondence."'

Third, there is a continuing debate as to whether knowledge can be attained by studying parts, or whether it is necessary to study complete systems in context (*holism*). Holistic analysts often view those who dissect phenomena into ever-smaller components as being guilty of 'reductionism,' that is, of being oblivious to the synergies and unpredictable interactions that can be comprehended only by taking a larger view.

Ontology refers not to how we know, but, rather, to what there is to know, that is, the nature of existence. Is 'reality' simply a product of the human mind, or does it exist apart from human knowers? Do humans make real choices, or are all actions determined, in principle, by prior causes? To what extent is existence individual, and to what extent is it collective or social? Is ultimate reality material and mechanical, in which case events may well proceed from prior causes, or is it immaterial and mental, in which case events may tend towards final purpose? Or is reality chaotic, in which case the order we think we discern is really a gross simplification, indeed an imposition of our imaginations onto infinite complexity? Ontological positions undergird most thought systems, even when not specifically acknowledged as doing so.

With these remarks in mind, let us now take a closer look at the epistemologies and ontologies in communication studies represented by the continuum between arts and sciences.

Arts

Marshall McLuhan, through his use of puns, aphorisms, metaphors, and other figurative devices; his juxtaposition of seemingly unrelated thoughts; his employing of qualitative analytical techniques such as figure/ground, 'probes,' and 'tetrads'; and his deferring to the authority of the poets and to the methods of literary criticism, was quintessentially an artist as a communication scholar. Implicit in his rhetorical strategies was the supposition that language, or the use of language, helps construct reality. How we describe things, McLuhan maintained, is as important, or more important, than what is described. McLuhan's research and analytical techniques, furthermore, were highly subjective and analogical, and his conclusions testable primarily through introspection and intuition, not through laboratory experiment and observation, pathways associated with science and social science.[18]

In general, the artistic imagination maintains that there is little to be discovered in terms of an objective reality. Inquirers are, instead, thought of as interacting with, and hence helping to construct, the phenomena they investigate,[19] making each statement about existence somewhat personal and unique, or, if shared, then by and large a social convention arrived at by consensus.[20] Hence, Van Gogh's *Starry Night* is both his singular interpretation of a starry night and an invitation to interpret starry nights in a manner similar to Van Gogh. The environment, or world, according to an artistic imagination is infinitely complex, and hence researchers unavoidably impose upon Nature, or create (rather than detect or discover), patterns and structures. Accordingly, knowledge is not deemed to be a correspondence between our thinking and the world; rather, it is *a strategy* to render the ineffable somewhat comprehensible. According to an artistic imagination, reality (if that term is at all apt in this context) is not confined to the merely material but extends to the imaginative. Plato provides philosophic justification for this view: for him, Ultimate Reality consists of Pure Ideas, that is, perfect shapes and forms – forms that we can imagine and towards which we can aspire, even though they are materially unattainable. To the extent that people strive for perfection, however, the imaginative is quite 'real,' and forms a part of everyday existence. Both George Grant and Northrop Frye dwelled at length on different aspects of this ontological question.

By at least the nineteenth century, however, the artistic imagination was superseded in status by science and social science – a condition persisting today. It is useful, therefore, to recount some virtues of the artistic imagination, since these are not always recognized in our scientific/technological society. According to the poet Shelley, for example, '[a] man, to be greatly good, must imagine intensely and comprehensively; he must put himself in the place of another and of many others; the pains and pleasures of his species must become his own. The great instrument of moral good is the imagination.'[21] These remarks do not just affirm poetry; they indict 'objective' science. Science, it is implied, has no empathy and no morality, a deficiency that grows in direct proportion to advancements in technology. Although giving birth to powerful means of doing things, science provides no insight into what should and should not be done, an existential dilemma elaborated on by Grant, Frye, and others.

It is ironic that even as the status of 'objective' science grew in relation to the arts and humanities through the nineteenth and twentieth centuries, science itself has increasingly been understood as partaking of the worldview of artists: Heisenberg's Uncertainty Principle, for example, proposes there can never be total objectivity, that the observer always affects the phenomenon being studied. Likewise, Thomas Kuhn, in a highly influential book, maintained that science is culturally specific, that scientists constitute particular communities which collectively compose and define their realities. Then, as well, eminent philosopher of science Jacob Bronowski proposed that scientific discovery is contingent upon the artistic (analogical) imagination.[22] These real and important qualifications notwithstanding, however, science and arts *do* differ – if not in kind, then at least in degree.

Humanities

Moving along the axis in figure 1.3, one finds the 'Humanities,' which denotes accounts of communication processes that are more rigorous and formal than, for instance, most of McLuhan's work. The 'Humanities' are also more intellectually penetrating than is mere craft instruction. With regard to the study of communication, the 'Humanities' encompass such diverse fields as the philosophy of communication, linguistics, literary criticism, history of media, intellectual history, biography, cultural studies, rhetoric, and semiology (the study of signs). The humanities often account for a much broader cultural context within which communicatory action takes place than does social science, although this is not always the case. Although the humanities lack the empiricism, objectivity, and refutability[23] claimed by science and some social science, they compensate for these deficiencies by their breadth and concern for history.

Social Science

Continuing farther along the axis in figure 1.3, one reaches 'Social Science.' Social scientists treat communication as phenomenal (i.e., observable). Communicatory acts, therefore, are thought to be discrete, measurable, and replicable. Social scientists engaging in communication studies conceive communication theory to be empirically testable. Empiricism in turn often gives rise to *methodological individualism*, whereby individuals, rather than social groupings or relations among or between individuals, constitute the units of analysis.

Exemplary of social science in communication studies is 'effects research.' According to U.S. historian of communication thought Everett Rogers, concern for effects has been 'the dominant focus of communication research' in the United States. Researchers conforming to this tradition explore the consequences for recipients of one-way transmissions. Although perhaps appropriate for certain questions (the relation between television violence and children's behaviour, for instance), the approach, according to Rogers, is 'inconsistent with communication as interrelationships and as processes of mutual influence.'[24]

Science

Communication as 'Science,' the starboard entry on the horizontal axis in figure 1.3, is typified by Shannon and Weaver's 'Mathematical Theory of Communication'[25] or, rather, by extensions and applications of that theory to physics, biology, computer science, and so forth. According to the mathematical theory, information is discrete, measurable, and subject to mathematical laws.[26] On the other hand, as Weaver himself remarked, the mathematical theory cannot account for *meaning* – a serious limitation indeed.[27] Science and social science alike, on account of their purported 'objectivity' and penchant for proposing unidirectional causations, tend to view human communication as conditioned stimulus–response. Interpreting human interaction exclusively through the paradigm of science or social science, therefore, can run the risk of lessening human dignity by marginalizing such notions as freedom, and hence responsibility for one's actions, surely a prerequisite for dignity. It can also lead to an undue emphasis on commandeering the means of power, whereby audiences are viewed by those controlling the means of communication predominantly as objects to which stimuli are applied for purposes of control.

Critical and Administrative/Pluralist Research

The other axis in figure 1.3 distinguishes between 'Critical' and 'Administrative' research. This dichotomy was formulated by Paul Felix Lazarsfeld, a distinguished social scientist and administrative researcher *non pareil,* in a seminal 1941 article.[28] Subsequently, Dallas Smythe and Tran Van Dinh, among others, have elaborated on the distinction.[29] Here I supplement Lazarsfeld's original dichotomy by adding the 'Pluralist' dimension.

Administrative Research

According to Lazarsfeld, administrative research is undertaken on behalf of administrative bodies to achieve well-defined purposes. These may be, for example, to increase sales, to educate, or to heighten understanding of government policies. But, in all instances, Lazarsfeld explained, knowledge or guidance is transferred by the administrative researcher to a message *sender,* who uses a medium for something.[30] Therefore, administrative researchers tend to focus on a standard set of problems: 'Who are the people exposed to the different media? What are their specific preferences? What are the effects of different methods of presentation?'[31] Smythe and Van Dinh concurred, adding: 'By administrative researchable problems we mean how to make an organization's actions more efficient, e.g. how best to advertise a brand of toothpaste, how more profitably to innovate word processors and video display terminals within a corporation, etc.'[32] It is evident that a good deal of present-day communication research is administrative: polling and market surveys, audience ratings, copy testing, focus groups, demographic analyses, motivational research, and so forth, are all of this class.

Critical Research

Lazarsfeld maintained that critical research differs from administrative research in two ways: First, he declared, critical research develops a theory of the prevailing social trends. In this regard, he referred specifically to increases in the concentration of media control and to the proliferation of techniques for manipulating large audiences. Present-day critical scholars, it may be noted, have identified additional, con-comitant trends: for example, increases in the commodification of infor-mation and communication,[33] the globalization of information systems,[34] increasing disparities between the information-rich and information-poor, and a decline in the public sphere.[35]

Second, according to Lazarsfeld, critical research implies 'ideas of basic human values according to which all actual or desired effects should be appraised.'[36] Indeed, it is from this notion of value that the very name 'critical' derives. Critical research is evaluative research, presuming enduring criteria for judging policies, activities, events, hu-man relations, institutions, and so forth, and as well enduring goals towards which we should strive. Critical researchers, Lazarsfeld con-tinued, 'have the idea ever before them that what we need most is to do and think what we consider true and not adjust ourselves to the seem-ingly inescapable.'[37]

One value or criterion for judging communication, then, is truthful-ness in media presentations, a standard, however, that becomes in-creasingly problematic the more one adheres to the notion of the 'active reader.' A second criterion is equity or social justice; equity presumes fairness, not only in accessing information, but also in the opportuni-ties for people to diffuse messages. Critical researchers also tend to favour communicatory practices that promote community, environ-mental health, and peace. Smythe and Van Dinh summarized the focus of critical research in writing: 'By critical researchable problems we mean how to reshape or invent institutions to meet the collective needs of the relevant social community.'[38]

It is a principal finding and conclusion of the present book that all ten theorists featured here as foundational were critical thinkers in Smythe and Van Dinh's sense of the term.

Pluralist Research
Today it makes sense to add the term 'Pluralist' to Lazarsfeld's typol-ogy. This is because much present-day communication research is nei-ther carried out at the specific behest of organizations, nor 'critical' in the sense of presuming, and opposing, enduring disparities in the power of people to communicate. Pluralist research rather *presumes*, at least implicitly, that there are few institutional, cultural, economic, ra-cial, age- or gender-related, occupational, linguistic, geographical, or other impediments to people making their way, the implication being that those not succeeding are 'unworthy.'[39]

A second, somewhat paradoxical meaning of 'pluralism' in light of the first is the notion that society is inexorably divided along demographic lines, implying that there is no *common good*. According to this view, society is made up of many 'special interest groups.'[40] Stuart Ewen has noted that this aspect of pluralism is tantamount to a strategy of divide and conquer.[41]

Yet a further variant of 'pluralism' is the doctrine of the 'active reader,' whereby interpretation of texts is held to be either specific to subcultures, which are seen as being multitudinous, or as unique to each individual in accordance with his or her temperament and life experiences. Accordingly, no generalization as to the meaning of a text is possible, a posture that denies power both to the text and to its disseminator – a serviceable notion indeed for media owners facing criticism over escalating levels of violence in media content and enjoying rising levels in the concentration of media ownership (but not to be emphasized when soliciting business from ad agencies!).

The notion of *consensus* illustrates well the differences between critical and pluralist thought. For 'pluralists,' mainstream media by and large *reflect* or *express* previously formed consensus, as when a media outlet commissions or publishes a 'public opinion' poll; sometimes media also are held to *facilitate* the formation of consensus by providing full and unbiased information on issues. For critical researchers, however, consensus is *a means of social control:* groups with power use media in all forms – advertising, news content, entertainment, 'public service' announcements, phone-in shows, contests, polls, and so forth – to manage opinion formation to further their goals. Critical researchers, therefore, concentrate on how media select, structure, and re-present 'reality' in an effort to form consensus.[42] Among the theorists treated here, the issue is addressed with particular cogency by John Grierson and Dallas Smythe.

Moreover, critical scholars, unlike pluralists, maintain that there is indeed a 'common good,' a healthy environment being an example. Rather than highlighting manifold divisions within society, therefore, critical theorists concentrate on one only – the conflicting interests between the wealthy, powerful minority and the rest.

Furthermore, critical analysts dispute 'postmodernist' contentions that meaning is inherently elusive and in the eyes of beholders, even though they do often acknowledge oppositional as well as dominant 'readings' to texts. This point is explored in more detail later in this chapter.

Pluralism, in the sense of each person being able to make his or her way to the centre if he or she chooses, and in the sense of tolerance of differences, is assuredly the *goal* of critical theorists. It is certainly not their view, however, that pluralism, in these senses, has been achieved, or that it is at all likely to be achieved within the prevailing economic/communicatory order.

TWO MODES OF CRITICAL ANALYSIS

Corresponding to the distinctions made previously between the humanities and the social sciences, we can in fact distinguish two branches of critical communication thought: an arts/humanities-oriented approach, often referred to as *cultural studies,* and a social-sciences orientation, more quantitative in nature, often referred to as *political economy.*[43]

Critical Cultural Studies
Critical cultural studies pays most attention to message encoding and decoding, that is, to the generation and circulation of meanings. Theorists writing within critical cultural studies contend that those controlling media heighten divisions within society by demographically targeting audiences. In addressing distinct groups, dominant interests endeavour to 'speak their language,' often with the intent of *naturalizing,* or making normal, the *dominator's* ideology or interpretation of public affairs. Theorists of critical cultural studies maintain, therefore, that a principal site of domination, and hence of potential struggle, is interpretation. Since most people are situated differently from those in charge of the mass media, any given message in principle can have diverse meanings, including a *dominant reading* that is the interpretation intended by those sending messages, and *subordinate or oppositional readings,* which would be truer to the life situation of message recipients. A report on enormous bank profits, for instance, might have a preferred or intended meaning that the economy is working well and that the banks are highly effective in providing needed services, whereas an oppositional reading could encompass such notions as monopoly control, unduly high fees, unnecessary layoffs, branch closures, low wages, and so forth.

Note, however, the important difference between the pluralist assumption of the 'active reader' and the critical cultural studies position concerning dominant and oppositional readings. Pluralists maintain that a given text or event can have in principle so many interpretations that the text or event itself is intrinsically meaningless – it is merely a stimulus, like a Rorschach test, to be interpreted. Critical cultural studies theorists, on the other hand, contend that, because a text is polysemous, it is a site of struggle as dominant groups endeavour to have their 'preferred' interpretation more widely accepted. Critical cultural studies analysts emphasize further that mass media often do this ideological work by 'entertaining,' that is, by providing enjoyment, as this simultaneously attracts audience attention and masks the deeper purpose of indoctrination. The term *hegemony* is often used to indicate that audience pleasure is a device used for manipulation and control. George Grant and Dallas Smythe were particularly insistent on this point.

Political Economy
Rather than exploring the possible range of meanings of a text and locating particular interpretations within a class or subculture, as do critical cultural studies theorists, political economists see the prime task of researchers as being the investigation of institutional, financial, political, and other pressures that shape message production and distribution in the first place. Why were Saddam Hussein and Manuel Noriega vilified by the Western press, for example, whereas Indonesian dictator Suharto, responsible for genocide in East Timor and mass murder in his own country, went relatively unscathed by mainstream media? For political economists, media's ideological function can be understood only when media are recognized as power sites within the larger political-economic system.

U.S. COMMUNICATION THOUGHT

We turn now to how these two typologies – transmission versus ritual views, and the 'fourfold classification' – are represented in U.S. communication thought. This brief overview of history will serve the additional purpose of distinguishing in their foundations Canadian from U.S. communication thought.

Dewey, Park, Cooley
A number of historians of communication thought propose that the field of communication study in North America was born, or at least was anticipated, during the earliest decades of the twentieth century with the writings of John Dewey, Charles Cooley, and Robert Park.[44]

Those three, often referred to as the 'Chicago School,' were humanist scholars who conceived society as an evolving organism. They viewed the means of communicating (telegraph, telephone, daily press) as ties that bind, or at least that should bind. They qualify as humanists, rather than as social scientists, on account of their penchant for analogical reasoning (society as organism; railways as blood vessels; telegraph and telephone lines as nerves), and because they concerned themselves with such difficult-to-quantify concepts as democracy and community. They were also very much in the idealist and pluralist traditions, as they preferred to speculate on the possibilities of new media enriching individual and community life, as opposed to addressing how media actually developed and functioned in the real world of asymmetric power relations. The Chicago School was encouraged by the possibility that emerging media could educate the public and help create a Great Community. They saw media as a cohesive force, dispensing enlightenment and facilitating dialogue. Through the notion of *instrumentalism*, Dewey seemingly contended that the human condition was bound to improve: technologies, he said, are instruments to solve problems, and as the problems change, so do the instruments. From instrumentalism it can be a short step to a doctrine of inevitable progress through evolving technology. For the Chicago School, moreover, people literally live in a nexus of communication. As Dewey expressed the notion: 'Society not only continues to exist *by* transmission, *by* communication, but it may fairly be said to exist *in* transmission, *in* communication ... Men live in a community in virtue of the things they have in common; and communication is the way in which they come to possess things in common.'[45]

Communities, then, for the Chicago theorists, are not composed of discrete people who merely transmit messages to one another. Rather, communities are defined by the *pattern of relations* among the members. Media of communication 'contain' communities and the individuals who comprise them.

Veblen

A contemporary of Dewey, Park, and Cooley, also for a time at the University of Chicago, was the maverick political economist Thorstein Veblen. Seldom acknowledged in the communication literature as being even a communication theorist, let alone a seminal and foundational figure, Veblen nonetheless was a writer with immense and original communicatory insight, and his thought figures prominently in the writing of the foundational Canadian communication theorist Harold

Innis. In his first book, *The Theory of the Leisure Class*,[46] Veblen detailed communicatory as opposed to utilitarian properties of consumer goods; people intentionally emit messages through their possessions, their hobbies, and their leisure-time pursuits, Veblen proclaimed. From him we learn as well that consumer goods not only *mean* certain things, but also *mediate* human relations. Clothes, modes of transportation, and housing are markers of class distinctions, for instance.

In subsequent books Veblen expounded on 'habits of thought.' He argued that *institutions* (i.e., 'habits of thought') undergird understanding and constitute every culture's (or subculture's) assumptions, or the ground upon which cognition and interpretation take place. If we are used to thinking of things instrumentally, for instance, we will approach nature much differently than if we conceive all elements of the world as being intricately related and interdependent. Veblen maintained also that each stage of societal development is typified by an archetypal system of preconception, socially constructed, that affects resource use and helps determine 'human nature' for that time and place.[47] These thoughts are all replayed in Innis's staples and communication theses, and to some extent in the thought of George Grant, C.B. Macpherson, and Northrop Frye. Veblen's analysis also included the study of technologies as *habits of action*, that is (as Massey lecturer Ursula Franklin put it), 'a *formalized practice*.'[48] Implicit in Veblen's work also is the notion that certain groups, to the extent that they control an important technology or practice, exert control over culture and cultural change; that, too, was a lesson absorbed by Innis, which he recast in terms of media theory.

Empiricism and the Chicago School
The Chicago theorists, however, fell out of favour in the United States in the 1920s and 1930s. The Great War and Great Depression tarnished all thought systems proposing inevitable progress. Moreover, media of communication during those dark decades were used unabashedly for propagandistic purposes and for advertising, not for enlightenment or for creating a Great, Democratic Community, as Dewey had hoped. Indeed, the chief failing of the Chicago theorists, notes communication historian Daniel Czitrom, was their 'refusal to address the reality of social and economic conflict in the present.'[49] While the Chicago School certainly recognized the political *possibilities* of communication technologies as a means to transform industrial society into a Great Community, they ignored the distribution of power – what Innis was to term 'monopolies of knowledge.' They were not, in other words, political economists.

During the 1930s, therefore, there arose a more statistically rigorous and experimental approach to communication study, narrower in focus, and far less optimistic. Leading U.S. communication theorists and practitioners then turned from grand questions of democracy, enlightenment, community, and the common good to more prosaic and testable concerns – persuasion, influence, control, effectiveness, advertising, propaganda, audience and opinion measurement, and so forth. Exponents of this empirical, administrative research included Paul Felix Lazarsfeld, Kurt Lewin, Harold Lasswell, Elmo Roper, Carl Hovland,[50] and, later, Wilbur Schramm. In some respects, then, these 'empiricists' were antithetical to the Chicago School.

But not in all! As noted by Hanno Hardt,[51] the Chicago School actually set the philosophic base of empiricism. Dewey, after all, was the leading exponent of *pragmatism*, the philosophic position which maintains that knowledge has value only if it can be applied. It is apparent that pragmatism, combined with progressivism and instrumentalism, constitutes a philosophic stance quite in accord with an administrative and pluralist orientation. It is therefore misleading to contend, as some have done, that, with regard to U.S. communication research, Dewey was 'the path *not* taken.'[52]

Although there certainly remains a lively humanist tradition, often critical, in U.S. communication research, today few would term this the mainstream. U.S. communication thought, rather, usually aspires to be scientific, 'value-free,' and statistically rigorous, and is often administrative. It is also noteworthy the 'founders' most often identified were empiricists – Lazarsfeld, Lasswell, Hovland, Lewin, Schramm – whereas humanists such as Dewey, Park, and Cooley are considered merely 'forerunners.'[53] Nor are critical theorists such as Adorno and Horkheimer accorded foundational status in U.S. historiographies. In Canada, however, the case is entirely different. One suspects there would be virtually universal assent that in Canadian communication thought three foundational figures were Innis, Smythe, and McLuhan – each in his own way a critical communication theorist. Below we speculate on reasons for these differences in foundations.

CANADA AND COMMUNICATION THOUGHT

Canada as Location

According to the celebrated U.S. sociologist Seymour Lipset, Canada is 'a more class-aware, elitist, law-abiding, statist, collectivity-oriented, and particularistic (group-oriented) society than the United States.'[54]

These fundamental distinctions, Lipset asserted, stem from what to him was 'the defining event' for both countries – namely, the American Revolution.[55] In Lipset's opinion, English Canada exists today because more than two hundred years ago English-speaking peoples in the northern regions of North America rejected the 'liberal,' 'democratic' values of the American Declaration of Independence.[56] (Likewise, according to Lipset, French-speaking Canadians, under the sway of the clergy, rejected the liberal, anti-clerical, democratic sentiments of the French Revolution.)[57] The result, according to Lipset, has been 'a conservative, monarchical, and ecclesiastical society'[58] in the northern half of North America.

Lipset is supported in these sentiments by Harold Innis. In 'Reflections on Russia,' Innis remarked: 'The Canadian has no revolutionary tradition – the influence of the Church in Quebec is that of pre-revolutionary France, the influence of the state in Ontario and in English-speaking provinces is that of the Loyalist – the counter-revolutionary of the American revolution. This is an island of counter-revolution in a world of revolutionary traditions.'[59]

Note likewise the comments of Northrop Frye: 'It would, I think, make for a clearer sense of Canada if we thought of it, not as British North America, but as a country that grew out of a Tory opposition to the Whig victory in the American Revolution, thus forming, in a sense, something complementary to the United States itself.'[60]

Citing Frye, Lipset maintained that a 'culture founded on a revolutionary tradition ... is bound to show very different assumptions and imaginative patterns from those of a culture that rejects or distrusts revolution.'[61] Americans, he suggested, look at governments through the eyes of the rebel; for them, governments are not to be trusted. For Canadians, on the other hand, lacking revolutionary history and zeal, government is less hostile; hence, Canadians have tended to welcome the provisioning by government of a greater range of services.

Not everyone would agree completely with Lipset, of course, particularly with his claim that Canada is more elitist and less democratic than the United States. Slavery did not figure as prominently in Canadian as in American history after all, and disparities in wealth and income even today are much greater in the United States than in Canada – surely a symptom of a gap in U.S. democracy. However, like Canadian political and moral philosopher George Grant, Lipset further proposed that, by retaining roots in an older tradition of British conservatism, Canadians value more highly than do Americans a sense of order and the common good[62] – a point echoed by Gad

Horowitz, who also suggested that Canada's social democratic/welfare state inclinations arose in the twentieth century from a tradition rooted in British Tory conservatism.[63]

To the extent that concern for the collectivity imbues the Canadian imagination more than it does the U.S. equivalent, we could expect leading Canadian economic theorists to be more critical than their U.S. counterparts of markets and the price system – a supposition certainly verified by the case of Innis and such contemporary Canadian economists as Mel Watkins, Ian Parker, and Abraham Rotstein; this is the case because market theory tends to justify individualism and to denigrate the collective provisioning of goods and services. Likewise, following Lipset, it is to be expected that mainstream Canadian communication theorists will show greater affinity to the 'culture as communication' model than their U.S. colleagues, who will be more attracted to the relatively more individualistic 'transmission model.'

Apart from ties to British conservatism, a further explanation for Canadians' greater concern for collectivity and the common good may be found in the geographic and demographic characteristics of the country. The bleakness of the Canadian landscape and the country's inhospitable climate are often said to have been of importance in configuring Canadian thought and the Canadian artistic imagination – from the journals of Susanna Moodie to the canvasses of the Group of Seven, for instance. 'Nature is consistently sinister and menacing in Canadian poetry,' according to Northrop Frye.[64] Whereas Puritans migrating to the Thirteen Colonies described their new homeland in paradisicial terms,[65] Frye remarked, settlers in the northern half of North America developed a 'garrison mentality.'[66]

The image of the garrison – that is, of collocations of settlers huddled in the wilderness for mutual support – helps distinguish Canadian thought generally from the rugged individualism typifying much of the U.S. discourse, whose writers often consider collective enterprise to be inconsistent with individual freedom. In Canada, however, artists and theorists alike have tended to view community and governmental provisioning of services as necessary for individual survival.[67]

The vastness and ruggedness of the landscape have meant other things too, according to Frye: a 'close relation of the people to the land,' for example, rather than an instrumentalist outlook whereby the environment is regarded solely in utilitarian terms. Indeed, he claimed, Canadian art expresses a deep sense of guilt at the 'rape of nature,' and at the 'death of animals.'[68]

Even more fundamentally, Frye averred, the Canadian landscape gave rise to a 'double,' or dialectical, vision: the bleakness of the landscape versus the imaginative purposefulness that people impute to it; the individual's struggle for survival versus the concomitant need for community; frontier versus farmland; wilderness versus metropolis.[69] Whereas the U.S. mythology posed 'a vast society slowly pushing a frontier westward until it reached the Pacific,' in Canada, he noted, spaces between Atlantic and Pacific are largely empty, and emptiness is reflected in Canadian art:

> Like islands lost in a frozen ocean
> The towns of Northern Ontario
> Spread out along an icy coast
> I'm tossed on a snowy sea
> On Highway 17.[70]

For a good number of years, possibly on account of the vastness and unsettled nature of the landscape, it was common to argue that the communication infrastructure is particularly important to Canada, indeed that this is a country existing 'by reason of communication.'[71] Beginning with the building of the Canadian Pacific Railway, there has been an emphasis in the policy literature and in government policy pronouncements that communication technology (railways, radio and television broadcasting, telephones, communication satellites, and most recently the 'information highway') is of vital importance for creating and maintaining Canadian national unity and sovereignty. So important, indeed, was the perceived connection between communication technology and national unity that, according to Frye, 'engineering modes of communication, the fantastically long and expensive railways, bridges and canals'[72] received much greater attention than did creative activity or media content. We return later in this chapter to a major paradox arising from this possibly undue emphasis on technology in the context of Canadian nationhood.

Undoubtedly the landscape has been a factor configuring Canadian communication thought. According to West Coast political analyst and playwright Herschel Hardin, however, the landscape provides but a superficial understanding of the Canadian identity, and to focus exclusively or intensively on that is sheer 'escapist fantasy.'[73] For Hardin, rather, the deeper contradictions concern: (1) French versus English Canada; (2) the regions versus the federal centre; and, most significantly, (3) Canada versus the United States,[74] a tension which, in Hardin's view, is most responsible for spawning in Canada an ethos of *public enterprise*. Hardin put it this way: 'We did not choose public enterprise freely. It was forced on us by American expansionism.'[75]

Canadian philosopher Leslie Armour adopted a similar tack. He contended that Canadian consciousness can best be described as that of a 'dispositional state,' an attitude often unconsciously held but manifested frequently in modes of social organization.[76]

Armour's search through Canadian political history and philosophy led him to propose two major, dialectically related principles as characterizing Canadian consciousness: communitarianism and pluralism. *Communitarianism* is evidenced by, according to Armour, the Canadian penchant for public enterprise – Canadian National Railways, Air Canada, the Canadian Broadcasting Corporation, Ontario Hydro, Hydro-Québec, the Manitoba Telephone System, and so on.[77] *Pluralism* (which Armour defined as tolerance, even celebration, of differences – a somewhat different meaning from that rendered earlier in this chapter) is in this context the dialectical counterpoint of communitarianism. In Armour's view, pluralism (i.e., tolerance) stems particularly from the existence of two founding linguistic groups. Armour remarked further that pluralism without communitarianism degenerates into rugged individualism, whereas communitarianism unmodified by pluralism enfolds people into a single community – a potentially totalitarian condition. It is important, therefore, he stressed, that Canadians endeavour to maintain *a balance*, that is, to retain the dialectic. This notion of balance between undesirable extremes recurs throughout Canadian communication thought.

In Canada, Armour advised, this tension is continually played out through regional loyalties. He wrote: 'Just as it has rarely seemed sensible to Canadians to suppose that the community is a mere aggregate of individuals, so it has never, I think, seemed even conceivable that we might form a single community.'[78]

Pluralism in the sense of respect for minorities is reflected today in multiculturalism as an official federal policy. With regard to multiculturalism the government of Canada declared: 'We believe that cultural pluralism is the very essence of Canadian identity. Every ethnic group has the right to preserve and develop its own culture and values within the Canadian context. To say we have two official languages is not to say we have two official cultures, and no particular culture is more "official" than another. A policy of multiculturalism must be a policy for all Canadians.'[79] Multiculturalism, or the 'Canadian mosaic,' is to be contrasted with the 'melting pot' or the notion of cultural assimilation that many ascribe to the United States. Canada's support of regionalism and multiculturalism, furthermore, implies greater resistance to the homogenizing thrust of advancing technology.

Another theorist who remarked on the pervasiveness of a dialectical cast of mind in Canada has been Concordia University professor Arthur Kroker, who, like Hardin, maintained that this can be explained primarily by the location of Canada at the periphery of the United States.[80] Being marginal to the U.S. economy and culture implies that Canadians have a 'double' or dialectical vision.[81] Canadians have long been cognizant of U.S. discourses, of course, but at the same time recognize that these are not completely their own. Dialectical modes of comprehension, then, according to this interpretation, can be expected to characterize Canadian scholarship.

Kroker endeavoured to document this 'great polarity' in discourse (between, as he put it, 'technology and culture, between economy and landscape')[82] by contrasting the works of George Grant, Marshall McLuhan, and Harold Innis. He maintained that Grant was a technological pessimist who longed for community and continuity in the face of rapid technological change; McLuhan he described as a technological optimist who welcomed the possibilities new media present for collapsing space; and Innis he depicted as a technological realist since he recommended achieving or maintaining *a balance* between undue pessimism and optimism, between older and newer modes of communicating, between the time bias of orality and the space bias of print and newer electronic modes of communication. It is the view presented in this book, however, that the Canadian dialectic on media or technology is much grander and omnipresent than Kroker recognized: that Innis, McLuhan, and Grant were *each* dialectical thinkers, that indeed Grant and McLuhan (like the other theorists treated here) developed and expounded upon variations of Innis's basic time–space dichotomy.

The central place of dialectics in Canadian thought and existence has been well summarized by English professor Robin Mathews:'Canadian identity lives in a process of tension and argument, a conflict of opposites which often stalemate, often are forced to submit to compromise, but which – so far in our history – have not ended in final resolution.'[83] Indeed, so fundamental is dialectic to the Canadian identity, Mathews continued, that, if it were to be broken or resolved, 'the country would be finished in the minds of many Canadians.'[84]

DIALECTICS

What then is the dialectic? As noted by philosopher Henry Giroux, the dialectic 'has an elusive quality.'[85] This is so because the term has been used, with varying meanings, by figures ranging from Plato and Hegel to Mao Tse Tung. Moreover, it has been defined both in purely idealist and in thoroughly materialist terms. As used in this book, the term 'dialectic' means both a mode of understanding and a way of describing human existence in the context of conflicting pressures.

Dialectical concepts and processes entail the clash or tension of opposites, out of which issues either a new synthesis or, at the very least, a balance or equilibrium. Dialectical logic sees contradiction as the primary means whereby higher truths are attained, and judges standard or analytical logic to be unduly static and rigid. When the term is applied to the phenomenal world, dialecticians claim that events, and indeed history, are largely the result of the interaction of contradictory forces.

In addition to proposing tension or struggle between opposing forces, however, according to Giroux, the dialectic comprises also several 'central categories' or characteristic features. One is *the social totality*: dialectics conceives *not* a world in which things, meanings, and relations are removed from human history, but rather one in which everything exists in a context of human action. In other words, there is no room in dialectical thought for fragmented, isolated, and ahistorical analysis. Moreover, social totality presumes that the irreducible unit of analysis is *the relation*, not the thing.

Second, the dialectic emphasizes *mediation*; in other words, it proposes that our experiences are not direct. Giroux writes: 'Social and political forces mediate between ourselves and the larger society; [mediation] ... replaces the myth of the autonomous individual.'[86] This in turn implies that dialectical modes of analysis are inherent, or should be inherent, to communication study inasmuch as communication is concerned with mediation and media.

Third, according to Giroux, dialectics concern *transcendence*, or synthesis, which constitutes a refusal to accept the world as it is. Transcendence implies both a normative (or 'critical') dimension, and a conviction that, from struggle or contradiction, better conditions can emerge. Some, Marx for instance, at times, seemingly have maintained that improvement is bound to happen, but few these days would be so sanguine.

Dialectical analyses are unpalatable to some. For one thing, the dialectic is inconsistent with linear causality as proposed by positivistic science and social science. Dialectics, rather, often propose that causation is bidirectional, implying indeterminacy. There is also a second reason for the unpopularity in certain quarters of dialectics. Dialectics single out *conflict*. Hence the notion of a dialectic can be and has been used as a rationale to support repressive ideologies and social systems.[87] Consider, for instance, the position of pacifist Kenneth Boulding in this regard: 'Dialectical philosophies such as Marxism, Fascism, nationalism, racism, and militarism are those which put a high value on conflicts as such and on "defeating the enemy." Nondialectical philosophies such as Christianity, Buddhism, psychoanalysis, social democracy, and social work emphasize love, empathy, resolution of conflict, the redemption and integration rather than defeat of the enemy.'[88] In some respects Boulding has a point. Certainly one should be careful not to bring about conflict where none exists, and not to exaggerate differences where they do exist. On the other hand, it is important to note that there are indeed significant elements of dialectics in psychoanalysis, Christianity, social work, Buddhism, and social democracy, Boulding's comments notwithstanding. Psychoanalysis, for example, maintains that psychoses arise from *conflicts* within the individual among the ego, id, and superego, as well as from conflicts in how the person relates to the social order; psychoanalysis further contends that a 'resolution' (or synthesis) can be achieved only by becoming aware of these conflicts. Likewise Christianity is immensely dialectical, as, for example, in the injunction 'He who would save his life will lose it, and who would lose his life for my sake will find it'; myriad other examples can be cited: good versus evil; light versus dark; the spirit and the flesh; truth and error.

Not to recognize conflict, tension, and opposition *where they exist* is to misconstrue a situation, and hence, in all likelihood, to perpetrate an injustice. Put positively, 'The dialectic functions so as to help people analyze the world in which they live, to become aware of the constraints that prevent them from changing that world, and, finally, to help them collectively struggle to transform that world.'[89]

It is understandable why pluralistic analyses are favoured over dialectical ones by commentators writing from privileged positions within dominant cultures. Unlike dialectics, pluralism obscures or fails to emphasize asymmetries and divergences of interest. In so far as Canada historically has been marginal to the United States, it also is easy to see why the dialectic is more prevalent in Canadian than in U.S. communication thought.

FURTHER CHARACTERISTICS OF
CANADIAN COMMUNICATION THOUGHT

Ontology

The Canadian preoccupation with connections, with community in the face of a barren land, linguistic duality, climatic adversity, and a powerful neighbour, may have contributed also to relatively greater attention being paid to ontology in Canadian versus U.S. communication studies. Ontology, as we have seen, concerns speculations or beliefs regarding the place of individuals and/or groups within the larger whole.

From a U.S. perspective, according to communication theorist Sandra Braman, researchers typically avoid specifying an ontological stance: although there may well indeed be 'significant ontological and deontological consequences of taking particular positions,' she writes, 'it is not on those grounds that the arguments [in communication theory or policy] are fought.'[90] To raise such issues within U.S. communication discourse could well be considered inappropriate or in bad taste. By contrast, we shall see that Canadian communication theorists place ontological concerns front and centre. Indeed, according to Margaret Atwood, anglophone and francophone Canadians alike have long had as their central concern 'survival' (la survivance),[91] certainly an ontological issue.

Technology and Nation

As remarked previously, communication policy is often driven, or perhaps more accurately is rhetorically 'justified,' by a presumed one-to-one correspondence between the development or deployment of technological means of communicating and national unity. The building of the Canadian Pacific Railway, the formation of the Canadian Broadcasting Corporation, the creation of Telesat Canada and the Canadian Radio-television and Telecommunications Commission, as well as recent policies ranging from claiming and exercising nation-wide federal jurisdiction over telecommunications to information highway initiatives, all have been couched in an assumed accord between national unity and the availability of nationally interconnected communication media. In making such simplistic associations, the Canadian government's policy literature is reminiscent of the idealistic and politically naïve writings of the Chicago School during the first decades of the twentieth century.

Not all Canadian media analysts see things so simplistically, however. Indeed, some have argued that technological endeavours such as the CPR did not and could not create a nation, since *nation* pertains to outlook, to history, to values, and to community. What the CPR did enable, according to Professor Maurice Charland and others sharing his view, was merely the formation of *a state* – that is, the common governance of people living in a defined territory.[92] The opposition or dialectic between governance over space ('state') and community (or 'nation') within time in the context of communication technology figures prominently in the Canadian communication literature, and this theme is explored in several of the chapters that follow. However, irrespective of whether Canada be a nation or a state (or, as Graham Spry would have it, a 'political nation'), a mythology of 'technological nationalism'[93] took hold and continues to receive emphasis in government policy documents,[94] and Canadian communication theorists have often tended to follow suit by casting much greater attention than their U.S. counterparts on the performance of media and on government's media policies.

Carleton University professor Heather Menzies goes even farther than Charland regarding the dialectic raised by the railway. She notes that the CPR historically increased tensions between Western and Central Canada.[95] Similarly, an antithetical case can made with respect to broadcasting. Although the CBC has long had a mandate to foster national unity and to reveal the regions one to another, surely the predominant use of television and associated technologies has been to import U.S. entertainment, advertising, news, and ideology into Canadians' living rooms. Communication technology, then, if anything, is dialectical, and this property of media is strongly reflected in Canadian theorizing.[96]

Communication Thought as Critical

In addition to being dialectical, holistic, and humanities-oriented, and expressing concern for ontological questions, foundational Canadian communication thought is critical in both the cultural studies and the political-economic traditions. Critical theory, we noted above, presumes the existence of enduring principles (an ontological position) whereby phenomena may be judged, and to the extent that equity or equality is one of these guiding principles, the Canadian penchant for political-economic analysis is readily understood.

Foundational Canadian communication writers, although eschewing pluralist assumptions (except in Armour's use of the term), also exhibit an abiding concern for democracy and for freedom. Their writing tends to be quite averse to advertising, and to media motivated primarily by profit. This corpus of thought also exhibits a strong attachment to the maintenance of culture through time in the face of commercial, political, and technological pressures. Moreover, foundational Canadian communication thought emphasizes the importance and the power of the human imagination, and it studies how our imaginations are moulded, or at least influenced, by prevailing institutions, by predominant media of communication, by our stories or myths, by our educational system, and by our place in the world.

Mediation

But, perhaps most significantly, foundational Canadian communication thought focuses on media, or *mediation*. This is part of the Canadian dialectic, and may be attributable in part to the vast empty spaces separating communities. Experience is seldom direct, according to Canadian communication theorists, and almost invariably relations among people are mediated by institutions, by technologies, by philosophies, by stories or myths, by property, by mass media, and so forth. Canadian theorists, furthermore, tend to inquire into who controls the means of mediation, how that control is exercised, and for what (whose) purposes: this emphasis again contributes to the political-economic dimension of Canadian communication thought.

THE CANADIAN THEORISTS

'Perception is the first step in resistance,' writes Heather Menzies.[97] Whereas control or influence over the means of communication is undoubtedly a major source of power, an understanding of factors that bias message production goes a long way towards neutralizing that power and perhaps encouraging resistance. By focusing on mediation and by employing dialectical modes of analysis, the foundational thought of these ten sages proves invaluable for understanding today's issues, and, in the end, perhaps for helping us to resist trends of which few of them would approve. Each writer has much to contribute to Canadian policy discussions on communication. Considered together, despite sometimes large differences in political and ontological understanding, they contribute to, and form, a distinctively Canadian way of understanding communication and communicatory processes.

A discussion of Canadian communication thought must include, and in a real sense begin with, Harold Innis, the pre-eminent University of Toronto economic historian who died at about the time many of the others featured here were coming into prominence. Innis began expressing explicitly his communication thought in the 1940s, and is seminal as a first-generation communication theorist.

However, Innis was actually predated by Graham Spry, who lobbied for public broadcasting in the early 1930s. Spry also outlived Innis by many years, and towards the end of his life was theorizing at a more abstract level on the meaning of communication. Spry, in fact, is a transitional figure in the expression of Canadian communication thought, since he combined scholarship with activism. Prior to Spry, during the nineteenth and early decades of the twentieth centuries, there were in fact a significant number of people devoting attention to Canadian communications – the pre-eminent engineer Sir Sanford Fleming, for instance, who prepared documentation on transcontinental railways, standard time, and public ownership of telegraph systems; and the feisty journalist/parliamentarian William F. Maclean, who wrote and spoke widely on public ownership of telephone systems.[98] These and other writers and speakers did not, however, as did Spry, combine scholarship with their involvement in public affairs. Spry, in contrast, wrote for such periodicals as *Queen's Quarterly* in addition to preparing briefs for Parliament and organizing a lobby group, the Canadian Radio League, making him well suited to represent the starting point for our review of first- and second-generation English-language communication theorists.

Another first-generation theorist is John Grierson – the Scottish-born founder of the National Film Board, who, like Spry, was a both a theoretician and a practitioner/activist, and whose institutional legacy, like that of Spry, persists to our day. Although Grierson's years in Canada were limited, they were eventful. In being brought up in a land marginal to a great power, Grierson shared the Canadian experience, possibly helping to make his thought consistent with that of the others considered here. From the late 1930s to the mid- 1940s, Grierson wrote thoughtful and provocative pieces on the relationship among communication media, education, and democracy.

The final first-generation theorist treated here is Dallas W. Smythe. In 1948, Smythe began teaching the first course anywhere on the political economy of modern (largely electronic) communication media. Few would deny Smythe's status as a foundational communication theorist in what has become a lively political-economic tradition.

Of these four, only Innis had 'disciples' among those we are treating here as representing the 'second generation.' Irene Spry and Marshall McLuhan both were avowed followers of Innis, although in McLuhan's case the differences are as pronounced as the similarities. Northrop Frye and C.B. Macpherson, both internationally acclaimed scholars, were certainly familiar with Innis's work (Macpherson studied under Innis, and Frye endeavoured to edit some of Innis's work), but neither shows direct indebtedness to him, even though, it is argued here, they elaborated variations of Innis's main space–time dialectic – as did all other of the theorists featured in this book.

Some readers may be surprised that C.B. Macpherson is treated here as a pioneer in communication theory. However, as has been too little recognized, that eminent University of Toronto political scientist and philosopher proposed explicitly that property mediates human relations; furthermore, he contended that property is both symbolic (and hence communicatory) and an artefact (and hence a medium of communication in McLuhan's sense).

Similar remarks apply to George Grant, who a decade after his death is still pre-eminent in Canada as a political and moral philosopher. Grant saw 'technology' as a general mediation, in terms of both our thinking and our doing. Unlike Macpherson, Grant also wrote directly about the more narrowly construed definition of media, giving explicit treatment to advertising, propaganda, mass communication, and so on. Those writings aside, however, Grant's discourse on mediation and on societies reproducing their ontologies through their technological extensions qualify him as being a foundational communication theorist.

In this book economic historian Irene Spry represents a bridge between Innis and Macpherson, in terms of both her intellectual output and her biography. She links also, of course, to Graham Spry, and parallels as well the thought of Dallas Smythe. Professor Spry's writings join explicitly the themes of staples (Innis), possessive individualism (Macpherson), private/public property (Macpherson and Graham

Spry), and advertising's impact on society (Smythe). Moreover, she furthers the discussions of the dialectic and ontology in unique ways, since it is only in her chapter (apart from brief reference in the Innis chapter) that indigenous peoples are considered, and particularly the tension between their 'time-biased' way of life and the space bias of the European settlers. Irene Spry also brings this time–space tension originally formulated by Innis into the present through her treatise on the conserver society.

Gertrude Robinson's chapter is also very important for this book. First, it opens up the topic of gender and communication, which is not treated elsewhere (except by personal biography in the case of Irene Spry). Second, her chapter revisits in a new way the issue of anglo-francophone communication by exploring press coverage of the October Crisis and the First Referendum. Consideration of French–English communication alone would warrant her being appraised a foundational writer. Gertrude Robinson was a student of Dallas Smythe at the University of Illinois, and undoubtedly he influenced her thinking, but certainly not to the extent that she should be considered a follower or disciple.

Northrop Frye remains perhaps the most celebrated of Canadian scholars. His thirty-some books point to a prodigious productivity. Hitherto, however, Frye has not been considered by many as being a communication theorist, despite writings focused directly on mass media. In this book, however, it is primarily Frye's thought on myth and social construction that is emphasized, and which, it is argued, should be considered foundational.

The last theorist considered here, Marshall McLuhan, was a contemporary of Frye's at the University of Toronto. For a brief period in the 1960s, McLuhan was probably the most famous intellectual alive, and the 1990s have seen a posthumous resurgence in his influence. No book surveying the foundations of Canadian communication thought would be complete without ample consideration of the writings of Marshall McLuhan.

The scholarship represented by these writers is remarkably diverse – theoretically, politically, and philosophically. Irene Spry was an ardent social democrat. Northrop Frye was a self-described bourgeois liberal even though he presented also collective, communitarian perspectives. George Grant and Harold Innis might best be thought of as 'Red Tories,' although ontologically there is a marked difference between them. Macpherson and Grierson, on the other hand, were 'Red Liberals,' both advancing the cause of individual freedom in the context of communal organization. Marshall McLuhan, in his later years, would seem to be a 'critical liberal-pluralist,' indicating, if anything, that McLuhan was contradictory. Political economist Dallas Smythe espoused a fundamental Marxism. Gertrude Robinson is a feminist scholar who has adopted a more conservative stance than her training in political economy would seem to warrant.

Moreover, these theorists came from an array of disciplines – economics and economic history, political science, literary criticism, theology, political and moral philosophy, and sociology. Consequently they cover both the social sciences and the arts/humanities. So heterogeneous indeed is their range of scholarship that, when commonalties are found (as many are), we must conclude that there indeed has developed or is developing a coherent if not unique mode of communication scholarship we can aptly term *Canadian*.

COMMUNICATION THOUGHT IN QUEBEC

Quebec, of course, provides a significantly different base for the development of communication thought. By its inhabitants, Quebec is often thought of as a 'nation' existing uneasily as part of the larger Canadian 'state.' Considered a 'homeland' for French-speaking peoples in North America, *la Belle Province* is often considered by francophones as more unified than the rest of Canada. This means that political and cultural problems for Quebecers have been and remain significantly different. According to Roger de la Garde, Professor of Communication at Laval University and long-time editor of the francophone journal *Communication*, beginning particularly in the 1950s Quebec intellectuals were intent on modernizing the province to ensure its place in the technologically advancing world. Hitherto, Quebec had been restrained both by the Church and by the ultra-traditionalist provincial government. In pursuing a modernity paradigm, de la Garde writes, Quebec communication researchers often adopted a 'developmental model' similar to that of such U.S. theorists as Ithiel de Sola Pool, Wilbur Schramm, and Lucien Pye; for them, the task in Quebec was less that of nation building and more one of 'development' – a much more 'American' proposition.

De la Garde continues: 'Such a contextualization favoured a definition of "communications" as an "object of scientific inquiry," as a "problematic." It encouraged an academic framework where communications were defined in mechanistic terms and seen as a "professional practice." In other words, communications issues were conceived as some sort of social mechanism that ought to be improved or repaired from time to time.'[99] Writing in the early 1980s, Professor Gaetan Tremblay of the Université du Québec expressed an opinion consistent with that of de la Garde:

> Properly speaking, there does not exist, at the present time, a Québécois theory of communications. [In Québécois] communications studies there are new researchers ... relatively young, and the research work is highly diversified ... You can find there all the major currents of thought active in the communications field in the West, from behaviorism to pragmatism, and including structuralism ... In general, however, communication theory is under-developed in Quebec.[100]

Tremblay next put forward the opinion that, in Quebec as elsewhere, theorizing communication is subject to strong capitalist pressures for internationalization and uniformity.

Not all would agree with de la Garde and Tremblay. Michael Dorland and Arthur Kroker, for example, have written that these pressures to adopt a U.S. frame for theorizing is but one part of a comprehensive dialectic, a dialectic that can be understood in Innisian terms. Referring to Quebec sociologist Marcel Rioux, they write: 'Rioux's Quebec is the tension between *time* (France as the past) and *space* (the future of the United States) in the New World or, what's the same, between Empire and Civilization as Quebec struggles between the possibilities of *popular culture* (rooted in a dialectic of remembrance and creation) and the *power* of technological society.'[101] Nonetheless, as Dorland and Kroker undoubtedly would agree, attenuation within a generation of Catholicism as the locus of Quebec's identity and the concomitant emergence of postmodernism decentring the culture, the unique status in the province of the French language, and the close sense of community, all serve to underscore the fact that communication and thinking about communication is different in Quebec than in the rest of Canada.

Regrettably, further consideration of French-language communication thought per se is beyond the scope of this book, although the dialectic of French–English communication is pursued in chapters devoted to the thought of Graham Spry and Gertrude Robinson. Perhaps patterns detected here among English-language theorists will prove sufficiently evocative to encourage other scholars to compare communication thought in Canada of these two language groups.

GLOBALIZATION

In recent years Canada has been experiencing seismic changes, beginning particularly with the Canada–U.S. Free Trade Agreement of 1988. Accompanying this and other moves towards borderless flows of goods, services, and capital have been the privatization of Crown corporations (including ones in the communication sector); deregulation of industry generally, and of communication industries in particular; dramatic cutbacks to social programs, to government assistance to the cultural industries, to health care, and to education; and a concomitant heightening in the significance of commercial considerations.[102]

One set of explanations for these changes is technological. Emerging communication media particularly, it has been argued, make people less apparently dependent on tight-knit community and expand their vistas to encompass the global community. Another set of explanations, however, of which technological ones can be understood as being subsets, can be understood through the analytical lens of political economy, that is, by considering outworkings of political, economic, and communicatory power – both domestically and internationally. Many of the theorists studied in this volume invoke political economy to aid understanding of communication processes, and, given the dramatic changes that continue apace, the time is now opportune to review the thought of these foundational writers to gain greater insight regarding the changes we are all experiencing.

2

The Communication Thought of
GRAHAM SPRY (1900–1983)

By nature I am compelled to be a reformer. I can always imagine improvements, always scent evils, and very easily hate some wrongly based institution.
– Passion and Conviction, 61

ABOUT GRAHAM SPRY

Graham Spry was exemplary in combining theory and praxis. On the
one hand, he was a historian, political analyst, and communication
theorist; in addition to articles on Canadian communication policy,[1] he
wrote on ancient and Russian history, on India and self-government,
and on francophone–anglophone relations within the Canadian Confederation.[2] This gentle, witty man was also, however, impassioned and
tenacious in pursuing institutional reform through voluntarist politics,
and his legacy continues to be felt in the fields of journalism, broadcasting, and health care. Graham Spry was born at St Thomas, Ontario, on
20 February 1900 to what his wife, Irene, termed a 'genteel' family. His
father, William Bigelow Spry, was a journalist and a high-ranking military officer with an authoritarian disposition. Graham's biographer,
Rose Potvin, reports on a 'schism' between them, and that Graham
'broke away as soon as he could.'[3] He was close to his mother, Ethelyn
Rich, though, and she doted on him, her eldest son.

In England with his parents during the First World War, Graham
Spry enlisted in the armed services shortly after his eighteenth birth-

Portions of this chapter were published as 'Canadian Communication and the Legacy of
Graham Spry' in *Queen's Quarterly* 100/4 (Winter 1993): 989–1004.

day, downcast that even then he was too young for active combat. With the Armistice, Graham returned to Canada, although his family remained in England, and he enrolled at the University of Manitoba, where he became editor of the student newspaper and won the gold medal in history (1922). He attained further journalistic experience as a reporter and editorial writer with the *Manitoba Free Press* (1920–2). A Rhodes Scholar, he earned a second BA in history from Oxford in 1924, and years later (1938) fulfilled Oxford's requirements for the MA.

His initial years at Oxford affected his subsequent life in many ways, but perhaps most importantly they made him aware of his deep love for Canada. Cognizant that all too frequently fine Canadian minds remain abroad, more intent on pursuing personal career ambitions than on contributing to their nation, Spry resolved 'to read everything with a view to application in Canada, [aiming] not to be a typical and good Oxonian, but a typical and better Canadian.'[4]

Back in Canada in 1926, Spry became national secretary of the Association of Canadian Clubs, adding significantly to his influential Canadian contacts. The Canadian Clubs were then experimenting with radio through the broadcast of luncheon speeches, whereby they could reach much larger audiences than could fit into a hotel banquet room.[5] Spry at this time also inaugurated and edited *Independence*, the monthly journal of the League of Nations Society in Canada, serving also on the League's executive.

In 1930, with Alan Plaunt (1904–1941),[6] Spry formed, and until 1936 worked vigorously on behalf of, the Canadian Radio League, a voluntarist association dedicated to establishing public broadcasting in accordance with recommendations of the 1929 Aird royal commission. Spry, Plaunt, and the League maintained that radio broadcasting, while important for certain limited commercial applications, should by no means be primarily a business. Rather, it should be treated as an instrument for cultivating an informed public opinion, for educating, and for entertaining; it should make the home 'not merely a billboard, but a theatre, a concert hall, a club, a public meeting, a school, a university.'[7] Spry admonished: 'Here is a majestic instrument of national unity and national culture. Its potentialities are too great, its influence and significance are too vast, to be left to the petty purposes of selling cakes of soap.'[8] Nowhere, in Spry's view, was the dichotomy between unrestrained private, commercial interest and broader public and national interests more marked than in Canadian broadcasting. As he wrote in 1931, commercial pressure within an unregulated, advertiser-financed broadcasting system leads inexorably to 'stultified educational uses of broadcasting,' to programming 'designed for and serving principally companies desiring to advertise themselves or their products,' to concentration of control in the hands of a few powerful private interests, to malformed and uninformed public opinion, and to an association of Canadian stations 'with the American chains to broadcast American rather than Canadian programmes.'[9] In the early 1930s, Spry coined his famous and oft-repeated aphorism 'It is a choice between the State and the United States'[10] to underline the fact that, in broadcasting (as in so many other matters), Canada as a nation, as a community, as a social organism, cannot survive without government actively coordinating and, in some measure, directing activities.

Much has been written about the voluntary efforts of the Canadian Radio League, and of Graham Spry, in bringing about public broadcasting in Canada.[11] To this day that campaign is considered a 'classic study on the art of lobbying.'[12] The League articulated clear and simple goals, most particularly 'the operation of Canadian broadcasting as a national public service';[13] it recruited members from all walks of life;[14] it studied the prejudices and idiosyncrasies of members of Parliament and of other influential citizens, and took these into account in forming its arguments and making its representations. The League needed just over eighteen months to convince the Conservative government of Prime Minister R.B. Bennett to inaugurate public broadcasting for Canada – despite Bennett's zeal in the depths of the Great Depression to cut back public expenditures in an effort to balance the federal budget! According to broadcast historian Margaret Prang, 'all the evidence suggests that the League's role was a major one, that it did much to prevent the radio issue from becoming a partisan question, and that it forestalled a postponement of the formation of a policy during the exigencies of the depression, a postponement which might have been fatal to the cause of public control.'[15]

In addition to his radio activism, between 1932 and 1934 Spry was also publisher of the *Farmers' Sun*, always a money-losing venture, renaming it *New Commonwealth* to reflect its new alignment with the newly founded social-democratic party, the Cooperative Commonwealth Federation (CCF). In 1935, Spry also purchased, for one dollar, the *Canadian Forum* (founded in 1920), thereby rescuing from bankruptcy that now venerable journal of arts and commentary. The early and mid-1930s also saw him join and become active in the League for Social Reconstruction (LSR), organized in 1931 by Frank Underhill and Frank

Scott as a 'Canadian Fabian Society,' and in this connection he became a contributing editor of *Social Planning for Canada*, published in 1935. As well Spry joined the CCF, was a signatory of the *Regina Manifesto* (1933), and served as vice-chairman of the CCF's Ontario Council. Twice (in 1934 and 1935) he was unsuccessful as a political candidate in the Toronto riding of Broadview. Of the first campaign, the *Mail and Empire* of 22 September 1934 reported: 'Mr. Spry, mounted on a truck, has held as many as a dozen street corner meetings in a single night.'[16] Years later, Spry recounted dryly that he lost both elections to Conservative candidate Tommy Church by 'large and enthusiastic majorities.' Lacking an income, Spry became forced to relinquish some of his voluntarist connections. Branded a radical, by 1936 he was simply unemployable in Canada.[17] Eventually he secured an executive position in England with a U.S. oil company, and thereupon wrote to his fiancée, Irene Biss: 'Here I am, the nationalist, working for Americans and in England. And here am I the socialist serving the biggest of big business. All contrary to my wishes, contrary to my hopes, and accepted by an act of will.'[18]

During the Second World War, still in England, Spry served as personal assistant to Sir Stafford Cripps of the British War Cabinet. He also became a member of the Home Guard, complete with tin hat, gas mask, and rifle.[19] In 1942 he accompanied Cripps on his mission to negotiate independence for India.

In 1948, endeavouring to re-establish formal ties with his native country, Spry became, at Saskatchewan premier Tommy Douglas's behest, agent general for Saskatchewan in Britain. Among other accomplishments, Spry recruited medical personnel to help neutralize the 1962 doctors' strike against the introduction of provincial medicare.

Whether at home or abroad, Graham Spry maintained a keen interest in Canadian public affairs – particularly broadcasting and francophone–anglophone relations. He secured leaves of absence as needed to return home to help influence policy. 'Retiring' in Canada in 1968, Graham Spry continued to lend his energy, engaging personality, and substantial intellect, both individually and through a revitalized Canadian Broadcasting League, to support his beloved CBC, until 24 November 1983, when he died peacefully while asleep at his home in Rockcliffe Park near Ottawa. He had spent the previous evening discussing broadcasting policy with his friend and collaborator Kealy Wilkinson.

Over his lifetime Graham Spry made many close friends, and of these many were extraordinarily influential individuals – Mike Pearson, Tommy Douglas, Frank Scott, King Gordon, Eugene Forsey, Walter

Gordon, Brooke Claxton, and, of course, Irene Biss, whom Graham met in 1933 at a LSR skating party and who was his spouse for forty-five years: 'We had such fun,' she exclaimed in our interview in 1993. Although moving easily in circles of power and wealth, Graham Spry retained an ability to empathize with the less privileged; perhaps his experience of penury and unemployment in the 1930s contributed to that capacity. In his eulogy, Tommy Douglas suggested that, although renowned for contributions to Canadian broadcasting, Graham Spry had achieved even more for the Saskatchewan farmer.

In this chapter we now recount Spry's communication thought as it concerns two related areas: anglophone–francophone relations, and the notion of community.

ANGLOPHONE–FRANCOPHONE RELATIONS

As a child Spry lived for a time in Montreal. As an adult he learned French by listening to recordings.[20] Throughout his adult life he retained a keen interest in the concerns of francophone Canadians, and in writings and speeches he addressed relations between French- and English-speaking peoples within Canadian Confederation. Some of his thoughts appear in notes prepared for two addresses given in England in 1966 and circulated privately to interested parties as a typescript bearing the title 'French Canada and Canadian Federation.'[21] Where not otherwise noted, this is the source document of this section.

According to Graham Spry, the Quebec separatist movement had origins in a traditional theory of nationalism as propagated in former years by the Church in Quebec. The theory maintained

> that as the family is a natural human unit, confirmed by the institution of marriage, so the nation is a natural unit, defined by a language group with a common history in occupation of a particular territory. A nation does not realize itself, thus the thesis runs, and is not a nation until it has been expressed through the institution of an independent State, encompassing within a single government the 'collectivity' of the language group and the territory the language group occupies.

But race and language, Spry continued, are dangerous foundations upon which to build political life: Race, he declared in 1929, is 'like a car left with its engine running; the slightest touch will put it in gear and set it speeding towards some bitter accident.'[22] 'Indeed,' he continued, an 'unqualified emphasis upon racial or linguistic factors ... [was] the right-wing and disastrous theory of nationalism which wracked Europe for at least the last 150 years.'

The opposite of racial and linguistic nationalism, according to Spry, is 'political nationality,' as advanced, for instance, by Lord Acton in 1862. A *political nation*, Spry explained, is 'a "moral and political being," wherein different races [are] embraced within a single state.'[23] Such was the philosophy that formed the Canadian Confederation in 1867, and was understood as such by both French and English leaders at that time. Their goal had been to create a community of two peoples – on the one hand, strong enough 'to resist continentalist pressures from the south,' and, on the other, sufficiently flexible 'to ensure the identity of each of the French and English societies.'

According to Spry, the essence of the Canadian *political nationality* ever since has been the ideal of 'two peoples living not separately but both differently and above all together.' Canada, for Spry, therefore, was 'a test case,' albeit on a modest scale, 'for the concept of a world-wide, multi-racial Commonwealth.'

However, it is precisely this concept that Quebec separatists oppose. Spry declared: 'Thus primitive, European theory [i.e., racially or linguistically based nationhood] threatens the more difficult but richer Canadian theory of "political nationality,"' due primarily to the primitive theory's deep, visceral, and simplistic appeal to emotions.

Quebec nationalism today differs in an important respect from the nationalism of former years. No longer is nationality expressed primarily through a Church intent on maintaining a pastoral way of life; rather, it is expressed through a political party intent on economic growth, trade, and development. Nonetheless, the current spirit of independence, Spry insisted, at a deeper level resonates with the past: the separatist party retains the longings for and attachment to ethnicity and language. Spry, then, proposed a dialectic composed of the racial and linguistic nationalism of Quebec and the political nationalism of Canada.

For Spry, however, the very existence of Canada as a political nation was and remains attributable to the French fact in North America, that is, continuance of that dialectic. Without French colonization of the St Lawrence valley during the fur trade, he stated, the region would have been swept into the American Revolution of 1776.[24] Likewise today: if Quebec were to secede, the 'larger vision of a Canadian nation of two languages and cultures peacefully mastering without bloodshed or hatred a territory as great as the whole of Europe' would be split into three geographic areas. He continued: 'The vision would dissolve, and the federal "political nation" disappear. In the course of time and of increasing economic and communications pressures, the several parts would almost certainly fall, whatever the political terminology, into total subordination to the United States.'[25]

SPRY'S THOUGHT ON INFORMATION AND COMMUNITY

Graham Spry often remarked that 'life is information.'[26] In a 1972 paper prepared for the Royal Society of Canada, 'Culture and Entropy: A Lay View of Broadcasting,' he went some distance in unpacking that three-word sentence.[27] 'Culture' and 'entropy,' he wrote, are opposing terms, the former being an expression for social organization or integration, the latter for disorganization or disintegration. These terms, he continued, although opposed, are joined through the concepts of information and communication.

Culture, according to Spry, *is* information, or at least is the product of information. 'Information is the prime integrating factor creating, nourishing, adjusting and sustaining society.'[28] Spry appears to have used the terms 'culture,' 'community,' and 'society' almost interchangeably, for he defined society as 'a people in communication,' and, citing cyberneticist Norbert Wiener, declared: 'Properly speaking the community extends only so far as there extends an effectual transmission of information.'[29]

The dual concepts of information and communication, for Spry, point to important parallels between the individual organism and society (the social organism). In this regard Spry recalls and updates the writings of the Chicago School. He declared:

> A society, a community, a nation, like any other organism, is a function of a network; society is organized, integrated and made responsive by information. In the human being, the central nervous system including the brain is that most powerful, most complex and highest of all networks of life – a network of 12,000 to 20,000 million neurons. [In a marginal note in 1981, Spry revised this estimate upward to 100 billion neurons.] Each of these cells is, so to speak, a two-way electric and chemical re-broadcasting station, creating by means of its axons, dendrites and synapses, an incalculable total of channels or inter-relationships.[30]

For individual organisms, Spry continued, life depends upon and may be defined in terms of the existence and continued use of the neural communication network; death, conversely, entails the disintegration or non-use of this neural network. Likewise, in society, communal vitality requires reciprocal transmission and reception of messages; social disintegration, the analogue of individual death, results from too much noise, from insufficient feedback (necessary for homeostasis), or from silence (breakdown or non-use of the communication system).

While significant parallels between individual and social organisms can be drawn, Spry averred, there is also an important difference. He explained:

> The wisdom of the community or society, balanced against the wisdom of the body, is elementary, rudimentary, inexperienced and very, very recent ... Whereas the human body, as inherited through the genetic code generation after generation, has millennia of experience as a single, unified system, sensitive and responsive to changes in the internal and external environment, human societies have only very recently developed rudimentary processes of social adjustment and social response.[31]

What, then, Spry asked, permits societies, made up of separate individuals, to attain and maintain organization (i.e., social homeostasis) in the face of entropic pressures inclining them towards social breakdown or social death? His reply: the means of communication, that is, the media. Media, and the individuals or groups controlling media, 'condition' and 'program' societies. Media as the 'central nervous system' of the social organism transmit instructions on how members are to respond to environmental change and regulate in a general way society's relationships with its environment. Society's 'genetic program' – its traditions, languages, laws, customs, institutions, and so forth – are continuously conditioned and modified (mutated) as new information is diffused through its media of communication. The implication is that media can either contribute to the vitality and growth of a society, or can be entropic, inducing disintegration and death.

SPRY'S VISION AND CANADIAN MEDIA TODAY

When Graham Spry set about forming the Canadian Radio League in the early 1930s, the challenge was clear: make room in a crowded and finite radio-frequency spectrum, dominated largely by U.S. commercial stations and networks, for a substantial, non-commercial Canadian presence. To this day the ideal has persisted, but the challenge has grown more severe. Technological trends, commercial pressures, and philosophical/political currents combine to undermine the predominance within Canada of Canadian and of public broadcasting.

In terms of evolving technology, three trends can be highlighted. First is the exponential expansion in transmission capacity: cable systems each year diffuse new packages of specialty (non-broadcast) television services; thousands of movie titles are now available on demand through video stores for playback on VCRs and digital-video-disc (DVD) players; Direct-to-Home satellite-broadcasting systems have been licensed whereby viewers can receive, by means of small and relatively inexpensive dishes, hundreds of television channels; and then, too, of course, there is the prospect of an 'Information Highway.' The spectrum of constraint of the 1930s, in other words, is increasingly a spectrum of abundance.

Second, through satellites particularly, but increasingly also through transoceanic and land-line fibre optics, the world shrinks into the proverbial 'global village.' Information increasingly can be gleaned instantaneously from geographically dispersed sites, while, conversely, programming/instructions are sent worldwide at lightning speed.

These foregoing technological trends combine with a third technological trend, and also with commercial considerations. In the 1930s the medium of communication of most concern to Graham Spry was relatively inexpensive radio broadcasting, which diffused indiscriminately programming to all within the coverage area of a transmitter. Today, radio has been largely superseded by much more expensive video, whose cost characteristics bestow tremendous financial advantage to programmers reaching large, often international audiences. Through cable and through scrambling/descrambling technologies (the third technological trend highlighted here), people increasingly are required to pay directly to access the bulk of the expanded programming fare. For both technological and financial reasons, therefore, electronically distributed information inclusive of all citizens, including particularly the financially underprivileged, is becoming marginalized, raising the prospect of yet further and more pronounced cleavages, domestically and internationally, between the information rich and the poor. As well, technological innovations permit people increasingly to receive and send messages in real time according to communities of interest distinct from and independent of location; *people-in-communication* (Spry's definition of community), therefore, is increasingly less likely to be defined by geographical or political boundaries. Moreover, due in part at least to information's inexhaustible economies of scale,[32] the pronounced tendency is towards heightened concentration of control internationally through formation of transnational informational conglomerates, exacerbating unidirectional flows from central, primarily American, production centres. This became particularly evident, and ominous, during the Persian Gulf War as citizens, political leaders, and news agencies alike relied on essentially a single news source.[33]

Technological and commercial trends in broadcasting and communication correspond to, help reinforce, and are in important respects dependent upon, prevailing ideology or thought systems. Theoretical neoclassical economics, for example, particularly as it emerged from long gestation in the economics department at the University of Chicago, has provided intellectual 'justification' for neoconservative policies – in particular privatization, deregulation, heightened commodification, reduction in social programs, increased user fees, reduced governmental activism, and globalization through deregulated international markets for commodities, capital, and information.

At the very heart of neoclassical ideology and of neoconservative policy, however, has been a conception of information/communication diametrically opposed to the perspective articulated by Graham Spry. One way to appraise the relevance of Spry's thought for the present and the future is to compare his depiction of information/communication with that of its opposite.

Neoclassicists have viewed information as mere commodity (akin to toasters, according to a former chairman of the U.S. Federal Communications Commission), while communication for them is but a variant of commodity exchange. Neoclassical economists George Stigler, Ronald Coase, and Gary Becker each won Nobel prizes in large part for expounding on this theme. Human relations, they have contended, are utilitarian and fleeting: autonomous economic agents come together briefly for trade and then go their separate ways, untouched and untouchable. Society is merely the summation of individuals, not an entity distinct in itself. For Gary Becker, social phenomena seemingly as diverse as marriage, family planning, racial discrimination, crime, divorce, drug addiction, politics, and suicide can be understood adequately through the principles and concepts of neoclassical economics (price, cost, individual utility maximization, supply, demand) – in brief, in terms of what Harold Innis described and warned of in his classic 1938 essay, 'The Penetrative Powers of the Price System.'

But, refusal to acknowledge, let alone highlight, society as a social organism and as an entity comprising groups and individuals in dynamic interaction, transforming one another and the social whole through informational exchanges, Spry would say, will inevitably result in entropy or social breakdown. Applying Spry's analysis, we could say that U.S. cities have long been experiencing entropy on account of the price system's penetrative powers. Those lacking money, that is, the means to communicate, in a society premised on the ubiquity of commodity exchange are precluded from meaningful participation in social affairs, leaving available only other, destructive modes for articulating their plight – riots, blockades, theft, vandalism, or, as the alternative, silence. For the affluent, too, although they are not likewise deprived of material comforts and delights, the price system can be erosive of hitherto permanent and deep-felt connections, commodifying one's sense of nation, of community, and of self.

For Spry, however, human relations are not, and should never be allowed to become, mere commodity-exchange relations. For him, rather, people influence and transform one another in unpredictable ways, and are as well components of, and participants in, an evolving social whole. Furthermore, Graham Spry feared that, in Canada, the commercial, commodified view of information/communication was achieving such ascendancy that his country could wither and be swallowed up in what today we might call the transnationalized, commercialized New World Order.

'What is the information upon which the Canadian society takes its decisions; who controls its selection and its distribution; and for whose purposes?' Spry asked. For advocates of information-as-commodity-alone, questions such as these cannot even be raised; they lie quite beyond the pale of thought. And hence, the immense utility of neoclassicism for the agencies of global commercialization and transnationalization.

In 1972 Graham Spry declared:

What we have today is a large measure of concentrated control over more and more of this great national instrument of stations and cable systems – a one-way node for distributing information and influencing public opinion by business and commercial interests. They are a part of the Canadian community but a conflict of interest is inevitable between using revenues for Canadian programming and using them to increase profits and push up quotations on the stock market ... In terms of Canadian purposes, strategy and Canadian reception of Canadian entertainment, education and information in the home, the trend seems to be irresistibly towards running down, disorganization, randomness, that is towards entropy.[34]

'Irresistible' this trend may indeed appear to be – and this from the person who persevered to help inaugurate Canadian public broadcasting against truly formidable odds! As we enter the new millennium, neoclassicism and neoconservatism seem more entrenched than ever. In addition, the commercial and technological trends described above remain and gather momentum. Given such ample cause for despair, note that it was also Graham Spry who admonished that '"Nothing is here for tears, nothing to moan." What the situation now commands is an urgent and renewed sense of the prime and essential purposes, ... a fresh and wise use of imagination and, above all will, will, will, the determination to achieve these purposes.'[35]

3

The Communication Thought of
HAROLD ADAMS INNIS (1894–1952)

Improvements in communication ... make for increased difficulties of understanding.

– The Bias of Communication, 28

ABOUT HAROLD INNIS

Harold Adams Innis was born near Otterville, a small farming community in southwestern Ontario, on 5 November 1894. His mother, Mary,
devoutly Baptist, named him 'Herald,' anticipating a life in the ministry
for her infant son. Although as an adult Innis became an agnostic,[1] he
retained lifelong both an interest in religion[2] and (according to his
colleague, friend, and biographer, historian Donald Creighton) many
aspects of his childhood faith: 'a strict sense of values and the feeling
of devotion to a cause,' for example; also a belief in the intrinsic worth
of the individual, and a distrust of hierarchies, organizations, and
pretentions.[3] In his maturity, Innis developed a 'Christian' or apocalyptic view of the future. Seemingly, then, it is not too much to suggest that
his early spiritual indoctrination and rustic beginnings had much to do
with his later engrossment in monopolies of knowledge, the oral dialectic, and centre–periphery relations.

Although his mother had attended college,[4] books and other reading
materials (apart from the Bible and the *Family Herald)* were scarce in the
Innis farmhouse. But nature was a wonderful teacher, and the youthful
Innis could tell at a glance the particular tree from which a hickory nut
had fallen, and identify by taste the source of a bucket of maple sap.[5]

For primary-level education, he attended a one-room school in

Otterville, a circumstance not without advantage: 'Specialization was avoided,' he confided to his diary, 'and the student given the best opportunity for rapid promotion.' After graduating from high school in 1912, he enrolled at McMaster, at the time a Baptist university located in Toronto, to major in history and political economy. There he encountered philosophy professor James Ten Broecke, who used to ask, 'Why do we attend to the things to which we attend?' – a question that Innis pondered for the rest of his life, and for which he formulated answers.[6]

Receiving his BA in 1916, Innis next enlisted in the armed services. Although religious zeal was instrumental in his reaching that decision,[7] the appalling slaughter encountered first-hand as a result undermined his faith and his naïve idealism alike. Innis became, by his own account, 'a psychological casualty.' Injured at Vimy Ridge in July 1917, he used his recuperation time to complete McMaster's requirements for the MA. His thesis was titled 'The Returned Soldier.'

Next he embarked on a doctoral program in political economy at the University of Chicago, where he encountered Professor Frank Knight, whose scepticism knew no bounds.[8] Also significant influences on him were C.W. Wright, who suggested a history of the Canadian Pacific Railway as a dissertation topic; sociologist Robert Park, a founder of the 'Chicago School' of sociology and pioneer in communication thought, who emphasized not only the bidirectional nature of interactions between culture and technology, a theme that Innis took to heart, but as well the notion that people inhabit both material and symbolic environments;[9] and Professor J.M. Clark, who emphasized the importance of overhead costs and encouraged students to invert standard economic doctrines as a way of testing their truth value.[10] Also, at Chicago, Innis absorbed the writings of Thorstein Veblen[11] – maverick political economist, founder of institutional economics, and, arguably, pioneer of North American communication studies.[12]

And, of course, there were the writings of Adam Smith (1723–1790), whose influence on Innis was probably much greater than is generally recognized. Smith's axial principle was that the division of labour, that is, task specialization in the production of commodities, is limited by the extent of the market. The size of the market, in turn, is constrained by the presence or absence of navigable routes of transportation.[13] Smith proposed also that money enables or induces expansion in the division of labour. Innis recognized the truth of these claims and spent many years elaborating them.

Furthermore, and more fundamentally, Innis's basic dialectic of time versus space as a dichotomous mode of organizing human activity was foreshadowed by Smith. On the one hand, Smith's *The Wealth of Nations* was a panegyric to the market, which he there extolled as a non-deliberative means of social and economic coordination, likening it to an 'invisible hand' that automatically brings buyers and sellers together for impersonal and self-interested exchanges of goods and services. Less well known, and certainly far less publicized in our day, however, was Smith's *The Theory of Moral Sentiments*,[14] a work that expounded upon the moral context needed for markets to function effectively.[15] In *Moral Sentiments*, Smith adopted the stance of the moral philosopher as opposed to that of political economist, and proclaimed that beneficence, or what he called 'sympathy,' is the highest of human virtues. He warned that competitive markets need to be constrained by a sense of community and shared values lest they undermine the social fabric. *Moral Sentiments* in other words extolled what Innis would later call 'time-binding' means of coordination, whereas *Wealth of Nations* emphasized impersonal, 'space-binding' means.

Innis received his doctorate from the University of Chicago in 1920. Also in that year he accepted an appointment to the Department of Political Economy at the University of Toronto, where he served as chair from 1937 until his death in 1952. He was also dean of the Graduate School (1947 to 1952). By all accounts he was a select member of the inner circle governing the university.[16]

By the 1940s, moreover, Innis had become the best-known and most respected academic in Canada. He was appointed to three royal commissions and elected president of both the Royal Society of Canada and the American Economics Association. He lectured overseas and received honorary degrees from several universities, including McMaster. Opinions varied, however, about Innis as a teacher. Arthur Ferri, today a retired consultant and business executive, took a fourth-year economic history course from Innis in 1949–50. Ferri recalls that Innis was so obviously a genius that students were quite in awe of him. When lecturing, Innis habitually jumped from point 'A' to point 'F,' leaving his auditors to make connections as best they could. While some, perhaps the majority, were enthralled by this, others were put off and dismissed Innis on account of his lack of clarity, monotone delivery, and formidable austerity (although in his office, Ferri remarked, Innis was highly approachable and modest). Fifty years later, Ferri retains the mental image of an angular Innis, hair tousled, standing behind a lectern for the entire period, neither fielding a question nor expecting one[17] – a pedagogical practice seemingly at odds with his championing dialogue and oral dialectic!

Always sceptical of concentrations of power and eager to lash out at abuses of privilege, at the end of his career Innis, in a sense, returned to the 'margin.'[18] In the late 1940s and early 1950s, he explored themes and issues that took him well beyond the security of his previous work and broke new interdisciplinary ground. In 1947 he addressed the Royal Society as its president, garbed in baggy pants and an old tweed jacket, on how Church and State monopolized knowledge by controlling the media of communication.[19] In 1948, invited by the administrators of the Beit fund to lecture at Oxford 'on any subject in the economic history of the British Empire,' he delivered talks on 'Empire and Communications,' hardly mentioning the *British* Empire at all; many walked out the first evening, so abstruse was his address, and audiences dwindled noticeably on subsequent nights.

Innis has been called the 'radical conservative of his day.'[20] On the side of conservatism, we shall see, he made 'a plea for time,' that is, an entreaty to remember things past and reinvigorate morality and community in the present. He cautioned against 'present-mindedness' and warned of the 'penetrative powers' of markets, which he saw as undermining morality and community. Prior to the Second World War, furthermore, Innis positively bristled at proposals for government planning, such as those set forth in the 1930s by Graham Spry and the League for Social Reconstruction.[21] In terms of education, Innis was not merely conservative, but élitist, claiming that in any community there is only 'a limited number capable of sustained mental effort'; although admitting that brilliant minds are to be found 'in all regions and in all strata,' nonetheless he also put forward the opinion that to thrive society must persistently seek out, encourage, and train the 'best brains.' Universality in higher education, conversely, according to Innis, means pandering to the lowest common denominator, in which case 'ideas must be ground down to a convenient size to meet the demands of large numbers.'[22]

Despite these conservative and occasionally aristocratic sentiments, Innis at heart, like Veblen, was a dissenter. He was the self-described 'dirt economist' who visited the regions he was writing about to mingle with the miners, trappers, lumberjacks, and fishermen.[23] In the summer of 1924, for example, preparatory to his book on *The Fur Trade*, he canoed down the Peace River to Lake Athabaska and, by the Slave River, to Great Slave Lake, and down the Mackenzie.[24] As a result of this trip, Creighton remarked, Innis not only recovered his health and spirits, but returned with a knowledge of the northlands 'such as none of his contemporary Canadian scholars would ever possess.'[25]

Innis disdained standard economic doctrine and railed at monopolies of knowledge, whether religious, political, technological, philosophic, or ideological. Consistently he was a critic of authority, warning of the dangers of concentrated power. By the end of the Second World War, he had become thoroughly radicalized, and worried deeply about the fate of Western civilization in general,[26] and of Canada in the face of U.S. commercialism in particular. Near the time of his own death, he wrote, for instance, that we Canadians

> are indeed fighting for our lives. The pernicious influence of American advertising reflected especially in the periodical press and the powerful persistent impact of commercialism have been evident in all the ramifications of Canadian life. The jackals of communication systems are constantly on the alert to destroy every vestige of sentiment toward Great Britain ... We can only survive by taking persistent action at strategic points against American imperialism in all its attractive guises.[27]

In his final writings, then, as Rick Salutin has suggested, Innis departed markedly from the more or less liberal philosophy he espoused previously.[28] He warned: 'The conditions of freedom of thought are in danger of being destroyed by science, technology, and the mechanization of knowledge, and with them, Western civilization.'[29] Capitalistic propaganda, Innis believed, had already overtaken the mass media and was then infiltrating the educational system. The university, for him a last bastion of resistance against insidious commercialism and unthinking acceptance of hegemonic doctrine, was under siege.

In 1945 Innis visited the Soviet Union, courtesy of the Academy of Sciences. Although highly critical of the journalism and Marxist dogma he encountered there, he also saw communism as providing a much needed 'balance' to the commercialism and present-mindedness of Western capitalism.[30]

Despite his growing pessimism, Innis's ironic and occasionally scatological wit saved him from sliding too deeply into the slough of despond. A famous Innisian aphorism – '[The] social scientist in Canada must have a sense of humour'[31] – tells us how he retained his sanity amid the absurdity and the deterioration he sensed about him. Insider/outsider, farm boy/scholar, liberal/socialist, moralist/agnostic, pessimist/humorist – these are but some of the contradictions of Innis the man and Innis the scholar

INNIS'S STYLE

Raised a farm boy, Innis remained most of his life untouched by literature, music, and the arts. 'I never heard him quote a line of poetry,' remarked friend and fellow historian Arthur Lower, 'and I suspect that to him poetry would have appeared not worth a serious man's attention.'[32] Nonetheless, Lower continued, in 1947 Innis did invoke Hegel's dictum that 'Minerva's owl takes flight in the gathering dusk,' indicating that perhaps he was then beginning to realize that there are indeed other matters of importance besides 'the stark facts of economics.'

Heather Menzies likewise speculates that, during his final years, Innis in fact was recovering the rich oral roots that had anchored him as a youth.[33]

Innis is not an easy read. Donald Creighton described the style as 'difficult, highly condensed, extremely elliptical, and not infrequently obscure.'[34] Northrop Frye found it 'impenetrable,' at least upon first perusal.[35] Innis's penchant for detail has been likened to that of a pointillist painter: from pages of amassed facts, patterns emerge.[36] *The Cod Fisheries,* one of his most celebrated works, required a full year of editorial assistance before becoming sufficiently coherent to warrant publication. His later works on communication are, if anything, less coherent still. Reviewing *The Bias of Communication* (1951), E.R. Adair berated the author for his 'intellectual shorthand,' complaining that the celebrated political economist 'rarely troubles to put in the words, let alone the phrases, that would show what connection there was in his mind between a sentence and the ones that precede and follow it.'[37] Indeed, Innis's infamous 'History of Communications' awaits publication to this day despite a long line of editorial efforts on the part of luminaries such as Mary Quayle Innis, Northrop Frye, Ian Parker, and William Buxton.

On the other hand, Innis's stylistic idiosyncrasies were precisely what attracted Marshall McLuhan, who expressed his enthusiasm by stating that each sentence in Innis's work 'is a compressed monograph [inviting] prolonged mediation and exploration.'[38] McLuhan explained, 'Were [Innis's mode of expression] to be translated into perspective prose, it would not only require huge space, but insight into the modes of interplay among forms of organization would also be lost. Innis sacrificed point of view and prestige to his sense of the urgent need for insight. A point of view can be a dangerous luxury when substituted for insight and understanding.'[39] Whereas McLuhan's reasons for endorsing the style, even to the point of emulation, will be addressed further in chapter 11, here speculation regarding Innis's motivation seems warranted. One possibility, of course, is that he simply could not write well, or at least only with great difficulty. The editorial rescue work required for *The Cod Fisheries* and the still unpublished 'History of Communications' lends credence to that proposition.

On the other hand, what might seem at first to be a lack of care or skill may actually have been a strategy. In what was otherwise an 'acerbic address,'[40] Innis once quipped that it was to escape enmity of powerful interests that he wrote in a manner 'no one can understand.'[41] Professor William Christian, one of Innis's editors, on the other hand, has proposed a more serious intent: through an enigmatic style, Christian suggested, Innis attempted to countervail the 'biases' of the written form,[42] 'bias' being Innis's code word for things inhibiting fullness or completeness, as well as tendencies towards some condition or mode of organization.

Christian probably has a point. Despite being himself a prolific writer, by the end of his life Innis expressed disdain for most written communication. Written texts, he pointed out, customarily lead readers through their authors' sequence of reasoning to preconceived conclusions, rather than opening up new possibilities and raising new questions for readers. He mused: 'The most dangerous illusions accompany the most obvious facts including the printed and mechanical word.'[43] In his preface to *Empire and Communications*, he went even further, cautioning: 'All written works, *including this one*, have dangerous implications to the vitality of an oral tradition and to the health of a civilization.'[44] However, writing ought not, *and need not*, stifle thought, Innis averred. Hence he esteemed the Platonic dialogues' preserving of 'the power of the spoken word on the written page' by eschewing a 'closely ordered system'; that is, they oppose 'establishment of a finished system of dogma.'[45] As well, they do not force closure on readers. Indeed, Innis remarked applaudingly, Plato did not even 'surrender his [own] freedom to his own books,' which is to say that he 'refused to be bound by what he had written.'[46] (In the hands of Aristotle, however, Innis lamented, all that changed: although retaining the dialogic form, Aristotle made *himself*, not Socrates, the interlocutor, thereby affirming his own control.)[47]

Given remarks like the foregoing, it is not inconceivable that Innis, on the one hand, scorning much written communication on account of its propensities to control readers' thoughts and stifle enquiry, and, on the other, admiring the enscribed Platonic dialogues for precisely their opposite tendencies, should himself have endeavoured to develop a style that would, if possible, evoke both thought and enquiry on the part of readers.[48] Although he did not employ the explicitly dialogic mode of Plato, nonetheless, through ellipsis and unexpected juxtapositionings, and also through a plethora of seeming contradictions, Innis encourages, indeed requires, 'dialogue.' As Professor William Melody has noted, 'studying Innis is a collaborative exercise ...; understanding comes from the interaction of the detailed descriptive analysis and the analytical insights of Innis, and the knowledge, experience and interpretive abilities of the reader.'[49] *The reader*, in other words, is not infrequently required to supply the connections, to resolve the contradictions, and to infer meanings.

One further point: The fact that Innis expressed *through writing* the idea that the printed word imprisons readers is indicative that he was arguing but one side of an implicit dialectic. His impassioned pleas for dialogue and for 'time,' by being presented in printed form, indicate that, for him, writing also can liberate.

SYNOPSIS

Three Phases
Innis's scholarship comprises three phases. The first culminated with publication in 1923 of *A History of the Canadian Pacific Railway*, his revised doctoral dissertation.[50] Unlike future endeavours, the main body of that work lacks communicatory insight. The focus there, rather, is on the financial intricacies of building and running the railway. Nonetheless, the book's introduction and conclusion are significantly broader in scope and elliptical in style, and presage work to come.

The second phase, occupying approximately the two decades to the early 1940s, was devoted principally to developing the 'staples thesis' of Canadian economic history. Two books in particular mark this period: *The Fur Trade in Canada* (1930) and *The Cod Fisheries* (1940). As well, papers addressing a broad range of themes, such as the importance of overhead costs in economic development, the role of the university in modern times, and 'the penetrative powers of the price system,' were prepared and have been gathered into essay collections: *Political Economy in the Modern State* (1946); the posthumously published *Essays in Canadian Economic History* (1956); and, more recently, *Staples, Markets, and Cultural Change* (1995).

Innis's final years were devoted primarily to the study of communication, and particularly to the differential impact of various media on the development and evolution of civilizations.[51] As noted above, some commentators have suggested a radical shift on Innis's part during this phase. Distinctions there certainly are, but in this chapter the continuities and similarities between the staples thesis and the communication thesis are also stressed. Remarking on the breadth of Innis's communication scholarship, Northrop Frye pronounced: 'Anything may be relevant to communication.'[52] This view is supported by the fact that, in these final endeavours, Innis moved from merely recounting economic history to considering 'all knowledge.'[53] Briefly, he postulated a dialectic of 'time-binding' versus 'space-binding' media, the former inducing or supporting local community and continuity, the latter fostering individualism, impersonal relations, change, and geographic empire. Major publications of these years include: *Empire and Communications* (1950), *The Bias of Communication* (1951), and *Changing Concepts of Time* (1952). A full bibliography of Innis's work can be found in Robin Neill's *A New Theory of Value: The Canadian Economics of H.A. Innis.*

Considering the full span of his career, it is evident that, for Innis, communication media were not confined to speech, writing, telegraph, telephones, radio, and so forth. For him, rather, the term *media* encompassed also modes of transportation – both those existing naturally, such as rivers, lakes, oceans, and horses, and those fabricated by people, for instance, canals, roads, railways, steamships, and chariots. As well, we realize retrospectively, the production or extraction of natural resources (or 'staples') constituted 'communication' for Innis. The extraction or production of staples creates environments, or ecosystems, that *mediate* human relations and otherwise affect a people's thoughts and actions.[54] Furthermore, trade in staples brings into contact peoples or civilizations previously isolated, setting up reciprocal relations of dominance and dependence, giving rise thereby to the dual dialectic of continuity versus change, and control over unbounded space versus local control. Although Innis seldom if ever used the term 'media' in his staples studies, retrospectively we can see that his communication thesis was germinating throughout this period.

Finally, and significantly, it is evident that, in his staples writings, Innis understood that money is a potent medium of communication.

Innis chafed at neoclassical treatments,[55] whereby money is viewed as a neutral (or 'unbiased') medium of exchange. For Innis, rather, money and prices 'penetrate' indigenous cultures, annexing them to an increasingly larger trading, financial, cultural, and political system. In the process, local relations based on hierarchy, kinship, tradition, love, empathy, culture, religious sensibilities, and intrinsic value (in Adam Smith's phrase, 'moral sentiments'), get wiped out and replaced by relations premised on money value and commodity exchange. Price becomes the primary if not sole indicator of value. Money, for Innis, indeed was preeminent as a 'space-binding' medium of communication.

In this chapter, two of Innis's main accomplishments in the field of communication are emphasized, corresponding respectively to the second and third phases of his career. First, we address his *staples thesis*, whereby he infused Canadian economic history with expansive notions of information and communication, constructing a dynamic, evolutionary, and highly original interpretation of Canadian economic, cultural, and political development. This feat alone would have assured Innis an abiding place in the annals of Canadian scholarship. That work, however, also led directly to his other major, and even more remarkable accomplishment: the *communication thesis*, which maintains that changes in the mode of communication lie at the heart of social, cultural, and economic evolution. As he summarized, 'I have attempted to suggest that Western civilization has been profoundly influenced by communication and that marked changes in communication have had important implications … In each period I have attempted to trace the implications of the media of communication for the character of knowledge and to suggest that a monopoly or an oligopoly of knowledge is built up to the point that equilibrium is disturbed.'[56]

Technological Determinism

Given the prominence of dialectics in Innis's work – particularly space versus time, and indeed (as we shall see) opposing notions of both time and space – and given as well the contradictions in his life noted earlier, there is little wonder that Innis has himself been interpreted inconsistently. To some, such as Everett Rogers and Daniel Czitrom,[57] Innis was a 'technological determinist.' According to this interpretation, Innis maintained that media condition the mode of social organization, whether towards an emphasis on community and continuity (i.e., 'time'), or towards an emphasis on spatial expansion and administration (i.e., 'space'). For others, however, such as Edward Comor and Paul Heyer, Innis was anything but a determinist:[58] Comor, for instance, insists that, for Innis, the predominance at any time and place of a particular medium is due to its consistency with, and contribution to, the knowledge, values, and goals prevailing in the society or power structure at that time. Furthermore, according to Comor, Innis purposefully selected the term 'bias' to indicate that media *emphasize* but do not determine.[59] Likewise, Heyer proposed that Innis chose words and phrases such as 'hastens,' 'facilitates,' and 'helps to define' to emphasize an absence of determinism.[60]

It is also worth noting that, throughout his career, Innis emphasized bidirectional causations. By applying that principle to media, he avoided technological determinism while at the same time affirming the influence on society of changes in the dominant mode of communication. The following captures well Innis's position on these matters: 'The impact of science [a way of knowing] on cultural development has been evident in its contribution to technological advance, notably in communication and in the dissemination of knowledge. In turn it has been evident in the types of knowledge disseminated; that is to say, science lives its own life not only in the mechanism which is provided to distribute knowledge but also in the sort of knowledge which will be distributed.'[61]

THE RAILWAY AS COMMUNICATION MEDIUM

From the very outset, Innis had in mind grand themes. Indeed the word 'civilization' appears in the opening sentence of *A History of the Canadian Pacific Railway,* his first book. There he declared that the CPR was a part of the 'technological equipment of Western civilization.'[62]

In fact Innis, like Veblen, saw technical equipment generally as being central to the study of civilizations. For one thing, technologies, or ways of doing things, arise *from* civilizations, and hence they manifest the prototypical concerns and thought patterns of the particular society. Second, technologies *have an impact upon* civilizations, and thus are key to understanding a civilization's evolution. Finally, according to Innis, technologies are the *means* (i.e., the media) whereby civilizations spread and contact one another. For such reasons, technologies generally, even ones not usually so construed, can be comprehended as constituting media of communication.

With regard specifically to the CPR, Innis argued that

> the history of the Canadian Pacific Railroad is primarily the history of the
> spread of western civilization over the northern half of the North Ameri-
> can continent. The addition of technical equipment described as physical
> property of the Canadian Pacific Railway Company was a cause and an
> effect of the strength and character of that civilization. The construction of
> the road was the result of the direction of energy to the conquest of
> geographic barriers. The effects of the road were measured to some extent
> by the changes in the strength and character of that civilization in the
> period following its construction.[63]

Let us look more closely at Innis's words here. The technical equipment
of the CPR was *a cause* of the strength and character of Western, that is,
European, civilization. This was so because the railway fostered industrialization – by moving energy supplies such as coal and building
materials such as iron ore to manufacturing sites. It was also *an effect*,
since the CPR was an outcome of industrialism and the knowledge that
the industrializing civilizations had acquired. Moreover, according
to Innis, the equipment of the CPR contributed to *the spread* in North
America of European civilization. It did this in at least two ways. First,
and perhaps most obviously, it was a medium for transporting across
the North American continent people and goods originating in Europe;
hence, it caused messengers (European immigrants, with their cultures,
goals, languages, priorities), and messages (for example, artefacts produced in Europe), to touch the lives of Native peoples and immigrant
settlers. Second, and even more fundamentally, the CPR was itself a
message: the equipment of the CPR comprised a massive, energy-
consuming, fast-moving, powerful, capital-intensive 'sign' dropped
into the very midst of indigenous peoples, whose entire way of life
was disrupted, and eventually shattered, as a result.

In the extract above, other, recurring Innisian themes and analytical
devices are evident too. Note, for example, the suggestion that control
over technology fosters relations of dominance and dependence. Own-
ing the technical equipment of the railway lent political, cultural, and
economic power to those in charge. In his later writings Innis often
emphasized that *monopolies of knowledge* (i.e., those large-scale truths,
systems of truths, or myths that allow groups to exercise control over
time or space),[64] inevitably accompany control of particular media of
communication.[65] In those writings, he drew attention also to competi-

tive pressures that inexorably arise as less privileged interests endeavour to bypass media controlled by dominant groups. In his introductory chapter to *A History of the Canadian Pacific Railway,* these analyses, too, were foreshadowed when Innis honed in on the monopoly enjoyed by the Hudson's Bay Company and the 'increasing strain' it experienced as others sought to erode it.[66]

Despite remarkable originality, particularly in the book's opening and closing chapters, Innis quickly became dissatisfied with his history of the CPR, and in the preface to *The Fur Trade in Canada* declared that the newer work was intended to help rectify certain defects of the previous one.[67] In part his dissatisfaction stemmed from his having adopted in *A History of the Canadian Pacific Railway* the view that Canada was an artificial country, an outcome of a heroic struggle and triumph of the will against both economic and geographic factors. In *The Fur Trade* and in subsequent works, however, he disavowed that contention, maintaining, rather, that the Dominion arose *from* geography, not despite it;[68] or, more precisely, that the *interaction* of landscape, technology, and the fur staple helped bring Canada into existence.[69] Innis's full thesis in this regard is presented below.

Some have referred to *A History of the Canadian Pacific Railway* as a work of the immature Innis. Be that as it may, the book's introduction and conclusion certainly make interesting reading, especially in light of the author's subsequent exploration of communication media other than the railway.

INFUSING ECONOMICS WITH COMMUNICATION

The Need for a Canadian Economics
When Innis moved to the University of Toronto, filled with the teaching of mentors such as Frank Knight, Robert Park, and J.M. Clark, and imbued also with the thought of Thorstein Veblen, he espied a dearth of materials dealing with *Canadian* economic history. He believed, furthermore, that economic models developed in older, industrialized economies should not, with impunity, be imported into emergent, peripheral ones. It was also his contention that economic history and economic theory should be closely integrated, that history provides the means whereby theory is tested.[70] He therefore set about developing a 'philosophy of economic history or an economic theory suited to Canadian needs.'[71]

The implications of Innis's position are enormous: if countries differ significantly in their economic histories, they ought then to develop their own, distinct economic theories. That position, of course, is anathema to the economics mainstream, which ascribes a universality and timelessness to economic 'laws.' It is also heresy to institutions such as the World Bank, the World Trade Organization, and the International Monetary Fund, which implement policies about the globe in accordance with an universalistic view.[72]

With regard specifically to *Canadian* economic history/theory, Innis identified three features as paramount – Canada's trading dependence on other countries; its geography, particularly the inland water systems and the pre-Cambrian shield; and the unique character of its natural resources, or 'staples.' Building on Veblen's work, moreover, Innis saw technological developments, particularly in the fields of transportation and communication, as interacting with geography and staples to disrupt established patterns of social interaction. Tensions result, according to Innis, when groups controlling the technologies associated with the staples trade enter traditional, time-bound cultures.

The Staples Thesis
Through the concept of staples (fish, fur, timber, mining, wheat), Innis perceived a way of linking modes of transportation, geography, social structure, culture, political organization, business and economic history, and technology to relations between imperial centres and colonial margins. His was an interdisciplinary analysis of cultures in collision, of societies brought into contact by the *media* of staples.

However, Innis did not posit staples as working their effects unidirectionally or in isolation. His analysis, rather, concerned the interaction of staples with the geographic characteristics of the regions and with the technologies used to harvest and transport them. These three factors – staples, geography, and technology – in Innis's view intersected to form distinct amalgams. Geography, for example, worked different effects, depending on the particular staple: The inland waterways, for instance, fostered east–west communication during the fur trade, but less so when lumber superseded furs. In part this shift resulted from the fact that furs are light in weight, with high value relative to their bulk, making them suitable for export to Europe, whereas forestry products are much heavier and cumbersome, hence favouring trade with the nearby United States. Furthermore, according to Innis, 'the effects of geography [could] be offset by capital and technology.'[73] He saw canals and railways, for instance, as countervailing the inland waterways, which had fostered east–west communication during the fur trade. Moreover, staples themselves begat these new transportation technologies, completing the 'triangulation' among geography, staples, and technology.[74]

Technology and capital, however, were treated dialectically by Innis, prefiguring his later analyses of communication media. On the one hand, some capital investments are small in scale, offering considerable flexibility: Wooden ships for the cod fisheries, for example, entailed small investment and were sufficiently mobile to permit exploration of alternative fishing grounds and markets. The contrast with the high and geographically fixed investment in a canal or railway system is readily apparent.[75]

According to Innis, the rise to predominance of a new staple, in combination with technological change, invariably produces a 'period of crisis.' Adjustments must be made, and new patterns of social inter-action must develop.[76] Groups controlling the new staple and the new technology ascend in power, whereas the group associated with the old staple and the old technology wanes in influence.

The Fur Staple

The Fur Trade in Canada has been described as Innis's 'first great work.'[77] There he developed fully the themes announced in embryo in *A History of the Canadian Pacific Railway*: for instance, the disruption or imbalance resulting when previously separate civilizations come into communica-tion. Like the railway, the fur trade, too, in Innis's view, brought 'a relatively complex civilization' into contact with 'a much more simple civilization'[78] – with dramatic consequences for each.

Europeans settling in North America, Innis remarked, brought with them 'cultural traits' derived from their own civilization.[79] This made them ill-equipped to survive in their new environment, and indeed many perished. Those who did prevail, however, through necessity borrowed 'cultural traits' from indigenous peoples, a very painful proc-ess, to be sure, since 'depreciation of the social heritage is serious.'[80] To mitigate their anguish, emigrants sought imports of manufactured goods from their homeland, thus setting up a legacy of dependence. To pay for the imports, settlers became reliant on harvesting primary products, or 'staples.' Relations between the colonies and Europe, consequently, were 'biased' from the outset.

According to Innis, 'the economic history of Canada has been domi-nated by the discrepancy between the centre and the margin.'[81] Concentrating on fur production, for example, meant that settlers lacked the motivation to develop indigenous manufacturing.[82] Moreover, the infrastructure (transportation, trade, finance), as well as government activities, were subordinated to the production of staples for export rather than being developed to encourage a broader economic and social base. The 'weakness' of the colony resulting from heavy specialization in staples in turn necessitated 'reliance upon military support from the mother country.'[83]

As Hegel understood, however, dependence is a two-way street. In the present instance, industries in the mother country became reliant on the hinterland, not only for a steady flow of raw materials, but also as a captive market for finished goods, making 'inevitable,' in Innis's view, 'the continuation of control by Great Britain in the northern half of North America.'[84]

The fur trade also had a drastic impact on indigenous peoples. In exchange for furs, Native peoples acquired 'iron goods' such as hatchets, knives, scissors, needles, and, most significantly, muskets,[85] quite disrupting their way of life. Guns, for instance, which replaced bows and arrows, required both periodic repair and a steady flow of parts and ammunition, making aboriginal people continuously dependent on Europeans. Rifles changed hunting practices drastically, diminishing to the point of virtual disappearance the supply of beaver in territories opened to the hunt; they also escalated the level of hostility among the various tribes that now competed for control over the prime hunting territories.[86] Innis lamented,

> The history of the fur trade is the history of contact between two civilizations, the European and the North American ... Unfortunately the rapid destruction of the food supply and the revolution in the methods of living accompanied by the increasing attention to the fur trade by which these products were secured, disturbed the balance which had grown up previous to the coming of the European. The new technology with its radical innovations brought about such a rapid shift in the prevailing Indian culture as to lead to wholesale destruction of the peoples concerned by warfare and disease.[87]

The Fish Staple

Innis's third book, *The Cod Fisheries*, focused on the fish trade off the Atlantic coast. Although giving rise to the fur trade, the cod fisheries differed in terms of centralization/ decentralization. The fishing trade centred on submerged land masses that formed multitudinous bays and harbours along the Atlantic coast, inducing decentralized control. Prior to settlement, law and order, such as existed in Newfoundland, for instance, was overseen in each harbour by an 'admiral,' the sea captain whose ship was first to arrive in the spring.[88]

Initially settlements in New England, Nova Scotia, and Newfoundland were limited to the sea coast, and were established on the basis of the European demand for fish, resulting in a relative isolation from the rest of the North American continent.[89] The shift westward of the fur trade, and the subsequent development of the timber trade, however, lessened and reversed pressures against more complete settlement, particularly in areas along the St Lawrence.[90] Economies in the St Lawrence and New England regions diversified, increasing 'the "pull" of the continent,' lessening the impact of the fisheries. In Newfoundland, however, geography and climate severely constrained agricultural development, and so specialization in cod continued.[91]

Climate and geography were not the only factors, however, inhibiting more balanced development in Newfoundland. Innis related that the English government imposed building restrictions on people coming to the colony as Britain did not want settlers competing with British ships for fish, or money from the fishing trade to be spent in Newfoundland instead of England.[92] Likewise, a powerful merchant class, whose members aspired to withdraw capital from the colony upon retiring to England,[93] discouraged fishermen from settling, since agriculture and other economic activities 'clashed with their own interests.'[94] Governments in Newfoundland consequently were forced to rely heavily on tariffs as their main revenue source, further limiting diversification. Apart from St John's, in fact, there existed virtually no local government in the colony.

Innis depicted life in Newfoundland as being filled with hardship, poverty, and oppression. To the Church fell responsibility for education, while private organizations provided such social and medical services as existed.[95] Whereas in Nova Scotia and New England growth in responsible government arose on account of 'the balancing of interests through divergent resources,' this was not the case in the single-staple economy of Newfoundland.[96]

In *The Cod Fisheries*, Innis anticipated his communication writings in several ways. He insisted, for example, that it was desirable to balance various items for export rather than to concentrate on a single staple, a notion that was subsequently recast as the need for balance between time-biased and space-biased media of communication. Moreover, in *The Cod Fisheries* he depicted desirable staples as being light in bulk and high in value, as these secured the most favourable terms of trade;[97] in his later writings he noted that a communication medium's bulk and weight help set its time-binding versus space-binding qualities, thereby affecting profoundly the development of the civilization. In addition, Innis's lifelong use of dialectic, his conception of two-way as opposed to unidirectional causation, and his perception that the price system possesses 'penetrative powers,' particularly in its capacity to split apart monopolies, are all emphasized, as is readily apparent in the following extract:

> An expanding commercial system broke the bonds of a rigid political structure defended by vested interests ... The activity of commercialism, which played its part in the disappearance of the colonial system but had also been intensified by it, loosened the powerful forces of competition in the Atlantic basin, and made it inevitable that systems of Imperial control should defeat their own ends. Competition, enforced by commercialism based on the fishery, and encouraged by Parliament with an interest in shipping and the fishing industries as a basis of naval support, was effective because of the mobility of labor, ships, and markets.[98]

The Forestry Staple

Although Innis did not complete a book on the timber trade, he did publish several papers centring on forest products, including lumber, pulp and paper, and journalism.[99] Perhaps more obviously than other staples, wood products connect directly to conventional communication media, what hereinafter may be termed *communication media proper*. Neatly combining Gresham's and Say's laws, Innis wrote: 'Cheap supplies of paper produce pulp and paper schools of writing, and literature is provided in series, sold by subscription, and used as an article of furniture.'[100]

According to Innis's historiography, timber supplanted fur as a key staple for export. Like fur 'it was adapted ... to the cheap water transportation of the St. Lawrence.' It contrasted to fur, however, in terms of weight, bulk, and value.[101] Whereas the manufacture of fur products, such as hats, was undertaken largely in Europe, timber's bulk and weight meant that manufacture 'took place close to its source';[102] Canada consequently exported square lumber instead of raw timber to the United States.

Timber's characteristics had further consequences for trade. Exports created immense pressures to utilize the large number of otherwise empty returning ships – either to deliver cargoes of processed goods or to transport new immigrants. Innis remarked, 'A heavy unbalanced trade [is] a source of constant disturbance.'[103] Imbalance in the case of lumber, Innis believed, presaged both the abrogation of preferential duties with Britain and the Reciprocity Treaty of 1854 with the United States.[104]

Paper is, of course, a major product of timber, and in Eastern Canada a large number of lumber companies shifted to the production of pulp and paper.[105] The production of newsprint, however, is an industry requiring 'enormous capital equipment, in mills and power plants, heavy fixed charges, and serious problems of overhead costs,'[106] resulting in a concentrated industry characterized by a few large production centres in order to realize economies of scale – a marked contrast from the smooth and flexible adjustments of supply to demand as pictured in the neoclassical economics model of pure competition.

Moreover, paper is a medium for written communication, and accordingly is part and parcel of modernity. Innis wrote: 'Expansion of the pulp and paper industry has supported intensive advertising and revolutions in marketing essential to the demands of the city. It has coincided with the decline of editorials and of freedom of speech, and the emergence of headlines and the modern newspaper with its demands for excitement, including wars and peace, to appeal to a large range of lower mental types.'[107] Exports of paper to the United States had dramatic consequences for the U.S. newspaper industry, and as a result for the whole of North America. Innis noted, for instance, that in St Louis, between 1875 and 1925, there was a decline in the space allocated to news, from 55.3 to 26.7 per cent, and a concomitant increase in the space devoted to advertising. The newspaper industry, perforce, given this development, needed to accommodate itself more thoroughly to the demands of advertisers. Thereby relations between the newspaper and the commercial world 'narrowed': on the one hand, large business organizations began to build up 'goodwill' through newspaper advertising; on the other, newspapers themselves became large, oligopolistic enterprises reluctant to rile advertisers.[108]

Furthermore, newspapers played a large role in transforming the conception of time – from continuity to sequential uniformity – and as well the conception of space – from one concerning locality where community resides, to borderless geographic extent organized through principals of commodity exchange. According to Innis, coupling the newspaper with the telegraph, in combination with faster presses, gave financial advantage to journals serving geographically extended markets with current 'news.'[109] Reliance on advertising added to the pressures since advertisers are interested in fast turn-overs. Hence, the 'bias' of the newspaper was set: journalism came to be written 'on the back of advertisements,'[110] emphasizing regionalism rather than localism, and functioning in a manner destructive of 'time and continuity.'[111]

THE COMMUNICATION THESIS

At the very pinnacle of his career as an economic historian, however, Innis turned to a field in which he 'mispronounced the names of even the most common authorities.'[112] His new focus: *communication* – a development stimulated, according to Innisian scholar A. John Watson, by contact with classicists on staff at the University of Toronto during the 1940s, particularly C.N. Cochrane, E.A. Havelock, and E.T. Owen.[113]

Minerva's Owl

Innis opened his most remarkable book, *The Bias of Communication*, with a quote from Hegel: 'Minerva's Owl begins its flight only in the gathering dusk.'[114] He used this quote to indicate that creativity and learning attain their zenith only when a civilization has begun its decline. Through the course of human history, Minerva's owl has taken several flights – 'in the gathering dusk' of classical Greece, Alexandria, Rome, Constantinople, the republican cities of Italy, France, Holland, and Germany.[115] In each case, Innis advised, there had been a decline in military or organizational power and this decline stimulated cultural activity. 'With a weakening of protection of organized force,' Innis explained, 'scholars put forth greater efforts.'[116] A clash between knowledge systems, and as well a greater balance between force, on the one hand, and intelligence, on the other, Innis viewed as stimulating creativity. More fundamentally, Innis proposed that changes in organization were accompanied by changes in systems of knowledge as each mode of organization had its own characteristic method of communicating.

According to Innis, new media of communication often are developed in the hinterlands, where organization is flexible. With time, new media penetrate the centre, undercutting conservative tendencies inherent in established power.[117] Each medium of communication is associated not only with a certain group, however, but also with a particular type of knowledge: hieroglyphics with spiritual knowledge and a priesthood; newspapers with advertising, current affairs, and big business. New media, therefore, engender struggles for ascendancy not only among groups of people, but also among types of knowledge. It is by dint of such conflicts or contradictions, Innis believed, that cultures flourish.

Continuity with the Staples Thesis

In the communication thesis, Innis was no longer concerned merely with Canadian affairs. His attention, rather, was now cast on the very rise and fall of civilizations.[118] Whereas the staples thesis proposed centre/margin as the overarching dialectic, in the communications thesis the chief antithesis was between space and time,[119] a dialectic, incidentally, that incorporates such further basic contradictions or tensions as empire versus custom (since empire accepts no bounds, whereas custom is local or indigenous), centralization versus decentralization, dependence versus autonomy, reason versus emotion (since administration of spatial empire entails calculation, planning, and social engineering, whereas continuity entails *feelings* of loyalty and belonging), the profane versus the sacred, and change versus continuity. In effect, Innis asked: What is the role of communication media in defining society, in maintaining social stability, in inducing social change, and in fostering empire and control? According to James W. Carey, in responding to these questions Innis 'founded the modern studies that now exist under the banner of media imperialism.'[120]

Implicitly at least, Innis regarded communication media as being in some ways similar to staples, or, as McLuhan put it: 'Media are major resources like economic staples.'[121] According to Innis, just as harvesting new staples helps bring about fundamental political, economic, and cultural struggle and change, so, too, do 'inventions in communication *compel* realignments in the monopoly or the oligopoly of knowledge.'[122] Regarding clay tablets and cuneiform script, for instance, he wrote:

> Dependence on clay in the valleys of the Euphrates and Tigris involved a special technique in writing and a special type of instrument, the reed stylus. Cuneiform writing on clay involved an elaborate skill, intensive training, and concentration of durable records. The temples with their priesthoods became the centres of cities. A culture based on intensive training in writing rendered centralized control unstable and gave organized religion an enormous influence.[123]

The point is made again with regard to Chinese pictographs. Although the Chinese developed paper, a most flexible medium for encoding messages, their symbol system was highly complex, consisting of well over 1,500 characters, and necessitated the emergence of 'a learned class,' which denigrated traditional knowledge. Complexity of the written language for Innis, in other words, explained the persistence of hierarchical political and religious institutions in the face of a light and flexible writing material.[124] In Europe, by contrast, albeit several centuries later, the much simpler phonetic alphabet combined with paper to hasten 'the growth of commerce.'[125] Innis, then, saw the physical materials upon which messages are inscribed as combining with the means of inscription to constitute distinct 'amalgams': paper-plus-phonetic alphabet was distinctly different from paper-plus-Chinese characters. In this, Innis's media analyses are again reminiscent of his staples thesis.

Furthermore, just as geography and water systems in his earlier writings were posited as directing the movement of particular staples, in his communications thesis he proposed that communication media (the material for encoding plus the means whereby the material is enscribed) 'bias' the movement of ideas. He declared: 'Writing with a simplified alphabet checked the power of custom of an oral tradition but implied a decline in the power of expression and the creation of grooves which determined the channels of thought of readers and later writers.'[126]

THEORY OF MEDIA

Innis's media analysis can be discussed in terms of four main principles.[127]

Time-bound/Space-bound Societies
A key factor distinguishing societies is the degree to which they are 'time-bound' or 'space-bound.' 'Time-bound' societies, in the purest form, are pre-literate, oral, and tribal. They emphasize continuity because the human mind, their principal repository of information and knowledge, is limited in storage capacity, compared with various materials used for writing; indeed, much time and effort, in the form of oral recitation and memorization, are required to conserve knowledge, reducing thereby the culture's capacity to develop new knowledge.[128] Moreover, the knowledge conserved will tend to be very practical (the

seasons, the floods, seeds and planting) and religious/magical. Hence, there is less possibility in an oral society for abstraction; stated otherwise, in oral society thought tends not to be separated from feeling, as it is in societies with writing, a particularly insidious consequence of typography according to Innis, as this resulted in a certain 'cruelty' to mechanized communication. Oral societies, moreover, are confined geographically by the distinctiveness of their languages and dialects. There is an emphasis on collectivity and the common good, and since many share the knowledge there is minimal individualization. Speech takes place in time and is inherently shared, so time-bound societies also tend to be consensual. Moreover, they are celebrative.

In comparison, space-bound societies, which by definition are ones in which either the price system has penetrated fully or the military exercises a major role in maintaining order, are secular in their concerns, materialistic in their interpretations, and impersonal in their social relations.[129] They accord high value to abstract knowledge and to exercising control over space, but place relatively little value on, even denigrate, tradition or continuity with the past. Their mode of thought differs from what characterizes oral societies, being comparatively more linear, more rational, more detached, less intimate or personal, and less reliant upon tradition.

It was Innis's position that space-bound cultures endeavour to 'spatialize' time, that is, to break it up into discrete, uniform, measurable chunks that can then be valuated in money terms.[130] Like Mumford, Innis recognized that the mechanical clock has been essential to this task. Through clocks, workers are summoned to factories, for instance, and can be recompensed according to the 'time' they put in. 'Measurement of time,' Innis added, 'facilitated the use of credit, the rise of exchanges, and calculations of the predictable future essential to the development of insurance.'[131]

This is not, of course, the only possible conception of time. 'Time-bound' communities by definition are not likewise engrossed in the moment. For them, time *flows*; human life is understood as 'a great stream of which the present is only the realized moment.'[132] Events are a succession of *recurrences* (the cycle of life), even though each instance may be charged with particular value and significance.[133] The biblical Book of Ecclesiastes captures well the conception of time as eternal recurrence: 'A time to be born, and a time to die; / a time to plant, and a time to pluck up what is planted; / a time to kill, and a time to heal; / a time to break down, and a time to build up ...'

Just as space-bound cultures have a particular concern with time, so, too, do time-bound cultures conceive space in a unique way. For them, space is neither unlimited nor something to be appropriated and annexed; rather, it is bounded and is to be protected. Boundaries are necessary for sustaining community and culture. Space for time-bound cultures is where the community lives, where it maintains its connections with the past, and where its future will unfold. This view is totally at odds with the notion of space maintained by space-bound cultures. There the desire is to conquer new territories, create larger markets, and organize land into efficient configurations (factories, assembly lines, territorial divisions of labour, and so on).[134] Space, like time, becomes commodified in space-biased cultures.

Change from one conception of time or of space to the other, according to Innis, is typically accompanied by conflict and struggle. The enclosure movements in England, the Oka crisis in Canada, Indonesia's genocidal treatment of the East Timorese, Innis would undoubtedly agree, are all examples of struggles between adherents to rival conceptions of space and of time.

Time-Binding and Space-Binding Media

Media of communication influence, and are influenced by, the character of knowledge of the civilization in which they prevail. Media are either relatively 'time-biased' or 'space-biased.' Media are predisposed to diffusing either space-binding or time-binding messages. Time-binding messages are ones that foster community and continuity, whereas space-binding messages help engender impersonal (commodified) exchanges, and are instrumental in territorial expansion and control.

Media can be broadly grouped as being oral, written, printed, or electronic, and may be depicted on a space/time continuum (see figure 3.1). Oral communication is pre-eminently time-binding since it emphasizes continuity and community. Orality builds social organization locally, tends to foster cooperation as opposed to competition, and directs activity in the interests of the community (the common good).[135]

The first modes of written communication also were time-binding, and indeed arose as an aid to memory. Moses, for instance, according to the biblical account, took charge of divine law by inscribing it onto stone tablets to guard against its loss upon the death of the elders. Writing not merely has been an aid to religious and cultural practice, however, but also has helped transform such practices. For the Jews, each written word came to be filled with meaning and mystery,[136]

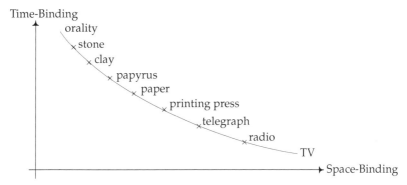

Figure 3.1 Time-Space Bias of Various Media

whereas graven images were denounced. The abstraction inherent in writing, moreover, opened the way to a universal ethics.[137]

Innis expressed the opinion, however, that writing as 'transpersonal memory' cannot long remain time-binding in its overall thrust, for it enables and requires readers to go 'beyond the world of concrete experience into the world of conceptual relations.' Writing, in other words, enlarges the time-and-space universe beyond things remembered and places known,[138] making the written word ultimately subversive of time-binding authority.

Furthermore, reliance on records inevitably displaces collective memory, subverting the communal aspects of oral society. According to Innis, the advent of writing caused poetry to become 'detached from the collective festival,'[139] and thereafter to be read silently, in solitude. Soon sword combined with pen, and together they served to help exert control over space.[140]

Successive innovations increased writing's space-binding properties, although Innis did not propose any rigidly linear chronology in this regard. 'Profound disturbances' were associated with the shift from stone to papyrus in Egypt around 2600 B.C., for example. According to Innis, 'a marked increase in writing by hand [on papyrus] was accompanied by secularization of writing, thought, and activity'; around 2000 B.C. a class of scribes skilled in writing overtook both royalty and the priesthood, whose power had been based on control over stone and hieroglyphics.[141]

Space-biased media are relatively flexible to work with, easy to transport, and abundant in capacity for storing information, but they are less durable than time-binding media. Compare, for example, the properties of papyrus or paper with those of stone tablets. Due to such inherent properties of time-binding media as intractability and durability, messages encoded on them will seldom be of merely passing importance in the eyes of the originating culture; they will, therefore, engender a sense of continuity. Messages encoded onto heavy media also will tend to have relevance mainly for the local culture, since transporting them is so difficult. Space-binding media, on the other hand, due to their flexibility and abundant capacity, need not carry messages that are so enduring. Frequently they carry messages that emphasize current, administrative, and, increasingly, marketing matters, as opposed to moral, metaphysical, mythical, religious, or community concerns.[142] Their messages are often directed at populations dispersed geographically, for purposes of administration and/or to take advantage of scale economies. Space-biased media, therefore, tend to erode local cultures and foster cultural homogenization. Moreover, by favouring one-way communication and centralized control, they contribute, in Innis's view, to a decline in democracy.[143]

Nonetheless, it is necessary at this point to recall previous discussions, for in writing of the *bias* of communication Innis meant that media emphasize or create tendencies in certain directions, but that they do not *determine*. It is also true, however, that Innis understood money, or the price system, to be a space-biased mode of communication *par excellence*, and the further the price system penetrates a culture, the more space-bound it becomes.

Impetus for Technological Change

In Innis's view, two forces lie behind technological change. One is the quest for power. At every stage of development, some try to bypass entrenched 'monopolies of knowledge' by innovating new media of communication. Innis believed that each medium is normally controlled by a particular élite – a priesthood, perhaps, in the case of certain time-binding media; press barons and advertisers, in the case of today's newspapers. Ecclesiastical demands in France in the sixteenth and seventeenth centuries, for example, for a time caused printing, a medium Innis believed to be subversive of priestly authority, to be suppressed. Nonetheless, it being the age of mercantilism, France was also intent to produce paper for export. Hence, France shipped cheap supplies of paper to The Netherlands and elsewhere, resulting in low costs for printed materials there, ultimately setting up The Netherlands as an important publishing centre. Eventually books printed in Holland were smuggled back into France, quite undermining the authority of the Church. By the eighteenth century, the evasion of censorship was pervasive. 'Freedom of the press in marginal free countries,' Innis pronounced, 'was supported by repression in France.'[144]

Alternatively, or additionally, Innis invoked the notion of *homeostasis* to explain the evolution of media. Pre-eminence of any medium in a culture, he maintained, carries with it inherent limitations, or 'biases,' and new media may arise to correct or compensate for these limitations, restoring balance or stability. As he explained,

> we may perhaps assume that the use of a medium of communication over a long period will to some extent determine the character of knowledge to be communicated and suggest that its pervasive influence will eventually create a civilization in which life and flexibility will become exceedingly difficult to maintain and that the advantages of a new medium will become such as to lead to the emergence of a new civilization.[145]

Innis illustrated this hypothesis by recounting, *inter alia*, the decline of the Roman Empire and the rise of Christendom. Note in the following account, however, that homeostatic pressures to innovate new media are inevitably supported by groups who would ascend to power at the expense of those controlling old media. Innis's thesis on homeostasis, therefore, may perhaps be regarded as supplementing his contentions concerning monopolies of knowledge, rather than as being a separate explanation.

According to Innis, administration of the Roman Empire depended upon a steady supply of papyrus. Papyrus, however, had inherent limitations: while flexible and light, it was fragile and could not be safely transported over land for long distances. As well, papyrus was produced only in a restricted area of the Nile valley, making its supply insecure.[146] A new medium – namely, parchment – consequently 'emerged to meet the limitations of papyrus.' For a time both papyrus and parchment were used, the advantages of one offsetting the limitations of the other. Parchment, being more durable, was of particular use to monks copying Hebrew scriptures and developing a new body of writing. Copying manuscripts onto parchment, however, was painstakingly slow; according to Innis, a skilled scribe needed about a year to make a single copy of the Bible, the normal pace being about two to four pages per day.[147] Books made of parchment consequently remained quite scarce, the few in existence being concentrated in small monastic libraries sprinkled over large territories. The copying process lent itself to censorship, and large amounts of pagan writings were lost. The ban on secular learning imposed by the Church gave preponderance to theological studies, making Rome dominant.[148]

Although for a time papyrus and parchment balanced each other,[149] that felicitous condition conducive to stability (homeostasis) did not last: the spread of Islam cut off exports of papyrus,[150] creating an imbalance in favour of time. Parchment alone was too intractable to administer an empire.[151] The time-biased monopoly of knowledge based on parchment therefore 'invited the competition of a new medium, namely paper from China.'[152]

The rise of paper – like papyrus, flexible for writing – in conjunction with the alphabet encouraged secular publications and facilitated administration over wider areas. According to Innis, 'the use of paper and the growth of trade favoured the development of cities and strengthened monarchies; the increasing importance of the vernacular and the rise of lawyers strengthened the position of political at the expense of ecclesiastical organizations.'[153]

The high cost of books produced by hand, even paper ones, in turn created pressures to develop machine processes, eventually resulting in printing.[154] Initially, for Innis, the printing press induced a movement back towards the oral tradition. This was because the flexibility of the alphabet with movable type facilitated greater use of vernaculars in written communication.[155] In the end, however, the printing press created pressures in the opposite direction; by inducing the rise of a secular, critical literature and thereby weakening the capacity of the State and Church to censor publications, it became 'a battering ram to bring [both] abbeys and castles crashing to the ground.'[156]

The printing press, then, was associated with, and gave rise to, a new 'monopoly of knowledge' – particularly with the advent of daily newspapers. According to Innis, mass-circulation dailies at the start of the twentieth century, facing high overhead costs, entered circulation wars to spread fixed costs across ever larger readerships. This meant, on the one hand, efforts to tap new, geographically contiguous markets, and, on the other, 'excitement, sensationalism, and capriciousness' in editorial content. As Innis put it, 'the news became a commodity and was sold in competition like any other commodity.'[157]

Despite intense rivalry, according to Innis, newspapers generally produced a new monopoly of knowledge: occurrences in space were emphasized to the utter neglect of time.[158] Newspapers were preoccupied with reporting events of the previous twenty-four hours, meaning that there arose a 'continuous, systematic, ruthless destruction of elements of permanence essential to cultural activity.' For Innis, indeed, 'the emphasis on change [became] the only permanent characteristic.'[159]

While from a homeostatic perspective, dominance by the printing press and journalism should have given rise to a new, time-binding medium of communication as a counter-irritant to re-establish balance or stability, this has been, in Innis's view, only superficially the case. Although radio broadcasting undeniably presaged a return of oral communication, Innis viewed radio as reasserting oral culture only in a shallow sense. He maintained that radio, on the one hand, through the immediacy of the spoken word, helped develop a new sense of community, and in so doing lent an emphasis to planning and the welfare state;[160] on the other hand, however, he argued, it contributed also to community breakdown since it substituted centralized, one-way communication for face-to-face, dialogic interaction.[161] Furthermore, by literally 'selling time,' radio radically extended the process of spatialization inherent in newspapers, permitting the price system to penetrate yet more deeply into human consciousness. Finally, again like newspapers, radio concentrates on ephemeral rather than on enduring matters, adding yet again to Western societies' 'obsession with present-mindedness.'[162]

According to Innis, therefore, since the emergence of the printing press at least, the tendency in the West to achieve homeostasis through the rise of alternative media has been superseded by an ever-escalating 'present-mindedness,' that is, by a succession of increasingly spatially biased media of communication.

Balance

Innis insisted that a balance between institutions, practices, and media exerting control through time and those managing control over space is essential for stability. Stated otherwise, *being* and *becoming* must be in dynamic equilibrium.[163] Undue emphasis on one mode of control or organization relative to the other inevitably leads to disorganization. [164]

According to Innis, orality is both pre-eminent as a time-binding medium and essential for democracy, creativity, and community. He wrote:

The oral dialectic is overwhelmingly significant where the subject matter is human action and feeling, and it is important in the discovery of new truth but of very little value in disseminating it. The oral discussion inherently involves personal contact and a consideration of the feelings of others, and it is in sharp contrast with the cruelty of mechanized communication and the tendencies which we have come to note in the modern world.[165]

However, time-binding media, although providing a sense of continuity and of intrinsic (timeless) value, ill-equip cultures to administer large territories. Moreover, time-bound societies tend to be static and rigid, even to the point of stagnation and boredom.[166] Space-bound societies, on the other hand, although dynamic, lack cohesion and a sense of intrinsic value. Personal worth in a thoroughly space-biased society, for instance, is appraised primarily in terms of income or wealth at the moment, not in terms of intrinsic humanness. It is in this light, it can be argued, that the apparent equanimity with which many middle-class Canadians today accept the diminution in social programs can be understood: after all, if the primary indicator of a person's 'value' is his or her monetary income or wealth, why should resources be spent enhancing the living conditions of those 'of little value'? For societies acknowledging the importance of time as duration and as continuity, by contrast, each member of the community is ascribed *intrinsic* value, and the community therefore strives to maintain a certain minimal living standard for all.

Likewise with regard to the environment: whereas a space-bound society (i.e., one penetrated fully by the price system) ascribes little or no intrinsic value to nature or to those endangered species lacking commodity exchange value, time-bound communities can be more nurturing.

For our present space-biased era, Innis's plea for balance amounts, in essence, to 'a plea for time.' He wrote: 'The modern obsession with present-mindedness ... suggests that the balance between time and space has been seriously disturbed with disastrous consequences to Western civilization.'[167] For Innis, however, *a real* sense of time is not simply to affirm that events and objects exist as a 'succession of particular states.'[168] Rather, it is to recognize, or believe, or have faith, that there exists 'a state of permanence beyond time,' [169]which is to say that value is intrinsic to the universe.

A concern for time, therefore, according to Innis, the economic historian, is not the same as a concern for history. Quite the contrary! Whereas historical analyses imply that events are unique and that all things change, a concern for time means that people look towards things that do not change. We will see this line of argument developed more fully in the writings of George Grant and Northrop Frye.

INNIS'S CONTRIBUTION

It is impossible in a few pages to give adequate summary to Innis's immense contribution to communication studies. Here I will but point to schools of thought that he inspired or anticipated. One of these is *communication and history*, that is, the practice of placing media of communication at the very centre of historical analysis. Innis certainly inspired Marshall McLuhan in this regard, and together they gave rise a still burgeoning literature.[170]

A second mode of media analysis that can be traced to Innis is *dependency theory*, or media imperialism. Control of media, for many present-day political economists, is basic, since from that stems control over symbolization and knowledge. Innis, however, was first to centre the analysis of political economy on communication media, and in so doing he again inspired a vast literature.[171]

Finally, Innis at least anticipated a third stream of thought – namely, *postmodernism* – inasmuch as he saw space binding media as more thoroughly commodifying life, and in the process eroding hitherto enduring meanings and distinctions. Moreover, according to Innis, reliance on mechanical means for diffusing information puts into question the reliability of that information; he mused: 'As modern developments in communication have made for greater realism they have made for greater possibilities of delusion,'[172] a sentiment eminently worthy of today's major postmodern writers. According to Jean Baudrillard, for example, we now live in a mediated world of *simulacra*, defined as 'copies' (theme parks, for instance) without originals.[173] Furthermore, due to a superfluity of information in this Information Age, there is a lessening of the value of information, an insight Innis put forth, and assented to by many postmodern writers.[174] Innis wrote: 'The printing press and the radio have enormously increased the difficulties of thought; … freedom of the press and freedom of speech have been possible [i.e., have been tolerated] largely because they have permitted the production of words on an unprecedented scale and have made them powerless.'[175] The devaluation of words, information, and knowledge can have tragic consequences, as the following extract from Aristotle's *Politics* would indicate: 'Speech … serves to indicate what is right and what is wrong. For the real difference between humans and other animals is that humans alone have perception of good and evil, right and wrong, just and unjust. And it is the sharing of a common view in these matters that makes a household or a city.'[176]

SOME QUESTIONS

A number of questions arise from Innis's work. Here I pose but three. First, is Innis's later media theory, what we have termed here his 'communication thesis,' an extension of or consistent with his staples thesis, or is it perhaps something quite different? Second, what is the relevance of Innis's thought to the early twenty-first century? Third, is it possible to attain a sense of balance or proportion in the modern, media-saturated world?

Communication and Staples Theses Compared

Innis formulated the staples thesis in the 1920s and 1930s in an effort to devise a distinctly *Canadian* economic history and economic theory. By contrast, through his media theory proper, which focused not on staples, but on orality and various means of inscription, he self-consciously followed in the footsteps of 'Spengler, Toynbee, Kroeber, Sorokin, and others [who] have produced works, designed to throw light on the causes of the rise and decline of civilizations.'[177] One might then ask why, if Innis is correct, *economic* theory and history are inherently particularistic, whereas *media* theory is or can be universalistic. This raises the further question of exactly how the staples thesis, economic theory, and the communication thesis are related. Staples and media proper, after all, were both addressed by Innis in the context of their consequences for the administration of large areas, for centripetal versus centrifugal forces, for centre–periphery relations, and for their implications regarding the penetrative powers of the price system. Recall also that, according to Innis, staples, in conjunction with geography and associated technology, could serve either to centralize or to decentralize governance in Canada. Highly significant in this regard were the bulk and weight of the staple relative to its value. These properties in turn established either an east–west or a north–south line of transportation and communication. On the other hand, irrespective of the lines of trade induced by their physical properties, according to Innis's analysis staples inevitably *deepen relations between a centre and its periphery.* Stated otherwise, trade in staples inexorably strengthens the penetrative powers of the price system. Some staples, of course, are more 'space binding' than others. The Newfoundland fisheries, for example, at first induced little permanent settlement, and thereafter only settlement along the coast. The fur trade was more 'space-binding,' fostering settlement in the interior. The lumber trade was more 'space-binding' still, spawning present-mindedness by facilitating growth of a news and advertising complex.

On the basis of this short recapitulation, one might conclude that staples, like media proper, can be arrayed on a spectrum of less- to more space-biased. On the other hand, however, unlike certain media proper, staples *are by definition space-binding* since inherently they serve to conjoin centre and periphery, albeit to greater or lesser extents, depending on the staple in question. There is no such thing, in other words, as a 'time-binding' staple, unless perhaps it is harvested exclusively for local use, in which case use of the very term 'staple' seems inappropriate. Staples production, Innis noted repeatedly, works its effects in conjunction with geography (principally the inland water routes), and with technology (the railway, canals, roads, pulp and paper mills, hydro-electric power stations, and so on). Coupled only to geography, staples production would certainly have produced space-binding effects, but effects much smaller than those produced when capital-intensive technology was applied to their extraction, processing, and distribution. Whereas geography was certainly important in the early years of staples' exploitation, it is also the case that technology, if anything, superseded geography in importance later on, heightening the space-binding character of staples.

In this light, Innis's staples thesis might very well be reformulated to the effect that *whatever* increases economic relations among regions or between hinterlands and centres – staples, money, inland waterways, oceans, ships, electricity, writing materials, printing presses, radio, and so forth – 'biases' indigenous cultures in the direction of space to the sacrifice of time. In this context, Innis's communication thesis can be seen as simultaneously broader and narrower than the staples thesis. It is broader because it addresses world history, not merely Canadian economic history. It is narrower because it concentrates primarily on various means of inscription, as opposed to recognizing the space-binding properties of other media, such as modes of transportation, energy, manufacturing, staples, and so forth.

Certainly staples cannot be reduced to (nor can they be enfolded within) a category called 'the means of inscription.' Equally clearly, however, staples *are* media of communication. Recognition of this latter point opens the way to an expansive definition for the term 'media of communication,' and makes Innis a progenitor, like Dewey, Park, and Veblen, of *mediation theory*. His discourse on staples and media proper, therefore, launches our study into the thought of other key Canadian communication theorists, particularly C.B. Macpherson, Northrop Frye, George Grant, and Marshall McLuhan, who likewise were very concerned with mediation, but whose focus was considerably broader than mass media or telecommunications systems.

RELEVANCE TO OUR DAY

Innovation at the Margins?
In some respects Innis's analyses, at least initially, seem quite inapplicable to our day, but in other ways they are most obviously prophetic. Here we address five issues. First is the question of whether new media are developed primarily by those at the periphery so as to erode established media power, as Innis suggested, or whether those at the centre are customarily the innovative ones as part of a continuing strategy to entrench their power.

Ours, it is often said, is an era of media *convergence*.[178] Global media conglomerates enfold under their control an increasingly wide array of hitherto distinct media operations – feature films, satellite television, news services, publishing, sound recordings, heavily advertised consumer products, and so forth. Looking broadly, one sees not an erosion in the power of established media, but concentration, and that on a global as well as a local basis.[179]

Moreover, mass media for decades have been conscious instruments of foreign policy on account of their 'space-binding' properties.[180] Writing recently in the influential journal *Foreign Affairs*, highly placed officials within the U.S. military-industrial establishment declared that information/communication is 'soft power,' more subtle perhaps than traditional military armaments but in the long run more effective.[181] It is at least partly for that reason that the Unites States insisted that information/communication be included in GATT (General Agreement on Tariffs and Trade) and World Trade Organization deliberations, and made it subject to bilateral and multilateral trade agreements such as the Canada–U.S. Free Trade Agreement and the North American Free Trade Agreement (NAFTA). Moreover, much of the innovation in communication media over the past fifty years can be traced to a single source – the U.S. military, which played a large role in the development of radio transmissions, satellites, computers, and the Internet.[182]

Some view the Internet particularly as a mode of communication that offsets the concentrated one-way communicatory power of mass media. Indeed, evidence supporting this position is presented in chapter 4 with regard to the delay, if not defeat, of the Multilateral Agreement on Investment (MAI). Regardless of its potential for democratic bidirectional communication, however, it is to be noted that the Internet, like so many other communication innovations, originated with the U.S. military, not in the periphery, as Innis's analysis might lead us to expect.

Mass Media versus Cyberspace?

Regardless of origins and initial development, emerging computer communication networks ('cyberspace') are seen by some as being in dialectical tension with traditional mass media – indeed, in a manner not unlike Innis's space–time dialectic.[183] According to this line of thought, mass media radiate messages from concentrated centres, whereas the Internet encourages lateral communication among communities of interest. Innis may therefore provide a key to understanding the present and predicting the future.

Within *both* mass media and cyberspace, however, we see contradictory trends. Consider, first, mass media. On the one hand, without question the global reach of concentrated media conglomerates is expanding, particularly through satellites and digitization. On the other, mass communication *seems* to be fragmenting through a proliferation of media outlets. The number of television channels available to those with satellite reception capability is now in the hundreds. In Innisian terms, however, this fragmentation of audience can be understood primarily as a *heightening* of the penetrative powers of the price system. The proliferation of channels segments audiences more precisely into demographically and psychographically defined clusters, thereby aiding the marketing of audiences to advertisers. Other channels are offered on a pay basis, further commodifying communication, that is, making it more space-biased. Audience members for each of the now multitudinous channels remain out of contact with one another and with members of other groupings as their attention is increasingly focused on narrow points of interest, discouraging dialogic communication. All news channels, sports channels, shopping channels, arts and entertainment channels, moreover, are, if anything, 'present-minded.'

Within cyberspace, too, there are apparently conflicting trends. On the one hand, cyberspace has been heralded as a new, global, democratic mode of communicating. Through e-mail messages are dispatched instantaneously from point to point, while through the World Wide Web any individual can 'publish' messages accessible by all with a computer, modem, and telecommunications link. However, only a small, relatively wealthy minority of the world's population currently accesses the Internet, belying the aptness of the term 'democratic' in that regard. Moreover, the Internet is increasingly commercialized; more and more it is a site for advertising, on-line sales and other financial transactions. The top ten web sites account for a disproportionate number of 'hits,' and if current trends continue the Internet will surely constitute yet another, even more powerful, mode of mass merchandising. Even with regard to electronic messaging within communities of interest, some foresee marketers as sponsoring (mediating) the communication;[184] others note that these activities contribute to surveillance generally and to market research in particular.[185]

Within an Innisian framework, then, there are a number of observations to be made. First, in terms of spatiality, converging mass media *and* emerging cyberspace make global communication more profuse than its local counterpart. In that sense, space and time are to be seen as being increasingly out of balance. Second, for both mass media and emerging cyberspace, there is fragmentation of communication; Innis would probably have interpreted this as a further breakdown in awareness of the *common good*. Third, globalized, converging mass media remain one-way, which is certainly consistent with space-biased communication, whereas emerging cyberspace offers not only the capacity for point-to-mass communication, but also two-way, lateral communication. This latter capability is why some see cyberspace as the dialectical opposite of mass communication. Apart from the relative strengths of vertical, one-way communication versus two-way, lateral communication within cyberspace, however, cyberspace inherently emphasizes communication over geographic expanse, and in that sense is fully consistent with the space-bias of mass media.

Cultural Ecology

In accord with John Dewey, Thorstein Veblen, Robert Park, and other mentors from his time at the University of Chicago, Innis insisted that the means of communication and the messages circulating in society at any given time constitute what we might call a 'cultural ecology,'[186] that is, a mindset or a shared system of meanings characterizing a culture. There in fact exists a voluminous literature on what has been variously termed the 'social construction of reality,' 'symbolic interactionism,' and 'the sociology of knowledge,' which contends that reality is not objectively given but is a product of the interaction of the knower and the known in the context of social consensus. One of Innis's major contributions was to argue that the means whereby signs, symbols, and messages are diffused and exchanged have a significant bearing on this cultural ecology, and in broadly predictable ways. As we contemplate various trends and crises – the political shift to the right in many industrialized countries, overpopulation, toxic wastes and spills, species extinction, greenhouse gases and acid rain, war, heightening gaps between rich and poor – we would do well to pause and consider the consequences of existing and emerging media of communication for our organic and symbolic ecosystems.[187] In this regard, it is instructive to bear in mind the dictum he advanced while thinking of German cinema during the Second World War: 'As modern developments in communication have made for greater realism, they have made for greater possibilities for delusion.'[188]

Ideology of Information Technology

Innis sounded the alarm against what has been described as 'the ideology of information technology,'[189] the notion that adoption of advancing communication technologies is essential for countries to maintain their place in the world. According to the Organization for Economic Cooperation and Development (OECD), for instance,

> IT [Information technology] is now regarded as indispensable to many economic activities, and industry experts consider broader IT production and use as a basis for further economic and social development (especially together with further development of relevant human resources). IT has become a strategic tool in the contemporary economic and political environment, as well for the opening up of new markets and patterns of demand.[190]

A reading of Innis, of course, would not make one so sanguine. First, the space bias of cultures, according to an Innisian analysis, is more than likely to increase through continual adoption of IT, with deleterious implications for geographically based communities. Of course, computer networks facilitate communication over distance, and so can help maintain relations previously formed, and develop new ones based on common affinities. On the other hand, our democratic political structures are all geographically based, and enhancing 'communities' that cross political boundaries is in effect to weaken local and national communities and political structures. The beneficiaries, as noted by Robert Chodos et al., are those entities that transcend national geographic structures – in particular, transnational corporations.[191] Thus we witness the decline in national sovereignty, and hence of democracy, which many summarize with the euphemism 'globalization.'

Concomitantly, dependence of third-world countries on the 'first world' deepens. Heightened commodity status for information, both a goal of those innovating IT and an effect of its use, means that information-rich, first-world countries can and do trade information in world markets to attain foreign exchange with which to purchase energy, natural resources, and the products of cheap labour – even while retaining the information/knowledge they sell once the trade is concluded! Information is a classic case of a 'public good,'[192] an issue to be broached again in subsequent chapters.

In conclusion, it is sufficient to note that Innisian-style analyses lead to conclusions significantly different from the more commonly expressed rhetoric of the technologically sublime.

Stability and Community in a Media-Saturated World?

Finally, we may ask, are stability and a sense of community still possible in an a world given over increasingly to space-binding media? Is abandoning the ideals of stability in favour of dynamic change, and of community in favour of commodity exchange, also necessarily to surrender to the 'cruelty of mechanized communication'? While at times Innis implied that a homeostatic principle exists whereby undue biases in the direction either of time or of space are automatically subject to correction, he also studied the rise and decline of civilizations and contended that Western civilization is now risking extinction on account of its neglect of time. To place complete faith in the inevitability of a homeostatic correction, or the 'invisible hand,' is tantamount to passivity, and one could argue this is precisely the spirit the commercial agencies of propaganda wish to inculcate. Pessimistic though Innis's writings became, they are nonetheless a clarion call to action, or redirection.

4

The Communication Thought of
JOHN GRIERSON (1898–1972)

By God, I am a fighting believer in democracy.

– Eyes of Democracy, 31

ABOUT JOHN GRIERSON

John Grierson, descendent of a long line of lighthouse keepers, was born in the tiny village of Deanston, just northwest of Stirling, Scotland, on 26 April 1898.[1] His mother, Jane Anthony, had been a teacher before her marriage. When John was two, his father, Robert Grierson, also a teacher, became headmaster of the school at Cambusbarron, today a suburb of Stirling. During the time the Griersons lived there, that mining community was replete with open sewers and middens. John's parents, both social democrats, strove to ameliorate the suffering in their community.[2] As a youth John Grierson inherited their social-democratic leanings and as well their religiosity; he even visited rural parishes by motorcycle as a lay preacher.

When he was seventeen Grierson entered the naval reserve. During the war he served as a telegraph operator aboard converted fishing trawlers used as mine-sweepers. According to his friend, editor and biographer Forsyth Hardy, for three years he sailed the North Sea 'with sudden death a constant possibility.'[3]

When the war ended, Grierson attended Glasgow University to study English literature and moral philosophy. There he joined the university's Fabian Society, which at his suggestion dissolved, to be replaced by the more activist New Labour Club. Upon graduation he lectured briefly, and with little satisfaction, at Durham University: he stated that, in-

stead of attending classes, the 'old clerks and spinsters' who were his
students ought to have been 'raising hell about the slums of the city, the
malnutrition of its children and its horrible schools.'[4]

In 1924, Grierson visited the University of Chicago as a Rockefeller
Research Fellow, initially to study how the press helped immigrants
meld into the American way of life.[5] There he encountered such eminent scholars as Charles E. Merriam and Robert E. Park (Innis's mentor), but, having grown weary of 'begoggled academics,'[6] he soon
moved on. Grierson travelled the country, visiting newspaper editors
in major cities and writing editorials for them without charge. During
these excursions he met both the celebrated political news columnist
Walter Lippmann and the documentary filmmaker Robert Flaherty.

Lippmann by that time had become an arch anti-democrat. His influential tome *Public Opinion,* published in 1922, argued that the practice
of democracy had 'turned a corner,' and that a new, more workable
version was now, of necessity, the norm. For pure or ideal democracy to
exist, Lippmann insisted, citizens need be rational, well informed, and
of generous spirit. Nowhere in the modern world, he declared, were
those conditions met. Common people, rather, he averred, are selfish
and on most issues ill informed, and possess no more than a rudimen-
tary capacity for reasoning. That being the case, he concluded, the old
'dogma' needed to be set aside and replaced by a more modern, 'prag-
matic' version – one that recognizes explicitly the need for an élite class
which alone possesses the knowledge, powers of reason, and goodwill
to make 'democracy' work. Moreover, it is the duty of these governors
to enlist the services of public persuaders who can 'manufacture the
consent' of the general populace for their cleverly contrived policies.
Lippmann's book at once enchanted and repelled Grierson (more on this
below).

While visiting New York, Grierson interviewed Lippmann, who advised the aspiring journalist to forsake press studies and investigate
instead the educational possibilities of the cinema,[7] guidance that caused
Grierson soon to visit Hollywood and Paramount Pictures. Granted
access to Paramount's files, Grierson prepared a report on the relation
between a film's content and the size of its box-office receipts.[8] There,
too, he met Flaherty, 'a poet of cinema,'[9] whose *Nanook of the North* gave
audiences a window from which to view *actual* hunger and *real world*
struggles for survival.[10]

Back in New York, Grierson began to write regularly on the movies,
his first articles appearing in the New York *Sun.* Many of these essays,

along with others written later in England, were compiled in a book entitled *Grierson on the Movies* (1981).

Slowly Grierson's life plan changed, and by 1927 his goal had clarified: to use the cinema to touch as many people as possible with the democratic ideal. He began, as he put it, to look upon the cinema 'as a pulpit, and use it as a propagandist.'[11]

Flaherty's pioneering work notwithstanding, the concept of *documentary* film was practically invented by Grierson. He variously defined documentary as 'the creative treatment of actuality,'[12] as film 'made from natural material,'[13] and as the cinematic presentation of 'drama that resides in the living fact.'[14] He chose *film* as his principal medium because it enabled him to reach a wide audience. And he selected *documentary* film because, he said, it is 'closer to the people and events.' Grierson's goal was to use cinema to increase people's awareness of reality, not to help them escape from it. He wrote: 'We believe that the materials and the stories thus taken from the raw can be finer (more real in the philosophic sense) than the acted article.'[15] To produce films with actors and scripts, he added, would inevitably mean that commercial considerations would be paramount. 'No service [is] so great or inspiring,' he remarked, 'and particularly for film-makers as a service which detaches itself from personal profit.'[16] Being relatively cheap to produce, documentaries also were within Grierson's limited financial means.

His first opportunity to actually work with the educational and propagandistic potential of film arose when he was hired by Sir Stephen Tallents, secretary of the Empire Marketing Board (EMB). The result was *Drifters* (1929), a film on the Scottish herring fisheries that Grierson wrote, directed, and edited. According to Hardy, *Drifters* for the first time brought British workers to the screen with dignity.[17] It was, in fact, first in a long line of British documentaries having, as Grierson put it, 'a theme in social observation – the ardour and bravery of common labour.'[18] For critic Joyce Nelson, however, *Drifters* was flawed: The fishermen, she complained, were presented solely from a 'middle class' or 'establishment' perspective, glorifying work perhaps, but avoiding basic issues such as wages and working conditions.[19] In weighing these comments, however, one ought to recall that the film's sponsor was, after all, the British government, meaning that Grierson's creative genius was not unconstrained.[20] Merely for representing working people with dignity,[21] Grierson was branded a Bolshevist by some.[22]

Rather than continuing to make films on his own, as he might well have done, Grierson next decided to head up the newly established

Empire Marketing Board Film Unit, thus inaugurating the British documentary-film movement. When the EMB folded in 1933, the film unit transferred, with Stephen Tallents, to the General Post Office (GPO),[23] where documentary production continued apace.

Many of the GPO films expressed sociological concerns. *Housing Problems,* for instance, presented *cinema verité* interviews with people in tiny slum rooms full of rats, with water running down the walls.[24] Grierson confided: 'The sense of social responsibility makes our realist documentary a troubled and difficult art in a time like ours.'[25] Always viewing his mission as that of educator first and artist second, he characterized his films as a *course of realism,* as opposed to the 'musicals and farces galore'[26] of the commercial cinema.

Meeting resistance from commercial distributors and exhibitors, Grierson devised novel ways to attract audiences. Through the Empire Film Library he arranged free loans of films by mail. He also organized exhibitions in the countryside by dispatching GPO travelling projectionists. He enlisted critics to review his films in the major papers. And he was instrumental in founding three journals – *Cinema Quarterly, World Film News,* and *Documentary News Letter* – to publicize the documentary-film movement.[27]

Grierson resigned from the GPO in 1937 to accept a commission from the Imperial Relations Trust to report on the film industries of Canada, Australia, New Zealand, and South Africa. This appointment coincided with a request from the Canadian government to devise a plan for the development of Canadian film. Grierson's proposal to the Canadian government was accepted in May 1939, and by Act of Parliament the National Film Board of Canada (NFB) was created, with Grierson as its first commissioner. During the war, Grierson served briefly also as the general manager of Canada's Wartime Information Board, the agency coordinating the government's information and propaganda activities.

For the NFB he recruited several key filmmaking colleagues from Britain, who formed the nucleus of the organization's wartime production staff. Grierson regarded cinema as a 'necessary instrument' of the war effort – 'a great instrument of propaganda ... one of the keys to men's minds.'[28] Through the series *Canada Carries On* and *The World in Action,* movie production in Canada increased dramatically. In 1945 alone the NFB produced 250 films,[29] most intended, in Grierson's words, to 'mobilize the patrol ships of the human mind.'[30] The large majority were compilations; that is, they contained little original footage. NFB filmmakers were, in other words, 'masters of montage,'[31] selecting sequences from other films and stock material, and editing these, typically adding 'a voice of authority' soundtrack.[32]

Unlike the propaganda issuing from other countries, the NFB's wartime films contained little or no hatemongering or violence. Grierson always adhered to the goal of keeping alive 'the decent human values.[33] He knew that, when the war ended, people would have to get along once more, and he wished to help make the peace stable. NFB films therefore focused on industrial preparations for war and on the peace that would ensue, not on the fighting.

NFB wartime films were shown not only in theatres, but in church basements, union halls, and community centres. Teams of itinerant projectionists visited up to twenty rural areas each month – travelling 'by car, train, tractor, dogsled, tug, water taxi or snowplane.'[34] By 1945 some 250,000 rural Canadians received monthly visits from the rural-circuit projectionists, 300,000 workers were called upon by industrial-circuit projectionists, and another 100,000 people were visited by the trade-union projectionists.

At the war's conclusion, Grierson resigned as Film Commissioner. He planned to establish a base in New York for international film production, plans that foundered, however, when the Red Scare broke.[35] On 6 September 1945, Igor Gouzenko, a cipher clerk in the Soviet Embassy in Ottawa, defected, turning over documents to the RCMP concerning a Soviet spy ring. Among those named was Grierson's temporary secretary for six months at the NFB. At an ensuing royal commission inquiry, Gouzenko denied that Grierson had been a Soviet agent and no charges were laid against him.[36] Nor was there a shred of evidence that Grierson had been involved in any way.

Nonetheless, as NFB historian Gary Evans put it, 'Grierson slipped and the prime minister [Mackenzie King] let him fall.'[37] When his application for a U.S. visa was being questioned on security grounds, for example, no prominent Canadian stepped forward to attest to Grierson's loyalty or to the service he had rendered the country during the war. Soon Grierson was barred from entering the United States.

In 1947, through the auspices of the British government (and much to the dismay of FBI director J. Edgar Hoover), Grierson was appointed adviser on Mass Media and Public Information to Julian Huxley, the first director general of the newly established United Nations Educational, Scientific, and Cultural Organization (UNESCO) in Paris. Grierson, though, stayed only one year. Much later he recalled that he had disagreed fundamentally with what he then saw as the U.S. government's plan to take over the financing of UNESCO and to use it as an instrument to implement its policy on the 'free flow of information.' Indeed, according to Grierson, the United States envisioned assuming control of 'all the radio stations, which had been set up by the great warring nations, and putting a radio network around the world.' He continued: 'This is against my principles ... We were handing over this vast machine to American know-how, to American technicians, to an inevitable American stranglehold on information.'[38]

Grierson next joined the Central Office of Information in London to plan, produce, and distribute government films.[39] In 1957 he launched a weekly program, *This Wonderful World,* on Scottish television, which for its eleven-year run received critical acclaim.

In 1968, almost destitute and suffering ill effects from years of alcohol abuse, he accepted an appointment at McGill University. Soon he was attracting up to 700 students for his introductory film course, and teaching a graduate seminar as well. Abstaining absolutely from hard drink, Grierson continued to teach at McGill until shortly before his death. Learning that his demise was imminent, he gathered belongings scattered on three continents and returned to his wife and home in England, where he surrounded himself with radio and television sets, newspapers, and books. He died in a hospital at Bath, on 19 February 1972, while dictating into a tape recorder.[40] His ashes were scattered into the sea.[41]

According to Harry Watt, a producer recruited at the GPO, John Grierson was an inspiration; he had 'the theory, the belief, and transmitted to us this faith and this belief that what we were doing was worthwhile.'[42]

The amount of time that Grierson spent in Canada was quite limited in comparison with the other theorists treated in this volume. During his later years, however, Grierson did not lose touch with the National Film Board, and he frequently remarked that he desperately wanted to return to Canada,[43] which of course he did at the end of his life. Moreover, it was during his time in Canada that he theorized extensively not only on the nature and function of documentary films, but also on interrelations among democracy, education, propaganda, and media practice. Born in a country marginal to England, Grierson well understood the problems smaller, indigenous cultures face, and that inordinate flows of communication across national borders pose severe challenges to sovereignty and democracy.[44] As a filmmaker and teacher, Grierson inspired thousands of Canadians, and his institutional legacy persists to this day. These considerations warrant the acclaim of his being considered foundational to Canadian communication thought.

DEMOCRACY, EDUCATION, PROPAGANDA

During his years as head of the NFB, Grierson theorized on media, democracy, education, and propaganda. Many of his ideas are contained in two books: *Grierson on Documentary* (first edition 1946) compiled by Forsyth Hardy, and *Eyes of Democracy* (written mostly in 1942 but published in 1990), edited and introduced by Ian Lockerbie.[45]

For readers unfamiliar with Grierson's thought, the Scottish filmmaker may at first seem highly paradoxical, indeed antidemocratic. He recommended, for instance, that in peacetime *propaganda* be a major instrument for furthering *democratic* practice. He deemed propaganda a cornerstone of a new, working-class *enlightenment*. Many, of course, think of propaganda as a perverse art, sinister in its purposes, and practised primarily (in peace time at least) by authoritarian regimes intent on subverting citizens, and by advertisers seeking to lure audiences into purchases they otherwise would not want and do not need. Not untypical is philosopher Gabriel Marcel's characterization of propaganda as a *technique of degradation:* 'An effective propagandist,' Marcel wrote, 'winds *into* the thought, and *under* the thoughts, of his auditor, in order to circumvent him.'[46] Likewise, according to Jacques Ellul, 'propaganda is a manipulation of psychological symbols having goals of which the *listener is not conscious.*' Ellul therefore added, 'Propaganda ceases where simple dialogue begins.'[47]

Nor did Grierson do much to enhance his claim to be a 'fighter for democracy' when he made such intemperate but eminently quotable pronouncements as the following: 'I am not going to pretend that I do not realize how "totalitarian" some of my conclusions seem, without the qualification I have just noted. You can be "totalitarian" for evil and you can also be "totalitarian" for good.'[48] And again: 'A mirror held up to nature is not so important in a dynamic and fast-changing society as the hammer which shapes it – it is as a hammer, not a mirror, that I have sought to use the medium that came to my somewhat restive hand.'[49]

Little wonder that some have seen Grierson as an apologist for autocracy.[50] But Grierson perceived himself much differently – as a veritable *democrat* and *educator*, who deployed his cinematic crafts *to emancipate* citizens and help retrieve *authentic* democratic practice.

The position advanced in this chapter, quite simply, is that Grierson was neither totalitarian nor, in the end, paradoxical. Rather, he strove above all to reconcile (or *synthesize* in the dialectical sense) the 'dilemma of democracy' as put forth by Lippmann, on the one hand, and the pure theory of democracy, on the other. Grierson seems paradoxical and at times tyrannical only because he was dealing with, and attempting to resolve, this gaping contradiction.

It is also important when reading Grierson to bear in mind disparate connotations inherent in the major terms he used: 'democracy,' 'propaganda,' 'education' – these words all are polysemic; different authors use them in remarkably different ways. It is essential, therefore, to understand Grierson's meaning in order to appraise the connections he forged among them.

Democracy

Democracy was Grierson's primary concern. But 'democracy' means different things to different people. According to the classical and agrarian (or Jeffersonian) conceptions, for instance, as described derisively by Walter Lippmann, democracy presumes that a 'reasoned righteousness' wells up 'spontaneously out of the mass of men'[51] whereby they are enabled to assume complete charge over their affairs. Classical theorists presume 'an unlimited supply of self-sufficient individuals'[52] who assemble together to discuss and decide on public affairs in an informed, reasoned manner, with goodwill.[53]

Once removed from total *participatory* democracy is *representative* democracy. In terms of how the latter is practised in the capitalist (liberal) states, attention tends to focus on the franchise and on such basic liberties as freedom of speech, assembly, and movement. Those freedoms nearly always exist, however, critics point out, alongside enormous disparities in living conditions. Leaders of the former *communist* countries, consequently, maintained that equity in the distribution of income is the *sine qua non* of the democratic state, not the formal freedoms, which mean so little if one is without basic needs. Others, for example Raymond Williams, have addressed the question of representation per se, arguing that, in practice, elected representatives are drawn almost entirely from a particular (i.e., propertied) class, a practice that undermines the democratic notion[54] and makes the practice of democracy a 'necessary illusion.'[55]

Given such marked disparities in conceptualization, what was *Grierson's* meaning of 'democracy'? For one thing, he insisted that democracy can never be 'cosy.' He declared, 'I never heard freedom talked about without the notion that it had to be fought for, or privileges without the notion that they carried responsibilities.'[56] True democrats, he confided, 'despise' the idea of security.[57] It is a humiliating sight, he averred, when people grow 'fat' upon attaining their heart's desire.[58] Put more positively, Grierson proposed that the essence of democracy is that 'constructive action shall bubble up all over the place.'[59] Democracies, in his sense, then, are political systems that encourage discussion, initiative, and activity at the local level.

This is not to say, however, that Grierson did not envisage an important role for élites. On the contrary, élites are needed, he said, to provide leadership in developing and implementing policies designed to meet the needs *expressed by the larger population.* At McGill he frequently exhorted his graduate students that, as society's future élites, they needed *to serve* the general public, and not merely look after their own interests.[60] 'To serve' requires that one continuously be in dialogue with the rank and file.

Moreover, for Grierson, democracy is, above all, a *faith* – 'the faith that we the people [can], with hand and brain, run the world we [live] in,'[61] and that *'a man is a man for a' that.'*[62] We can speculate that ultimately it is acceptance or rejection of this 'faith' that separates democrats such as Grierson from autocrats such as Lippmann. Lippmann, after all, had no notion that leaders should be bound by the needs and aspirations of those they govern; rather, he proposed that élites should 'manufacture consent' for policies they had themselves devised.

In some other respects, however, Grierson agreed with Lippmann. Both disputed the 'dogma of democracy.' People simply *cannot* be experts on all matters of public concern. Nor are people necessarily the rational decision-makers the pure theory of democracy requires. Furthermore the press cannot adequately inform people on public issues to the extent that the pure theory of democracy demands. But, it is to be emphasized, Grierson disputed fundamentally Lippmann's conclusion that these conditions necessitate that consensus be 'manufactured,' and he was equally dismayed by his mentor's all-too-ready acceptance of autocracy. Grierson therefore set out to 'fill the gap in educational practices' as his way of retrieving authentic democracy.

Education

Grierson was, according to his self-appraisal, a democratic pragmatist: he was willing to modify democratic practices as needed in light of contemporary conditions without, however, sacrificing discussion and initiative at the grass-roots level – for him the essence of democracy. Grierson described his proposed synthesis between the cynical auto-cratic realism of Lippmann and the agrarian/classical democratic ideal-ism of Thomas Jefferson as bringing the latter 'down to the realm of practical consideration and achievement.'[63]

In an effort to accomplish this, Grierson recommended that educa-tors and artists devise *democratic propaganda* – what he also called *the necessary education* – to enlighten and motivate citizens. No, Grierson attested, the average person is not sufficiently aware; nor can he or she be expected to be an expert in much. But, if guided by democratically inspired educators and artists, people *can* make wise decisions in choos-ing their goals, and they *can* act in ways that lead to the realization of them.

Speaking to the American Library Association in 1946, Grierson rec-ollected his childhood in the mining village in Scotland, where resi-dents faced continual deprivation.[64] Of what possible use to them, he asked, were the philosophical musings and poetic insights dispensed by the schools? Are educators not fixated on making of everyone a 'gentleman in the library'? He added tellingly, 'If the people of my village can now look forward to better lives and better conditions of work, it is certainly not because of the ideals which education set before them. It is because they thought out their economic problems for them-selves and because they organized and struck and fought and finally voted the conditions of their own future.'[65]

For Grierson, then, it is not in imparting what he called the 'genteel grace notes of human thought' that the real value of the library and the school lies for working people, but rather in equipping them with practical tools for everyday living.[66] Indeed, he laid at the very door-step of traditional education part of the blame for the waning of democ-racy, charging:

> We think the theory of education itself is wrong, and that it proceeds on an altogether false assumption. The false assumption is the mystical demo-cratic assumption that the citizen can be so taught to understand what is going on about him that he and his fellows in the mass can, through the electoral and parliamentary process, give an educated and rational guid-ance to the conduct of the state. In its extreme form, it is the false assump-tion that a man can know everything about everything all the time. This assumption, we say, has led education woefully astray and is continuing

to do so. We say quite precisely that education has set itself an impossible task and therefore a wrong task; and we add that, by so doing, it has blinded itself to what is possible and therefore right. We even add that, by bringing democracy to a state of disappointment, discouragement, impotence, and frustration, it has put the survival of democracy itself in jeopardy.[67]

If education is to be of value to workers and be supportive of democracy, he contended, it must become *less* rational, *less* analytical, *less* dispassionate, *more* emotive, *more* synoptic, and *more* persuasive: in sum, *more propagandistic*! In making these pronouncements he anticipated Marshall McLuhan by over twenty years. Grierson declared: 'Education has concentrated so much on people knowing things that it has not sufficiently taught them to feel things'; and again: '[Education] gives them facts but has not sufficiently given them faith'[68] – faith in themselves, faith in democratic modes of decision making, faith in the goodness of their fellow citizens. Education *for* democracy, he insisted, requires that issues be simplified and presented in dramatic ways, first to attract attention, and second to stir people to action, initiative for him being 'the heart and soul of the democratic idea.'[69]

Grierson maintained further that there are 'basic dramatic patterns' or recurrences in public affairs, of which citizens need to be apprised. He termed these the 'shorthand method[s] for world observation';[70] McLuhan was to call them 'myths.' 'Revelation of these dramatic patterns,' Grierson insisted, 'is a first essential in the process of modern education.'[71]

Grierson recognized that his proposals departed significantly from traditional views of education, that in recommending that educators emphasize through narrative the *patterns* (meanings) of facts, as opposed to the facts themselves, he was further 'politicizing' education. He argued, however, that as far as democracy is concerned *there is no neutral ground*. The options for education, he exhorted, are either to be 'for democracy and against authoritarianism, or … for authoritarianism.'[72] Given that premise, Grierson concluded, 'propaganda, so far from being the denial of the democratic principle of education, becomes *the necessary instrument* for its practical fulfilment.'[73] He predicted confidently: 'Much of what we now know as education will become what we now know as propaganda.'[74]

However, more is at stake, Grierson cautioned, than merely democracy. The whole of human history to the present, he attested, has been racked by wars over the material means of living. Unless greed and self-centredness are deliberately redressed through education, inequities will surely become more pronounced, particularly as new technologies of transportation and communication proliferate. It is vital, he concluded, that educators and creative workers inculcate in citizens a sense of heightened interdependence and an ethic of the common good.[75]

Propaganda

Democracy being a faith as well as a practice means that democracy's proponents can aptly be termed 'propagandists' – albeit in the original sense of those who spread a faith. In the context of Grierson's thought on media and democracy, then, *propaganda* has a meaning far different from that of Marcel and Ellul. In using the term, Grierson meant not lies or attempts to subvert audiences, but inspirational and dramatic approaches to public education. His intent was to uplift, not 'circumvent'; he strove to stimulate dialogue, not stifle it.

Grierson might very well have been further ahead had he simply termed himself an advocate and publicist of democracy, rather than its propagandist. The period during which he wrote, however, provides an important clue as to why he insisted on characterizing himself as he did. He thought of himself as engaging dialectically in a struggle with Goebbels, the Nazi master of propaganda, for people's hearts and minds, and in that context he distinguished propaganda for democracy, such as he recommended and practised, from what he termed 'propaganda on the offensive.' Both types, he recognized, simplify and repeat in order to persuade; also, they appeal in the first instance to the emotions, for only after the emotions have been enlisted does the intellect come into play. ('The heart has reasons that Reason will never know,' wrote Pascal.)

Despite such commonalties, though, Grierson insisted that there are profound differences. First, democratic propaganda does not lie.[76] Second, whereas propaganda on the offensive spreads antidemocratic, authoritarian values, democratic propaganda spreads democratic, humane ones. In Grierson's opinion, democratic, humane values include: internationalism, cooperation, service, the dignity of the working person, fraternity, equality, dialogue, local initiative, and an ethic of the common good. Finally, democratic propaganda is constrained as to its permissible sphere of persuasion; with respect to his own films, for example, Grierson explained: 'Where we stopped short was that, with equal deliberation, we refused to specify what political agency should carry out that will or associate ourselves with any one of them. Our job specifically was to wake the heart and the will: it was for the political parties to make before the people their own case for leadership.'[77]

The ethos of democracy, Grierson believed, requires that decisions as to means come from the citizenry.[78] Documentary filmmakers ought only to stimulate 'a phase of criticism,' out of which would arise 'a phase of creation.'[79]

MEDIA AND DEMOCRACY

Authentic democracy, Grierson emphasized, requires a 'quick and living system'[80] of communication – particularly for a country so vast yet sparsely settled as Canada: 'Getting together is important. Getting our ideas together is important. Once good feelings and good ideas move like wildfire across the democratic sky, we are half-way towards building a community worth living in.'[81]

Grierson maintained that democracies rely more heavily upon an effective communication infrastructure than do authoritarian regimes. Dictators, he pointed out, can routinely supplement persuasive communication with force, an option not as readily available to leaders in democracies.[82] Moreover, he conjectured, 'it is your democrat who most needs and demands guidance from his leaders.'[83]

Guidance requires, however, that communication take a form that people can readily understand. And in his view there is no form more readily understandable than narrative. Gary Evans relates that, in graduate seminars, Grierson would often remark on 'active' verbs used by newspapers: somebody does something to somebody.[84] Elsewhere Grierson rhapsodized, '[the Hearst press] turned into a "*story*" what we in Europe called a "report." They had in fact made the *story* – that is to say, a dramatic form – the basis of their means of communication ... I saw in it a necessary instrument not only of education and illumination in our highly complex modern world, but an instrument necessary to a democratic society.'[85]

Although, for Grierson, drama is an essential tool for democratic communication, he also realized that it could be used, and in fact predominantly was being used, to spread antidemocratic values – for example, consumption, acquisition, leisure, individualism, entertainment, passivity, and submission to authority. He added, highly skilled media professionals

have formulated story or pictorial or dramatic shapes. They have evalu-
ated the good and the bad, the heroic and the unheroic, the exciting and
unexciting, the desirable and undesirable. They have observed the things
that interested people; they have researched into the patterns of report
that commanded men's understanding, attention and desire. They have
done so in the name of entertainment, news reporting, salesmanship and
public instruction and ... they have done it for profit. They have ... in fact,
provided a system of evaluation for men's daily experiences where such a
system was lacking. They have consequently created loyalties and formed
the pattern of men's thought and action.[86]

The crisis of democracy, therefore, for Grierson, stemmed in large part
from patterns of ownership and control of the mass media – precisely
the position advanced by Graham Spry with regard to the crisis of
culture.

Grierson felt, of course, that documentary film was admirably suited
for propagating democratic values. Near the end of his life, he also
addressed the democratic potential of television, of which he was a
practitioner but about which he was very sceptical. On the one hand, he
conceded, television is a marvellous device since it reaches people right
in their homes; in that sense it is superior even to the cinema. And being
nestled within the dwelling, television is immensely propagandistic:
'Where more notably than in the home,' he asked, 'does the power of
suggestion operate?'[87] However, on the other hand, he pointed out,
television's immense powers of suggestion have not been, and likely
never can be, put to the service of democracy. In an interview with the
National Film Board, Grierson remarked:

There are limitations to this ... *théâtre intime* of television. There are limitations. And the limitation is the effect that you get cosy. And the people
themselves like television to be cosy. And they don't like to be hurt. When
you show brutal things on television they have no effect. They haven't
the effect you think. McLuhan thinks there is a great effect from this television ... He says it's a massage. Yes it's a massage that medium. It puts
you to sleep. It doesn't brace you. It puts you to sleep. And the people
want to be put asleep, and they object to anything that revokes their
infinite comfort. It is a thing of the home and not an explosion in the
home ... It is an instrument of domestic ease.[88]

Such remarks, however, are atypical. Grierson's major writings, prepared in the 1940s amid the din of the Second World War and prior to the onset of television, express an exuberance about how artists and educators, through their selected media, can be agents for democracy. As Gary Evans notes, it was Grierson's heartfelt position that the democratic élite – the teachers, artists, politicos, and so forth – occupy 'a pulpit,' and that from a pulpit one must never preach despair. With Grierson, 'there is always hope and optimism,' Evans summarized; 'this is the messianic Judeo-Christian ethos which was at his core.'[89]

Given the burgeoning of 'home entertainment' since Grierson's death, it is germane to inquire as to whether such optimism is warranted in our day.

ART AND DEMOCRATIC PROPAGANDA

Art should not be a device for escaping intolerable reality, Grierson insisted, although he recognized that often it is used for precisely that purpose. In an early essay he described well polar-opposite approaches to art, which for him were so well exemplified in the dialectic of documentary versus commercial cinema:

> There are, as I understand it, two paths of imagination and beauty. There is the path which enters bravely into the affairs of men and of nature, and separates the golden rhythms of life from the slip-shod of mere events. And there is the path of fantasy which begins where one's insight has failed. It winds its way in the moonlight and the half-light and presents a vision to its wanderers only when things are already fantastic and obscure. It is the path in the end to sentimentality, for while it pleases our nostalgia for a different world, it reveals nothing about this one.[90]

For Grierson, then, art was to be, first and foremost, a means *to heighten awareness of the real*, no matter how cruel, how unjust, how objectionable that reality might be. Although himself an artist, Grierson certainly was no aesthete. He insisted that if there was ever a contradiction between beauty and goodness, one must always choose goodness, and he urged that governments do so as well. Referring to *Triumph of the Will,* a masterful propaganda film by Nazi filmmaker Leni Riefenstahl, Grierson declared: 'The first test of a film is not whether it is attractive or not, but whether it is good or evil. The work may be very beautiful, but it must not be allowed to lead people to destruction or to pervert youth. I think there are lots of beautiful films going around today that shouldn't be presented because they are teaching people defeatism ... The protection of its youth is a nation's foremost duty.'[91]

Grierson emphasized *intended* effects. One need not hunt around for subliminal and unintended effects, he argued, because 'there is so much evidence available, to reveal and discuss, of purposes actually intended and served by the popular newspapers, loyalties deliberately inculcated and processes of propaganda of one sort or other – and overtly – imposed on the news.'[92] His approach in the classroom, therefore, was to present students with 'the organized appearance ... of actual practitioners.'[93] That strategy, he claimed, referring obliquely to McLuhan, helps 'debunk some of the more "mystical" speculations which presently derive from the communications enthusiasts.'[94]

Although acknowledging certainly the *creative* role of the artist in bringing home to audiences knowledge of their circumstances, Grierson's was not the fanciful imagination of, say, a Northrop Frye. Grierson insisted that filmmakers and other artists are never completely free in constructing their versions of truth: 'You've got moral laws to affect it, you've got social laws, you've got aesthetic laws. What is truth isn't a nasty question at all,' he insisted. 'It's a question that is forever with you when you're a film maker. It's to make your truth as many-faceted and as deep, as various, as exciting, as possible.'[95]

SOME QUESTIONS

This section endeavours to place Grierson's writings within the context of Canadian communication thought generally, and to compare it to that of Innis in particular. The section also assesses the relevance of his work for the future, and revisits that apparent oxymoron 'democratic propaganda.'

Democratic Propaganda?
Foreshadowing McLuhan, Grierson proposed that educators ought to adopt the dramatic, rhetorical, and emotional tactics of the commercial media. He charged that, in refraining from doing this, educators had largely abandoned to advertisers the 'socially necessary' education of giving social direction and providing interpretive patterns. In a media-saturated world, Grierson maintained, the 'fight for democracy' requires that educators take up all 'necessary instruments.' Grierson's stand on education could well be repugnant to some – particularly those who rank rationality ahead of emotion and believe that it is in

expanding the capacity for critical thought that the key to resisting indoctrination by self-serving autocracies is to be found. Granted people today receive disproportionate amounts of information on public affairs from television, a medium in which the 'image' is supreme; nonetheless, one can argue, education for democracy requires that educators *supplement*, not replace, as Grierson recommended, analytical and factually based pedagogy. There should be, in this view, an *augmented* effort to teach 'media literacy'[96] so that citizens become more cognizant of the limitations and biases of various media, particularly television.

Representative of this latter view is the egalitarian educator Paulo Freire, who wrote: 'The special contribution of the educator to the birth of the new [democratic] society would have to be *a critical education* which could help to form critical attitudes.'[97] Freire insisted that the development of critical faculties is the *sine qua non* of education for democracy. Otherwise, Freire advised, people continue being treated in less than fully human ways. Without a critical component to education, the teacher remains the one who 'knows best,' a posture paving the way for the continued manufacture of consent later in the student's life. Freire insisted that it is impossible to square propaganda with true, democratic education. For propaganda, even of the type proposed by Grierson, always implies 'fundamentally, a Subject who persuades, in some form or other, and an object on which the act of persuading is exercised.'[98] He added: 'To substitute monologue, slogans, and communiques for dialogue is to attempt to liberate the oppressed with the instruments of domestication.'[99] For Freire, therefore, dialogue – not persuasion – is the path to an authentically democratic education. Through dialogue, the student wins back the right 'to say his own word, to name the world.'[100]

Grierson's response in this instance undoubtedly would be that we live in the world as it is, a world in which we confront persuasion at every turn. In a world increasingly interconnected across broad geographic expanse, where face-to-face discussion is often impractical, democratically inspired artists and educators simply *must* use media and persuasive tactics if democracy is to become more than merely a 'necessary illusion.' One senses that Grierson would perhaps have looked on Freire as being unduly romantic, at least if that great pedagogue's proposals, intended to guide educators in the illiterate tribal communities of Brazil, were deemed appropriate for the modern, industrial world. For democratically inspired educators in modern circumstances to rely solely on dialogic interactions, Grierson might say, is unrealistic and hence self-defeating. Better that they use both their authoritative, persuasive powers and the mass media to inspire dialogue at the local level.

Grierson further maintained that, with modernity, the challenges facing democracy are growing. Most of us now live in what he termed a 'monstrous new metropolitan world.' To re-establish democratic community in the face of the anonymous and utilitarian social relations characterizing our megalopolises is indeed a daunting task,[101] one requiring extraordinary skill and effort. For this struggle, *the necessary instruments* of radio, the photograph, the poster, the story, and, of course, the cinema, are vital.

In *Eyes of Democracy*, Grierson met head-on the criticism that propaganda or persuasion is inherently antidemocratic due to its appeal to the emotions. The belief that '"smart" operators' can jockey people into thinking and acting against their will or interest, he argued, hinges ultimately on 'the respect with which one holds public opinion.'[102] Grierson, the populist democrat, maintained that the public cannot be played the fool forever, that eventually the trickster will be found out. He added, 'in this matter the memory of the public is so long as to be frightening.'[103]

More can be said on the issue. Persuasive communication is not inherently unethical or untrue. The rhetorician of economics, Donald (now Deirdre) McCloskey, wrote: 'Why should the latest facts not be persuasive? They will not speak for themselves. Why should new theories not be articulate? They will not be heard otherwise.'[104] If change is to come, whether in terms of scientific understanding, environmental practice, economic theorizing, human rights, or democratic decision making, persuasive discourse must come first.

And yet, disquietude persists at Grierson's insistence that élites be charged with the task of inculcating democratic values through emotional appeals. Is this not likely to entrench the old autocracies, which through 'trickle down' and other rationalizations are able to convince others, if not themselves, that the common good is congruent with their own material welfare?

Paulo Freire appears to agree wholeheartedly with Grierson on one thing, however: democratic education must encourage people to assume an 'intimacy' with their problems, rather than merely repeating 'irrelevant principles' and 'inert ideas.' Freire, like Grierson, maintained that democratic education 'moves people to experiment and discover for themselves.'[105]

GRIERSON AND CANADIAN COMMUNICATION THOUGHT

In his analysis, Grierson set in opposition two types of propaganda, democratic and authoritarian; two types of education, democratic (or 'propagandistic') and traditional; two modes of governance, democratic and autocratic; two types of cinema, imaginative and realist; and two perceptions of reality, holistic and individualistic. It is this latter dichotomy particularly that aligns Grierson's thought with Innis's.

Innis and Grierson both maintained that innovations in the media of communication provide explanation for societal change. Innis distinguished between time- and space-bound societies, the former being interdependent and organic, and the latter individualistic, with interpersonal relations mediated largely by the price system and by commodity exchanges. Grierson likewise distinguished between individualism and an organic interdependence and cooperative spirit.

Grierson's analysis differs from Innis's, however, in several ways. First, Grierson maintained that modern technologies of transportation and communication *heighten* material interdependence, and hence render anachronistic individualistic modes of thought, whereas Innis emphasized that these space-binding media fragment hitherto organic (communitarian) societies. Grierson contended that new media which heighten *material* interdependence can and should be used to increase awareness of this new condition on the part of citizens. Each medium of communication for Grierson is itself dialectical, having, on the one hand, a material effect either of heightening or of lessening interdependence, and, on the other, of fostering or obscuring awareness of these material conditions.

Innis and Grierson disagreed fundamentally about yellow journalism and new media. Grierson saw the Hearst press as boldly innovative, whose tactics should be mimicked by democratic propagandists, whereas Innis saw only diversion and a new monopoly of knowledge that robs people of their capacity for independent, critical thought. Much of what Grierson saw as untapped potential, Innis disdained. Where Grierson saw the emergence of a new tool for democracy, Innis saw the collapse of civility, even of civilization. Like Innis, Grierson was a realist concerned with the material conditions of people's lives. On the other hand, he was also a social constructionist who declared: 'There is no such thing as truth, until you've made it into a form; truth is an interpretation of a perception.'[106] In making that declaration, Grierson draws closer to the theorizing of McLuhan and Frye than to Innis.

Like other writers with whom we are concerned, Grierson adopted a broad definition of communication media. Because they foster heightened material interdependence, Grierson argued, all sorts of technologies can be considered media. He wrote: 'The patterns of inter-relationship which lie at the root of modern citizenship and therefore challenge us to new ways of management have all a technological basis and I cannot think of a gas pipe or electric wire or road or ship or plane or factory that has not something to say.'[107]

A main contention of Grierson, then, was that *technology* has caused Western societies to enter a new era of interdependence and internationalism. Since he did not investigate forces giving rise to technological innovation, there is an implied technological determinism. On the other hand, however, certainly when dealing with film, radio, and the press, Grierson was far from espousing technological determinism, for he insisted that the *use one makes* of particular media is vitally important; that new media give rise to new possibilities for democratic thought and action, but, equally, if wrongly used, can heighten authoritarianism. Repeatedly, like Graham Spry, Grierson drew attention to the importance of modes of ownership and finance on content, demonstrating thereby an acute awareness of the political economy of media.

Like other theorists we shall visit, Grierson distinguished sharply between two world-views – namely, realism versus social constructionism – and in that context wrote at length on the role of the artist. Whereas Northrop Frye (as we shall see) maintained that the legitimate function of the arts is to divert people's attention from intolerable and unalterable reality, and whereas Dallas Smythe charged that in the real world of money and power artists generally are forced to obscure real conditions, Grierson advanced the notion (as did McLuhan) that true artists heighten people's awareness of their lived conditions and hence are indispensable agents for reform.

For Grierson, as for other theorists in this book, human nature is not static. And, he insisted, for democracy to be authentic in a world that is increasingly interdependent, human nature *must* change. It must become less individualistic and more cooperative. Through the ages, Grierson proclaimed, it has been the task and responsibility of poets, priests, artists, teachers, and political leaders 'to change "human nature" to fit the facts,' and, he added, in carrying out that responsibility 'their instruments have been culture, law, religion and education.'[108] Writing in the 1940s, Grierson saw the cinema as but the latest in a long line of instruments and practices that could be employed to make human nature fit the facts of existence. This is why cinema was for him a 'necessary instrument.'

RELEVANCE FOR TODAY

Some believe that media practices since the Second World War have caused or at least have contributed to an erosion of democracy.[109] On the one hand, the well-honed arts of advertising and public relations have refined the construction of *pseudoenvironments* (Lippmann's phrase) as a precondition for manufacturing consent:[110] simulations, simulacra, photo-ops, sound-bites, imagineering, virtual reality, and other terms testify to the ubiquity of such practices. And, on the other hand, given the proliferation of home entertainment systems, people may increasingly feel 'cosy.' Citizens can easily find other, less troubling, albeit simulated, worlds with which to 'engage.' If this were the complete story, Grierson would despair, were he still alive. Fortunately, it is not, and a most telling case in point concerns the mobilization to resist efforts by the Paris-based Organization for Economic Cooperation and Development (OECD) to implement the Multilateral Agreement on Investment (MAI). Let us look briefly at this encouraging experience as it concerns media practice.

From 1995 to 1998, Canada and twenty-six other OECD members endeavoured to negotiate an agreement that, in the name of increasing the international mobility of capital and the rights of investors, would have severely constrained the capacity of nation-states to control investment within their borders. Critics charged that, if the proposed agreement were signed, governments would be hamstrung in devising and implementing domestic social and environmental policies, in establishing indigenous labour standards, and in forming or continuing domestic cultural policies. Environmental, labour, social, and cultural groups saw the MAI, in brief, as a treaty for 'corporate rule.'

Although the agreement was scheduled for signature by May 1998, the Canadian mass media, largely controlled by transnational corporate interests through ownership and advertising, gave it scant attention. The Ottawa *Citizen*, a Conrad Black paper, was virtually silent on the issue until mid March 1998, when it announced on its front page that the deal was probably dead. One interesting exception to the paper's self-imposed news blackout was an article appearing in its 14 February edition which reported that Trade Minister Sergio Marchi had 'lashed out at critics';[111] more on this below. Coverage in the

Thomson-controlled *Globe and Mail* was somewhat more extensive, but the few stories that appeared were mostly confined to the business section. (The publicly owned CBC, however, it should be noted, carried a number of special reports on the MAI.)

Exactly why the MAI was shrouded in secrecy by privately owned mainstream media is of course subject to conjecture. However, a memorandum leaked from then prime minister Brian Mulroney's Office in September 1985, outlining a strategy for manufacturing consent of Canadians for a free-trade agreement then being proposed with the United States, may be of relevance:

> Our communication strategy should rely less on educating the general public than on getting across the message that the trade initiative is a good idea. In other words, a selling job. The public support generated should be recognized as extremely soft and likely to evaporate if the debate is allowed to get out of control. At the same time a substantial majority of the public may be willing to leave the issue in the hands of the government and other interested groups, if the government maintains communications control of the situation. Benign neglect from a majority of Canadians may be the realistic outcome of a well-executed communications program.[112]

Controlled information resulting in benign neglect by the majority of citizens was one of the things Walter Lippmann had in mind when he declared in the 1920s that the practice of democracy had turned a corner.

But, despite a virtual news blackout by the daily press, the MAI did become an issue for some, even if not for most Canadians. The Council of Canadians, a nationalist lobby group, in 1997 obtained a leaked, draft copy of the agreement, which it promptly posted on its Internet site. Tony Clarke and Maude Barlow of the council then published a highly disturbing book in the fall of 1997 that analysed in detail after depressing detail the antidemocratic implications of the MAI; that book eventually made it to the *Globe and Mail*'s bestseller list! Opposition worldwide became organized, and through the Internet pertinent information, documentation, and analyses were exchanged instantly. In Canada, speakers such as Maude Barlow and Tony Clarke criss-crossed the country.

On 13 February 1998, an all-day conference in opposition to the MAI was held at Carleton University in Ottawa, with Tony Clarke as the keynote speaker. Announced at the last minute, probably to pre-empt media coverage of that conference, Trade Minister Sergio Marchi held an 'informal breakfast' at which, according to the *Citizen*, he 'lashed out' at critics, also assuring reporters that Canada would not sign a deal that sold out the country's sovereignty or its cultural rights. Articles in both the *Citizen* and the *Globe and Mail* the next morning dutifully reported Marchi's spirited remarks, but were bereft of any reference whatever either to the anti-MAI conference at Carleton University or to Clarke's speech, despite the fact that critics like Clarke were the reason Marchi held the 'breakfast' in the first place. Government, seemingly, had retained 'communications control of the situation' in an effort to ensure that the debate did not get 'out of control.'

Although the virtual news blackout by the mainline press was successful in keeping most Canadians blithely unaware that a treaty of gargantuan proportions was being negotiated,[113] in the end that did not suffice. 'Propagandists for democracy,' such as Clarke and Barlow, utilized alternative media, and played at least a part in causing the deadline to pass without the agreement being signed. At which point the *Globe and Mail* carried a front-page story entitled 'How the Net Killed the MAI: Grassroots Groups Used Their Own Globalization to Derail Deal.'[114] According to the *Globe*, 'by pooling their information they [grass-roots activists] have broken through the wall of secrecy that traditionally surrounds international negotiations, forcing governments to deal with their complaints ... "This is the first successful Internet campaign by non-governmental organizations," said one diplomat involved in the negotiations. "It's been very effective."'[115] Were Grierson alive, one senses that he would consider the Internet today to be one of democracy's 'necessary instruments.'[116]

5

The Communication Thought of
DALLAS W. SMYTHE (1907–1992)

Control of the means of communications is the basis of political power.

— *Dependency Road*, 209

ABOUT DALLAS W. SMYTHE

Dallas Walker Smythe was born at Regina, Saskatchewan, on 9 March 1907 – an only child and, he judged, 'a rather pampered one.'[1] His father, John Walker Smyth [*sic*], had left elementary school at twelve, upon the death of *his* father, to provide for the family. Beginning his working life as an errand boy at a hardware store in St Mary's, Ontario, John Smyth eventually became a partner in a thriving Regina hardware business. Dallas's mother was a nurse, although she did not long practise her profession. Towards Dallas she was overbearing, as the following anecdote indicates. The hills in the Qu'Appelle region near Regina are less than seventy-five feet high, yet, distrustful of the steering and brakes of automobiles, she insisted that she and her child walk, not drive, up and down every one. In his autobiography Dallas related: 'She would get out, taking me and we would walk behind the car as Dad drove it up or down the hill. When we would get back in the car she always seemed to regard it as exceptionally good luck that it had stayed on the road. Dad just smiled.'

With but little formal education, Dallas's parents developed 'an intense devotion' to learning. From the time he began to read, young Dallas found himself surrounded by books. At Christmas, year after year, he would receive up to fifty of them. The family avoided the public library, however, as his mother was convinced that books from that source harboured 'germs.'

Overprotection meant that, as a child, Dallas tended to handle inter-personal conflict through words 'rather than with my fists.' Later he rebelled furtively. Only in middle age, he confided, did he manage to make 'a final rebellion against manipulation by my parents.'

As we will see, though, Dallas remained a rebel all his life, although in maturity it was from an unjust political-economic order that he recoiled. Indeed, his father and mother had always encouraged him to 'identify with the underdog,'[2] and Smythe recalled their reading aloud to him passages concerning social justice from the New Testament; he assessed that the 'formula for primitive socialism' found there 'made an early imprint in my mind.'

Recollections of his early Regina years included a tornado that ripped the house off its foundations with the three Smyths huddled inside, and much pleasanter ones too – for instance, of 'smelling the air and the earth and feeling the sun and wind on those hot summer days.' In his autobiography he wrote, 'without realizing it those relations to my environment were to fix a definition of "home" for me of which I was unaware in later years in the United States and which I would retrieve from the subconscious half a century later when I returned to Regina to live.'

After the flu epidemic of 1918, which young Dallas barely survived, the family settled in Pasadena, California, a locale his parents judged to be of a healthier clime. There they lived in a modest but comfortable house.

Smythe's undergraduate years were at the University of California, at Los Angeles and at Berkeley. Receiving an AB in 1928, he entered directly into Berkeley's PhD program. Most influential among his pro-fessors was Melvin H. Knight, brother of Frank H. Knight, Innis's mentor. Smythe assessed that Melvin Knight 'probably had more to do with everything else I did in later life.' A 'radical in the best sense of David Hume,' until his death in 1981 at age ninety-two, Knight re-tained, according to Smythe, 'a sensitive empathy with the poor of the earth.' In the preface to *Dependency Road*, Smythe's great work of syn-thesis, prepared in the late 1970s, he noted touchingly that, even in old age, Knight provided 'cogent and lively advice ... when I was writing this book.' Another influence at Berkeley was Marxian economist Leo Rogin, who taught economic theory. Smythe described Rogin's lectures as 'invaluable,' but this view reflects the fact that Smythe had already formed an antipathy to mainline economic theory: 'I could never claim to be a specialist in economic theory because the particular field with its emphasis on abstractions turned me off; the real world of people, processes, power and poverty, seen in its natural setting attracted me much more.'

Three events in the 1930s helped shape Smythe's political orientation.[3] First was the 1934 gunning down by the National Guard of several striking longshoremen who had been picketing the docks in San Francisco. Smythe remarked, 'That really demonstrated the realities of class struggle in a way that no amount of reading did.' Second was the burning by the sheriffs of shantytowns in California inhabited by 'Okies' and 'Arkies' during the drought years of the Depression. In his autobiography, Smythe recalled: 'I *saw* the reality portrayed in Steinbeck's *Grapes of Wrath*.' Third was the Spanish Civil War, and especially the U.S. embargo, disabling the Spanish government in its fight against fascism.

Completing his thesis in 1936, Smythe moved to Washington to work for the Central Statistical Board. There he organized a small, five-member local in the first Congress of Industrial Organizations (CIO) union in the government. He also became active in the American League for Peace and Democracy, which was pressuring the government to lift its embargo on Spain. Although Mrs Roosevelt was a member, the League was probed by the House Un-American Activities Committee (HUAC), which named Smythe and seven others of the Washington branch as ringleaders. Thereby Smythe became known to security agents as a PAF – 'a premature antifascist.'

Smythe's interest in communication grew out of his government work. In his position with the Central Statistical Board, he ensured that government questionnaires were technically competent and did not duplicate information elicited by other forms. Next, as senior economist in the Department of Labor, which acquired responsibility for implementing the Fair Labor Standards Act of 1938, Smythe reviewed the labour practices and market characteristics of the *Dallas Morning News*, and as an expert witness presented evidence establishing that the *News* engaged in interstate commerce. During the Second World War, Smythe returned to the Central Statistical Board, but as a labour rather than an agricultural economist, and in that capacity studied, among other things, the labour practices of the Western Union Telegraph Company. In 1943 he moved to the Federal Communications Commission

(FCC) as chief economist, initially to work on labour–management problems in the communication industries, but also on other economic issues as they arose after the war. Thereby he became a 'communication economist.'

At the FCC one of Smythe's major projects was to prepare the economic section of the 'Blue Book' – *Public Service Responsibility of Broadcast Licensees* (1946). Maintaining that broadcasters have public-service responsibilities because they use publicly owned radio frequencies, the 'Blue Book' elicited howls of protest from broadcast-industry executives. It proposed, for instance, that the FCC should actually compare the programming of licensees at licence-renewal time with the promises the owners had made in their original licence applications![4] A couple of years later, the House Un-American Activities Committee challenged Smythe's appointment at the University of Illinois, partly on grounds that he had helped write the 'Blue Book.'[5]

Smythe remained with the FCC until July 1948 – one of the last New Dealers, he mused, 'to leave Washington with his scalp still on.' That August he moved to Urbana–Champaign to join the newly forming Institute of Communications Research at the University of Illinois, under the direction of Wilbur Schramm. The following year, the institute launched the first-anywhere PhD program in communication. It was miraculous that Smythe attained this appointment, and, having received it, that he was ever able to take it up, so outrageous were those times in the United States. At Illinois he immediately became the subject of continuous surveillance and surreptitious reports to the FBI by (according to Smythe) campus informant Wilbur Schramm![6] Over time, Urbana became more congenial though, and there even developed an informal dinner circle, which included Smythe and his wife, the Gerbners, and the Schillers: of this, too, the FBI was cognizant, and wary.[7]

In 1948 Smythe began teaching the first course anywhere on the political economy of communication, although discretion dictated that for several years the course bear the title 'The Economics of Communications.'[8] In the course, Smythe focused primarily on electronic communication – telegraph, telephone, radio broadcasting – and on radio spectrum allocation.[9] He was concerned primarily with how these fields were organized, how they interrelated as industries, and the development of public policy, particularly at the domestic (U.S.) level, but internationally as well.[10]

Political economy for Smythe, furthermore, meant not merely studying communication industries from an economic point of view, but also *integrating* communication studies and economics into a new approach. According to Smythe, standard economics is woefully deficient because it does not recognize the dynamic power implications of communication. Likewise, mainstream communication studies are lacking as they seldom acknowledge the economic base of much communicatory activity. Hence, *the political economy of communication*, as Smythe formulated it, draws out the economic base of communicatory activity while at the same time showing the power repercussions of communicatory control for the economy and economic organization. According to Smythe's formulation, capitalism must produce people ideologically willing to support it, and mass media are tools to that end.[11]

Undoubtedly Smythe's most celebrated studies from his years at Urbana were content analyses of commercial television programming undertaken on behalf of the National Association of Educational Broadcasters (NAEB) to bolster their representations to the FCC to have broadcast frequencies reserved for educational television. His findings are summarized in his 1954 article 'Reality as Presented by Television.'[12] Those studies not only were successful in achieving the purpose for which they were intended, but also were instrumental in Smythe's appointment a couple of years later as economic adviser to Canada's Royal Commission on Broadcasting (the Fowler Commission), for whom he again analysed content; Smythe not only authored the chapter on content in the commission's main report, but also was responsible for Volume 2, consisting of basic tabulations.[13] Smythe recalled, 'throughout I was treated with sensitive courtesy and generosity ... My experience with the Fowler Commission ... raised in my mind the possibility of migrating back to Canada.'

Other work undertaken during his years at Urbana included studies for the National Council of Churches concerning the nature and effect of religious broadcasts. Smythe spoke often to the council, and in his autobiography he disclosed: 'I had found an area [i.e., seminaries] where political activity had substantial freedom in the 1950s. Indeed it was only at lectures in Divinity Schools where theologians were not afraid to discuss capitalism, socialism and communism frankly and with enthusiasm and self-confidence.'[14]

While at Urbana, Smythe also published *The Political Economy of Communications* (1956) and *The Structure and Policy of Electronic Communication* (1957). However, the U.S. foreign and domestic policies assaulted his conscience, and so 'on a hot sunny day in late August 1963,' hard on the heals of the Cuban Missile Crisis, 'two cars drove into Regina, Saskatchewan; one, a Ford, contained Jennie and our daughter, Carol, then a little more than two years old; in the other, a Mercedes, were our son, Pat, then nine, and me.'[15] With the aid of Graham Spry, Smythe had attained an appointment as chairman of the Division of Social Sciences at the Regina campus of the University of Saskatchewan. Smythe and his family had decided to begin a new life in the city and country where he had been born fifty-six years earlier. As he put it, he and his wife 'had rejected the United States as a country to respect or to live in, and looked eagerly to a better life in Canada.'[16]

In 1971–2, a time when few in the West were allowed to enter the People's Republic of China, Smythe spent a month there. One outcome of that trip was his paper 'After Bicycles What?,' written in 1973 but not published until 1994. Circulating as in photocopied form for twenty years, this piece was nonetheless one of his most famous.

'Retiring' from University of Saskatchewan after ten years of service, he moved next to Simon Fraser University in Burnaby, British Columbia, first as chair of the Department of Communication Studies for two years, next as professor until 1980, and finally as emeritus professor. During the 1980s Smythe lectured and was a visiting professor at over a dozen universities around the world.

As the years passed, Smythe's radicalism intensified; he referred to this shift in perspective as moving 'counterclockwise,' since normally people become increasingly conservative as they age. Moreover, his analyses grew broader, more holistic, and more systemic. Beginning, in the early 1950s, with tightly focused analyses of television programming in selected communities over brief periods of time, he turned next to the history, development, control, and performance of various sectors of the evolving electronic communications industry. His next qualitative leap was even greater: he began linking electronic communication to the entire capitalist order! Finally, ever curious and innovative, his last, incomplete, and to date unpublished writings explored questions of ontology, venturing into implications of quantum physics and chaos theory for information and communication.

Over an academic career that spanned more than forty years, Dallas Smythe published more than two hundred articles, monographs, and special reports. His grand work of synthesis, *Dependency Road*, appeared in 1981. Published posthumously (but benefiting from Smythe's advice) was *Counterclockwise* (1994), a compilation edited by his former student Thomas Guback. In 1993, a festschrift honouring Smythe, *Illu-*

minating the Blindspots, appeared; edited by, among others, his former student Manjunath Pendakur, now a dean at the University of Western Ontario, that volume consists of contributions by many of the world's leading critical scholars, and contains a bibliography of Smythe's published work for the period 1948 to 1992.[17]

When they last met in 1991, and recalling his work on behalf of the National Council of Churches, Guback asked whether Smythe thought there was a 'much closer connection – than would be superficially apparent – between radical and Christian points of view.' Guback reports that Smythe responded unequivocally, 'Yes!' Guback continued, 'Although his current work was in other areas, I think he would have approved the growing links between radical political-economics and Christian theology, between economic justice and religion, between the struggle to end oppression and a Christian economic ethic.'[18]

Dallas Smythe died at Langley, British Columbia, on 6 September 1992.

CONTENT ANALYSES

As Director of Studies for the National Association of Educational Broadcasters (NAEB), Dallas Smythe was a major reason why educational broadcasters in the United States succeeded in having channels reserved for educational broadcasting. He selected New York City, which then boasted seven commercial stations, for which to perform a content analysis of commercial television programming, and, with collaborator Donald Horton, tabulated data for the first full week of January 1951; they presented the results to the Federal Communications Commission (FCC) later that month. So revealing was the initial study that the NAEB urged Smythe to continue the work. In subsequent years he completed content analyses of television programming in Los Angeles, Chicago, New Haven, and, again, New York. Smythe's classic 1954 article 'Reality as Presented by Television' summarizes much of the data and conclusions of these NAEB studies. In the article, Smythe disclosed, among other things, that one of every five minutes of big-city television, and one in every four minutes in smaller markets, was devoted to advertising. To him, therefore, 'the most basic and subtle dimension of television's "reality" is the commercial context in which it is presented; ... [it] more or less subtly conditions even the non-advertising content of programs.'[19] Smythe found also that by far the largest class of programming was drama, which accounted for up to 47 percent of total broadcast time.

Even in those early years, Smythe disclosed, the television world was violent: in a full week's programming in New York, 3,421 acts and threats of violence were observed, an average of 6.2 per hour. And the most violent television fare was children's programming, for which he detected 22.4 acts or threats of violence per hour, compared with only 6.0 per hour for adult drama.[20]

Smythe also discovered that television disproportionately represented males (by a ratio of two to one), and certain age groups: whereas at the time more than half the U.S. population was younger than twenty or older than fifty, only one-quarter of television characters were within those age brackets. Heroes in television drama, he estimated, averaged thirty-two years of age, whereas villains averaged forty-three years. Although men on television on average were older than women, female villains were older than male villains (forty-seven vs forty-two years, on average). Americans of colour constituted only 2 per cent of television characters, although they made up several times that percentage of the national population. Whereas white Americans comprised 83 per cent of television heroes, they made up only 69 per cent of television villains. Whereas there were three times as many white male heroes as white female heroes, heroes from other races were females rather than males by a ratio of almost two to one; Smythe remarked, 'Such results could happen by chance less than two times in 100.'[21]

Introducing the study, Smythe outlined the import of the data. For him, 'reality' concerns 'the flow of representations of the human condition.' Television programs represent symbolically the human condition, and in so doing can be thought of as comprising a 'stimulus field 'that affects audience's perceptions, motivations, and learning. Smythe, however, was no proponent of simple-minded, mechanistic 'effects.' He wrote: 'Audience members act on the program content. They take it and mold it in the image of their individual needs and values. In so doing they utilize not only the explicit layer of meaning in the content but also innumerable latent or contextual dimensions of meaning.'[22]

Likewise producers, according to Smythe, consciously and unconsciously build in meanings, both contextual and explicit. Consequently, program material on television consists of a group of symbols that mediate exchanges between the mass media and the audience.[23]

Smythe's methodology in undertaking these content analyses was

completely quantitative. Years later he related to Guback that he chose
not to pass beyond strictly quantitative studies into more interpretative
('cultural studies') approaches because, to him, 'the textual approach,
the exegesis of text in media, is an excellent way of devoting an awful
lot of energy, from an awful lot of people, for no purpose worth a
damn – because it ends up where it began, with speculation. It doesn't
have any relation to behavior – and I'm not a behaviorist in the psychological special use of that term – but I think that action is the name of
the game.'[24]

Industry Studies and Public Policy

Two seminal monographs exemplify well Smythe's work on the political economy of electronic communication. Both *The Structure and Policy
of Electronic Communication* (1957), written at Urbana, and the masterful
yet rather cumbersomly titled *The Relevance of United States Legislative–
Regulatory Experience to the Canadian Telecommunications Situation* (1971),
prepared for the Canadian government while he was a professor at
Regina, illustrate Smythe's historical, materialist, and institutionalist
approach. In the former study, Smythe first recapitulated the history of
wire telegraphy in Europe and the United States from the 1840s, emphasizing particularly the role of government policy, industry practices, and 'technology'[25] in structuring the industry. A second chapter
addresses the advent and development of wire telephony, emphasizing
also its relations with telegraphy. Running through both chapters is a
summary and analysis of international developments to coordinate
worldwide the provision of telegraph and telephone service. A third
chapter summarizes the development of radio services, both point to
point and broadcast, in the context of power arrangements among
government, providers of the older electronic communication services,
and other interests such as equipment manufacturers. The monograph
provides extended discussion of the principles of radio-frequency allo-
cations and of organizations coordinating this activity globally. The
second monograph covers much the same territory, albeit updated to
include regulatory initiatives of the 1960s and excluding broadcasting.
It is, however, a much more critical document. It positively bristles with
accounts of the telephone industry's unfair trade practices and of gov-
ernment/regulatory inadequacies. Prepared in a period of under two
months to meet a short-term deadline, this masterful 216-page report
sets out the author's thinking to that time on the interrelations among
technology, organizations, and public policy in North American tel-

ecommunications. It is of course impossible to give adequate summary to such a comprehensive document in the short space available here. However, extracting but three of Smythe's major conclusions should indicate the flavour of his analysis:

First, whereas in the nineteenth century, nation-states depended on monopolistic corporations to act as agents in domestic telecommunications, that was a period in which technology and markets were unique to each corporation. By the early 1970s, the computer-satellite revolution had rendered this industry structure obsolete and, Smythe proclaimed, 'public policy could not re-establish the era of the monopoly firm even if it wished to do so.'[26]

Second, spectrum management, that is, licensing of users of the radio spectrum, therefore now supersedes control over the monopoly corporation as the prime tool for national telecommunications policy.

Third, attempts by the FCC to regulate AT&T after 1934 were generally 'futile,' as was the 1956 application of antitrust to AT&T. Smythe recommended segregation of monopoly and competitive markets in telecommunications, thereby anticipating by over a decade developments in U.S. telecommunications policy through antitrust.

MEDIA AND MONOPOLY CAPITALISM

Mass Media

Smythe's close analysis of the content of commercial television paved the way for his later claim that mass media are the ideological apparatus of the capitalist system. For him, monopoly capitalism would have been impossible without the mass media. Indeed, he attested, monopoly capitalism *invented* mass media.

'Monopoly capitalism' refers to the increasingly global private enterprise system, dominated by just a few hundred gigantic corporations. It arose in the 1890s. Prior to that time, capitalism consisted principally of small competitive firms.[27] The transition from competitive to monopoly capitalism, Smythe claimed, was made possible by the emergence of the mass media, beginning with mass circulation daily newspapers.

Under a regime of monopoly capitalism, mass media 'manage demand,' a task not required prior to the onset of mass production, but essential since the turn of the century. More generally, mass media set 'the daily agenda'; [28]that is, they inform and guide not only 'consumers' in their day-to-day activities, but also citizens and other institutions, for example, small businesses.

For Smythe, however, the *prime* task of the mass media is 'producing *people*'[29] – people with a set of 'correct' beliefs. 'Correct' beliefs include such (to Smythe erroneous) notions as the following:

- that personal possessiveness is essential to human beings;
- that the main goal of life is to consume commodities and services;
- that freedom and conflict are individual, not collective matters;
- that commodities and services do not educate or form values; they merely contribute to people's comfort and pleasure;
- that a conflict of ideas need not be resolved; every person to his or her own taste and belief;
- that it is possible and desirable to be neutral or objective while working in the mass media, educational institutions, government and business; it is not, as Mark Twain put it, a question of 'Who are you neutral against?'; and,
- most important, 'You can't change human nature'; the status quo is timeless.[30]

In addition to inculcating *beliefs* such as these, media 'screen in' *values*, for instance:

- *that private is better than public*; private business is clean and efficient, whereas public and governmental affairs are dirty and inefficient;
- *that prices charged by private business are good*; taxes, however, since they fund public goods that do not meet the market test of profitability, are by definition bad;
- *that private property is virtually sacred*; hence, public planning and the public regulation of business are inherently bad;
- *that technology and winning are of utmost importance*. 'As we learn from professional sports,' Smythe explained '"nice guys finish last"; our high moral ends will justify our means.'[31]

Smythe admitted that such a brief summary of beliefs and values o versimplifies, to a degree, the texture of ideology propagated by the media. In television, for example, family values and small groups are positioned more favourably than raw individualism. Nonetheless, the foregoing encapsulations are instructive, and many readers will recognize recurrences of such values and themes in the news and in media entertainment.

Consciousness Industry

It is not merely mass media, however, that inculcate capitalist values and beliefs. Fronting the relatively few gigantic corporations is a 'cluster of institutions' that Smythe called the 'Consciousness Industry' (CI). The 'Consciousness Industry' is 'most directly concerned in the design of consumer goods and services, their packaging, audience production, advertising, and marketing.'[32] It consists of

> the advertising/market research agencies plus the mass media. Backing them are the educational system, photography and commercial art. In the next rank are professional and pre-professional sports, comic books, parlor games (such as Monopoly), recorded music, tourism, restaurants, hotels and transportation. In the next rank are other consumers goods industries– the Homogeneous Package Goods (soaps, soft drinks, etc.) and the consumer durables (such as household appliances, motorcycles and automobiles). As backdrop for CI are the industries which bind together the whole Monopoly Capitalist system: the Military-Industrial Complex, telecommunications, banks, insurance, finance, real estate, the gambling industry, and crime, both organized and unorganized.[33]

CI, in brief, is wide-ranging and, according to Smythe, the 'indispensable foundation of the capitalist politico-economic system.'[34] Smythe maintained that the Consciousness Industry has largely superseded military power as the primary means of imperial control.

Smythe contended further that consumer goods are particularly important instruments of the Consciousness Industry. Consumer goods are *teaching machines*, a term that can be traced to behavioural psychologist B.F. Skinner. They *teach* because they 'appeal to and cultivate possessiveness in users'[35] through their design, packaging, and the sales appeals used in their marketing, which address individual insecurities and latent aggression.

Characterized by a 'genuinely mysterious mixture of use values and insubstantial images,' many consumers items have propaganda value not just at home, but abroad. In a memo written to the Chinese government in 1973, Smythe elaborated: 'To adopt capitalist luxury goods such as private automobiles, family-sized washing machines, family-sized refrigerators, one-way TV, etc., [would be] to equip Chinese families with that many *educational instruments* leading to the capitalist cultural road.'[36] This result is predictable because the power of capitalism stems ultimately from its ability to develop *capitalist consumption relations*, that is, human relations mediated by 'style changes, imitation of happy, wealthy people, fear of loneliness, sexual appeals, etc.' Therefore, Smythe continued insightfully, 'consumer goods and services ... mass produced under capitalism are *designed,* made and sold not primarily to serve the people, but to keep the people in a "rat race" in which they work as hard as they can to buy as many consumer goods as they can so that they generate the necessary profits to satisfy the system.'[37]

THE AUDIENCE COMMODITY

For Smythe, mass media 'produce' audiences in two senses. First, they assemble audiences for sale to advertisers and other professional persuaders. To do this, media offer 'free lunches' – TV programs, news stories, recorded music, and so forth. The program or editorial content therefore is an *input,* or a cost of producing the real output – *the audience commodity*. Different types of content produce audiences with different demographic and psychographic characteristics, thereby meeting more closely the needs of particular advertisers and public persuaders.

Audiences are 'produced' also in a second sense. People are worked upon by mass media. Their consciousness is altered. (Smythe went so far as to contend that audiences themselves 'work' at the task of making over their consciousness by viewing TV programs, reading newspapers, and so on.)

This, however, gives rise to a contradiction. On the one hand, people are persuaded or otherwise conditioned into conforming to the demands of capitalism. On the other, they must 'live as human beings.'[38] Hence, people seek out institutions, for instance, churches, political parties, trade unions, families, and communities, which support such basic human qualities as love, creativity, and the affirmation of individual dignity.[39] Although such institutions, born in a previous era, persist in the present, they have in Smythe's view grown frail: they have 'been stripped' by the impact of mass media of much of their traditional effectiveness. [40]

The basic contradiction, nonetheless, persists, and Smythe hoped it would eventually overthrow monopoly capitalism and replace it with a more humane and just economic/political system, one based on equality in which commodity-based relations are minimal.

DIALECTICS

Smythe maintained there are fundamentally two types of knowledge. One is *idealist*. Standard economics, he claimed, is of this type, since it pays little attention to 'oligopolistic reality,' that is, to concentrated power in the real world, choosing rather to use deductive logic premised on unrealistically competitive assumptions.[41] Likewise, in Smythe's opinion, much of the communication- studies literature is idealistic, particularly when addressing media 'outputs.' Usually communication studies defines output in non-materialist terms such as 'information,' 'messages,' 'images,' 'education,' 'advertising,' or 'programs.' According to Smythe, these are at best ill defined (i.e., idealist, subjective) *inputs* that help produce the real output – namely, the kind of audiences capitalism requires. Smythe termed that output 'audience power.' Audience power can be observed and measured through the buying practices and other behaviour of audiences, and hence is objective and realistic.[42]

Nor is idealism versus realism the only tension or contradiction running through Smythe's thought. Contradiction, he maintained, permeates all things and all relations, and is the source of most change. Usually contradictions are asymmetrical; that is, there is a dominant or more powerful force or tendency and a subordinate, often repressed one. Nonetheless, these forces struggle with one another, at least incipiently, and issuing from these struggles is the possibility of transformation.[43] Some of the more important dialectical relations proposed by Smythe are the following.

- *People and Commodities*. Smythe submitted that there is a contradiction between people as members of audiences and people as participants in more traditional social formations (families, churches, labour unions, political parties). Furthermore, he suggested, a contradiction is built into commodities whereby their physical and symbolic properties can both improve individual or collective welfare and damage that welfare;[44] so, for example, power-generating stations (a producer's commodity) improve well-being by reducing dangerous and irksome work but at the same time cause ecological harm. Furthermore, for Smythe, these distinct sets of dialectical tension – that is, those within the individual and ones within the commodity – 'intersect' to constitute a third set of dialectical tensions – between people and commodities.[45] Smythe wrote that we must stop thinking of people and commodities as disconnected, again a basic premise of neoclassical economics, and view them rather as forming *'relationships in social processes.'*[46] Commodities, in other words, 'bias' or *mediate* human relations.

- *The Rich and Poor.* Of all the social contradictions, the most enduring and universal in Smythe's view is that between rich and poor. He wrote: 'As one looks at the reality of the world in historical time, it is clear that the most universal, durable cleavage is the contradiction between the rich and the poor in terms of their respective control of the means of living – i.e., their power relations.'[47] Change or development in any society, Smythe declared, arises from struggles for ascendancy among rival groups. Important in those struggles in our day, and hence helping to set the trajectory of social change, are the mass media, which play an agenda-setting role.[48] Smythe always insisted that 'control of the means of communication is the basis of political power.'[49] Hence seizure of the media is 'an immediate imperative' of every revolutionary movement.[50] Resistance, for Smythe, in part entails establishing *horizontal* communication networks to countervail hierarchical domination.[51]

- *Consciousness Industry and Cultural Screens.* Smythe defined 'traditional societies' as those in which central place is afforded activities for which the use of commodities is marginal or absent: 'Sexual activities, child-rearing, making and enjoying the subtleties of communities, healing, consoling, learning, artistic, religious needs,' for Smythe, all are instances of 'central activities' for which, in traditional societies, the use of commodities is limited or absent.[52] For capitalist societies, by contrast, the commodity form predominates, even in meeting these 'central needs.' There, the price system, and concomitantly the mindset promulgated by the Consciousness Industry, *invades* activities and institutions that had developed over the millennia, and endeavours to transform them into relations of commodity exchange. Traditional institutions and practices that manage to survive this onslaught, however, in Smythe's opinion, are bulwarks against the capitalist offensive. They offer intimations of a cultural reality different from, and inconsistent with, that proffered by the Consciousness Industry.

To defend against CI incursions, Smythe recommended *cultural screens*, which he defined as aspects of a national culture or ideological system that serve to protect its *cultural realism*, that is, its central values as expressed in artifacts, practices and institutional policies.[53] Examples of cultural screens include: language; religious and mythical beliefs; customs; and border control over the movement of people and things.

Although cultural screens are as old as humanity, in most areas of the globe today they are being undermined through the 'free flow' of investment, technology, goods, information, and tourism. According to Smythe, 'if the idea of cultural screens, and the necessity for them, is today novel or strange, that shows how far modern capitalism has undermined them in its ceaseless quest for profits. The worldwide expansion of the capitalist system since about the sixteenth century necessarily involved the systematic penetration and liquidation of cultural screens of traditional societies.'[54]

A case in point, according to Smythe, is the unwarranted disdain many in the West afford *censorship*. Censorship became opprobrious in seventeenth-century England when the emerging business class was keen to cast off ecclesiastical and governmental restraints on commercial publication; the term continues to be applied today to all manner of government regulation, even when designed to protect indigenous cultures from foreign domination. To argue in this manner, however, Smythe insisted, is to miss the main point, for under capitalism (i.e., the Consciousness Industry) decisions are made all the time on what to publish and not publish, what to broadcast and not broadcast, what to produce and not produce. Although such decisions are seldom called 'censorship,' they amount to just that – decisions about which messages will circulate in society and which ones will not see the light of day.

On commercial television, for example, self-censorship means that programs must contribute to the sales of advertised products and to the hegemony of monopoly capitalism. Likewise, in the daily press, media analysts such as Noam Chomsky, Edward S. Herman, and James Winter have documented systematic omissions in news coverage: stories inconsistent with dominant political-economic interests are not distributed by commercial media.

In fact, censorship is pervasive in 'democratic' society. As Walter Lippmann observed, 'events' being virtually infinite in number means that the press *could not* cover everything, even if it wanted to. Furthermore, the absence of a right to initiate speech over media is tantamount to censorship. As University of Windsor professor Myles Ruggles remarks, 'the general citizenry of North America has no rights to express itself in the mass media; … there are no enforceable citizen rights to initiate speech or to reply to speech, whether as an editorial or paid advertising content, in the public fora of the mass media.'[55] For reasons such as these, Dallas Smythe concluded that judgments concerning censorship should be made on 'the merits of the decision [to publish or not publish] rather than whether it is a public or a private organization that makes it.'[56]

ARTS AND SCIENCE

Smythe defined *culture* as 'all that people use and value in their daily lives.' Culture always exists, he proposed, 'in a context of social relations.'[57] Control of culture, furthermore, is required for monopoly capitalism to flourish, since that political-economic system is premised on the ubiquity of commodified social relations. Smythe saw the arts, sciences, and technology as important components of culture, and hence, like mass media, as being loci of struggle.

Art as Propaganda
While much attention was paid in the West to 'socialist realism' as practised, for instance, by the former Soviet Union, much less has been afforded 'capitalist realism.' According to Smythe, however, art in the West is immensely propagandistic. One aspect of this is art's status of commodity. In that capacity, art cultivates 'possessive individualism,' meaning that art objects, like other commodities, exist to be accumulated, and hence they manifest and contribute to the growth of class structure.[58] Moreover, consistent with the individualism of capitalist ideology is the notion of artist-as-genius. According to Smythe, this outlook serves to depoliticize fine art. Under capitalism, art is not seen as a means for expressing political statements or providing social commentary; its function, rather, is merely to evoke feelings. *Objets d'art*, under capitalism, exist to be contemplated and to give pleasure. According to Smythe, then, aesthetics subverts political economy.

The myth of the gifted, albeit often alienated artist, likewise depoliticizes art by engendering the notion that only the cultured bourgeoisie or the gentry are capable of appreciating high art.[59] Whereas the upper classes, then, appropriate the often heavily subsidized 'fine arts' to substantiate their sensibilities and superior class position, the unwashed masses receive 'popular culture,'[60] which likewise, for the most part, is controlled by the CI. Like the fine arts, the lower arts 'provide the spark of novelty' that is incorporated into the marketing of consumer goods and contributes also to their planned obsolescence.[61]

But art, in Smythe's view, is dialectical. On the one hand, whether high or low, art normally contributes to hegemonic ideology. On the other, when Canadian artists and artisans organize and struggle in support of indigenous values, they serve the interests of the large majority of Canadian people.

Science and 'Technology'

According to Smythe, the word 'technology' rivals '"free flow of information" as the propaganda term of greatest value to monopoly capitalism.'[62] As popularly conceived, *technology* is a neutered term, an autonomous force, the practical out-working of disinterested, apolitical science.[63] It therefore serves as a convenient scapegoat when things go wrong and invites people to accept as normal the way things are, masking power relations embedded in engineering designs.[64]

In his meetings with Chinese government officials, Smythe asked why, if technology is value-neutral, did railways in China all run east and west. 'The railways were built during China's era of colony,' Smythe observed, 'to serve the interests of compradors who came and wanted to penetrate China … to exploit your resources, labor, minerals, and everything else … When you took over … you couldn't travel or send freight from the north of China to the south of China. There were no means to do it. Everything was penetrated from the coast.'[65]

Technology, Smythe insisted, *never* can be neutral. Power relations are *always* embedded in industrial design. For one thing, money is the most important term in every engineering equation, and for that reason alone technology never stands or evolves independently of the economic system: inventions and practices that forward the goals of the ongoing system will be developed, and, conversely, those not serving the purposes of the economic system are suppressed, no matter how useful they might be otherwise. By way of illustration, Smythe recalled the 'failure' of broadcast facsimile as a means of distributing text to the home.[66] Broadcast facsimile was tested as early as 1943 and, if implemented on a large scale, could have utterly transformed the U.S. newspaper industry. By Smythe's reckoning, it could have allowed communities with only one or two daily newspapers to support as many as fifteen or twenty. But a competitive news industry, according to Smythe, would have disrupted the mass marketing of consumer goods since audience shares would be volatile.

More generally, according to Smythe, technological innovation normally serves to concentrate communicatory power within the existing power system. This means that new media will tend to accentuate information flows from the core to periphery and minimize lateral communication. To continuously innovate such undemocratic means of communicating, therefore, Smythe assessed, the Consciousness Industry must do its work. This it does by hammering home a number of axioms so that they become 'common sense.' Examples of these common-sense but 'false' axioms are:

- *the law of comparative advantage,* which maintains that specialization and free trade increase the wealth of all nations;[67]
- *the notion that technology is neutral,* that its introduction and use have no particular political consequences;[68]
- *the principle that information is a commodity alone,* that it can be regarded 'objectively' and that it has no particular cultural or political consequences;[69]
- *the claim that the 'free marketplace of ideas' is democratic;*[70]
- *the assertion that private corporations are individuals,* and that they therefore deserve the 'same' rights (for example, to freedom of speech) as people ;[71]
- *the doctrine of possessive individualism,*[72] the claim that humans are by nature selfish accumulators.

INFORMATION OR COMMUNICATION?

In a book on which Dallas Smythe was working at the time of his death, he asked why we use the term *Information* Society rather than the *Communication* Age or the *Communication* Society.[73] How and why, he queried, have we come to consider information so much more important than communication? The answer, he maintained, lies in the notion of commodity, in power, and in control.

In this unpublished manuscript, Smythe defined *information* as a 'particular state of patterned energy.' Information therefore has certain parameters – energy, matter, structure, time, and location (or space). As 'an actual state of energy,' information is omnipresent in the universe. When identified or recognized, moreover, 'particular states' may be referred to as signs or symbols, or preferably 'marks.'[74] As 'marks,' the scope of information is limited to the organisms and structures that sense it through vision, hearing, touch, smell, taste, and/or electromagnetism.

Information does two things, he continued. First, it constitutes structures of all kinds – from single-celled animals or plants to the very cosmos. All entities, both individual and collective, are organized in terms of information. Information serves also a second function: for sensate creatures, it directs attention to 'the probable future motion of patterned energy to, within, or from one structure to another.' Stated otherwise, *information predicts the movement of information*. Information, then, is a 'tendency to motion,' or 'evidence of impending motion.'

Drawing some political-economy implications of this second function of information, Smythe advised: 'The interest of Paleolithic humanoid institutions and individuals, no less than the interest of present TNCs [transnational corporations] and their captive nation-state hosts, has been to acquire and use information as predictive of tendencies to motion and of the character of structures ... prepatory to taking interested actions in relation to those features of the environments.'

Whereas information is an actual state, according to Smythe, *communication* pertains to motion, that is, to exchange and sharing of patterned energy between and within structures. He defined *structures* as 'energy perceived practically as being in a quiet condition.'

Structure, then, *is* information. Structures have origins and destinies. They are not interminable. They change as information enters them and as information is dispelled. Communication, then, may be defined as 'patterned energy between nodes of densified energy (structures), or to or from unbounded space.'

Communication therefore differs from information. Communication implies interdependence, relationship, flux, and totality, whereas information implies structure, temporary rigidity, quantification, and commodification. For Smythe, information is in accord with a nineteenth-century (Newtonian) view of the universe whereby matter was deemed to be partionable into static, fundamental building blocks. *Communication,* on the other hand, is much more a twentieth-century concept, quite in tune with modern quantum physics and systems theory. At the subatomic level, Smythe noted, basic phenomena are seen as 'relations and connections in processes.'

To exemplify in everyday life this altered (non-Newtonian) understanding, Smythe pointed to boundaries. From a Newtonian and from an atomic point of view, which we associate with *information*, boundaries define and enclose separate structures that can be analysed in and of themselves in the absence of context, interaction, or change. The holistic view, by contrast, which we associate with *communication*, looks at boundaries as zones where exchanges take place, examples being the skin of mammals and their sense organs, which exchange energy in various ways with the environment. Within structures, too, patterned energy (information) is exchanged among components.

Communication, furthermore, usually is both *reciprocal* (i.e., bidirectional) and *asymmetric* in the quantity and quality of patterned energy exchanged. One implication of non-linear, bidirectional exchanges is the importance of initial conditions. Following Gleick, Smythe asked: Can the flap of a butterfly's wing in Brazil form a Tornado in Texas? This seems less unlikely if one accepts the principle that a small-scale initial event can expand recursively through rapid reiteration to develop points of crisis. Smythe further remarked that the revolution in communication and information during the twentieth century comprises exponential increases in the speed with which people move patterned energy, potentially heightening the importance of small events with regard to future states.

Although the old Newtonian view of reality as linear and divisible has been immensely productive, giving rise to innovations ranging from internal-combustion engines to pesticides, plastics, and synthetic rubber – even designer DNA – it has generated also imponderable environmental problems: the Greenhouse Effect, the foreseeable disappearance of fossil fuels, deforestation, the erosion of the ozone layer, contamination of groundwater, and deterioration of air quality.

Most fundamentally, according to Smythe, whereas 'the Newtonian paradigm was focused on the character of *being,* the focal point today of non-linear [holistic] science is on *process,* that is on *becoming.*' Furthermore, change in non-linear, recursive processes is context-dependent, in marked contrast to linear (Newtonian) change. In the scientific and philosophical debate concerning chance versus necessity, Smythe found a 'basic contradiction in which the unity of opposites, contending with each other, is pervasive and inclusive of life processes.' This notion of unity in opposites – or, stated inversely, that syntheses can form from antitheses – is, of course, a dialectical position encountered time and again in this survey of Canadian communication thought.

In his final works, Smythe indeed sought syntheses, and in that regard he proposed integrating information and communication into a dialectical study to be known as *infocom.* Smythe explained:

'Infocom' (the integration of communication and information) is a way of describing the states of energy in all systems at whatever scale of size or complexity in the process of change. The communications aspect is the state of (usually patterned) energy in motion over time and space, between and within structures (eg. radio waves carrying TV programs or computer data, motions of bodies in air under high and low pressure …). The informational aspect is the state of energy in leaving, or entering a system/body/structure/institution. In such systems it is concentrated, or solidified in structures of varying degrees of hardness (skeleton, fat, soft organs, or the 'reserve funds' of a TNC [transnational corporation]). In the process of leaving or entering a system the information aspect moves through exchange to produce changes in the system and in its relation to other systems.

Smythe's emerging analysis of 'infocom' was not, of course, devoid of political-economy implications: Information, he wrote, always serves the values of the host structure, and on leaving carries those values. For that reason, information is never value-free. Moreover, when information is exchanged, the sharing or exchange is usually asymmetric: 'equality and equilibrium … are *not* typical.'

Furthermore, if a superior structure controls information and the policies governing communication, it then may extend control 'toward global proportions.' And this, Smythe remarked incisively, is precisely the 'posture and intent of the political/economic formation which generated the drive for the Information Society.'

At this point we must leave the thought of Dallas Smythe concerning 'infocom.' Had he lived to complete and publish these last works, he might well be remembered by the communication studies discipline not only for his pioneering work in the political economy of communication, but for transcendent theorizing as well.

SOME QUESTIONS

Smythe's 'Realism'
In this section we consider, first, whether Smythe was successful in implementing a thoroughly materialist (or 'realist') analysis, and whether, if feasible, that would have been desirable. Smythe, it will be recalled, criticized both mainstream economics for promulgating idealist models devoid of power considerations, and communication studies for specifying *idealist* outputs of media. To make communication studies more concrete, he proposed that *audience power* be recognized as the

media's main output. He defined audience power as people ready, willing, and able to purchase advertised goods; to vote for advertised candidates; and to support the existing economic order. Audience power is materialist, he contended, because people's *actions* (the manifestation of their indoctrination) can be observed and measured, whereas 'programming' and 'messages' lead merely to interpretative (i.e., subjective and speculative) analyses. Audience power is indeed less idealist (more materialist) than 'information' or 'messages' or 'programs,' and so in that respect Smythe indeed was successful in pursuing his goal. On the other hand, one of his central points was that the *Consciousness Industry*, fronting monopoly capitalism, produces audience power. Having materialized the product, in virtually the same breath he may have idealized the agent or producer. Certainly, "Consciousness Industry" is a huge abstraction, as confirmed by the range of institutions, objects, and practices that Smythe said comprise it. 'Consciousness Industry,' therefore, is not unlike 'technology,' standing as a surrogate or as a code word for an entire economic order. Certainly, CI in its entirety is not observable, and hence is "idealist" in Smythe's sense of the term.

That this should be the case is easily understood. Scientific (in Smythe's terms, 'materialist') analysis entails the partitioning of a system so that one component (the 'cause') is deemed responsible for changes in another component. Smythe's point, however, was that there is an entire system at work, which he called 'monopoly capitalism,' and it is this system that produces 'audience power.' The Consciousness Industry is a part of monopoly capitalism, but it is neither a small nor an autonomous part; it is the agent acting for the whole. To disassemble the Consciousness Industry into its components and study them separately would undermine Smythe's main point.

Given the foregoing, Smythe's major accomplishment was not so much substituting objective/materialist for subjective/idealist analysis, but rather simply (yet importantly) identifying more accurately the output of media – namely, audiences with inclinations to act and think in certain ways and to accept certain doctrines.

What then can be said for his key idealist terms – namely, Consciousness Industry and monopoly capitalism – compared to the idealist notions he derided – principally 'technology,' but as well ideology, messages, meanings, persuasion, and the like? For Smythe, 'technology' is a cover-up for 'monopoly capitalism'; technology *is* what monopoly capitalism *does*. Smythe noted, though, that most people seldom recognize this. For many, 'technology' connotes, and is frequently intended by users of the term to connote, an autonomous by-product of a self-sustaining scientific enterprise. In that semantic field, 'technology' can be at once a goal, a cause, and an explanation. Smythe's insight was brilliant and heuristic – that 'technology' is neither autonomous nor bereft of political-economy consequences. On the other hand, though, it is also worth mentioning that, in addressing the *meaning* of the word 'technology,' Smythe engaged in *interpretative*, not materialist, analysis.

But once again, this is as it must be. It was, after all, the point, or rather an implication, of the semiotics of Ferdinand de Saussure that humans are forever located in a world of material objects ('signifiers'), which they *interpret* ('signifieds'). Taking de Saussure seriously means believing that humans are forever engaged, dialectically, in the tension between idealism (interpretation) and materialism (observation). Idealists (such as Northrop Frye) and materialists (such as Smythe), remarkably dissimilar in their epistemological predilections, ineluctably must observe *and* interpret.

SMYTHE AND CANADIAN COMMUNICATION THOUGHT

Smythe and Innis

Smythe was critical of Innis, who, he complained, 'conspicuously missed the main point of Canada's industrial development.' [75] By this Smythe meant that Canada has always been a colony – first, of France; then, of England; and, now, of the United States – yet Innis appeared to believe that Canada enjoyed a brief interlude of independence. Moreover, Smythe held the opinion that, when Innis dealt with 'technology,' it was 'in idealist terms, unfocused on the going concern [i.e., monopoly capitalism].'[76] Indeed, Smythe charged that Innis 'helped popularize the myth' of technology, meaning that Smythe regarded Innis as being a technological determinist.[77] Smythe also claimed that Innis 'did not address the significance of mass communication in either his economic or his communication writing.'[78]

Such criticisms seem unduly harsh. Actually, Smythe and Innis had much in common. Both concerned themselves with centre–periphery relations – Innis, through the staples thesis and his concept of space-binding media; Smythe, through his notions of the Consciousness Industry and audience power. Innis thought of the price system as 'penetrating' time-bound cultures, while Smythe saw the 'Consciousness Industry' as 'invading' institutions of pre-capitalist formation (the church, political parties, and the family). Innis saw the daily press as spreading 'present-mindedness' over increasingly larger geographic areas, and Smythe viewed the mass media generally, including the daily press, as enculturing people into possessive individualism. Innis warned that Canadians were 'struggling for our lives' in face of a flood of U.S. advertising, while Smythe in the same context summoned up the image of King Canute vainly trying to hold back a flood of foreign-originated, commodified cultural products. Whereas Innis saw message-propagating properties in staples, railways, stirrups, clocks, and media proper, Smythe saw them in consumer and producers goods of all kinds, as well as in the products of mass media. Finally, Innis made 'a plea for time' whereby he hoped that such time-centred institutions as family and church could countervail the pre-eminence of the price system; Smythe, too, expressed the hope that the 'contradiction' between markets and those very same pre-capitalist institutions might ultimately result in the overthrow of monopoly capitalism. In all these matters, the distance separating Innis and Smythe was not great, and one wonders why Smythe chose not to be more complimentary of Innis. This is not to say, of course, that there were not important differences. Perhaps most significantly, Innis remained always the economic/cultural historian who in his communication writings addressed the sweep of time, explaining time or space biases in civilizations by the mode of communication, whereas Smythe was a historian only in a much narrower sense. Although certainly cognizant of, and writing about, the histories of the industries in which he had an expertise – telephone, telegraph, and broadcasting, for instance – Smythe focused much more directly on material relations today. Historical analysis for Smythe was but a means for better comprehending material conditions in the present. Smythe, then, was not a 'meta-historian,' as was Innis.

It is interesting to compare Innis and Smythe with regard to the innovation process. Innis maintained that innovations in media often are undertaken at the margins, and that, as a new medium diffuses into the core, instability occurs: the existing power structure is challenged by the new medium and its associated monopoly of knowledge. Smythe, in contrast, saw the existing system of power as playing a huge role, either in supporting or in subverting innovations, depending on whether they were anticipated to extend or diminish existing hegemony. Nonetheless, he was in agreement with Innis in maintaining that for power to shift from one group to another there must also be a shift in control over the predominant means of communication.

Smythe and Grierson

Interesting parallels also can be drawn between the work of Smythe and Grierson. If Smythe's central category was the Consciousness Industry, Grierson's was propaganda. CI for Smythe, though, was a more expansive category than propaganda was for Grierson, who confined its application largely to the mass media and, in the future, he hoped, to education. Nonetheless, CI and propaganda serve much the same function for these two theorists – namely, creating and sustaining a 'human nature' suitable to the needs of the power structure. Grierson recommended, however, that the techniques of propaganda be taken over and applied by those with a more democratically inclined philosophy so as to engender pursuit of the common good; Smythe, one senses, would look on Grierson's proposal as naïve in the extreme since, he insisted, democracy requires that the means of communication be used 'horizontally,' not vertically, as Grierson recommended. Grierson, we might say, was the gradualist who felt that increases in democracy could be attained by individuals fighting for it within the current system; Smythe was the revolutionary who believed that democracy can come about only through concerted class struggle and the seizure of the means of communication by oppressed peoples.

On other key points, though, these theorists were agreed – on the principle that aesthetics displaces political economy, for instance. Grierson always insisted he was an educator first, and an artist only second, and that, when beauty and truth conflict, one must always opt for truth no matter how tempting the other option may be. Smythe went even further, charging that aestheticism serves hegemony by trivializing the political-economy import of artistic works. Both Smythe and Grierson looked at art dialectically: most often, they believed, art serves to inculcate anti-democratic values in unwary audiences, but also it has the potential to energize and make people aware.

Smythe and Grierson were agreed, furthermore, that on important issues one can never be neutral; as Grierson expressed the point, one can either be 'for democracy and against authoritarianism, or … for authoritarianism.'[79] There is no middle ground.

SMYTHE'S RELEVANCE TODAY

Smythe's work certainly sharpens our critical awareness and analytical skills. Merely recalling his pronouncements concerning consumer goods as 'teaching machines' and the ideological obscurantism inherent in the term 'technology' enriches our capacity to understand current affairs. But Smythe contributed much more.

Smythe's central tenet was that 'the power to control information flows (or communications) is the basis of political power and an attribute of sovereignty.'[80] In the case of Canada, he judged, the country historically has been 'schizophrenic on several levels,'[81] attempting to attain or regain control here while ceding control there. Smythe's dictum retains importance as we now witness hitherto domestic telecommunications firms 'partnering' through ownership and contractual agreements with foreign-based carriers, with much domestic telecommunications policy increasingly subordinated to international agreements and to rulings by the World Trade Organization.

Smythe's analytical stance casts new light also on technological trends in communication. There is a myth propagated in popular communication discourses that the Internet, for example, is levelling hierarchies, that this uncensored, 'anarchic' medium is a powerful force for democracy. Smythe's dictum that only those technological devices and systems that augment and extend existing power relations are allowed to persist and develop, however, should cause us to pause and ponder this blithe interpretation. Rapid technological change in communications, the perceived need to upgrade computer systems every couple of years; to add sound cards and ever-faster Internet links; to purchase CD 'Burners'; to add digital video and surround sound to home entertainment systems – all this is part and parcel of the growing hegemony of a worldwide infotech business. Each new device is a 'teaching machine' prophesying its own obsolescence. Technological changes in computer communications keep consumers for ever on the treadmill of continual purchases and dissatisfactions, just as Smythe described for the entire capitalist order.

Furthermore, the Internet is, if anything, a means of extending and speeding up commercial transactions in general. On-line advertising, e-commerce, and the electronic marketplace all take capitalism to a new order of magnitude, integrating markets worldwide. And accompanying every purchase is a record that facilitates direct advertising to increasingly well-targeted consumers.

Moreover, gaps between information rich and information poor grow exponentially as increasingly sophisticated devices are needed to access and send information, and as information is increasingly commodified. Smythe understood, of course, that perhaps the most significant and continuing dichotomy in human history has been the disparity between rich and poor, a disparity that swells daily with the proliferation of new information technologies and the heightened commodification of information that those technologies enable.

Since Smythe's death, the hegemony of the Consciousness Industry has, if anything, increased. Meanwhile, the institutions of family, trade union, and church, which Smythe held to be sites of resistance, reel under the penetrative powers of the price system and the relentless invasion of people's minds by the Consciousness Industry.

Smythe's analyses certainly deserve to be read today as they increase our understanding of our times. True to his Marxian faith, Smythe prophesied that crises and contradictions will continue to mount so as, eventually, to bring about a new, more just political-economic-cultural order. In that matter, only time will tell.

6

The Communication Thought of
C.B. MACPHERSON (1911–1987)

Life is for *doing* rather than just *getting*.

– The Rise and Fall of Economic Justice, 83

ABOUT C.B. MACPHERSON

Renowned as a political philosopher, C.B. Macpherson ought also to be remembered as having been an innovative communication theorist. He wrote extensively on *mediation*, and, in particular, how different modes of property shape (or 'bias') human interactions. Moreover, Macpherson was a masterful analyst of rhetoric. Long before social scientists such as Donald McCloskey and Arjo Klamer began studying 'economics as rhetoric,'[1] Macpherson was busy deconstructing classical discourses on property, the market, and human nature, and was proposing alternatives to the mainstream.

Crawford Brough (pronounced 'Bruff') Macpherson was born in Toronto on 18 November 1911. His mother was a music teacher, and his father taught at the Ontario College of Education.[2] Their summers, his spouse, Mrs Kay Macpherson related,[3] were spent at the family cottage in the Thousand Islands, near Gananoque, Ontario.

Brough Macpherson attended the privately run University of Toronto Schools (UTS) before enrolling at the University of Toronto in 1929. At U of T he sat in on some lectures by Harold Innis, which he found less than inspiring: 'He went on and on about the bloody fur traders,'[4] Macpherson complained years later. It was as an undergraduate that Macpherson's left-of-centre views began to form, and these he retained for the rest of his life. He received his BA in 1931.

Next he moved to England to study at the London School of Economics under Harold Laski. Laski, a prolific writer, was by Macpherson's reckoning one of the few theorists then trying to combine liberal values with some kind of socialism,[5] Macpherson's lifelong project! Through Laski, Macpherson met other left-of-centre academics, including R.H. Tawney, whose influence is not to be underestimated. Tawney's most celebrated works were *The Sickness of An Acquisitive Society* (1920), a devastating critique of capitalism published originally as a Fabian tract,[6] and *Religion and the Rise of Capitalism* (1926), which, among other things, censured the debasement, indeed inversion, by latter-day Calvinism of authentic Christian ethics. 'Puritans,' Tawney scoffed, see in the poor 'not a misfortune to be pitied and relieved, but a moral failing to be condemned, and in riches not an object of suspicion – though like other gifts they may be abused – but the blessing which rewards the triumph of energy and will.'[7] In an interview years later, Macpherson affirmed that he developed his own account of *possessive individualism* to give 'a more precise expression [to] Tawney's notion of acquisitiveness.'[8] The University of London awarded Macpherson a MSc in economics in 1935 and a DSc, also in economics, in 1955.[9]

In 1935, Macpherson joined the Department of Political Economy at the University of Toronto, and thus became a colleague of both Harold Innis's and Irene Biss's. Macpherson and Innis, along with political scientist V.W. Bladen and sociologist S.D. Clark, formed the nucleus of an informal Faculty Club lunch-table discussion group.[10]

Macpherson evidently was an exemplary teacher. According to his former student and later Canadian federal political party leader Ed Broadbent, rather than merely summarizing the thought of great political theorists, Macpherson routinely presumed (not always correctly, no doubt) that his students had read the original texts, enabling him to devote class time to unpacking the authors' often tacit presuppositions concerning human nature, the nature of economic life, and their view of history.[11] Indeed, it was one of Macpherson's primary tenets that, when studying political philosophy, one ought always to 'keep a sharp lookout for two things: [the] assumptions about the whole society ..., and [the] assumptions about the essential nature of the people who are to make the system work.'[12]

Macpherson's sole non-academic appointment was during the war, when he served in Ottawa under John Grierson in the Executive Office of the Wartime Information Board. One can but speculate on whether wartime atrocities, had he experienced them more directly, would have wrought as deep an effect on Macpherson as they did on Innis (and on George Grant, for that matter). He spent another year during the war as an acting professor of Economics and Political Science at the University of New Brunswick, but returned to the University of Toronto in 1943, where, apart from accepting visiting-professorships in Britain, the United States, and Australia, he remained until retiring in 1977.

Neither a utopian nor a determinist, C.B. Macpherson chose equity or justice as the theoretical and moral base from which to mount critiques of capitalism and of individualist philosophies, and from which to propose social and political reform. 'Socialism is not intended to put people on a level,' he wrote from England during the Depression; 'it is to remove the system which prevents people from finding their own level.'[13] Macpherson was, in brief, a 'Red Liberal.'

In the estimation of Daniel Drache and Arthur Kroker, Macpherson was 'one of the twentieth century's foremost socialist critics of liberalism.'[14] Never strident, Macpherson was exemplary in his scholarship, always giving opposing systems of thought and their expositors fair treatment. His commentaries and analyses were invariably grounded on eminently sound logic. His strategy of refutation was often to state explicitly the assumptions upon which antagonistic thought structures are based, and only then to challenge them. 'The final effect,' according to Broadbent, 'was as satisfying as variations on a theme by Bach'[15] – Bach being, incidentally, Macpherson's lifelong passion.

Likewise William Leiss has remarked that Macpherson successfully carried out his resolve 'to write with clarity of expression' so that his works, like those of his model Voltaire, would be accessible to a wide audience.[16] Deeply committed to social change, Macpherson believed that, to be effective, political philosophers must write not only rigourously, but with clarity and integrity.

Macpherson's first book, *Democracy in Alberta*, was published in 1953. There Innis is mentioned but once, and then only in passing. Nonetheless, that work could accurately be characterized as an application of the staples thesis to the administration of a province. Macpherson analysed Alberta's unique 'quasi party' system of government, which began in 1921 with the ascent of the United Farmers of Alberta. He used the term 'quasi party' to denote dominance in a jurisdiction by a single party; for Alberta, he attributed this to the region's staple economy, its relatively homogeneous class structure, and its inhabitants' disaffection with remote financial interests.[17]

Notable as *Democracy in Alberta* is, it was only with publication of *The*

Political Theory of Possessive Individualism in 1962 that Macpherson, then fifty-one, secured a worldwide reputation as a distinguished scholar. There he reinterpreted English political theory, in particular, that of Thomas Hobbes and John Locke, critiquing their views of property, society, and human nature; he also lauded the 'morally superior' views of John Stuart Mill. Macpherson's Massey Lectures for the CBC, entitled 'The Real World of Democracy,' were published in 1965. Perhaps his most widely read work, these lectures describe non-liberal (i.e., communist and third-world) conceptions of democracy, and compare these to liberal/capitalist conceptions. Macpherson there remarked in detail on what he saw as a basic contradiction in liberal democracy – that, although it was within capitalism that basic human rights arose, capitalism is now eroding those rights through ever-increasing concentrations of wealth and power.

Macpherson's other books include *Democratic Theory: Essays in Retrieval* (1973), a collection of essays enlarging on themes he developed elsewhere; *The Life and Times of Liberal Democracy* (1977); *Property: Mainstream and Critical Positions* (1978), an edited volume containing two seminal pieces by Macpherson; *Burke* (1980), in which he reconciles and critiques the thought of that apparently self-contradictory eighteenth-century conservative/liberal philosopher and parliamentarian;[18] and *The Rise and Fall of Economic Justice* (1985). A full bibliography of Macpherson's work appears in *Powers, Possessions and Freedom: Essays in Honour of C.B. Macpherson,* edited by Alkis Kontos.[19]

C.B. Macpherson was a member of the Royal Society of Canada and an Officer of the Order of Canada. He died in Toronto on 21 July 1987, peacefully, with his wife, Kay, and daughter, Susan, at his side.

SYNOPSIS

Whereas Innis proposed that staples, money, and various means of inscription mediate human relations, and Smythe that consumer goods, mass media, and, more generally, the Consciousness Industry do this, Macpherson pointed to the institution of property. He saw property as a human-made institution that creates and maintains relations among people. Changes in the system of property alter fundamentally the pattern of human relations.

Macpherson also emphasized the role of political philosophers in justifying systems of property. For that reason, political philosophy, too, at least indirectly, mediates human relations. Moreover, political philosophies often propose *an essential human nature* that, if commonly accepted, also helps shape the manner in which people act and relate to one another. For both these reasons, Macpherson contended that the major problems of our time are not primarily material but ideological, which is to say they are symbolic, and hence communicatory.

Property as Mediation

Property and Democracy

C.B. Macpherson devoted his academic career to theorizing on capitalism, socialism, democracy, and property. He defined *capitalism* as an economic/political system based on private ownership of the means of production (i.e., land, machinery, supplies, and so forth), whereby individuals, calculating their most profitable courses of action, enter into contractual exchange relations. By *socialism*, he meant a condition whereby everyone possesses as a right the capacity to access the means of production; consequently, in socialism, labour is not a commodity as it is under capitalism. *Democracy* for Macpherson denotes an entire way of life, 'a whole complex of relations between individuals,' and not simply a system of government.[20] A truly democratic society, in his view, is one that ensures that all can develop and exert their capacities or potential, that each may live, as he put it, 'as fully humanly as he may wish.'[21] Tying these concepts together for Macpherson is *property*, which he defined as 'an enforceable claim of a person to some use or benefit,'[22] and hence also as 'a man-made device which establishes certain relations between people.'[23] Property, therefore, is of immense importance; indeed, he announced, 'all roads lead to property.'[24]

Property as Concept and Institution

Macpherson viewed property dialectically, as being both a concept and an institution.[25] These dual aspects of property are in continual interaction, either reinforcing or contradicting each other. He wrote, 'What [people] see must have some relation (though not necessarily an exact correspondence) to what is actually there; but changes in what is there are due partly to changes in the ideas people have of it.'[26] During times of stability, property as a concept and property as an institution are mutually supportive, the concept justifying the institution, and the institution verifying the concept. During times of transition, however, conceptions of property inconsistent with the institution arise and may foretell change in the institution. Therefore a good starting point for those interested in reforming property (i.e., changing social relations) is to challenge property's justificatory theories and its commonly accepted meanings.

Changes in the conception or meaning of property do not occur randomly or without cause. According to Macpherson, they invariably spring from 'changes in the purposes which society or the dominant classes in society expect the institution of property to serve.'[27] In making this statement, Macpherson hinted at two ways whereby meanings and purposes ascribed to property can change. First is the 'democratic way,' whereby meanings emerge as a consensus from the grass roots; in this regard he pointed out how pollution of the air and water, and depletion of natural resources, could very well cause people to revise fundamentally their thinking about efficacy of private property.[28] Alternatively, meanings can be imposed from above, whether through educational systems, philosophic writings, religious indoctrination, or other modes of persuasion such as the mass media, in which case meanings change only as the dominant class changes, or at least as the perceived self-interest of the dominant class changes.

Whenever the meaning of property is in transition, property becomes controversial. People at such times disagree about what the institution of property is and the purposes it should serve. For Macpherson, these issues constitute the most essential debate in which a society can engage.

The Properties of Property
If property as an institution and property as a concept are inextricably linked, and if both these aspects of property are changeable, Macpherson asked rhetorically, can anything of general validity be said about property? Not a great deal, he replied, but some things indeed can be said. First, property is not a thing. It is, rather, an enforceable right. It is 'a claim ... of a person to some use or benefit ... that will be enforced by society or the state, by custom or convention or law.'[29] This aspect of property, according to Macpherson, has been acknowledged by all major theorists. Second, through the ages, property as an enforceable right has been justified on one of two grounds – either as being necessary for people to realize their 'fundamental nature,' or because it has been deemed a 'natural right.'[30] Disputes concerning what type of property is best, therefore, are usually couched in terms of 'human

nature,' or with regard to what comprises a 'natural right' to property. The historical significance of philosophers and theologians in this regard is apparent.

Third, being an *enforceable* claim, property is inherently a *'political relation between persons.'*[31] Every system of property sets out the rights, enforced by the state or community, of persons in relation to other persons.[32] Property, in other words, enables, causes, induces, encourages, shapes, biases, filters, and/or censors material and symbolic exchanges among people; *property mediates human relations.*

Fourth, property has been conceptualized historically in two basic ways: *Private property* is a right to exclude others from some use or benefit; and *common property* is the right of an individual *not* to be excluded from some use or benefit. For example, the right to access streets and parks, according to Macpherson, is a property right common to all; in Canada so is Medicare, access to a public library, and education up to and including the secondary level.

It is precisely because property can be set as either an enforceable right to exclude or as a right not be excluded that Macpherson can state that property helps define and redefine relations among people. To have property is to be able to participate in social/communicatory life; to have no property is to be barred from this. Property signifies the *selective protection of interests,* and hence denotes the selective capacity to participate in social, economic, and communicatory life.

Finally, although both private and common property are created and enforced by the state or community, these are rights of *individuals* (including corporations as 'artificial persons'). According to Macpherson, 'in neither case does the fact the state creates the right make the right the property of the state ... The state *creates* the rights, the individuals *have* the rights.'[33]

Property and the Common Good

In Macpherson's view, over time there has been a continuous 'narrowing' in both the concept and the institution of property; by this he meant that considerations of the common good have continuously been stripped away from property. In the writings of Plato, Aristotle, St Augustine, and Thomas Aquinas, common property was treated as an important mode of ownership. However, by the 'early modern' period (the seventeenth century) and the arrival of the 'full capitalist market society,' common property dropped 'virtually out of sight.'[34] Theorists of the marketplace (Hobbes, Locke, Bentham, James Mill, among others) focused attention almost exclusively on *private* property. But, even in their writings, property remained broad enough to include rights to life and liberty. A subsequent narrowing, however, has confined the conception of property to some use or benefit of a material thing or to revenue, and it includes virtually unrestricted rights to sale or disposal.[35] Regarding land, for example, ownership no longer is conditional, as it once was, upon performance of any social function.[36] According to Macpherson, 'narrowings' like these were precisely what the capitalist market economy needed to operate fully.[37]

Political Philosophy as Mediation

Property and Philosophy

Macpherson maintained that modes of ownership always require justification. He declared: 'Any institution of property requires a justifying theory. The legal right must be grounded in a public belief that it is morally right. *Property has always to be justified by something more basic*; if it is not so justified, it does not for long remain an enforceable claim. If it is not justified, it does not remain property.'[38] Political philosophers, therefore, have a special social role – namely, a class interest to serve. Only rarely, Macpherson assessed, are political concepts shaped by theorists 'who are simply grammarians or logicians.'[39]

It is not only one or other of two modes of ownership that political philosophy endorses, however. It also promotes a particular view of human nature, and in doing this it again mediates human relations. How people see themselves surely affects their interactions. If people believe themselves to be by nature infinitely acquisitive, for example, as some political philosophers (and most neoclassical economists) have claimed, they will surely behave differently than they would otherwise. Indeed, in their justifications of a class interest, Macpherson continued, it is most common for political philosophers to propose that the essence of personhood is *proprietary individualism,* by which he meant a 'conception of the individual as essentially the proprietor of his own person or capacities, owing nothing to society for them. The individual [is] seen neither as a moral whole, nor as part of a larger social whole, but as an owner of himself.'[40] *Proprietary individualism* means, furthermore, that people are considered, and consider themselves, to be divisible: in other words, aspects of the person, such as skills and energy, can with equanimity be hived off for sale to others. Labour power, therefore, can and should be sold in the marketplace as a commodity. Proprietary individualism, in other words, constitutes an ontological justification for the market economy and for relations of commodity exchange.

Many types of relations besides those of commodity exchange are conceivable, of course: As Macpherson remarked, 'there are relations of love, of friendship, of kinship, of admiration, of common interest';[41] there are also relations of customary status. But, in each case, the ontological premise or justification would be other than proprietary individualism.

From proprietary individualism, there follows a concomitant axiom, also fundamental to the market society – namely, that humans are by nature *possessive individualists*. Possessive individualism means that humans are intrinsically covetous, implying that in principle there should be no restraint on a person's right to accumulate. There are, of course, other, more traditional or communitarian conceptions of personhood – ones that maintain, for instance, that a person's capacities derive from the community, making each community member dependent upon and obligated to the community as a whole[42] – but these sentiments tend not to be recognized or valued in market-driven economies.

To the extent that traditional, communal social relations are marginalized or denigrated by individualistic political philosophies, a society's institutions and its philosophers are instrumental in *creating and maintaining* a distinct acquisition-oriented 'human nature.' In fact, according to Macpherson, such is the real business of political philosophers! Furthermore, in as much as the state is in charge of enforcing private property rights and generally maintaining conditions conducive to commodity exchange, it too is inexorably involved in creating and maintaining 'human nature.'[43]

Personhood conceived as proprietary individualism, Macpherson attested, arose during the age of mercantilism and persists to this day. In *The Political Theory of Possessive Individualism*, he traced the origin and development of this doctrine, focusing particularly on the writings of Thomas Hobbes and John Locke. Let us then turn to Macpherson's analysis of the rhetoric of classical political philosophers, and, in particular, to their treatment of 'human nature' and how they thereby 'justified' human relations in the mode of commodity exchange.

Hobbes and Possessive Individualism
Thomas Hobbes (1588–1679) was one of the first to posit human nature as possessive individualism. According to Macpherson, Hobbes saw people as 'self-moving and self-directing appetitive machines'[44] – that

is, as organisms *driven* to seek their own good and to avoid their own harm. Anticipating alike Jeremy Bentham's 'felicific calculus,'[45] modern behavioural psychology,[46] and neoclassical economics,[47] Hobbes contended that people's behaviour is *determined* by their 'appetites.' And, since people are inexorably 'driven' to seek their own welfare, what better, more peaceable way of doing this than through markets and commodity exchanges?

Furthermore, in Hobbes's view, since markets aggregate decisions on the part of a multitude of individuals, they express consensus on *value*. Market prices thereby become the primary indicator of goodness, since they denote quantitative, collective judgments on gradients of worth. The postulate of possessive individualism, it follows, implies ultimately that the marketplace is the primary ground of morality, since morality is, after all, a judgment with regard to value. If and when the marketplace is fully dominant, *intrinsic* value, that is, value inherent in the subject or object, is effaced. This is in part what Innis had in mind when he wrote about the price system's penetrative powers.

Macpherson by and large accepted *the logic* of Hobbes's argument. Indeed, at the close of *Possessive Individualism*, he stated boldly: 'The individual in market society *is* a proprietor of his own person; however much he may wish it to be otherwise, his humanity *does* depend on his freedom from any but self-interested contractual relations with others. His society *does* consist of a series of market relations.'[48] Nonetheless, he disputed fundamentally Hobbes's contention that there is a givenness or inevitability to all this. In particular, he disputed the permanence or innateness of possessive individualism, and hence the inevitability of human relations based primarily on the mode of commodity exchange. Macpherson proposed instead that the appetitive nature described by Hobbes, while accurately portraying people *in* capitalist society, was *produced by* capitalist society. No conception of human nature as being infinitely desirous existed in feudalism, he attested. Nor need any such conception persist in the future, provided society's institutions are altered in appropriate ways. We discuss below his position on 'a new system of property.'

Locke and 'Inherent Inequality'

According to Macpherson's account, John Locke understood that proprietary individualism inevitably gives rise to gross inequalities. In a possessive market economy (that is, in an economy where labour power is a commodity), there *must* be, by definition, both a class with sufficient resources to employ the labour of others, and a class with so few resources as to necessitate its members offering themselves for employment.[49] Whereas the sale of products, at least according to the theory of competition, may entail a *quid pro quo* such that there is no net movement of power from one side of a transaction to the other, in the labour market, Locke recognized, this is never the case. There *the means of labour*[50] (i.e., the land, machinery, and materials that workers require in order to be productive) are owned by the employer. Owners of the means of labour, therefore, set the terms and conditions upon which workers access these means. A major way 'of transferring another man's power to oneself,' Macpherson observed, 'is by denying him free access to what he needs in order to use his capacities, and making him pay for access with part of his powers.'[51] There is, in other words, a systematic flow of power in the labour market from workers to employers. All this Locke understood, and approved.

Indeed, so great and manifest are the inherent class-based differences in living conditions that result from asymmetric power relations in the buying and selling of labour power that Locke espoused the notion that there are, in fact, class-based differences in human nature! He proposed that workers, living hand to mouth, are in no position to cultivate abstract powers of thought, making them *intrinsically* less rational than people of property. Locke cautioned, however, that should workers actually begin to understand their plight – namely, that the government, employers, and indeed the whole economic order, are not their benefactors but their oppressors – they would surely revolt. To avert that situation, so calamitous to the people of property, Locke proposed that workers' wages be kept to the bare subsistence so that their energies would continue to be devoted exclusively to the task of eking out a living.[52] Similar sentiments are expressed in the writings of other classical British political economists – Jeremy Bentham and Thomas Malthus, for instance.[53]

Cognizant that gross inequality is endemic to the possessive market society, but believing also that mere reason can never suffice to keep the peace, Locke further recommended propagating a simplified and distorted religion that would transform biblical moral precepts into binding commands. Locke believed that workers would submit readily enough to 'supernatural sanctions.' He wrote: 'For the day-labourers and tradesmen, the spinsters and dairy-maids ... hearing plain commands is the sure and only course to bring them to obedience and practice; the greatest part cannot know, and therefore they must believe.'[54] Even for the people of property, Macpherson noted, Locke saw much merit in a simplified Christianity, declaring, 'The view of heaven and hell will cast a slight upon the short pleasures and pains of this present state; ... upon this foundation, and upon this only, morality stands firm, and may defy all competition.'[55]

From this brief account one may conclude that, for Macpherson, religion, like political philosophy, mediates human relations; that both of these symbolic systems can be used to support particular systems of property and hence particular modes of human interaction; and that groups in charge of religious practice and belief (propagators of a 'monopoly of knowledge,' in Innis's terms) may very well exercise their symbolic or ideological power in ways that secure material advantage for themselves and their allies.

An Altered System of Property

C.B. Macpherson claimed that historically democracy and the freedoms we associate with it arose in capitalist countries because, for markets to work effectively, certain individual freedoms were required – for instance, freedom to own and accumulate property, freedom to enter into contracts, a limited freedom of speech and of thought in order that owners of capital could seek out profitable opportunities and use the most efficient means of production.[56] Gradually, and not without considerable agitation, freedom to vote and the right to legislative representation were extended even to the lower classes, and hence did liberal democracy arise.

Although the practice of democracy extending beyond the propertied classes was born in capitalist states, Macpherson insisted, capitalism and democracy are no longer compatible. The reason is that capitalism inexorably increases concentrations of wealth and power, and exaggerates class divisions. Competition in the marketplace means survival of the fittest, giving rise to monopolies and tight oligopolies, and to ever-increasing disparities in wealth. More than most of the theorists considered in this book, C.B. Macpherson proposed a positive plan of action to overcome factors eroding justice and democracy. His proposals centred on reforming the institution of property and, in particular, on guaranteeing access by workers to the means of labour.

Macpherson saw two possible ways of guaranteeing access to the means of labour. One is a system of property supportive of independent producers whereby all persons or households own their own means of labour. Under such a system there would be no commodified labour. However, for the modern era, Macpherson deemed this handicraft mode of social organization impractical because producer-households would be unable to avail themselves of scale economies.[57] (See, however, E.F. Schumacher, for instance, for a dissenting opinion.)[58]

The practical alternative, according to Macpherson, is common ownership of the means of labour, that is, a socialist economy. In a socialist economy, again, there would be no transfer of powers through the sale of labour power since labour power would not be bought or sold. Although common ownership of the means of labour (for instance, through co-ops) would curtail the right to unlimited accumulation, this limitation on people's freedom would not be important if people conceived themselves as doers and exerters instead of as infinite consumers and acquirers.

Dichotomous views of human nature, Macpherson maintained, support radically different systems of property. If to be human is to be infinitely acquisitive and desirous, then restrictions on the right of individuals to accumulate property are hard to justify.[59] But if people by nature are exerters, doers, creators, and enjoyers of their attributes, then the property system should guarantee access for all to the means of labour.[60]

To effect property reform, ultimately, people's conception of human nature must change. This, Macpherson acknowledged, entails persuasion, and hence is a task of communication.

Media and Democracy

Macpherson used the term *technology* to refer primarily to the discovery and application of new sources of energy and to the invention and use of new means of communication.[61] Macpherson did not address media, and, more generally, technology, to nearly the same extent as Innis; nonetheless, like Innis, he did accord them a pivotal position.

Moreover, Macpherson treated technology dialectically. On the one hand, he saw technology as potentially freeing people, or at least those in the industrialized nations, from 'compulsive labour,' that is, from having to devote the bulk of their time and energy to eking out a living. Labour-saving modes of production enable people for at least part of their day to think and act 'as enjoyers and developers of their human capacities.'[62] New technology, in other words, is a prerequisite for the developmental human nature he recommended. That precondition, however, Macpherson averred, is already fulfilled in the industrialized world: the means are available *now* to free people from toil for several hours a day.

However, he warned, in the absence of an altered human nature continued technological development will serve not to help people to fulfil their potential, but rather to increase concentrations of wealth and power. As long as wants are deemed infinite, he explained, 'no increase in productivity, however great, will put an end to scarcity.'[63]

Macpherson discerned, therefore, a 'race' between ontology and technology.[64] By 'ontology,' he meant the predominant conception, at any particular time, of the human 'essence.' By 'race,' he implied not only that ontology and technology are both subject to change, but also that it really matters which changes the more quickly, and in which direction. Only if the conception of the human as doer, exerter, and developer of capacities replaces quickly the view of people as infinite desirers and accumulators will technological advance become consistent with democratic freedoms.[65] That is the case because the latter view of human nature leads inexorably to greater and greater concentrations of wealth and power perpetuating and increasing class divisions within society. Common property is inconsistent with an unlimited right to accumulate.

Today, of course, we indeed see a heightening in economic concentration, both globally and domestically. Macpherson saw this too and concluded pessimistically: 'In the West the immediate effect of the technological revolution will be to impede the change in our ontology which it otherwise makes possible.' He took this view because those controlling the industrial and communicatory system are doing everything in their power to confirm people's self-image as infinite accumulators and desirers, *this conception of personhood being the very basis of their power*. As Macpherson wrote, 'efforts in that direction are evident enough in the mass media now.'[66]

SOME QUESTIONS

Much of Macpherson's thought is captured by the poet Wordsworth:[67]

> The world is too much with us; late and soon,
> Getting and spending, we lay waste our powers:
> Little we see in Nature that is ours;
> We have given our hearts away, a sordid boon!

Given our discussion thus far, at least four questions deserve attention. The first concerns Macpherson's ontology, by which I mean here what, if anything, he believed to be ultimately real. Is 'Reality,' for Macpherson, entirely a social construction – in other words, culture-specific and arising from communicative interaction – or is he, at the very least, a structuralist, that is, someone who claims that, despite cultural differences, there are essential truths upon which all cultures are or should be based? The second question concerns gifts, and the similarity and differences between a gift (or 'grants') economy and the notion of common property. The third question for discussion pertains to differences and similarities in Macpherson's thought and that of other theorists. Finally, we must consider his relevance for today and for the future, and particularly the possibility of applying his analysis of ownership and democracy to mass media.

Macpherson's Ontology

C.B. Macpherson agreed with Innis that the price system erodes morality – in other words, that, in a market society, money and prices are the primary standard or measure of value. Prices are forever in flux, due to supply and demand, and hence value in market-dominated societies is both relative and subject to constant change. In this light, it is understandable that advocates of the market – Hobbes and Bentham in times past, and in our day advocates of free trade and of global investment – wished and wish to 'jettison hitherto prevalent Natural Law limits on property.'[68] These proponents well understand that markets can abide 'no other criterion of a man's worth than what the market will give him.'[69] Markets in capitalist societies do not acknowledge intrinsic value, only money price; and instead of 'Natural Law,' the basis of morality is supply and demand.

Macpherson, however, unlike most 'natural law' theorists, agreed that morality *is* inherently changeable – and not just in capitalist societies. He wrote, 'It can then be seen that man can in principle choose and impose what moral rules he wishes, and can change them as circumstances seem to him to call for. This is what men in different societies commonly have done.'[70]

In his essay on Burke he remarked further that, provided the social order had changed sufficiently long ago, 'Natural Law' can be invoked to support virtually any existing social arrangements, even ones contrary to what previously had been taken to be 'Natural Law.' He explained:

[Burke's enlisting Christian Natural Law] did no violence to the Christian Natural Law. It had always upheld a traditional social order against any threats. Now the content of the social order had changed, and in England it had changed long enough ago that the new covenant had already become traditional. So the Natural Law could now appropriately be used to defend the new traditional order against new threats, the more so since the new covenant utilised the old forms.[71]

Although it is clear that Macpherson viewed morality, including certain pronouncements on 'Natural Law,' as being socially constructed, it also appears that he believed there is an intrinsic moral order against which human morality and positive laws can be judged. At no point did Macpherson, the admirer of Voltaire, actually appeal to or invoke Natural Law, and understandably not, in light of the text quoted above. However, belief in an intrinsic moral order certainly seems implicit in much of his work. The very fact that he challenged so relentlessly the thought of Hobbes and Locke would indicate this. Let us, therefore, look briefly at three specific examples.

First, Macpherson lauded John Stuart Mill for devising 'a moral model' of democracy. What distinguishes the younger Mill's model from the position of Bentham and his father, James Mill, Macpherson declared, is its *'moral vision* of the possibility of the *improvement* of mankind, and of a free and equal society not yet achieved.'[72] What entitled Macpherson, one might ask, thus to speak of a 'moral vision' in the context of an 'improvement of mankind,' if morality and value are merely social constructions, or if, even worse, they are merely products of market forces?

Second, comparing 'possessive individualism' to John Stuart Mill's developmental notion of human nature, Macpherson remarked that declarations concerning 'man's essence' are neither true nor false, they are simply postulates of value.[73] As such they need be neither proven nor disproven, but simply accepted or rejected. On what basis, however, can or ought one choose between opposing postulates of the human essence if neither is 'true'? Macpherson's rejoinder was that the postulate of the human essence as exerter, enjoyer, and developer is 'more morally pleasing'[74] than, and is 'morally preferable'[75] to, the conception of people as infinite acquirers and appropriators.[76] That Macpherson nowhere attempted to justify this claim indicates that, for him, it is *axiomatic*, requiring no further rationale or justification. It is simply self-evident, an ideal to strive for even if not perhaps fully to attain. Whereas morality and 'human nature' in the here and now, for Macpherson, are indeed social constructions, it was also evidently his view that the human spirit can transcend the determinisms, not only to recognize, but to strive for, a higher order of goodness.

Third, Macpherson accorded his book *Democratic Theory* the provocative subtitle *Essays in Retrieval*. What, though, is it that we are to 'retrieve'? For Macpherson, it is the classical conception of humanness as denoting 'a doer, a creator, an enjoyer of his human attributes.'[77] That conception, familiar to the ancient philosophers, was all but wiped out of human consciousness with the rise of the market economy and its justifying philosophy. *Utilitarians* such as Bentham viewed the human essence as 'essentially a bundle of appetites demanding satisfaction.' In reaction to this, Macpherson wrote, 'the idea of man as activity rather than consumption [was] brought back,' or retrieved, by a wide range of writers, for example, Carlyle, Nietzsche, J.S. Mill, Ruskin and Marx.[78] This, too, is what *we* need to retrieve.

Macpherson, therefore, it is argued here, implicitly contemplated an intrinsic, universalistic moral order in which equality, human development, and creativity are transcendent values. Beyond the all-too-apparent inequalities of position, wealth, and capability that confront us daily, Macpherson intimated, there is the supreme value of equality – equality of opportunity for people to develop and apply their capacities.

Gifts

As we have seen, Macpherson held in dialectical tension private property and common property, and concomitantly human nature as acquisitive/consumptive versus developmental/creative. However, although Macpherson devoted much attention to common property, his analysis in fact remained rooted in the rhetoric of individualism and individual rights. Macpherson maintained that common property, that is, the right of each *individual* not to be excluded, is required for the *individual* to attain and exercise his or her potential.

An alternative schemata, however, was developed by the eminent economist Kenneth Boulding, and it provides an interesting counterpoint to Macpherson's. Boulding suggested a triad of communicatory modes consisting of threat, exchange, and love. 'All social organizations without exception,' Boulding attested, 'are built by processes that can be classified into these general types ...'[79] One of Boulding's many remarkable achievements was in fact to analyse the 'gift' or 'grants' economy as an economy premised on 'love' or empathy, and to compare that with the exchange economy.

Lewis Hyde, too, contrasted the transmittal of gifts with the exchange of commodities. For Hyde, the cardinal difference is that a gift establishes a feeling bond between people, whereas the sale of a commodity leaves no such connection.[80] Hyde wrote incisively: 'Because of the bonding power of gifts and the detached nature of commodity exchange, gifts have become associated with community and being obliged to others, while commodities are associated with alienation and freedom.'[81] He added: 'the freedom of the free world tends toward the perfect freedom of strangers.'[82]

Much could be said on the topic of gifts and how gift relations differ not only from commodity-exchange relations, but also from relations based on common property. In the context of Macpherson's thought, though, two points seem essential. First, gifts cannot be fitted into his schemata since true gifts consist neither of a right to exclude nor of a right not to be excluded; they are, rather, voluntary transfers to which recipients have no legal claim. Second, although Macpherson writes of common property, he does so in the context of individualism, not of community; common property gives *individuals* the right not to be excluded, and it is justified by a presumed human nature whereby the *individual* is thought of as a developer and exerciser of his or her own talents and attributes. Again the contrast to the gift economy is clear, as there the giver voluntarily surrenders to another or others a part of the self. True community, it can be argued, arises from and is sustained by gifts as well as (or more than) rights.

It matters quite a bit whether one views social institutions and policies as common property or as gifts. Medicare, public education, unemployment insurance, public housing, and so forth, can be thought either as 'rights' won through struggle by hitherto oppressed people, or as the society as a whole undertaking to care for its members in such a way that 'gifts' become inscribed in law as 'rights.' In this latter case, since 'gifts' become enacted as rights, individualist language can be used, but these social programs nonetheless retain qualities of gifts, with the attendant notions of caring and community.

There is, as well, a marked difference in the conception of 'human nature' associated with the logic of rights versus gifts. Although the developmental view of human nature assuredly differs from possessive individualism, as Macpherson took pains to point out, these two conceptions do not differ as much as Macpherson may have believed. For *both* propose the maximizing individual – in one instance, an individual who maximizes his or her talents and skills; in the other, one who maximizes his or her acquisitions and consumption. In both cases, however, we see self-interested individuals. The gift economy, by contrast, requires and proposes a much greater communal sensibility, and self-sacrifice by individuals.

Macpherson's analysis would have been much enriched had he considered the gift as part of a triad consisting also of private and common property.

MACPHERSON AND CANADIAN COMMUNICATION THOUGHT

Macpherson and Innis

As we have seen, Macpherson proposed a dialectic of private property (as a concept and an institution) versus common property (also as a concept and as an institution). His thought in this regard certainly links up closely with that of Innis. Common property is, of course, subversive of commodity exchange and the price system, both of which Innis associated with space-bound cultures. Common property, on the other hand, is consistent with Innis's notion of time-bound society, especially if it is premised on the gift concept as opposed to an individual right.

Moreover, Macpherson detected a movement historically from common property to private property, just as Innis posited a trend from time-binding to space-binding media of communication. Furthermore, Macpherson's dialectic concerning rival conceptions of human nature – namely, people as infinite accumulators and consumers rather than users and developers of their talents and capacities – is quite consonant with the thought of Innis. Whereas Innis urged a balance between time-binding and space-binding media of communication and made 'a plea for time,' Macpherson urged that we 'retrieve' common property and the sense of people as doers and exerters of their capacities.

Innis and Macpherson had similar notions of mediation. Neither saw communication as merely the dispatching of messages by autonomous senders to recipients. Rather, senders, recipients, messages, and media, for both these writers, are simultaneously parts and products of an ongoing political, economic, cultural, and social order. If, as message senders, we conceive ourselves to be infinite acquirers and accumulators, Macpherson charged, it is because the philosophical/propertied order into which we have been born tells us that this is who we are, and requires that we act accordingly. Likewise, Innis conceived people as being born into cultures that take their shape, in part, from the predominant media of communication. Whereas Macpherson attached great importance to the symbolic order, in particular, schools of political philosophy, Innis devoted much greater relative attention to the means (media) whereby messages are exchanged and diffused.

Finally, it is in the context of mediation that asymmetrical power relations are treated by both writers. Innis focused on relations between centre and periphery, and ascribed these to the mode of communication, whereas Macpherson concentrated on relations between owners and workers, and ascribed these to the mode of property. However, in this regard, both emphasized relations of dominance and dependence. Innis declared that relations between centre and margin, between time and space, must be readjusted to restore balance and prevent chaos; Macpherson asserted that the ratio between private property and common property must be altered to fulfil the human potential, to prevent environmental collapse (more on this below), and to create a more humane, more just social order.

Macpherson and Grierson
Both Macpherson and Grierson were political theorists keenly interested in democracy and social justice. Both advocated the cause of workers in the belief that democracy must take into account the needs and desires of people from all strata. Certainly there is a greater ring of authoritarianism in Grierson's work than in Macpherson's, but both insisted with equal vigour that old-style market-based liberalism is inconsistent with democracy in the modern era.

There is, nonetheless, a fundamental difference in approaches between these seminal thinkers. Macpherson was, if anything, the impeccable scholar, highly analytical in his analysis of the base assumptions of the classical philosophers, and faultless in his logic and documentation. He maintained that political philosophers, as well as the institutions they serve, are a prime cause of the lapse of democracy in our era. Grierson, in contrast, was a self-avowed propagandist who maintained that close analyses (of the type Macpherson engaged in) do little to help the condition of working people, and that, as far as ideology is concerned, it is the mass media that are primarily responsible for capturing the imaginations of common people in ways that erode democratic participation.

Both writers expounded on how mediation affects democracy. Grierson addressed traditional media, principally the press and film, whereas Macpherson looked primarily to the mode of property and underlying political philosophies. But both agreed that the prevailing conception of human nature goes a long way in influencing how people interact (or 'communicate'), and both chose to advance conceptions of human nature that are markedly different from the mainstream.

Macpherson and Smythe

Macpherson's concept of 'possessive individualism' is a core building block in Dallas Smythe's communication thought. Macpherson and Smythe both contrasted that acquisitive and hedonistic view of human nature with what Macpherson termed the 'developmental' view. Macpherson, of course, noted only in passing the influence of mass media on the human self-concept, whereas, for Smythe, the influence of the media, and more generally of the Consciousness Industry, was an abiding concern. The Consciousness Industry, as Smythe explained it, embraces education as well as mass media, and a plethora of other practices, institutions, and objects, and hence includes the writings of the political theorists to which Macpherson devoted such critical attention.

Macpherson and Smythe were alike also in setting in opposition two modes of social organization, one characterized by private ownership and commodity exchange, the other by common ownership and relations based on a fuller range of human characteristics. Both saw the price system as alienating people from nature, from one another, from their work, and above all from themselves.

THE RELEVANCE OF MACPHERSON'S THOUGHT TODAY

The competitive market society, according to Macpherson, is premised on personhood as possessive individualism and on human nature as 'a bundle of appetites demanding satisfaction.'[83] It is also premised on the notion that people are averse to any form of exertion; in the language of neoclassical economists, exertion is a 'disutility.'[84] Based on these premises, *the good society* is one that maximizes individual satisfactions through acquisition and consumption and minimizes the effort required to attain these satisfactions. This outlook, moreover, 'justifies' the continuous introduction of 'labour-saving' technologies that displace workers and give rise to structural unemployment. There is, however, Macpherson insisted, an alternative view of human nature whereby a person's activities are deemed to be purposeful and enjoyable, in and of themselves. Human attributes, according to this latter view, consist not of an innate desire to accumulate and consume, but of a capacity 'for moral judgement and action, for aesthetic creation or contemplation, for emotional activities of friendship and love, and, sometimes, for religious experience.'[85] According to Macpherson, activities consistent with these attributes are, in and of themselves, 'a satisfaction ..., not simply as a means to consumer satisfactions.' According to this developmental world-view, in other words, 'life is for *doing* rather than just *getting*.'[86]

Writing in the 1970s, Macpherson declared that several factors *require* us now to discard the notion of human nature as possessive individualism *and to retrieve* the developmental model. At the time he was writing, Western capitalist and communist regimes were 'competing' for the esteem of third-world peoples and for the favour of their own citizens. This rivalry was predicated, in part, upon the quality of life the opposing political and economic systems made possible. In terms of political and civil liberties, Macpherson acknowledged, the West was far ahead of the Communist Bloc, indeed, so much so that the communist world could do little but improve relative to the West in that regard. Such being the case, however, it followed that the West was likely to lose some of its relative advantage in the area of civil liberties, making it important that it strive to improve its conditions of access to the means of labour, the area in which communist nations were markedly superior.

Since the time of that assessment, competition from communism has, of course, waned. Meanwhile, in the West, we have witnessed an ongoing dismantling of the welfare state and an intensification in the commodification of labour as transnationals increasingly pick and choose from a worldwide labour pool.[87] Can one therefore still maintain, on the threshold of the early twenty-first century, that there remains an urgency to rethinking human nature along the lines Macpherson suggested? Several responses, each at least implicit in Macpherson's writings, support the affirmative.

Anomie

First is Durkheim's notion of *anomie*. If doing, exerting, and developing are indeed closer to the 'essence' of humanity than are consuming, accumulating, and desiring, then an economic or social system premised on the latter activities must, in important ways, fail to satisfy. (Above we noted that Macpherson denied that one could make true or false statements about essences, including the human 'essence'; it is also quite clear, however, that Macpherson believed firmly that the former view is morally superior to the latter, and therefore it seems consistent with Macpherson's thought to posit that continued adherence to a 'morally inferior' conception of human nature will be alienating).

Having a thoroughly inculcated 'morally inferior' view of human-ness, people may attempt to alleviate their inevitable frustration, or degradation, by whatever means are available, or seem to be appropri-ate. In a possessive market society, that, of course, entails yet further accumulation and consumption, leading perhaps to addictions of vari-ous sorts,[88] but, in the end, augmenting the frustration that the addi-tional consumption was intended to relieve.[89] Alternatively, people may engage in violent behaviour if the opportunity for increased con-sumption is denied them, as it so often is for the poor and unemployed. Violence could result also if and when profligate consumption and accumulation are recognized as failing to satisfy, but what really does satisfy (in Macpherson's terms, exerting, doing, and developing one's capacities) remains unknown or is unattainable. To the extent that such malaise grows and becomes widespread, society deteriorates.

We can only speculate on how far Macpherson would have agreed with this analysis, but it does seem consistent with the general thrust of his writings. With regard to the next three propositions, however, specu-lation as to Macpherson's concurrence is not required since he ad-dressed directly these issues, albeit not in the detail one might perhaps have wished.

Environment

Macpherson saw environmental collapse as a possible, indeed likely, outcome of the possessive market society. Obviously people cannot forever be infinite consumers in a finite world. Macpherson therefore applauded opposition to 'the cult of economic growth at whatever cost to the environment and the quality of life.'[90] Ecologically speaking, it makes great sense to think of human nature in terms of developing skills and exerting talents, rather than as consuming and acquiring infinitely. The very continuance of the species may depend upon such a shift in our thinking about ourselves. [91]Macpherson pointed with hope to ecological movements, anti-pollution movements, anti-nuclear and disarmament movements, as well as to neighbourhood and women's movements, as sources for social change.[92]

Justice

As well, there is the question of justice. Macpherson was certainly convinced that the competitive market society is unjust since it *system-atically* robs certain groups of their power and concentrates wealth in the hands of others. In his view, this 'transfer of powers is a continuous transfer between non-owners and owners of the means of labour, which starts as soon as and lasts as long as there are separate classes of owners and non-owners.'[93] Rethinking human nature along the lines suggested by Macpherson would be a first step in making society more just, as no longer would infinite accumulation (and hence disparate classes) be 'justified' by a false underlying ontology.

Democracy

Finally, there is the question of democracy. Macpherson maintained that with capitalism there are ever-increasing concentrations of wealth, and that this is quite inconsistent with democracy. In this final discussion, let us build upon Macpherson's analysis to consider specifically trends towards concentration of control of the media, and the implications that this locus of control has for democracy.

Like other sectors, media worldwide are becoming highly concentrated. One Canadian gentleman, Mr Conrad Black, in 1997 controlled more than 650 daily and weekly newspapers on four continents, with a combined circulation of 10 million,[94] including 60 of Canada's 105 daily newspapers. David Radler, president of Hollinger Inc., Mr. Black's holding company, related: 'I am ultimately the publisher of all these papers, and if editors disagree with us they should disagree when they're no longer in our employ.'[95]

Studies have suggested dramatic changes in the nature of news coverage once Mr Black takes over a paper. With regard specifically to the *Windsor Star*, Maude Barlow and James Winter relate:

> The *Windsor Star* saw a dramatic decrease in labour coverage. In 1991, before Black's involvement with Southam, 21 percent of all front page items dealt with labour issues. By 1996, that figure had dropped to 1.8 percent. On the editorial pages of the *Star*, labour coverage in columns, letters, and editorials dropped from 9.2 percent in 1991 to just 2.9 percent in 1996. At the *Vancouver Sun,* labour stories fell from 11 percent in 1991 to 5 percent in 1996. Business coverage increased dramatically.[96]

Monopolizing the press is inconsistent with basic democratic freedoms of speech and inquiry. British theorists Graham Murdock and Peter Golding have remarked,

> Liberal democrats have long recognized that access to adequate information and to a diversity of debate and representations is a basic precondi-

tion for the effective functioning of a democratic polity and for the full exercise of citizenship rights. Accordingly, they have seen the communications system as essentially a public set of institutions charged with a duty to provide the necessary resources for effective citizenship.[97]

Trends in media concentration, as well as those towards privatization and deregulation, which further commodify information, would be regarded by Macpherson, one suspects, as being highly anti-democratic.

Issues of concentration aside, however, even more fundamental is Macpherson's association of common property with democracy, and of private property with autocracy, and nowhere do these associations find greater applicability than with regard to mass media. Private ownership of mass media, Myles Ruggles has pointed out, is akin to a new 'enclosure of the commons'; it is tantamount to denying the general citizenry expression through the mass media.[98] In North American mass media, Ruggles writes poignantly, 'there are no enforceable citizen rights to initiate speech or to reply to speech.'[99] Publishing letters to the editor, for example, is entirely at the editor's discretion.

For those struggling to increase democracy in the twenty-first century, application of Macpherson's notion of common property to the field of mass communication should be a top priority.

7

The Communication Thought of
IRENE SPRY (1907–1998)

I think it is impossible not to be a communications theorist if you are trying to understand what is going on in the world of economics.

– Interview with Irene Spry, 29 January 1998

ABOUT IRENE SPRY

Irene Mary Spry (*née* Biss) was born on 28 August 1907 at Standerton, in the Transvaal, South Africa. Her father, Evan E. Biss, came to South Africa after the Boer War (1899–1902). At the time of her birth he was chief inspector of schools in the Transvaal, where he set up a school to train teachers. Before Irene reached the age of three, however, he moved with his family to Bengal, India (now Bangladesh), sensing 'there was no future for Brits in South Africa.'[1] There he again rose to be chief inspector of schools. As an educationist, his goal was to organize and promote education on a massive scale.

Irene's mother, Amelia Johnstone, had an abiding interest in natural history and was skilled at carpentry, and also in instructing her children. Irene Spry would often recount the story of her mother standing under a tree, saying 'Go higher, go higher,' while Irene's brother was climbing up. 'That's the kind of person Irene was,' commented her longtime friend Paddye Mann, '– always urging someone, especially herself, to go higher.'[2] Both parents had strong, social-democratic views–'a sort of missionary impulse to feel that one should do anything one could to help other people.'[3]

When Irene was about six, she and her family moved to England, where she spent her formative teenage years. In our interview she recalled vividly how her father 'scandalized' the conservative town of Tiverton, Devonshire, one election day by coming out 'wearing red colours.'[4]

When she was about fifteen, Mr Biss took Irene out of school, requiring her instead to study economics by correspondence, evidently convinced that the local teachers were not adequately exploring her potential. This proved to be a wise decision, as at seventeen she was admitted to the London School of Economics, and a year later, on a scholarship, to Cambridge. There she attended lectures by John Maynard Keynes, became a lifelong friend of fellow student and soon-to-be world-renowned economist Joan Robinson, joined the Labour Club, and through her American tutor was exposed to international scholarship.

Receiving a BA in 1928, she moved directly to Bryn Mawr, in Pennsylvania, for MA studies, hoping thereby to acquaint herself with what people in other countries were thinking. That desire helps explain her acceptance of an appointment as a lecturer in the Department of Political Economy at the University of Toronto in 1929. She was only twenty-one at the time.

One of her students at the University of Toronto was C.B. Macpherson. Asked if she had perhaps nudged Brough Macpherson in the direction of his future scholarly endeavours, Professor Spry replied: 'Well we frequently discussed problems. I think we nudged each other ... I certainly always learned more from my students than I ever taught them. It is very difficult not to understand that if you are a teacher.'[5] At Toronto she also became a don-in-residence and a doctoral candidate.

Irene Biss's original intent had been to stay only a few years in Canada, but encountering Harold Innis at U of T changed that. Indeed, Innis became the most significant figure in her scholarly development, making her certain 'that this is where I wanted to be.'[6] Innis was, she remarked, 'absolutely an incredible standard bearer; he showed us what it meant to be a scholar.'[7]

Irene Biss worked closely with Innis, travelling on his behalf to Nova Scotia, for example, in support of his researches on the cod fisheries. She also assisted him in his researches on the forestry industry. Furthermore, she contributed a chapter to a book he edited on one of his favourite themes: rigidities and overhead costs.[8] Innis, in return, introduced Irene Biss to the study of Canadian economic history. Of equal significance, he informed her of the importance of studying matters first-hand to find out what *people* – trappers, miners, farmers, engi-

neers, aborigines, teachers, bush pilots, in fact anyone living and working in her areas of research interest – might have to say.

Consequently, for her doctoral research on the development of electric and other forms of power in Canada, she made a cross-Canada field
trip in 1935 – travelling by train, pontoon airplane, canoe (with some
portaging), stern-wheel steamer, and motor boat – to power stations
and mines, and to talk to people in communities such as The Pas,
Dauphin, Cranberry Portage, Fort McMurray, Fort Smith, Resolution,
Yellowknife, Fort Simpson, Aklavik, Rampart House, Dawson, Skagway,
and Vancouver. During this trip, Miss Biss took particular interest in
'the human element.'[9] According to University of Ottawa professor
John Batts, who chanced upon her journal among some uncatalogued
documents at the Heritage Centre in Yellowknife, only occasionally did
a word such as 'formidable' appear in her diary that would indicate she
was then still 'a young woman on a rather daring expedition to gather
information in a predominantly male environment.'[10]

Innis contributed in other ways also to Irene Biss's formation. He
affirmed, for example, her lifelong disaffection with standard modes of
economic analysis.[11] In our interview she remarked,

> I find [standard microeconomic analysis] rather arid ... I don't find math-
> ematical economics very illuminating or helpful or having anything much
> to do with the actual world. And one of my feelings about economics and
> economic thought is that it is *so* important that one should stick close to
> what is really happening in the world and try to develop an understand-
> ing of that rather than just being a theoretician.[12]

In 1938, however, much to Innis's chagrin, Irene Biss decided to marry;
move to England, where her betrothed, Graham Spry, had secured
employment; and raise a family. These plans, in Innis's view, signalled
the end of a highly promising scholarly career. In that foretelling, hap-
pily, Innis was mistaken. But marriage certainly did end her career at
the University of Toronto, which then had a policy that when a female
faculty member married she must resign, a policy, incidentally, that
likely delayed Irene's marriage several years on account of Graham's
protracted unemployment. Although circumstances precluded comple-
tion of her thesis, through several articles[13] her work on electrification
did become available.

Back in Canada during the war, Irene Spry took up a position in

Ottawa with the Wartime Prices and Trade Board. She saw little of her husband during those years. When the fighting finally ended, however, she rejoined Graham in London, where he was to become for two decades Saskatchewan's agent-general. It was in that capacity that Graham received a letter in 1957 from Saskatchewan's provincial archivist, requesting documentation on John Palliser's expedition to the Canadian West (1857–60), it then being the one-hundredth anniversary of that momentous trek. Graham passed the letter on to Irene,[14] as was his custom in such matters, and thus was launched her second major research project, an inquiry that again took her on field expeditions to the Canadian West. She recalled: 'The first big trip I did of the west my oldest son came with me and we scoured the plains and the mountains which was very interesting and great fun. And then later I was back and forth continually ... I travelled around; I had a little red Volkswagen I travelled around in, but a good deal of it was simply foot jogging. ... I could tell you stories about that!'[15]

Although massive documentation relating to the Palliser Expedition existed, it was not complete and was sometimes inconsistent. There have been controversies – for example, regarding some portions of the route taken. This constituted one reason for Irene Spry's 'on the spot' studies of 1960 and 1964. Although much of the topology had changed over the intervening hundred years, she nonetheless was able, through direct observation, to resolve certain controversies.[16] In other instances she interviewed extensively people familiar with the areas, and gleaned from them knowledge of the landscape as it had existed in the earlier period.

In 1963 Irene Spry's first volume, *The Palliser Expedition*,[17] dedicated to the memory of her father, was published. That was followed in 1968 by her edited work *The Papers of the Palliser Expedition 1857–60*.[18] It is significant that Irene Spry, an emigrant from the British Isles and one who so delighted in exploring the vast regions of Canada, devoted such detailed scholarly attention to Palliser, himself an explorer of British North America who likewise hailed from the British Isles and a person who decided, in Irene Spry's words, to 'forego personal emolument'[19] in the interest of scientific discovery.

Resulting also from her work on the Palliser Expedition have been important articles concerning the 'great transformation' of the Canadian West – from a 'native-dominated, non-industrial society to a European-controlled capitalistic economic system.'[20] And, finally, also consistent with her historical research has been her work on the 'conserver society.' These research areas are discussed below.

In addition to her love of scholarship and her enduring social-democratic sentiments, Irene Spry also shared with her late husband a lifelong commitment to social activism, of helping to increase social justice in the world. In fact, Graham and Irene first met in 1933, the heart of the Depression, through their activities with the activist League for Social Reconstruction – forerunner of the Cooperative Commonwealth Federation (CCF) Party and Innis's particular bugbear. The Depression radicalized many. Irene Spry recalled, 'Here were millions of people unemployed. Here were people starving and going ragged and going cold, and yet there was food going to waste because nobody could afford to buy it. You had surpluses of grain, surpluses of milk being thrown away. It was just repugnant to common sense, and this had to be a part of the background of anybody in the social sciences.'[21] For many years Irene Spry was active also in the Associated Country Women of the World (ACWW), an organization dedicated through literacy and other programs to the intellectual development of women everywhere. With the ACWW she travelled twice around the globe and worked with women in Africa, Asia, and Europe.

In 1967, Graham's duties in England ending, she accepted an appointment at the University of Saskatchewan, but within a short time moved with Graham to Ottawa, where he pursued his interests and activities relating to broadcasting policy. There she joined the Department of Economics at the University of Ottawa, where she continued as emeritus professor upon her retirement. Professor Spry received honorary doctorates from the University of Toronto and the University of Ottawa, and in 1993 became an Officer of the Order of Canada.

The years during which Professor Spry was most active were not ones of sexual equality. However, as her daughter, Lib, noted in a video honouring her,[22] 'she was a woman who by her actions showed other women that they could do things.' At the conclusion of our interview in January 1998, Professor Spry volunteered, 'My travels around the country, which as I say extended from the Maritimes to the Pacific coast, to the north, to the Yukon, were very interesting and I feel so lucky that I had this opportunity to see what Canada really is like. Such an amazing country! … Coming from a little country like England to this *huge* expanse of country – very exciting.'

On 16 December 1998, after a brief illness, Irene Spry died peacefully at her Rockcliffe home, her daughter and surviving son at her bedside – but not before she had received, just a couple of weeks earlier, confirmation that *From the Hunt to the Homestead,* the book on which she had laboured for twenty years despite near blindness, would be published in 1999 as a joint undertaking of the University of Alberta and University of Calgary presses.[23]

THE PALLISER EXPEDITION (1857–1860)

As Irene Spry noted, the Palliser Expedition was all about communication. From the very beginning, Palliser's intent was to investigate possible lines of communication between the prairies and the Pacific coast. Moreover, at the instigation of John Ball, under-secretary of state in the Colonial Office, a 'second problem of communication'[24] was added to Palliser's mandate – namely, discovery of a route between Lake Superior and the Red River Settlement. Failure to discover such a route, Ball fretted, would mean that communication with the British prairies would need to pass through American territory, increasing the likelihood of annexation.

Media used to forge lines of communication on the Palliser Expedition included canoes (to journey from the Lakehead to Fort Garry), Red River carts, horses, and dog sleds. Equipment employed in assessing these routes included thermometers, barometers, a microscope, geological hammers, telescopes, magnetic sensing devises, and related surveying equipment. The explorers took with them also supplies of tobacco to ease communication with indigenous peoples.[25]

The Palliser expedition was to be primarily for scientific purposes. It was to test and add to existing maps; record natural features of the country and its altitudes; study fauna, flora, climate, and geology; and make note of resources such as timber and minerals. It was to inspect the quality and character of the soil, and to appraise the region's capacity for sustaining agriculture. The value of the expedition, therefore, was highly contingent upon the quality of its record-keeping. But, as Irene Spry noted, there were in the first year grave concerns. Palliser was distressed that their record-keeping had been inadequate and wrote in a letter to James Hector, physician and the expedition's naturalist-geologist: 'I hope you are helping Sullivan with the Journal – Pray put your shoulders to it for I tremble for it ... I fear we have not been as diligent as we ought to have been ... But all I implore is – Get up the Journal and spare no pains with it.'[26] In fact, no official 'log' had been kept during the first season; consequently, the formal journal covering the period was compiled only during the winter of 1857 from notes made in the field.

Irene Spry remarked also on the qualities of Hector's field notes and diary, which were made 'in blurred pencil in his execrable writing,' with the consequence that 'page after frustrating page is totally illegible.'[27] Palliser, however, sent eight dispatches from the field to the secretary of state, and these, combined with letters, field reports by colleagues, and instrumental observations, provide a 'first-hand freshness that gives them special interest.'[28]

In the end there were bountiful materials upon which to base the final report, and some nine months were required for its preparation. Publication of the report made available for the first time detailed information about the vast territory explored by the expedition, and that work became 'the basis of all subsequent surveying operations in the Northwest Territories.'[29]

Palliser's expedition went some distance in foreclosing annexation of Rupert's Land and the British northwest by the United States. To many, when the expedition set out, it seemed unlikely that the territories would long remain in British hands, so obstructed were the lines of communication and transportation connecting the western territories with the Canadas, so sparsely settled were the territories, and so aggressive were American traders and entrepreneurs in crossing the unmarked boundary in pursuit of economic gain. The expedition, as Mrs Spry put it, 'was at least a gesture of official interest.'[30] She added, 'If Palliser had done no more than constitute himself the instrument which extracted this evidence [of interest] from the reluctant imperial government, his work would have had considerable significance in preserving the vast western lands to be the keystone of the nation which was ultimately to reach from coast to coast, north of the as-yet-unidentified border.' Yet, Palliser accomplished more than this. The expedition helped forge a 'great chain of regular communication from the Atlantic to the Pacific,'[31] foreshadowing the building of the Canadian Pacific Railway – the topic of Innis's doctoral dissertation and first book. From Mrs Spry's work on the Palliser Expedition, then, we come to understand more thoroughly some political-economic implications of communication, and in particular the importance of the communication infrastructure to geopolitical organization.

THE GREAT TRANSFORMATION

Palliser as Precursor
The Palliser Expedition was not, however, just about forging east–west lines of communication within British North America. It meant also

heightened contact between the nomadic peoples of the plains and industrial civilization – definitely an Innisian theme. Fiercely proud in their self-sufficiency, based largely on the plenitude of buffalo,[32] some tribes of the British Northwest resented intrusions onto their land. Indeed, the Blackfoot country that Palliser traversed was generally regarded as being so dangerous as to be virtually impassable. Yet there Palliser experienced no violent clashes – in fact, not so much as a stolen horse or a pointed gun. Remarkably, Palliser achieved peaceful passage not by avoiding the Native peoples, but by mingling with and befriending them.

Factors helping to shield traditional ways in the British territory were weakening, however, even before Palliser's expedition. For one thing, liquor, ammunition, and tobacco proffered by the fur traders and the Hudson's Bay Company were breaching the independence of Native peoples. For another, the monopoly enjoyed by the Hudson's Bay Company, which to that point had inhibited settlement, was crumbling – in part due to the swelling numbers of country-born 'freemen' of mixed blood (Métis) who often collaborated with the American traders.[33] Palliser was convinced that the Company's monopoly could not be sustained much longer in the face of the then burgeoning 'free trade.' He also was concerned that the ways of life of the aboriginal and Métis populations would be severely disrupted when free trade was officially sanctioned. Once the Indian Territories were opened to all comers, Palliser predicted, debauchery and destruction by the whites would be uncontained.[34] He sent a confidential report to the British secretary of state to this effect after the first season of the expedition, thereby going well beyond his official terms of reference. The remedy he proposed was technical assistance. Some of the Native peoples, he wrote, already wanted to farm, and thus were in need of education, seeds, and equipment. Through agriculture, he advised, they could adapt to the new way of life then being thrust upon them.[35] According to Professor Spry, Palliser practised his ideals by providing a plough for the use of the Indian mission at the Qu'Appelle Lakes.

Hector, too, submitted a report, pleading that aboriginal peoples not be regarded as 'so many wild beasts ... which are in time to be removed in the process of settlement.'[36] Rather, he urged, there should be installed immediately a system of governance that would account for the interests *both* of indigenous peoples and of the settler populations.

Despite the exemplary nature of the Palliser Expedition, however, it certainly 'spearheaded' less-than-savoury things to come.[37] Palliser's good intentions and honourable comportment notwithstanding, the expedition blazed a trail for white invaders, whose coming destroyed cherished ways of life.[38] Even as Palliser was finalizing his general report, the 'Canadian drive for westward amplification'[39] was well under way.

The Disappearance of the Commons

The Palliser Expedition led directly to 'a great transformation'[40] in the Canadian West: 'from common property resources, to open access resources, and finally to private property.'[41] The transfer of Rupert's Land and the Indian Territories to Canada in 1870 was an important watershed in this regard.

Prior to that time, apart from the Red River Settlement, most of the population on the prairies still roamed and hunted; people's livelihood was based on freely accessing common resources scattered over a wide territory. Nature's bounty, generally, was open to all who could access the land, much of which remained unbounded. Outside the range of possible raids by hostile groups, anyone could pitch a camp, use the water, cut wood, eat berries, and hunt.

Within the context of the surrounding commons, tribes did set out and enforce boundaries. These were generally in flux, however, shifting as the strength of the tribes waxed and waned as a result of epidemics, access to European technology, and other consequences of contact with Europeans. Friendly tribes often hunted one another's territories, and travellers were sometimes permitted to use the land's resources on their journeys.

Within the context of the vast commons, Mrs Spry remarked, the Hudson's Bay Company established 'tentative and fragmentary claims to property.' It built pickets about its outposts; it fenced fields for planting; it guarded pasture land.[42] Indigenous people, of course, were not acquainted with, nor always respectful of, such private-property claims as the whole notion of exclusive and permanent property in land and other 'gifts of the Great Spirit' was quite antithetical to their thought and values. Not infrequently, therefore, they trampled crops, stole horses, and tore down outposts.

Knowledge, skill, resourcefulness, and courage were essential on the prairies before 1870, as nature's bounty at that time 'could not be purchased.'[43] Although on occasion nature was not generous, usually there was an abundance, and the Native peoples lived 'a good life.'[44]

Nor were they by any means profligate in their consumption. Irene

Spry remarked that there is no evidence to indicate that aboriginal peoples hunted any animal so heavily 'as to cause severe depletion and possible extinction prior to the arrival of the white man.'[45] Nomadic life, after all, did not encourage the accumulation of material possessions, and for that reason alone undue exploitation of the land and its resources would not be expected.[46] Indeed, quite the opposite; Spry speculated that strict rules surrounding the buffalo hunt were devised in part for the purpose of conservation.

However, the steady influx of outsiders, in particular, entrepreneurs intent upon seizing opportunity from a vast land rich with 'unappropriated resources,'[47] strained the finite resource base of the prairies. Buffalo robes and buffalo tongues began to acquire value in export markets, leading to wholesale slaughter. By 1879 buffalo were virtually extinct, with only a few stragglers remaining. The price system, Innis might say, had 'penetrated' the British Northwest! Some Native peoples made valiant attempts to prevent overhunting by strangers; in the American territory, these efforts resulted in long and bloody wars, but in the British Northwest 'settlement' was achieved largely through the negotiation of treaties between 1871 and 1877, the full import of which the indigenous peoples at the time ill-understood. Spry wrote: 'How could interpreters find words ... when they discussed white men's ideas of "property" and "sale"?'[48]

When the treaties were being negotiated, the commissioners were at pains to give the Indians assurances that they would be able to continue practising their traditional ways of life: Spry noted, for instance, that a specific clause in the Blackfoot Treaty afforded Indians the perpetual right to pursue their vocations of hunting throughout the surrendered territory, subject only to 'such regulations as may, from time to time, be made by the Government' and excepting only such tracts of land as might be required and taken up from time to time 'for settlement, mining, trading, or other purposes.'[49] This might today be termed the 'Mac Truck clause'! Little could the indigenous peoples then have foreseen the degree to which those exemptions would be invoked.

As private ownership of the land increased, customary common rights to hay, wood, water, and other resources diminished, and Native peoples were pushed increasingly onto reserves. The exigencies of their wandering life simply were at odds with the requirements of the private-property claims of settlers. Spry wrote bitterly: 'The age old rights of the commons gave way before the advance of exclusive salable property rights; only the private owner, supported by the police, might now use the gifts of the Great Spirit.'[50]

Concern soon became widespread that all game, not just the buffalo, would disappear from overhunting and overfishing. A new Fisheries Act in 1884 proved to be a hardship for the Native peoples dependent on fish for their sustenance; yet, as Irene Spry notes, it was not people fishing for their own use that had created the problem, but rather commercial fishing, 'especially when more efficient – and so more destructive – gear was used.'[51]

Besides game and fish, timber diminished rapidly. Swelling populations consumed part of this resource, but as well commercial loggers began transporting lumber out of the territory.

Apart from occasional clashes and formal protests, however, the indigenous peoples could only look on in disgust as the price system penetrated ever more fully. Lacking the desire and acquisitive skills needed to prosper within an economic and cultural system based on private property and commodity exchange, their halcyon days of abundance gave way to a century of penury.

As Irene Spry remarked, prior to European settlement the Indians and Métis formed a remarkably egalitarian society wherein all could access 'the common riches provided by nature,'[52] and whereby the strongest (or luckiest) shared the bounty with the less fortunate. The newcomers, of course prospered, but their prosperity was due not so much to the *abundance* of the land, as it had been for the indigenous peoples, but to *scarcity*; scarcity enriches property owners living within a system of commodity exchange. Egalitarian society thereby gave way to immense disparities in the means of living.

THE CONSERVER SOCIETY

Irene Spry's scholarship regarding the settlement and great transformation of the Canadian West foreshadowed her interest in the 'conserver society.' In work for the Conserver Society Project, a collaborative effort between the University of Montreal and McGill University, she appraised the social and environmental costs in the late twentieth century of continued mining and harvesting non-renewable resources, addressing at length the extreme deficiencies of markets and the price system as indicators of appropriate rates of extraction.[53] She concluded that, although forecasts of resource depletion, such as those made by the Club of Rome, were grossly overstated,[54] ineluctably there are severe environmental and social costs seldom factored into the profit calculations of individual decision makers. Her recommendations point firmly towards conservation of resources.

Significant though this study is, of even greater pertinence to this volume is a follow-up piece in which she addressed the ecological consequences of increased leisure. It is to that paper we now turn.[55]

Capital has long been a substitute as well as a compliment for labour. 'Since Adam and Eve left the Garden of Eden,' Professor Spry began, 'human beings have dreamed of a life free from drudgery.'[56] And, in the twentieth century, she continued, at least in the affluent West, 'the burden of incessant toil has largely been lifted from human shoulders.' Indeed the combination of capital investment and technological change has decreased for many the amount of time devoted to paid employment as well as lessening the physical irksomeness of work. Between 1890 and 1960, the average work week in manufacturing declined from fifty-nine to just over forty hours, with further significant reductions since. Pension plans have made possible earlier retirements for some, while the young now stay in school and university longer before entering the paid workforce. Even in the home, capital investment and technological change have reduced the time required for household chores. Ostensibly, then, the time available to pursue leisure activities has increased. However, she remarked, in practice this change in the amount of leisure time 'is by no means clear.'[57] Many people, especially the self-employed, put in many more hours per week than the average. Women in this century in particular have taken on work outside the home in addition to domestic chores, reducing significantly their leisure time. Then, too, time spent commuting and waiting in line-ups detract from time available to pursue interests unrelated to paid work.

Professor Spry next inquired into how Canadians actually spend their leisure time. Much of it, of course, is spent with television (twenty-four hours a week on average) and with other mass media. But underlying mass media, she remarked, is 'the proliferation of sales promotion and advertizing,'[58] a main purpose of which is to convince people on how they should fill their remaining leisure hours, and on their need to purchase equipment and other 'necessities' in pursuing these suggestions.

Of the varied ways of spending leisure time, Professor Spry advised, many 'entail very heavy demands on material and environmental resources.'[59] She noted:

Travel means jet planes, the fuel they use, and the cloud cover they create; automobiles mean gasoline and smog. Television means cameras and

klieg lights, congested air waves, production studios, elaborate transmit-
ting and receiving equipment, including satellites and other technology ...
Even unassuming personal participation in sport has become the *raison
d'être* for promoting sales of elaborate equipment and clothing ...[60]

Paradoxically, then, increased leisure augments pressures on people to
increase their earnings so that they can afford the equipment they have
come to be believe their leisurely pursuits require, or even to pay the
installments on the domestic labour-saving devices that ostensibly were
intended to increase their leisure time.[61] As she put it: 'The choice does
not seem to be a choice between more consumption and more leisure
time, but between more consumption for leisure time activities and
more consumption of other sorts.'[62] Parallels are readily apparent here
with the thought of Dallas Smythe and C.B. Macpherson.

The heightened attention afforded leisure-time pursuits, and the notion that one must work harder and longer to be able to afford 'quality'
leisure time, reflect poorly on the priorities of modern society. Spry
wrote: 'The TGIF ('Thank God It's Friday') view of the working week
suggests that few of us get much satisfaction out of what we do to earn
a living.'[63]

Persuading people that satisfaction and enjoyment come not from
work, but from consuming, is of course the stock-in-trade of the mass
media. Indeed, 'ideas as to the good life absorbed from television
programs and advertisements combined with conspicuous consumption to keep up with the Joneses mean continued, open-ended increases
in consumption.'[64] But 'open-ended consumption' to keep up with the
Joneses is not only environmentally unsound, it also yields little satisfaction to consumers. 'Emulation in consumption satisfies no one and
there is no limit to the burden which it imposes on scarce environmental and material resources.'[65]

There are, fortunately, less costly possibilities: jogging, trail skiing,
cycling, yoga and meditation, gardening, crafts, carpentry, do-it-your-
self repairs that combine recycling of materials with the satisfaction
derived from fulfilling the 'instinct of workmanship' (an expression
borrowed from Thorstein Veblen). There is, in other words, wide scope
for activities that are simultaneously satisfying and low-consumption.
Most fundamentally, time spent for 'recreation' should allow us to
explore our individuality and self-expression, to exercise our 'cramped
and atrophied bodies, exercise and develop powers of intellect and

imagination and of independence of thought and character.' It is a sad commentary that few of us find in our working lives opportunities for these varied satisfactions; it is even sadder that many may not find them in leisurely pursuits either.[66]

Television and the Quality of Leisure Time

Particularly problematic is television. Many people whose living conditions do not afford them requisite amounts of comfort, tranquillity, and agreeable surroundings *escape* 'into the image world of television,' where they may 'effortlessly join the jet set in gracious living.'[67] But this engrossment, Professor Spry advised, cultivates discontent: 'It is a world in which the importance of having more and more consumer goods is relentlessly driven home, a world in which the emphasis is constantly on the *apparatus* of living, not on the quality of life itself.'[68] The accent, in brief, is 'on *having* things,' not on '*doing* things.'

Although some programs on television and radio do provide food for thought, these are the exception; for the most part, viewers are, and are intended to be, 'passive spectators or auditors, whose imaginations are neither challenged nor stimulated.'[69] In Professor Spry's view, having one's imagination and thought stimulated is much more likely if one attends the theatre or a concert, or visits an art gallery or a historic site, than if one views sitcoms and soaps.

More particularly, she said that 'the active enjoyment of beauty is a creative, not a passive experience.' And what, she exclaimed, can give satisfaction even richer than *enjoying* beauty, is *participating in its creation*. Leisure-time arts and crafts give outlets for the 'instinct of workmanship,' but this is precisely what television deadens. To maintain an excitement and joy throughout our lives, Spry advised, we need to pursue 'some unfolding interest, achieving new skills, discovering new creative possibilities,' and not just view passively escalations in television violence and entertainment-sports.[70]

It was Professor Spry's hope that, as the idea of the conserver society takes hold and spreads, indicators of social status and self-esteem will shift from ones of conspicuous leisure and conspicuous consumption to low-consumption activities that contribute to the individual's sense of significance through the development of skills and capacities. If that shift were accompanied by a decrease in the emphasis afforded competition, then pressure for ever-more-elaborate equipment would be still further reduced, and leisure occupations could begin to play a significant part in moving us towards a conserver society.[71]

RECAPITULATION

Irene Spry's work on the Palliser Expedition and on the subsequent disappearance of the commons in the Canadian West is seamless with her later work on television, leisure, and the conserver society. Palliser blazed the trail whereby the price system and private property came to displace an egalitarian society premised on the commons and the common good. In the process, aboriginal peoples were displaced, the land and its resources were laid waste, human relations were mediated by money and by commodity exchange, and a new emphasis was accorded the accumulation of wealth by those with property. In her work on the conserver society, she noted that the price system, even today, systematically fails to account for the environmental and human costs that ensue from resource exploitation; as a communication system and as a system of valuation, she stated, the price system is woefully inadequate. In her work on television and the leisure society, Professor Spry noted how the medium's primary function is not to enrich the capacity of people to create and enjoy their attributes, but rather to further extend the penetrative powers of the market, so that instruction in how and what to consume, and consumption itself, fills greater and greater portions of available time, thereby erasing vestiges of a more communal way of life, and with devastating implications for the environment.

IRENE SPRY AND CANADIAN COMMUNICATION THOUGHT

'Since Jacques Cartier sailed up the St. Lawrence, the inland waters of Canada have been of vital importance ... They have given access to the interior and have made it possible to transport the harvest of furs, lumber, wheat and minerals to the seaboard for export to outside markets.' Thus begins Irene Spry's entry on 'Water Power' for the *Encyclopedia Canadiana*,[72] well demonstrating the stamp of Harold Innis. Both scholars maintained that transportation and communication media permit the penetration into communal, indigenous societies by more technically advanced ones. Both noted how the price system subverts communal, egalitarian ways of life. Both proposed a dialectic between two modes of social organization. Both intimated that victory by the more technologically advanced society increases disorder or entropy.

Professor Spry did more than simply extend Innisian analysis into new facets of Canadian economic history; she also formed a bridge between Innis and C.B. Macpherson. As the price system penetrated the Canadian prairies more deeply, she noted, the commons was replaced by private property, and human nature was increasingly conceived as 'possessive individualism'" Irene Spry, colleague and friend of both Innis and Macpherson, through her work on Palliser and the conserver society, showed how economic and communicatory power (Innis's focus) commingles with ideology or philosophy (Macpherson's focus) to effect a new order and/or deepen an existing one.

And just as she extended Innis's thought, so did she extend Macpherson's. Macpherson concentrated on the writings of influential political philosophers, whom he saw as being decisive in reconceiving human nature in a way supportive of the capitalist system; Professor Spry, in contrast, afforded much the same function and power to the mass media, in particular, television. Spry and Macpherson alike bemoaned that, in conceiving people as passive consumers, the human potential is far from being realized.

Furthermore, Professor Spry linked Innis and Macpherson to other theorists into whose thought we shall also delve. Northrop Frye, George Grant, and Marshall McLuhan, like Irene Spry, distinguished between the deadening effects of television and the energizing influence of other media such as literature, theatre, and fine art.

In my interview with Irene Spry, I asked if she had ever thought of herself as a communication theorist. She responded no, she had always thought of herself as an economic historian. But, on further questioning, she volunteered, 'I think it is impossible not to be a communications theorist if you are trying to understand what is going on in the world of economics.' Her scholarship testifies to the acuity of that observation.

SPRY'S RELEVANCE FOR TODAY

The story of the Palliser Expedition and the ensuing demise of the commons in the Canadian West can be read as an allegory for understanding our own time. Just as the landed commons then was transformed into private property, with stark consequences for the distribution of wealth and income and for ecological balance, so, too, at present are there immense pressures to privatize and commodify today's social commons – education, health care, park lands, and public broadcasting; in all cases, for-profit providers stand ready and eager to enter fields that hitherto have been considered a common right of citizenship.

George Grant, whose work is discussed in the next chapter, maintained that the historical and philosophical justification of Canada has always been a greater emphasis on the common good than was possible under American pragmatism and philosophic individualism. Professor Spry's analysis helps us understand, however, at least some of the reasons why the current, ongoing 'great transformation' seems to be acceptable to many Canadians. The single most important leisure-time pursuit in this country, after all, is viewing commercial television, which, in the hands of commercial interests, is an ideological apparatus without equal in the history of humankind.

Professor Irene Spry maintained that hedonistic individualism bears a life-threatening environmental burden, that it gives rise to huge disparities in living conditions, and that ultimately it is unsatisfying even for people of wealth. At the dawn of the new millennium, her analysis of the previous century and a half is well worth considering.

8

The Communication Thought of
GEORGE GRANT (1918–1988)

Beyond time and space there is order.

– George Grant in Conversation, 49

ABOUT GEORGE GRANT

George Parkin Grant was born in Toronto on 13 November 1918 to a distinguished family of educators. His maternal grandfather, Sir George Parkin (a self-described 'wandering evangelist of Empire'),[1] was principal of Upper Canada College, an exclusive private school in Toronto; he was also the first secretary of the Rhodes Scholarships at Oxford and Sir John A. Macdonald's first biographer. George P. Grant's paternal grandfather was George Monro Grant, a minister in the Presbyterian Church, who in 1877 became principal of Queen's College at Kingston, Ontario.[2] His father, William Lawson Grant, was for several years a professor at Queen's, but became principal of Upper Canada College at the time of George's birth. George's mother, Maude Parkin, his 'most important formative figure,'[3] was one of the first women to graduate from McGill and later headed its Royal Victoria College; regarding Maude, Grant confessed to an 'Oedipus complex the size of a house.'[4]

According to biographer William Christian, even as a youth George Grant was 'passionate, sensitive, intellectual.'[5] Attending Upper Canada College, he became a pacifist and began writing poetry. Indeed, Christian remarked, Grant always saw things 'through the eyes of a poet.'[6]

At Queen's University from 1936 to 1939, Grant majored in history and attended his only formal philosophy course.[7] Awarded a Rhodes Scholarship in 1939, he next studied law at Oxford. Since wartime conditions made it impossible to continue his studies after that first year, he volunteered to be an Air Raid Precautions Warden in a frequently bombed, working-class district of London. 'I helped wounded people,' he wrote home at the time; 'I carried the dead – I evacuated shelters – I lost some good friends – I told people that their relatives were in hospital when I had just seen them taken to the morgue. I told others the truth. For myself I was up 36 hours on end and while it [the Battle of Britain] lasted was very near death. I put out innumerable incendiaries.'[8]

One night a shelter for which Grant was responsible suffered a direct hit, killing possibly 300 people. To his mother he wrote, 'One of the most fascinating speculations I know is the wondering at the way a bomb can descend &, in the space of a second, destroy even the most intricate, delicately balanced human personality. Not only is the beautiful mechanism of the body torn, ripped, masticated by the tiger-like violence of the high explosive, but the existence of the person knitted with his thoughts, passions, ambitions, inhibitions is destroyed.'[9]

As it had for Innis, war transformed utterly Grant's outlook. In Grant's case, it meant rejection absolutely of 'progressive liberalism'[10] – the political philosophy which maintains that humans can and almost inevitably will improve their condition by resolutely applying their minds in freedom to technological innovation. How can one possibly believe in inevitable progress through technological means, Grant queried, given the manifold atrocities wrought in the War through technological devices? By 1945 he had resolved to dedicate his scholarly life to drawing out the implications 'of *not* thinking progressive liberalism.'[11]

When Hitler turned his fury on Russia, Grant despaired even more. Although the Nazi tactic eased the threat to his adopted British community, it was at the cost of spreading evil elsewhere. 'It is a brutal world,' he lamented, 'when our success is mainly due to others getting it.'[12]

Social and family pressures, in addition to the abatement in the bombing of London, induced Grant, passivist principles notwithstanding, to enlist in the Merchant Marine. When the United States entered the war upon Japan's attack on Pearl Harbor, however, Grant became virtually suicidal. Diagnosed tubercular, he was about to be discharged when, in panic and despair, he deserted and was declared missing for a time. Darkness, it seemed, was enveloping the globe. But, in the pre-dawn of an early December morn, Grant experienced a profound renewal. Riding his bicycle in the English countryside, he approached a gate barring his way. Years later, he described the experience: 'I got off my bicycle and walked through a gate, and I believed in God. I can't tell you more, I just knew that was it for me. And that came to me very suddenly ... I think it was a kind of affirmation that beyond time and space there is order ... And that is what one means by God, isn't it? That ultimately the world is not a maniacal chaos.'[13]

Thus also was born Grant's 'red toryism.' According to author Charles Taylor, so-called Red Tories, or 'radical conservatives,' believe there exists 'something greater and more enduring than ourselves.'[14] For some, the sublime or ineffable may be nature or the landscape; for others, culture or tradition; for others still, natural law or divine will. But in all cases, according to Taylor, Red Tories believe that humans participate in something greater than themselves, of which they are but a part and which they do not control. This belief, Taylor advised, is what in essence distinguishes philosophic conservatives from liberals, the latter maintaining that *humans* are the creators of all value and the measure of all things.

Grant incarnated Taylor's depiction of the Red Tory, even though he disdained being so labelled. Recalling his epiphany, he remarked: 'If I try to put it into words, I would say that it was the recognition *that I am not my own*. In more academic terms, if modern liberalism is the affirmation that our essence is our freedom, then this experience was the denial of that definition, before the fact that we are not our own.'[15] Grant thereby came to define *philosophy* as 'faith seeking understanding,'[16] and as 'the extreme human presumption of claiming to be open to the whole.'[17] *Faith* for him meanwhile, following philosopher and theologian Simone Weil, meant 'intelligence ... enlightened by love.'[18] Intense thoughts indeed!

Grant was at pains, however, to distance himself from present-day 'conservatives.' For him, true conservatism means a desire to keep (i.e., to 'conserve') or retrieve the 'good.'[19] Contemporary 'conservatives' by contrast, he bristled, stand merely 'for the freedom of the individual to use his property as he wishes, and for a limited government which must keep out of the market-place.'[20] In other words, contemporary conservatives are, in fact, 'liberals.'

Grant convalesced in Toronto, then spent a couple of years with the Canadian Association of Adult Education, where, among other things, he helped inaugurate *Citizen's Forum* on CBC radio. That venture was prologue to a lifelong association with the public broadcaster. In fact two of Grant's seven books were originally prepared as lectures for the CBC;[21] Grant always wanted his work to be accessible to a wide public.

When the war finally ended Grant returned to Oxford, this time to study the philosophy of religion. In 1947, degree not yet in hand, he moved to Halifax to teach philosophy at Dalhousie University. In 1961 he joined the faculty at McMaster's Department of Religion as chair. Distraught at the 'social scientific' or purportedly 'value-free' empiricism of many of his McMaster colleagues,[22] Grant returned to Dalhousie in 1980, where he remained until retiring in 1984. He died at Halifax on 27 September 1988.

As a student Grant had few truly influential mentors. Austin Farrer at Oxford, who introduced him to the writings of Descartes, was perhaps one. But even of Farrer, he remarked, 'I hardly ever spoke to him, I just heard him lecture.'[23] On the other hand, the writings of Plato and Kant certainly made deep and lasting impressions. After Grant graduated, contemporary authors Leo Strauss and Jacques Ellul,[24] and the modern 'saint' Simone Weil, as well as existentialist philosophers Nietzsche and Heidegger, all were highly influential.[25]

In the first edition of *Philosophy in the Mass Age* (1959), Grant also lauded Hegel as being 'the most remarkable of modern philosophers.'[26] At that time Grant felt that Hegel provided a key for synthesizing the wisdom of the ancients (particularly the Greek and Christian-Judaic heritages) and Western science and technology. However, as Grant's belief in progress waned, so did his enthusiasm for Hegel, with the result that, in 1966, in the preface to the new edition of the same work, he declared: 'Hegel was not correct in his claim to have taken the truth of antique thought and synthesized it with the modern to produce a higher (and perhaps highest) truth; ... on many of the most important political matters Plato's teaching is truer than Hegel's.'[27] It is worth remarking at this point, however, that both these mentors – Hegel and Plato – were dialectical thinkers.

Over the course of his career, this 'burly man with an impressive corporation'[28] published seven books, the first being *Canada – An Introduction to a Nation* (1943). His major works in political philosophy, however, were not inaugurated until 1959 with the appearance of *Philosophy in the Mass Age,* and they culminated in 1986 with *Technology and Justice.* All his books on political philosophy were slender in size, but rich in content. *Time as History* (1969), perhaps his densest work, is merely fifty-two pages in the original edition.[29]

Despite renown as a broadcaster and political theorist, and the responsive chord he sounded and continues to sound for many, the voice of this 'brooding philosopher'[30] was by and large an isolated one.[31] For artist Alex Colville, designer of Canada's centennial coins, George Grant *was* the lone wolf depicted on the fifty-cent piece. [32]For example, defining philosophy for the 1950 Massey royal commission as 'the analysis of the traditions of our society and the judgment of those traditions against our varying intuitions of the Perfection of God'[33] won for Grant little but enmity from fellow philosophers.[34] Likewise, his appraisal that philosophers generally are handmaidens to the military-industrial complex did not endear him to his colleagues.[35] Grant once remarked: 'To think outside this [liberal] faith is to make oneself a stranger to the public realm.'[36]

One further illustration: Despite being the sole breadwinner for a family of eight in 1960,[37] Grant resigned his post at York University before teaching even a single class – this in order to avoid adopting a text he felt was contemptuous of his faith. 'Not being his own' meant that Grant was obliged to act according to his conscience. Lone voice notwithstanding, books about Grant,[38] festschrifts in his honour,[39] and Canadian Studies courses dealing with his thought continue to enhance the reputation of this 'touching, unguarded' scholar.[40]

SYNOPSIS

Just as Innis proposed that human artefacts, in particular, modes of transportation, means of inscription, and technologies for extracting staples, constitute milieus within which human communication and social organization are shaped, likewise did George Grant regard 'technology' as a general mediation affecting decisively modes of human interaction and, most significantly, the formation of values and ontological perspectives. Whereas Innis contrasted time-bound and space-bound societies as alternative modes of social organization, Grant distinguished between 'antiquarian' and 'technological' (or modern) societies. Antiquarian societies differ from technological societies, according to Grant, due to: (1) contrasting conceptions of time; (2) rival conceptions of justice; (3) different conceptions of law; and (4) marked differences in conceiving the relation between fact and value.

Grant maintained further that our technological order is sustained by the mass media, the arts and the educational system, which together ensure that antiquarian conceptions of time, community, equality, continuity, justice, and law remain largely unarticulated, leaving people rather oblivious to the prisons in which we live. For Grant, therefore, it is through political philosophy and remembering the wisdom of the ancients that our best hope for freedom lies.

ANTIQUITY AND MODERNITY

Like Innis, Grant took Hegel's dictum that 'the owl of Minerva only takes its flight at twilight'[41] as indicating that people begin to understand their culture only when it is being challenged or replaced. Whereas Innis held the opinion, however, that Minerva's owl has flown many times – from Babylon, Egypt, and Greece, for instance – for Grant, the flight has occurred but once; for him, there have been but two major époques in human history: antiquity and modernity.

By *antiquity*, Grant meant all civilizations prior to the rise of Western science, that is prior to 'the age of progress.' People of antiquity believed that meaning is intrinsic to the universe. Accordingly, by repeating, imitating and fulfilling divine acts as revealed in sacred stories and myths, people understood themselves as participating in a fixed order of meaning and goodness. Actions not conforming to or re-creating the sacred were of, at best, little value to the people of antiquity.

However, with the 'age of progress,' Grant reflected, all that changed. 'Mythic consciousness,' that is, belief in a fixed order of goodness, all but disappeared. Attention became riveted instead on 'unique and irreversible events.'[42] People came to believe that *humans* make all meaning, that *people* create all value,[43] and hence that *we* are 'the measure of all things.'[44]

In place of myths or systems of meaning through which people understood a given order of goodness or value, therefore, there arose 'the last great myth' – namely, 'the myth of progress.'[45] According to Grant this dramatic shift in world-view entailed fundamental change in conceptions of time, justice, and law. As well, it gave rise to the notion that fact can be separated from value.

Time

Antiquarian Conception
Grant referred to Plato's antiquarian conception of time as '*the moving image of an unmoving eternity.*'[46] Through his doctrine of pure forms, Plato maintained that the most real and perfect order is an ideal, noncorporeal one. Although perfection, being an ideal, exists by definition

in the immaterial realm of ideas,[47] it does have material consequences. As Grant expressed the point, 'the desire for good is a broken hope without perfection, because only the desire to become perfect does in fact make us less imperfect.'[48]

Attempts to achieve perfection, however, are bound to be frustrated, if for no other reason than the fact that matter is inherently in motion, whereas 'perfection' in principle cannot change: something that is perfect cannot become 'more perfect'; were perfection ever to be achieved, all movement would necessarily entail a departure from it. Therefore, materiality, in the Platonic view, is at best a shadow or a pale (but moving) image of perfection.

Hence, Socrates – for Grant, 'the supreme figure in all philosophy'[49] – approached his demise with equanimity. For him, death meant passage 'from the shadows and imaginings of the world to the *reality* beyond change.'[50]

The antiquarian view of time incorporates particular conceptions of justice and of law. For the ancients, according to Grant, *justice* meant rendering anything its due[51] and doing what one is fitted for.[52] Justice meant also implementing in everyday life a 'transcendent, eternal model of justice,'[53] and hence participating in a goodness which people neither measure nor define.[54] Therefore the ancients accorded precedence to *natural law*, that is, law deemed to be intrinsic to the universe. Natural law ought never to be constrained or contradicted by *positive* (or legislated) *law*.

Time in the Age of Progress
Since the essence of matter is movement (or 'becoming'), materialistic cultures tend to denigrate all that is constant or slow to change. Time for such cultures *means* change, which is to say that time *is* history, history being, after all, the recounting of change. 'The infinite for modernity,' Grant declared, is no longer 'the ancient eternal-beyond-time,' but rather 'the limitless possibilities of men for action in space and time'[55] – that is, wide-open possibilities *to do*.

This modern conception of time as change, or what Grant referred to as *time as history*, carries over into altered conceptions of justice and law. The thoroughly materialist mindset recoils, of course, at the antiquarian conviction that *justice* means doing what one is fitted for, since that implies that people ought to be content with their 'lot in life.' Grant, a staunch egalitarian, was likewise dismayed by this implication. Nonetheless, he found also great, perhaps even greater, deficiencies in the modern (liberal) conception, particularly as formulated by the eminent Harvard political theorist John Rawls.

In his celebrated tome *A Theory of Justice,* Rawls defined as 'just' those political systems that maximize individual freedom and equality. Echoing Adam Smith's doctrine of the 'invisible hand,' Rawls went so far as to claim that 'just' political systems arise spontaneously from voluntary negotiations among 'rational' individuals.[56] 'Rational,' according to Rawls, means that people know where their interests lie and they act accordingly. Since 'rational' people understand that a degree of social organization is necessary for achieving their goals, he continued, they will submit voluntarily to a degree of governance. In Rawls's view, therefore, one need not rely on 'metaphysical presuppositions' such as the highest good or the common interest to justify governance.[57]

Countering Rawls, however, Grant questioned whether in technological society self-absorbed individuals can *even think of* the complex apparatus needed to introduce and extend liberty and equality.[58] He asked in effect: Is not a selfless consideration of the whole also required? Moreover, according to Grant, Rawls's analysis was premised on a model devoid of power considerations: in his naïvety Rawls had not even considered whether corporations and governments would freely shed their concentrated power to permit the emergence of a system based on liberty and equality.[59]

Even more important, Grant saw dangers in a legal system bereft of natural-law considerations – of what Rawls derisively termed 'metaphysical presuppositions.' Natural law, Grant insisted, protects the weak through doctrines of equality and the sanctity of human life.[60] *Positive law*, on the other hand, being enacted by or at the behest of the most powerful, entitles the leaders to designate who exactly is 'worthy' of their protection and who is not.[61] For Grant, ultimately, positive law devoid of considerations of natural law is tyrannical. He prophesied: 'If tyranny is to come in North America it will come cosily and on cat's feet. It will come with the denial of the rights of the unborn and of the aged, the denial of the rights of the mentally retarded, the insane and the economically less privileged. In fact it will come with the denial of rights to all those who cannot defend themselves. It will come in the name of the cost-benefit analysis of human life.'[62] For Grant, it would appear, fascism is the fulfilment of liberalism.

This is not to say that Grant did not find much merit in modern conceptions of law and justice. He acknowledged that the freedom-to-do inherent in the modern conceptions has brought about multitudinous improvements – modern medicine and a plethora of labour-saving devices, for instance. No sane person would doubt this, Grant affirmed. That being the case, modern accounts of law and of justice *must* be true. And hence Grant's dilemma.

For while *both* modern and antiquarian accounts of law and of justice are true, Grant saw them as being mutually exclusive. In *Philosophy in the Mass Age*, he expressed his perplexity by asking how these two 'true' accounts could even be 'thought together.'[63] Difficulty there may be, he there averred, but assuredly they *must* both be 'thought,' since each on its own is 'wholly unacceptable.' On the one hand, antiquarian conceptions of law and justice encourage people to justify horrendous conditions as being the 'will of God.'[64] On the other, 'the worst crimes of the twentieth century have been perpetrated in the name of progress and man's right to make history.'[65]

Technology and the Dialectic of Time

What then causes societies or civilizations to move from one conception of time to the other? Grant pointed first to Judaism and Christianity. By maintaining that God acts in history, Christianity and Judaism increased for people the significance of unique, irreversible events as compared with cyclical, repetitive ones.[66] Paradoxically, then, these religions contributed the replacement of 'mythic consciousness' by a historical and more secular consciousness. People's attention shifted from a preoccupation with the world beyond time to the here-and-now. Indeed, by emphasizing the importance and orderliness of the material world, both religions engendered Western science and the quest for continual technological advance.[67] Today, however, 'continual technical achievement' is the major agent perpetuating modern consciousness. Technological change weakens our sense of continuity, and therefore necessarily attenuates considerations of the eternal.[68]

The 'moulding' of our actions and imaginings, Grant continued, has in fact recast technical achievement itself as the supreme value of our civilization. Technology has become not only a basic feature of our being, but the prism through which we comprehend and judge our existence. There has arisen, in his phrase, a 'theology of technique'[69] to which most people, irrespective of political, religious, or philosophic persuasion, adhere. Technology, Grant claimed, burns its 'brand ... deeply into the flesh.' It does this by imparting many messages, mostly subliminal. Some of these implicit and often subconsciously perceived messages are the following:

- *The message of automatic progress.* Technical achievements inform us that humans have accomplished much in the past, implying that they can and will accomplish much in the future. People's attention, therefore, is riveted on the future.[70] By concentrating on *becoming* rather than on *being*, people lose sight of venerable, extrinsic standards or 'values' by which technical achievements can be judged. Moreover, orientation to technical achievement and the future obliterates our awareness of deprival.

- *The message that* people *are the makers of events and of history.* By innovating new technologies, people see themselves as taking charge of their future. Consequently, there arises a new primacy of the will. The scientific and social-scientific project today is to gain mastery over both non-human and human nature, not merely to understand or appreciate them. Controlling human nature is required, Grant writes, 'so that we can be shaped to live consonantly with the demands of mass society.'[71]

- *The message of a distinct subject–object dichotomy.* Technology implies that the world is 'a field of objects' over which the thinking subject stands and upon which he or she acts.[72] A concomitant implication is that *fact* (the objective given) can be separated from *value* (a subjective assessment of the gradient of worth). Below we enlarge on Grant's critical analysis of these principles.

- *The message that meaning is illusory, the search for purpose futile.* Given that technology augments the capacity of humans to alter their environment, 'horizons' (i.e., limitations, taboos, restrictions, values, laws) are increasingly perceived as being merely *human* constructs, not as givens of a divine or natural order. Referencing Nietzsche, Grant wrote: 'The historical sense teaches us that horizons are not discoveries about the nature of things; [rather] they express the values which our tortured instincts *will to create.*'[73] In such circumstances it is 'upon our will to do … [that] the whole burden of meaning' is placed.[74]

- *The message that equality as a goal is neither attainable nor desirable.* Again referencing Nietzsche, Grant remarked that a society intent on technological mastery will find unacceptable a doctrine of equal rights because this is based on the antiquarian premise that, before God, all persons are equal. Grant, the outspoken egalitarian, asked rhetorically, 'Why should we limit that shaping [of human and non human nature] by doctrines of equal rights which come out of a world view that "history" has swept away? Does not [technological society] require a legal system which gives new range to the rights of the creative and the dynamic?'[75]

- *The message that nature is unimportant compared with technology.* Technology, after all, separates people from nature.[76] Confronted with environmental crises, Grant argued, people can conceive only of technological responses: 'More technology is needed to meet the emergencies which technology has produced.'[77] In fact, even recognizing what constitutes an environmental crisis can be problematic for an order devoid of intimations of the sacred. Species may become extinct, but what is it exactly that makes worthwhile their continued existence anyway? After all, are not all life forms merely 'necessitous chances of natural selection'?[78]

- *The message that all cultures are, or should become, the same.* Technology homogenizes cultures.[79] This, in fact, is the grand motif of *Lament for a Nation*, and is addressed below at greater length.

- *The message that individual initiatives are insignificant in the public sphere.* Modern technology requires increasingly large corporate and governmental institutions, causing people to be 'less organically related' to their institutions and to become less effectual as individuals in bringing about change.[80] Hence, increasingly, people confine their seeking out of satisfactions to their private lives, recognizing that it is in the private domain alone that freedom is to be found. Technology, then, induces the privatization of experience and diminishes the conception of the common good. It causes people more easily to 'surrender to passivity and the pursuit of pleasure as a commodity.'[81]

- *The message that speed, efficiency, and power are the main criteria for judging.* For Grant, people today have become so immersed in scientific, technological culture that there is seldom even an awareness of deprivation – at having lost the sense of unalterable goodness that the ancients thought permeated the universe. To be aware of loss, of course, requires *remembering*, which is very difficult after centuries of enlightenment.[82] Our present criteria for judging technological innovations – speed, efficiency, and power – are themselves products of the technological society. Since technological society has given rise to these ideals, 'improvement' means simply getting further along with the technological project. Other, antiquarian standards – a sense of community, a human pace and scale, wholeness, meaningfulness of work, an ethics of non-power[83] – seem, if not ludicrous, then at least inappropriate or impractical nowadays.

It must be emphasized that Grant disagreed thoroughly with all of the foregoing messages. Next we review his arguments rejecting two of them – namely, that separation of fact from value, and the distinction between objectivity and subjectivity.

Fact/Value, Objectivity/Subjectivity

Grant noted that Heidegger[84] proposed that *technology* is the means whereby people act upon and transform the world around them, and that, as technology becomes more powerful, the world increasingly is viewed as comprising objects, including human objects, to be acted upon for purposes of manipulation and control. Although technological innovations may at first be intended for human betterment and may initially have that effect, ultimately, according to Grant's reading of Heidegger, technology leads to human degradation on account of an inexorable process of objectification. Grant assessed that this posture of objectification is not merely dangerous, which is apparent enough in our day, but also false. He argued that true objectivity is impossible because value can never be separated from fact. *All* knowledge, he insisted, even the most 'scientific,'[85] is couched in value, in personal experience and in belief.[86] Presuppositions concerning the nature of reality, the ground of being, and hierarchies of evidence, although often inchoate, bear upon how every individual experiences and interprets the world.[87] It is always a *subject* who knows. Once subjective aspects to knowledge are acknowledged, purportedly hard and fast distinctions between 'fact' and 'value' disappear. 'Facts,' or what we often take to be discrete phenomena, are selected, according to our value system, from an infinite array of possible phenomena, and once selected are interpreted through the screens of belief and value. We look for and see primarily what is important (or of value) to us, and tend not to look for or even notice myriad other possibilities.

In addressing objectivity/subjectivity and the problem of knowledge, Grant engaged the existentialist tradition of philosophers such as Kierkegaard, Dostoevsky, Marcel, Heidegger, Sartre, and Nietzsche. Grant defined existentialism as 'the problem of subjectivity,' and as concern 'with human existence as subject in a world of objects.'[88] According to him, existentialism, at bottom, is 'a protest' against the

propensity of Western science and technology to objectify. Put positively, existentialism affirms subjective knowledge, including the knowledge of value and of history. In affirming value and subjectivity, Grant
believed, existentialism reaffirms human freedom, that is, the individual's capacity to choose.[89]

For Grant, an implication of our innate subjectivity is the invincibility
of the human spirit.[90] He wrote: 'Freedom and subjectivity mean the
same thing [due to] the ability to transcend ourselves.'[91] We can think
about ourselves thinking about ourselves, for instance – an infinite
regress. This innate capacity for transcendence, Grant believed, is what
distinguishes humanity from other species and is the source of our
inherent moral responsibility.

Existentialism, for Grant, however, is itself dialectical. On the one
hand, there are theistic existentialists such as Kierkegaard, Dostoevsky,
and Marcel who, with Grant, affirm that the values people in their
subjectivity *choose* to accept and adhere to can be known as being (or as
not being, as the case may be) in conformity with the basic principles of
the universe. Grant wrote: 'There are certain things that one can know
in advance should never be done.'[92] On the other hand, there are also
atheistic existentialists such as Sartre and Nietzsche who espouse in
Grant's view a *pure* subjectivity, since values for them are purely social
constructions, the universe being for them indifferent to human action.[93] Scientific objectivity and atheistic existentialism alike, in Grant's
view, cause people to 'lower [their] sights,' that is, to neglect considerations of time (eternity), which, for Grant, 'is man's greatest need.'[94]
Grant, therefore, commended a balance, the middle way, between scientific 'objectivity' and 'pure subjectivity.'

Communication as Propaganda

Since rapid technological change and scientific modes understanding
encourage objectivity and the separation of fact from value, Grant saw
the modern technological project as being essentially nihilistic and
totalitarian. However, in his view, these implications have not yet sufficiently penetrated human consciousness. Indeed, powerful agencies of
propaganda inhibit people from becoming aware. Grant wrote:

> Every instrument of mass culture is a pressure alienating the individual
> from himself as a free being ... The individual becomes (whether on the
> assembly line, in the office, or in the department store) an object to be ad-
> ministered by scientific efficiency experts ... Modern culture, through

the movies, newspapers and television, through commercialized recreation and popular advertising, forces the individual into the services of the capitalist system around him.[95]

Grant identified, in particular, the mass media, the arts, and the educational system as instruments of mass persuasion and coercion working at the behest of powerful interests to obscure and/or soothe over totalitarian and nihilistic implications of technological society.[96] Grant claimed that through flickering images *mass media*, for example, 'kill' memories, and that the seeming intensity of events[97] inhibits individuals from 'identifying life as it is with life as it ought to be.'[98] Newspapers and television with 'capitalist associations'[99] spew forth misinformation, making very difficult the attainment of 'independent views.' Media continually propagate 'fictions,' some so blatant that 'one must begin to question motives.'[100] In the mass media the existing economic and political system is invariably depicted as good, normal, the one best way; alternatives are either dismissed or ignored. Media are highly selective in what they cover, giving primacy to ideas that strengthen the existing power structure but affording scant attention to, for example, the 'great egalitarian principle [that] the community has an obligation to ease by compensation the insecurity of those sacrificed to economic progress.'[101]

Advertising, for Grant, is tantamount to 'brainwashing' and its intention is to enslave. [102]He noted sourly that advertising is the principal content of privately owned media (Smythe's position again), and that it accounts for higher expenditures than education. 'Much of our cleverest talent,' he grumbled, 'receives a high reward for ... entrapping people into believing that they need a new kind of car or soap.' Even more significantly, advertising persuades audiences that production should be concentrated on goods that can be produced privately for profit, rather than on services to meet pressing social needs.[103] Advertising is, in other words, a powerful force opposing the 'common good.'

Art, too, in a technological/capitalist society, according to Grant, serves an essentially oppressive power structure.[104] Art enfolds us into accepting what we are[105] rather than enlightening us as to who we might become, and it convinces us that meaning and purpose are to be found only in the 'fun culture.'[106] For Grant, the contrast with 'great art' is stark. 'Great art,' he attested, manifests the artist's position respecting the human condition, which one can infer by studying the particulars of the artist's work.[107] This Grant, in fact, did with works by Fyodor

Dostoevsky, wherein he discovered an omnipresent dialectic not unlike his own, comprising a tension between freedom of the will and the need for redemption arising out of the exercise of that freedom; as well, oppositions between faith and doubt, between good and evil, and, as Grant expressed it, the 'agonizing struggle of the believer to reconcile the necessary with the good.'[108]

Finally, Grant charged, the *educational system* moulds students' consciousness into supporting the goals and projects of the power élite. Rather than providing a place where students are encouraged to think deeply about their world, schools and universities are given over to training specialists. 'Even the traditional humane subjects such as history, the classics and European literature,' he complained, 'are in many cases taught as techniques by which the student can hope to earn a living, not as useful introductions to the sweep of our spiritual tradition.'[109] Curriculum, Grant stated further, indoctrinates students into a 'paradigm of knowledge'[110] based on the false dichotomy between fact and value. This dichotomy, rife with political-economic consequences, is of immense value to the 'great corporations'[111] by making it 'illegitimate' to consider publicly any criteria that could restrain technological applications. 'Facts,' being 'objective,' become, according to the dominant paradigm, the proper subject matter for schools and universities; 'values,'' by contrast, being merely 'personal' or 'subjective,' *ought* (note the value judgment!) be kept strictly private. For the modern paradigm to work well, Grant advised, proponents know full well that we must not reflect too long or too deeply.[112]

CANADA AS ALLEGORY

In his most famous book, *Lament for a Nation*, Grant recast the dialectic of ancient versus modern accounts of time, law, value, meaning, and justice into an allegory featuring Canada and the United States. Grant maintained that the Canadian Confederation was founded on an older, more 'conservative' conception of justice, that in refusing to wage a war for independence as had the Americans, Canadians retained roots in a tradition of British conservatism based on the premise of the *common* as opposed merely to the private good.[113] Justice as the common good, Grant insisted, is antithetical to the spirit of capitalism since capitalist ideology, as represented, for instance, by the works of Adam Smith and John Rawls, maintains that the common good need not even be considered for purportedly it results automatically as an unintended by-product of the myriad, self-interested actions and interactions of individuals pursuing single-mindedly their private gain. Adam Smith went even further: he admonished that if the common good were to become a conscious goal, the beneficent automaticity of the market mechanism would be weakened, and so too, necessarily would advancements toward the common good![114]

The Canadian hope, however, according to Grant, had been to build within North America *a community* with 'a stronger sense of the common good and of public order' than was possible under American-style individualism.[115] By 'community' Grant meant, in part, a social order that respects the dignity of every person and works on ways towards fulfilling that dignity as conditions change.[116] In identifying conservatism with pursuit of the common good, Grant found a close affinity with socialism. He asked: 'What is socialism, if it is not the use of the government to restrain greed in the name of social good? ... In actual practice, socialism has always had to advocate inhibition in this respect. In doing so, was it not appealing to the conservative idea of social order against the liberal idea of freedom?'[117]

Socialism, 'conservatism,' communitarianism, and Canadian nationalism, in Grant's estimation, were all bound together in Canada's formation and development. Major publicly owned enterprises such as the CBC and Ontario Hydro were founded by Conservative governments, which understood that private enterprise inherently is antinationalist. 'No small country can depend for its existence on the loyalty of its capitalists,' Grant snapped; 'only in dominant nations is the loyalty of capitalists ensured.'[118] That insight means that Canadian nationhood requires a strong central government to counterbalance continentalist, today global, business pressures. Limiting the civil service 'in the name of free enterprise,' Grant remonstrated, 'simply strengthens the power of the private [transnational corporate] governments.'[119]

According to Grant, however, in the 1960s Canada turned from conceiving justice as pursuit of the common good, and towards the capitalistic conception of justice as unrestrained individual freedom to pursue private profit. Chief protagonists favouring the former and resisting the latter, according to Grant, were Conservative prime minister John Diefenbaker, and External Affairs minister Howard Green, both of whom struggled vainly to keep nuclear warheads off Canadian soil. Agents of capitalism, and of justice as individual or corporate liberty, included U.S. and Canadian business leaders, Liberal party officials (notably

C.D. Howe and Lester Pearson), and U.S. president John F. Kennedy, all of whom, according to Grant, strove to tear down restraints interfering with the pursuit of profit, including Diefenbaker's ban on nuclear warheads. What was at stake in that struggle, as Grant saw it, was the very survival of 'the Canadian hope' in the face of 'the American capitalist dream.'

To lament, Grant declared, 'is to cry out at the dying of something loved.'[120] Grant lamented 'the end of Canada as a sovereign state.' He bemoaned also the passing of the Canadian hope that a country in North America could pursue justice as the common good. And, most fundamentally, he bemoaned the demise in North America of the notion of time as the moving image of eternity. The proximate cause of Grant's lamentation was capitalism and the will to pursue power and profit through technological mastery.

SOME QUESTIONS

Grant had the mind of a poet. No few lines of poetry can do justice to his thought. Nonetheless, the following from John Donne reflects accurately Grant's love for and belief in the common good:

> All mankind is of one author and is one volume ... No man is an island, entire of itself; every man is a piece of the continent, a part of the main. If a clod be washed away by the sea, Europe is the less, as well as if a promontory were, as well as if a manor of thy friend's or of thine own were. Any man's death diminishes me because I am involved in mankind, and therefore never send to know for whom the bell tolls; it tolls for thee.[121]

A number of questions arise from a study of George Grant's work. One broad area of inquiry concerns similarities and differences between his thought and that of the other theorists we are concerned with in this book. In this section I extensively compare Grant with Innis, and more briefly with Smythe and Macpherson.

Second, much has transpired since Grant's death in 1988, the very year Canada signed a free-trade agreement with the United States. More recently, the World Trade Organization has become a powerful promoter of global free trade. There has been also the rise of the Internet and plans are under way to implement a globally interconnected 'Information Highway.' Moreover, neo-conservative/neo-liberal policies, often under the guise of deficit reduction, have pared social, educational, cultural, and environmental programs to the bone, with a concomitant waning in consciousness of 'the common good.' In this context, one may well ask, just what of Grant's analysis remains of relevance?

Finally, are there messages of hope or of action to be gleaned from the works of this brooding political philosopher?

Grant and Canadian Communication Thought

Innis and Grant

Innis and Grant alike were holistic thinkers. Each based his enquiries into the evolution of societies on a value-oriented or critical perspective. Both made strong connections between societal evolution and technological change, and warned that society cannot survive if, in Grant's words, it puts 'its faith in techniques and not in wholeness.'[122] Innis and Grant alike railed at growing control over educational curricula by business interests, and were appalled at the prospect of narrow, technocratic instruction increasingly becoming the norm. Like Innis, Grant elucidated an all-encompassing dialectic concerning opposing conceptions of time; despite differences in terminology, the basic understanding of the two was similar: Grant's 'time as history' corresponds well to what Innis meant by 'space bias,' and Grant's 'time as the moving image of an unchanging eternity' can certainly be subsumed into Innis's category of 'time bias.' Both scholars attributed movement from one mode of organization to the other to technology – in Innis's case, to the means of inscription and electronic media; in Grant's, to technology and technological innovation as a general mediation or milieu.

Both Innis and Grant, furthermore, attacked liberalism. Innis, the political economist, critiqued commodity exchange as an economic practice and mainline economics as its justificatory knowledge system; he was particularly apprehensive lest commodity exchange displace or render trivial other modes of interacting. Grant, the political philosopher, while also castigating undue commodification of human relations,[123] accorded relatively greater attention to 'contractarianism' as both a practice and a political philosophy, particularly as it was expounded by John Rawls. However, the doctrines of commodity exchange and contractarianism, although distinct, are closely related and consistent. Both are premised on individualism, selfishness, calculation, and negotiation/exchange. Both deny that people should strive consciously for a higher, collective good. In the theory of commodity exchange, for example, all 'value' is deemed to arise from market activity;[124] in the marketplace, there is no such thing as intrinsic value.[125] Likewise contractarianism posits 'rights' as set out in contracts to be of higher priority than natural law or conceptions of natural justice.[126] To the extent that these two libertarian doctrines acknowledge a higher good at all (the 'wealth of nations' in the case of economic liberalism, maximum freedom in the case of contractarianism), this good will be attained automatically, adherents to the doctrines propose, through the multiplicity of individual transactions and contracts (the doctrine of the 'invisible hand'). Innis and Grant, however, both took great exception to these liberal doctrines, and both investigated at length their dark side. Each thinker was deeply troubled that North America generally, and Canada in particular, were becoming increasingly depersonalized and alienating due to the growing predominance of these libertarian modes of thought and action. Grant wrote: 'When everything is made relative to profit-making, all traditions of virtue are dissolved, including that aspect of virtue known as love of country.'[127] Canadian governments, both theorists felt, were opting increasingly for power/objectivity/technology/profit over equality/love/community/continuity. These choices, they attested, were ripping apart the social fabric: 'Values' (how Grant hated that term; he felt it denotes something that people create, rather than something given) were being effaced or reconstructed in accordance with the nihilism of technological society.

Undoubtedly, on account of such commonalties, early in his career Grant lauded Innis, singling him out, along with Northrop Frye and classicist Charles Cochrane,[128] as one of the few Canadian thinkers 'who have shown themselves willing to go beyond scholarship to more general questions of human import.'[129] Grant, however, became dismissive of Innis (and of Frye, too, for that matter),[130] referring derogatively to the former as a 'scientist' who questioned only how things work, and as one who was unconcerned about 'more essential, ultimate questions.'[131] Asked, 'How did Harold Innis influence you?' Grant responded tepidly, 'The person who educated Innis in his later life was Cochrane, because they went for walks around the University of Toronto. He helped Innis move beyond the fur trade, etc., into deeper subjects. I hardly knew Innis and have only read his books in recent years.'[132] Given the ample likenesses to their thought, the disdain, or at least the chill, evident in Grant's remarks is surprising. So, a question arises: What were their main points of departure?

Innis, the economic historian and agnostic, had rooted most of his life in the material, the concrete. Nature to him, certainly in his staples period, was basic (one might say prior) to thought and human activity. Human activity, he maintained, at least for peripheral economies, depends on what resources or 'staples' abound in the environment. The properties of staples, in combination with geography and technology, help mould human organization and human thought. As people innovate new ways of extracting staples, new environments arise that help transform social and economic relations and human consciousness. Likewise, Innis addressed in somewhat the same materialist manner the various means of inscription. For him, writing materials, like staples, have intrinsic properties that help steer the cultures that use them. The material means of carrying symbols, he thought, are basic to understanding a culture. In Innis's schemata, however, behind technological change and the exploitation of staples is a quest for wealth and power. That quest led, for example, to settlement in the new world; likewise, attempts to overcome marginality lie behind many innovations in media. Always in Innis's analysis there is the notion of an imbalance or asymmetry – whether between the motherland and the colony, between dominant and subordinate groups within a culture, or between time and space as principles of organization and control – and these imbalances, this dialectic, gives rise to movement or change.

For Grant, much of this is different. For him, there was no notion of the material or phenomenal world being prior to the ideal; indeed, he believed that, once a culture begins conceiving the material realm in that way, trouble is sure to arise. 'The beginning,' for Grant, was not a superfluity of natural resources, or the availability of a potential medium of communication, but ideals and ideas – of God or gods, of existence, of justice, of goodness, of natural law, and of time.

Materiality and political economy do, of course, enter Grant's analysis (and in *Lament for a Nation* he is, indeed, a virtuoso political economist). But Grant, it appears, engaged in political economy reluctantly – because, in the West, according to his estimation, time as history has superseded time as the moving image of eternity, and we must understand the world in that light.

For Grant, Innis was a tragic figure, trapped in his own dialectic: although able to penetrate and reject the false claims of modern, space-bound cultures, Innis remained unable, in Grant's view, to accept the truth claims of time-bound culture: '[Innis] took methods from the moderns, but his motives for doing science came from the ancients. He was at one and the same time both toughly cynical about social science, and sadly doubtful about the claims of the older science. The result is a kind of sadness in his work – even if it is a sadness well penetrated by wit and anger.'[133]

But, it is to be emphasized, differences between Grant and Innis can be overdrawn. For, despite his materialist outlook, Innis also remarked that an authentic conception of time means recognizing or believing that there exists 'a state of permanence beyond time.'[134] And Grant, despite affording such great emphasis to perfection, also was of the opinion that we need to comprehend through science the world as it is, since 'we can only know how we should live if we know what kind of a universe it is.'[135]

One other point is extremely important. How remarkable that these two great communication thinkers held so much in common, despite ostensibly different starting positions: Innis the farm boy, Grant born to privilege; Innis the agnostic, Grant the believer; Innis the 'dirt economist,' Grant the poetic, idealistic philosopher. Of that, Canadian policy makers and students of policy should take particular note.

Smythe and Grant
Dallas Smythe also shared many sentiments with George Grant, particularly regarding mass media, technological change, and Canada–U.S. relations. However, whereas Smythe emphasized the role of the Consciousness Industry in conforming human beings to the requirements of monopoly capitalism, Grant's concerns were more existential; part of capitalism's project of indoctrination, he believed, is a concerted effort to cause people not only to lose touch with themselves and their roots (to this Smythe would agree), but to become forgetful also of eternal or ontological questions. Apart from an abiding concern for equality, one looks in vain in Smythe's work for Platonic Ideals, and it is in this regard, one suspects, that Smythe would level his sharpest criticism at Grant, and Grant find Smythe most lacking. In reading Smythe, one senses that life is a continuous struggle between oppressor and victim, whereas, for Grant, beyond the maniacal chaos of everyday existence, 'there is order.' Grant wrote that it is not through internal contradictions that justice is to be achieved, but through thinking, remembering, and loving. Both Smythe and Grant saw the quest for power as dominating society. Likewise, each pointed to the industrial arts ('technology') as a major means by which power is sought and exercised. Indeed, both saw technology, or as Smythe preferred 'the

industrial arts,' as conditioning people's minds. Smythe, though, emphasized how industrial products inculcate 'capitalist values,' whereas Grant, although certainly not oblivious to this aspect of liberal capitalist society, was even more concerned about the existential lessons regarding fact, value, time, history, and being versus becoming, which are implicit in the technological project.

Smythe and Grant were both concerned about the hegemony exercised by the United States over Canada, and the Canadian government's complicity in this dominance. Whereas Smythe detailed myriad instances and means whereby Canada became increasingly dependent upon the United States – though film, broadcasting, telecommunications, spectrum management, the arts and sciences, and generally through 'technology' – Grant focused intensively on but one instance as exemplifying, in particular, Canada's capitulation to technological and market forces – namely, the implanting of nuclear warheads on Canadian soil. Whereas Smythe related that Canada had fallen under the sway of the United States and international capitalism in large part through the operations of the Consciousness Industry, Grant appears to have believed that *all* countries and all peoples, the American people included, are more or less willing victims of an oppressive and ultimately nihilistic mindset, a mindset that he called 'time as history.'

Both Smythe and Grant in profound ways were idealistic – indeed, utopian – thinkers. However, whereas Smythe looked to the future and to revolution as the means for implementing a classless, egalitarian society, Grant (likewise a staunch egalitarian) recalled the past, when people were steeped in Platonic notions of goodness and perfection; therefore, Grant looked not to revolution or to dialectical materialism, but to recollecting ancient wisdom, reaffirming natural law, and reinstating natural justice as the means for implementing a just and peaceable society.

Macpherson and Grant

Unlike Grant, C.B. Macpherson did not emphasize the 'common good,' the proposition that we are 'all part of the main.' Socialism, for Macpherson, rather, was required so that each *individual* could employ and develop his or her capacities. Macpherson was essentially a liberal who thought that socialism is necessary for *individual* freedom.

However, Macpherson shared with Grant the belief that there is an intrinsic moral order against which human morality and positive laws can be judged. Although the content Grant and Macpherson ascribed to the eternal moral order differed in some respects, in other ways it was similar. Both writers, for instance, ascribed high intrinsic value to equality. However, their notions of equality differed. For Macpherson, equality meant equal opportunity for people to develop their talents and express their skills; for Grant, it meant absolute equality before God. In *In Conversation with George Grant*, by David Cayley, Grant affirmed: 'I have no doubt that within Christianity everyone is equal before God. I don't think you can hold Christianity for a minute without believing this. There are inequalities that represent some truth in the world, as well as ones that represent untruths in the world, but ultimately, before God, people are equal.'[136] Macpherson was zealous to bring about the political/economic order best suited to fulfil human potential, which he defined in terms of skills and creative activities. Grant, by contrast, was less concerned with fulfilling the human potential in these terms, and more with fulfilling divine law, which is summarized as loving one's neighbour as oneself.

Macpherson perhaps saw in technological advance greater potential for contributing to human development than did Grant, although both were dialectical thinkers in this regard. Macpherson saw technology as potentially freeing humankind from the drudgery of eking out a living and thereby enabling people to devote their talents and energies to self-development; Grant, to the contrary, saw technology as transforming human nature in a negative way, inducing people to concern themselves with power above all else. On the other hand, Macpherson's optimism was modified significantly by the political economy of the present economic order, and Grant's negative assessment was qualified by technologically based benefits in terms of health care and labour-saving devices. Finally, Macpherson and Grant were alike in insisting that human nature is not set. Macpherson saw political philosophy as a major means for transforming human nature in a positive direction, whereas Grant, although emphasizing the negative impact on human nature of technological change, also held out the hope that, by remembering the ancient wisdom, people could recapture their essential human traits.

GRANT'S ANALYSIS TODAY

George Grant warned of the dangers inherent in pursuing power for the sake of power through technological means. Technological innovation governed solely or primarily by technologically inspired values of speed, efficiency, and power, he warned, place humankind at grave risk. The separation of fact from value, and the objectification of human beings in an era characterized by a diminished sense of community and on an ever-larger scale, increase the likelihood of injustice – indeed, of atrocity. Individualism and self-gratification, as promoted by the mass media, may induce extremely destructive behaviours in a world already environmentally challenged.

Referring to the development of the atomic bomb in the 1940s, Grant quoted J. Robert Oppenheimer as stating that the invention was too 'sweet' to reject. One suspects that, in our day, Grant would understand the Human Genome Project likewise as being too 'sweet' in the minds of the military-industrial-technological establishment to reject.

But, in engineering life at its very conception, are not humans fulfilling the Nietzschean prophecy of negating horizons and thereby collapsing values and meanings – except for the supreme value of aggrandizing power for its own sake? Are we in the West not thereby re-entering a new era of fascism, an era from which there is little prospect of escape? George Grant's analysis, therefore, is indeed a discourse for our time.

George Grant has been criticized for being unduly pessimistic, and it is easy to see how readers could come away with that impression. His avowed intention as a philosopher, after all, was to bring 'the darkness into light as darkness.'[137] What enabled him to do this consistently and effectively for so many years was his deep conviction, acquired in England in the midst of war, that beyond the seeming maniacal chaos and apparent relativity of time and space, 'there is order.'[138] Ultimately, therefore, paradoxical though it may seem, Grant wrote from a foundation of great hope.

Theologian and philosopher Simone Weil and Plato seem to have helped Grant most in this regard. Weil invoked a statement of Plato's positing 'an infinite distance which separates the order of necessity [i.e., human history, linear causality] from the order of good [i.e., God, perfection].' That infinite chasm, however, by Plato's account, *can* be bridged. Grant restated Plato's position: 'The order of good enters the human world when human beings are moved by their love of perfection.'[139] Love of perfection enables people to transcend their mundane existence and thereby partake of the eternal.

For Grant, however, even more than Plato, Christian doctrine provides a compelling reconciliation. Self-surrendering love is *the perfect means* of bridging that chasm.[140]

Grant has also been charged with providing few solutions to the profound problems he raised. To 'lament,' after all, is to imply that it is already too late to do much. And after exquisitely unfolding Nietzsche's thought, Grant admonished that we remember what has been handed to us from older traditions, in particular, from the Jews and the Greeks, and to sift 'by loving and thinking' their truth from their error, thereby opening ourselves up 'to the whole.'[141] Grant assessed, however, that 'this is to say very little.' One might wish that he had been able, or had been more inclined, to couple his deep analyses and profound faith with plans for action. While Grant was himself a social activist in the sense that he devoted his life to teaching and writing about injustices, inconsistencies, and moral dilemmas pervading our society, in calling readers and listeners only to remember, to think, to love, and to believe (hugely important as these are), he may in the end have helped inspire passivity; such is the main difference between Grant and, say, John Grierson, Dallas Smythe, or Graham Spry.

The paradox of Grant runs deeper still. On the one hand, he always insisted that it truly matters what one does, that each individual ultimately is responsible for his or her own moral comportment. On the other, 'necessity' and 'fate' are recurrent, often explicit, themes in Grant's writings. Fatalism would seem, however, to detract from the significance of human action. Grant's penchant for fatalistic interpretation was perhaps ultimately the source of his apparent lack of revolutionary zeal.

Nonetheless, for readers able to retain a spirit of hope and activism in the face of Grant's evident resignation, the writings of this brooding philosopher of modernity can be of immense aid for comprehending our own time and, inferentially at least, pointing us towards what we should be doing.

9

The Communication Thought of
GERTRUDE JOCH ROBINSON (B. 1927)

There are no neutral media systems.

– 'Binational News,' 149

ABOUT GERTRUDE ROBINSON

Gertrude Joch ('Gee-Gee') Robinson was born into a bilingual family in Hamburg, Germany, on 15 November 1927.[1] Her father, Frederick W. Joch, from Munich, operated an international shipping business that required of him extended absences; his first ship, a wooden schooner, was named *The Gertrude*. Her mother, Sarah Blaisdell, of Chicago, known as 'the American' in the small town of Reinbek, just outside Hamburg, 'set the tone' in the Joch household. Each year she would travel to the United States and bring back American clothing for her two daughters.

Childhood for Gertrude Joch meant living in 'a bubble in a foreign environment.' For one thing, the family listened frequently to BBC radio broadcasts – a dangerous pastime in those years of German fascism. The children learned never to speak outside the home on matters learned inside. For another, for a time, at least, the girls managed to keep out of the German youth organization: their mother produced health certificates of various kinds to that end. Even when the girls were finally forced to join, the parents forbade them to wear the German youth uniform, with the result that, in the school parades, they were embarrassingly conspicuous. Discounting completely the education the girls received at school, the parents, both avid readers, encouraged their daughters to read omnivorously, which they did. They thereby gained exposure to international literature, an advantage unique for the time and place: Dostoevsky, Tolstoy, Shakespeare, Jewish writers, *The Red and the Black*.

Gertrude Robinson characterizes her youth as that of an 'insider/ outsider,' a status profoundly affecting her subsequent scholarship. In our interview in 1998, she attested: 'I think as an insider/outsider you are forever critically observing where you are, and are aware of the fact you are critically observing it, so it becomes a way of leading one's life.' Although her formal schooling in Germany was lacklustre, there were other pedagogic venues. During a year of study for confirmation in the Lutheran Church, for example, she was required to respond to profound ethical questions: 'How does one know one is doing the right thing?' and 'What does it mean to build an ethical life?' Upon the close of the war, moreover, she attended a school set up in the ruins of Hamburg by Jewish teachers returning from concentration camps, and studied, in her words, 'totally unorthodox philosophy, aesthetics, world history, world literature, sciences, geography in a manner that was completely mind boggling because it was so eclectic; ... it was the first time that I got sort of intellectually challenged.'

In 1947 Gertrude Joch enrolled at Swathmore College in the United States, concentrating on ethics and aesthetics, motivated, she declared, to pursue answers to the questions posed by her Lutheran pastor. Swathmore was and remains a Quaker college, and Robinson soon became interested in Quakerism. She found particularly appealing their 'silent meetings,' social activism, and pacifism.

In 1950, Gertrude Robinson, now married, was accepted in the MA program in philosophy at the University of Chicago. An influential mentor there was C.I. Morris. According to Robinson, in *Signs, Language and Behavior* (1946) Morris built upon the semiology of Charles Sanders Pearce. Another of her professors was the logical positivist Rudolph Carnap. However, she rejected outright Carnap's philosophic stance: 'I have to find myself in contrast to him, and primarily for the reason that ... logical positivism has no place for ethics or for aesthetics ... So Carnap for me has never been a model because ... you simply cannot say that ethical statements or aesthetic statements are meaningless statements.'

At Chicago, Robinson also studied the writings of John Dewey, a leading philosophic pragmatist. Her MA thesis, 'The Concept of Verification in Russell's and Dewey's Theory of Knowledge,' was, as she put it, 'a study in dialectics between structure and process, that is, between the proposition that truth is static versus the claim that it is contextual and evolves.' Although at the time opting for Dewey's dynamic notion of truth, subsequently she became disenchanted with his pragmatism because, she related, it provides no foundation except 'majority rule' for evaluating truth. Years later she located in the works of the seminal symbolic interactionist George Herbert Mead, and later still in the writings of Clifford Geertz, the powerful concept of 'interpretive communities,' an explanation of how different discourses become meaningful (i.e., 'truthful') for different groups. We will return shortly to Robinson's ontological position as exemplified by the construct, interpretive communities.

During the 1950s, Robinson bore five children, placing her professional and intellectual aspirations on hold. In 1960, though, shortly after the birth of her last child, she was diagnosed as tubercular and forced to convalesce for six months in a sanitarium at Urbana, Illinois (her husband having attained a teaching position at the University of Illinois in 1956). 'Totally cut off from the outside world,' including her five children, and confined to bed, this enforced respite was a blessing in disguise. Being 'extremely interested in the negativity of [American] people towards Eastern Europe,' and intrigued particularly by the work of two faculty friends, both of whom were interested in the different versions of communism as practised in their birthplaces,[2] Robinson undertook to study systematically the Russian language, Russian sociology, and Russian politics. Even more significantly, she began, as she put it in our interview, to think of herself again as an individual, not simply as a mother of five and the wife of a university professor. In the process she rediscovered that intellectual pursuits 'were absolutely at the essence of who I was.' She added: 'So I attribute this very difficult period to my renewed understanding that I as an individual had an additional identity to socially constructed identities of wife and mother.'

The next year she registered as a part-time student at the University of Illinois and, in 1962, upon the suggestion of eminent communication professor George Gerbner, she became a doctoral candidate in the university's Institute of Communications Research. Among her instructors were political economist Herbert Schiller, cyberneticist Ross Ashby, political sociologist Joseph Gusfield, and political economist Dallas Smythe.

Robinson's first recollection of Smythe is that he urged students to 'think dirty,'[3] meaning that they should 'expect the worst' when studying organizations involved with the communication business. In our interview she attested that Smythe was seminal in acquainting her with the importance of political economic considerations: 'I learned that it is fundamental and you cannot understand anything if you do not investigate the institutional structure and the power relationship and the economic base of a particular situation.' Even at the institute, however, Robinson was an 'insider-outsider':[4] she was only a part-time student, and was older than many of her cohort, which included but one other female; moreover, she was the spouse of a faculty member; even her friendship circle of Dallas Smythe, George Gerbner, Herbert Schiller, and their wives was an 'out group' on the campus. Then, in 1966, now divorced, she became essentially a single mother, further marginalizing her status.

Robinson's doctoral dissertation, completed in 1968, was entitled 'Tanjug: Yugoslavia's Multifaceted National News Agency.' In it she explored that communist agency's news-production methods, and its strategic role in founding President Tito's 'non-aligned nations group.' Her dissertation led to a book, *Tito's Maverick Media: The Politics of Mass Communication in Yugoslavia*, published in 1977, as well as to numerous articles.

Even while preparing her thesis, however, Robinson was already shifting somewhat from the firm political-economy stance of her mentors, and towards what she termed a more 'flexible,' 'less deterministic' systems-theoretic/symbolic-interactionist approach. In our interview she stated that political economy can be too rigidly unidirectional, attributing all phenomena, including the distribution of symbols and the interpretation of texts, to the intention of message senders singlemindedly pursuing power and profit. Her position, therefore, became, and remains, one of proposing that, while information systems may spring out of power contexts, interpretation is culturally or subculturally specific. Below we expand on these notions.

In 1968, Professor Robinson became a research associate with the institute, and the next year she joined the Department of Sociology at Illinois as an assistant professor. In 1970 she was hired by McGill's Sociology Department, where she began teaching a course on Canadian mass communication. Totally unfamiliar at the time with the Canadian institutional context, she told her first students that, if they supplied the Canadian content, she would provide the theoretical questions and the ways in which those questions might be addressed. In our interview she confided, 'It was a complete cliffhanger but it was marvellous.' Canadian course materials were sparse at that time, and the little that was available in English rarely mentioned Quebec, 'so one of the challenges I've had ... was to incorporate Quebec into my teaching and to point out how totally different the development in Quebec was.'

At McGill, Robinson immediately became involved in an interdisciplinary faculty group intent on establishing a communication program. McGill's Graduate Program in Communication was launched in 1974, and during its formative years (1974–8) Robinson was its associate director. In 1979 she became its acting director, and over the next twenty years served four terms as director. As well she was the third president of the Canadian Communication Association (1983), and between 1987 and 1993 served as editor of the *Canadian Journal of Communication*.

Professor Robinson is author of three books: *Tito's Maverick Media* (1977); *News Agencies and World News in Canada, the United States and Yugoslavia* (1981); and *Constructing the Quebec Referendum: French and English Media Voices* (1998). She is also editor or co-editor of three volumes[5] and author or co-author of some fifty articles.

Gertrude Robinson's life has not been without tragedy. Twice within the space of a year (1969–70), she was informed by telephone of auto accidents; in each instance, one of her children had been killed.

Growing up in a bilingual 'American home' in fascist Germany, Robinson was made aware at an early age how powerful the mind is in its capacity to construct alternative realities. Fighting tuberculosis and experiencing the heartbreaks of divorce and death of offspring may also have been factors inducing her to opt for, in Hannah Arendt's words, 'a life of the mind.' Interpretation, for Gertrude Robinson, is all-important; to her, there is no way to apprehend directly a reality that may exist separate from the human being. She is fully in accord with the proposition expressed by theorist Stephen Littlejohn that 'communication is the process whereby [social] reality is constructed.'[6]

In 1999, Professor Robinson retired from McGill University. For her, the prospect of 'retirement,' however, is in fact an enhanced opportunity to write, and thereby to make further contributions to Canadian and international communication thought.

ONTOLOGY AND EPISTEMOLOGY

As an afterword to her collection of essays on world news agencies, Professor Robinson positioned herself firmly and explicitly in the social constructionist camp. She declared:

Following Berger and Luckman,[7] I believe that social reality is not immediately apprehended, it is instead actively created and recreated through the different meanings people attach to it. Human activities furthermore are dynamic and take place in 'settings' which contain both structural and interpretive elements. Settings, actors and actions accordingly are systematically interrelated. There is a dialectical interdependence between human beings and their natural and social environments. This interdependence is unique because the human organism selectively perceives and responds.[8]

Robinson explained that she views 'the symbolic not as context but as *the most important* factor in understanding human behaviour,' terming her approach both holistic and cybernetic. When studying news agencies, for instance, it is not sufficient to study the parts in static isolation one from another; rather, 'non-linear relationships, feedbacks and learning strategies' must be anticipated and accounted for. In addition, attention must be given to organizational constraints. Likewise, in perusing recent literature, 'the social setting' needs to be studied, since it 'structures the way in which an actor [i.e., an author] behaves.'[9]

Underlying Robinson's symbolic-interactionist approach is the proposition that people are not finished products of biological evolution: through humans' propensity to symbolize and conceptualize, rather, 'human nature' is subject to incessant and radical transformation. (On the other hand, though, she agreed that there is a permanence to the human proclivity to seek out meaning and to 'make sense' of experience.)

Robinson contended further that her symbolic- interactionist stance 'turns the stimulus-response paradigm on its head.' Rather than focusing exclusively on the individual, as do behavioural psychologists in the tradition of John Brodus Watson and B.F. Skinner, symbolic interactionism 'asserts that humans are born into a culture, and that it is the culture which supplies the various symbol systems which convey meaning in given social situations. Consequently, these symbol systems are ... public inscriptions of a communal sensibility, which those who wish to understand human behavior need to study.'[10]

For Robinson, moreover, there are no 'raw data' – not even in the physical sciences. Interpretation, rather, is key. But interpretation is always couched in a social context.[11] Referencing historian of science Thomas Kuhn, she attested that scientific work, being but a 'human activity' like all other intellection, is necessarily situated in a particular place and time, and involves groups of people developing schema to explain selected disciplinary issues. Referring to Northrop Frye, she proposed further that all authors, including scientists, are 'member[s] of a professional group with identifiable characteristics, practising [their] craft in a particular economic and social context.'[12] For her, therefore, *membership* is key in determining the nature of an author's creative output as well as its validity or truthfulness.

A startling implication of her position, therefore, is that the 'value' or 'truth' of a scholarly contribution can be assessed only by the author's peers: 'Truth,' in the sense of correspondence to a reality existing outside the verbal structure, she insists, cannot be a criterion. In personal correspondence she elaborated:

> I reject, in other words, a theory of 'truth' defined in terms of a one-to-one correspondence, because humans are 'symbol using animals' whose *understandings* [sic] of their social realities change not only themselves, but what these realities *mean*. Example: The [1999] nurses' strike in Montreal was initially interpreted as being about pay and working conditions. Now, seven days later, the nurses have turned the meaning of the strike into one about 'the safety of patients in a hospital system which has been badly mismanaged by the PQ government.' This government induced the scarcity of doctors and nurses through a buy-out and is perpetuating unsafe conditions by not paying nurses enough to attract new ones.[13]

Social constructionism, then, makes problematic knowledge and truth. Robinson recognized this explicitly in her seminal study of the first Quebec referendum. There she pointed out that, by maintaining that symbol systems construct and reconstruct social reality, one challenges 'four of the methodological assumptions of mainstream social science: [namely,] the strict separability of theory and data; the availability of a formal language of analysis purged of subjective references; the researcher's claim to moral neutrality; and the availability of an Olympian view from which to judge the evidence.'[14]

Consistent with her stance on knowledge as social construction, Robinson has taken a keen interest in contributing to the 'historiography' of her field, which she defines as 'the placing of idea structures in their historical time and place.'[15] Historiographies include accounts of 'masters' recruiting disciples and institutionalizing themselves at universities and institutes, of students and associates spreading out and perpetuating ideas through conferences and publications, and of false starts, archaic doctrines, and discarded theories. Those ignorant of the context within which ideas arise and flourish, Robinson charged, lack understanding.[16]

PRESS STUDIES

Like C.B. Macpherson, Robinson has insisted that practitioners of academic disciplines and subdisciplines ineluctably participate in the continual reconstruction of symbolic environments, and hence, whether purposefully or inadvertently, help redefine social reality. So, too, however, Robinson affirmed, do journalists. Furthermore, just as different academic disciplines and subdisciplines provide rival accounts of social reality, likewise do different press systems. Professor Robinson, therefore, has spent considerable time exploring differing accounts of social reality as provided both by competing domestic press systems (particularly English- and French-language press systems in Canada), and by international press systems. In her recent study on press coverage of the 1980 Quebec referendum, moreover, she went well beyond her previous press studies to show how coverage is influenced strongly by the political/economic interests of media owners.

French and English Press Systems: The October Crisis
The October Crisis in the autumn of 1970 entailed the kidnapping and eventual release, fifty-nine days later, of British trade commissioner James Cross, by the Front de Libération du Québec (FLQ), and within that period also the kidnapping and murder of Quebec's Labour and Immigration minister, Pierre Laporte. The FLQ had demanded, *inter alia*, release of twenty-three 'political prisoners.' In a study published in 1975, Robinson reviewed differences in how Canada's 'two solitudes' construct reality by comparing coverage of the crisis by the English- and French-language press. In Canada, she claimed, French and English cultural/symbolic systems 'rarely intersect,' and differences in media portrayals of the crisis provided 'a unique opportunity for exploring in greater detail how English and French Canadians conceive of their alternative realities and what implications these conceptions have for theories of communications and political behavior.'[17] More generally, she intended her study also to test Innis's thesis that increases in the

speed of communication and reduction in costs narrow media content and homogenize people's conception of reality. As Robinson put it, 'the media with their monopolies of knowledge, Innis argues, have acquired the social power to produce official versions of the world which are fashioned from values stressing market perishability and political control rather than human adaptation needs.'[18]

According to Robinson's content analyses, coverage by the two press systems differed fundamentally with regard to themes, geographic sources of items, and personalities. Although the English and French dailies afforded approximately equal front-page space to stories focusing on 'kidnapping' and 'security,' the French dailies devoted significantly more attention to: 'negotiations,' 'religious aspects/funeral,' 'the position of the Federal Government,' 'the position of the Quebec government,' and 'time.' English papers, in contrast, emphasized 'manhunt,' 'the War Measures Act,' 'murder,' and 'Parliament.' For the French papers, the crisis was about whether negotiations could be completed in time to save the lives of the captives, whereas, for the English papers, the crisis concerned terrorism and police activity in tracking down and arresting criminals. In addition, the French press paid far greater attention to the lapse in civil liberties. As well, there was far greater emphasis on background stories in the French press, indicating, for Robinson, 'greater French media involvement in politics through interpretative pieces.'[19]

Robinson concluded that her findings affirmed the 'social construction of reality' thesis, which proposes that people learn about themselves and their world through a stock of symbols that are consistently selected and used by those living in the culture. 'Reality,' according to the thesis, is not something external or separate, but comprises *selected* aspects that our culture teaches us are important and to which therefore we should pay attention.[20]

Robinson further suggested that her evidence provides partial confirmation of Innis's thesis that the technology distributing symbols has a cultural impact. She remarked that the broadcast media, being more amenable to central control, were more homogeneous in their coverage than were the print media.

Media and Divisiveness in Yugoslavia

Robinson remarked that two types of theoretical models have been proposed to explain relationships among ethnicity, modernization, and media. The most widely accepted model suggests that 'modernization neutralizes and submerges ethnic, racial or tribal politics with their attendant conflict.'[21] According to Daniel Lerner, Lucien Pye, Wilbur Schramm, and others, by propagating materialist values and reinforcing commodity-based modes of human interaction, mass media are instrumental in the processes of cultural homogenization and assimilation. On the other hand, however, Robinson noted, there is a counter-model which asserts that mass media increase differences and heighten tensions. As a result of media publicity, for example, everyone comes to want the same things, but goods being in short supply means that some people will become increasingly frustrated. Robinson declared that Yugoslavia 'provides an unusual setting for testing these two models and discovering what kind of role the mass media have *in fact* played both in modernization, nation-building and in bringing about psychological change among the country's multinational population.'[22]

Following Karl Deutsch, Robinson noted that countries divided linguistically, ethnically, or along religious lines tend also 'to be characterized by a more or less complete set of parallel institutions and sub-cultures.' Members of linguistic and ethnic subgroups consequently have the capacity to communicate more effectively with their own members than with others. During the periods of Robinson's analyses, Yugoslavia indeed had parallel and compartmentalized newspapers, publishing houses, and electronic media; these were, according to Robinson, 'organized regionally within the country's six republics and run by personnel speaking different languages, trained in different journalism schools and belonging to separate professional organizations.' She added: 'the culture and outlook of these communicators is further diversified by religion and history.'[23]

Analysing the content of Yugoslav media and media practices confirmed for Robinson the thesis that mass media can be ethnically divisive. Only 2 per cent of the Croatian population read a daily newspaper from Serbia, for example. Likewise, she found that broadcasting transmitters were not strong enough to carry programming across republican boundaries. Furthermore, the media system was subdivided into six republican networks, each managed by ethnically distinct communicators who wrote and broadcast in separate languages. These communication systems stressed local and regional content. Robinson quoted Milovan Djilas, ex-Communist Party 'ideologist,' as remarking: 'In Yugoslavia all writers are fighters,' pointing to the stark difference in the political power of writers in Belgrade versus, say, New York.[24]

Quebec Referendum (1980)

Competing Narratives

Robinson noted that Quebecers are provided with two dialectically opposed 'symbol maps' [25]– what Northrop Frye has called 'myths.' It is through one or other of these symbol maps that most citizens interpret current events and social reality.

One of these symbol maps was presented by the Parti Québécois (PQ) in its pre-1980 referendum White Paper. That document contended that Quebecers are *un peuple* occupying an ethnic 'homeland.' The *peuple québécois,* furthermore, according to this narrative, have since the British Conquest been systematically oppressed by the English-speaking majority. In order to be free, Quebecers therefore must break the hold of Canadian federal institutions, an action that would at once affirm the mythic persona of a *peuple québécois* and destroy the condition of dependence.

The other narrative in the pre-referendum campaign was promoted by the federalist-oriented Liberal party. Responding to the PQ's document, in their Beige Paper the Liberals maintained that *Canadiens français* have always constituted a 'distinct and unique society, with all of the attributes of a national community.'[26] Furthermore, far from a history of subjugation, this second narrative proposed that there have been in Canada two 'founding peoples,' and insisted (as did Graham Spry) that the continued existence of both peoples is contingent upon survival of the broader Canadian Confederation. In the federalist narrative, then, the emphasis is on Canada as 'homeland' for *all* Canadians.[27]

Both of these stories are 'true,' Robinson would say, in the sense that evidence can be marshalled to support each one. On the other hand, however, as symbolic maps, they are mutually exclusive, and by the rules of logic both cannot simultaneously be 'true.' Nonetheless, the stories provide backdrops for, and hence colour in their different ways, events occurring within Quebec. In particular, they affected press coverage of the first referendum.

Press coverage of the referendum, Robinson argued, *even in principle* could not be 'neutral' or objective: one or other of two mutually inconsistent stories unavoidably formed the implicit context. Likewise readers perusing press accounts will have at the back of their minds one or other of these narratives, affecting in dichotomous ways their interpretations of events.

Political Economy of Press Coverage

Apart from the narratives that reporters and readers bring to events, there is a second aspect as well that colours the news. Although in previous analyses Professor Robinson downplayed power considerations affecting news reporting,[28] in her treatment of referendum coverage she gave fuller play to the tendency of the press to select and present material in accordance with the owners' political-economic predilections and aspirations. Although a majority of French-speaking journalists favoured sovereignty-association ('Oui') during the 1980 referendum campaign,[29] media owners were opposed ('Non'),[30] and consequently both newspaper and television media (according to Robinson) presented material partial to the federal, or 'Non' side. Robinson concluded that the referendum case studies demonstrated unequivocally that 'corporate control extends beyond political activity to editorial publication.'[31] Although stylistically conforming to the ideals of balance and objectivity, she continued, media personnel (as guided and constrained by media owners) maintained 'total control over their own performance space,'[32] and thereby were able *unobtrusively* to favour the 'Non' side.

Robinson identified several ways whereby media in their coverage maintained *stylistic* objectivity and *ostensible* balance, all the while unobtrusively favouring the 'Non' side. In her book she addressed these means exhaustively, and here we note briefly but several of them:

- *Linkages.* Release of the Parti Québécois's White Paper coincided with a one-day walk-out by Quebec civil servants over wages; English-language television stations linked the two stories, making the unveiling of the referendum paper seem chaotic.[33]
- *Voices.* Both English- and French-language dailies chose only Liberal ('Non') sources to comment on the tabling of the Parti Québécois's White Paper.[34] Ample reprinting of the White Paper gave an air of balance or objectivity to the news coverage, although it would have been a dedicated reader who would wade through the mass of material. Regarding television coverage, Robinson noted that separatist premier René Lévesque's statements were generally used as a basis for interpretation by television commentators, whereas those of federalist opposition leader Claude Ryan remained uninterpreted. She observed the same practice in treating party spokespersons: 'Statements from the Parti Québecois were interpreted while those from the Liberals

were rendered verbatim.'[35] The press's quoting practices, she added, 'are rhetorical devices.'[36]

- *Framing.* Every reported event is 'framed,' which means it is given a context. On the one hand, context provides material for interpreting the reported event and encourages a particular interpretation; on the other, the reported event serves to illustrate or 'prove' the frame.[37] Referendum coverage was framed as an election, and consequently it 'lacked all historical perspective and ... featured a small number of arguments made over and over.'[38] Emphasis was accorded campaign events, personalities of the leaders and strategies, rather than the substance of the issue.

- *Imagery.* On 7 March 1980, one of the English-language television stations began its newscast with the image of a car struggling up a slippery hill; the visual was accompanied both by dramatic music and by graphics referring to a long-standing strike of blue-collar workers that prevented snow removal; the next shot was of people walking on unshovelled sidewalks in a snow storm, and the headline on the screen linked that image to results of a referendum poll released that day.[39]

- *Stereotyping, labelling.* In the referendum coverage diverse social groups, political party representatives, business people, and others were grouped or stereotyped into polarized teams or camps. Likewise the leaders' personae 'became stereotyped into the smoke-surrounded, populist orator René Lévesque ... and his stern, intellectual adversary, Claude Ryan.' In one news segment both Ryan and Lévesque were asked to comment on poll results; in the clip the Liberal leader, Ryan, was alone and shot at eye level in front of an office building; Lévesque, by contrast, was shot from above, surrounded by a chaotic crowd of reporters inside a radio station. 'This manner of shooting,' Robinson commented, 'evoked the reason–emotion opposition that was recurrent throughout the referendum campaign.'[40]

Despite the common objective to support the 'Non' side, French and English coverage differed remarkably. Robinson attributed this primarily to differences in audience characteristics. The French press, she explained, had a heterogeneous audience comprising not only those favouring sovereignty-association, but also those opposed, and as well people wavering who perhaps did not know (given an ambiguous referendum question) exactly what the issue was. Therefore, in her view, the French-language *La Presse* opted for a 'documentary approach' to give stylistic balance, quoting verbatim large portions of the Quebec government's policy document with but little commentary. The audience for English-language media, in contrast, was uniformly against the provincial government's initiative, and so the English *Gazette* chose 'an oral approach,' affording space to provincial opposition leader Claude Ryan to speak in his own voice against the document even while denying Quebec premier, René Lévesque, an opportunity to speak in favour of it.[41]

Robinson concluded that news discourse constitutes part of the symbolic environment whereby reality is defined. As she put it, 'symbol systems impact on social reality.'[42] These news discourses, therefore, are part and parcel of the 'processes of political persuasion.'[43]

FEMINISM AND COMMUNICATION STUDIES

Consistent with her press studies and general ontological stance, Professor Robinson placed the 'feminist perspective' in communication studies, which she has helped pioneer, within the context of competing intellectual paradigms.[44] Reviewing three broad approaches to the study of women – conservative/functionalist, feminist, and Marxist – Robinson declared that the three, although making important contributions, 'leave out key issues in human behavior, [namely] the nature of ideology as symbolic production, and its role in the human enterprise.'[45] Once ideology is recognized to be important for gender studies, it follows that the discipline of communication has much to contribute to feminist scholarship: gender roles and stereotypes, after all, are socially constructed through communicative interaction. Sex and gender are 'different things,' Robinson pointed out, the first being fixed and defined biologically, the second being culturally constructed and unstable.[46] The complete study of gender therefore must encompass symbolization, media, and patterns of social communication.

Robinson's approach to gender is 'critical' in so far as it explores the conjunction between gender and power, and how this conjunction plays out in *all* communicative situations. Symbolic approaches to the study of gender raise questions concerning both the *control* of ideological production and the *content* of ideological forms.[47] Studies concerning ideological *control*, Robinson affirmed, show that women are significantly underrepresented in institutions where ideology is produced: in Canada and Europe 'women are virtually absent from the ranks of media owners'; nor do they figure prominently in the top ranks of the Canadian civil service; moreover, they are 'virtually absent from the managerial level of daily newspapers'[48] and they continue to be found 'overwhelmingly' in the lower ranks of the university professoriate.[49]

Concerning the *content* of ideological forms, Robinson remarked that men and women consistently are depicted as differing with regard to occupation, behavioural patterns, personality traits, and marital and parenting status. Women are but rarely covered in daily news shows, and when they are it is usually from traditional viewpoints. This 'taken-for-granted world of sex role portrayal,' she commented, socializes women in the matter of life goals. Women's 'objective inequality' is thereby masked as 'mere gender specialization.' Furthermore, due to the media-control aspects (reviewed above), women have been 'denied access to the very instruments by which an alternative ideology can be constructed.'[50]

Symbolic approaches to gender studies, Robinson affirmed, have helped open up completely new areas of inquiry. Following Kenneth Burke, symbolic interactionists have developed notions of 'frame' and 'script' and have employed the metaphor of drama to analyse social behaviour. The implication is that men's and women's behaviours are 'scripted' and that 'common sense' or habitual interpretations of these behaviours make 'objective inequalities'[51] seem normal – that is, it's just the way things are, and must be!

In their detailed empirical studies of employment trends in Canadian media, however, Robinson and colleague Armande Saint-Jean reported 'resounding' improvement in the status of women over the past two decades regarding overall participation in the media labour force, remuneration, and news assignments and positions within the managerial hierarchy.[52] (This is not to say, of course, that women have yet attained parity with men; for example, in the mid 1990s only 27 per cent of print journalists employed by dailies and 9 per cent of the editors-in-chief in the Canadian Daily Newspaper Association were women.)

Expanding on her feminist interests in women's status in the power structure, Robinson investigated changes in media narratives regarding female politicians for the Royal Commission on Electoral Reform. There she took the changes in media narratives as being indicative of continued male/female power differentials, not only in public life but also in the ideological preconceptions of reporters.[53] Three narrative strategies demonstrate these preconceptions and the consequent marginalization of women leaders in the political realm. Up to the 1960s Robinson found that women politicians were depicted as the 'wife of ...' or 'widow of ...,' 'spinster,' 'femme facile,' and 'club woman,' indicating that women's political legitimacy was narratively established either in relationship to a male partner or as an accepted public role for single women. The 'transitional narrative' between 1970 and 1985, however, as influenced by the emerging ideology of feminism, began to create a new descriptive regime that was superficially more egalitarian. In this period women politicians were described as 'superwomen,' 'champions,' and 'members of a male opposition gang.' Such labels, however, Robinson commented, either turned female politicians into unattainable icons or described their contribution to party politics in relation to male role models (e.g., good 'team players'), rather than in terms of their own leadership capabilities. In the 1990s, Robinson concluded, the narrative changed again; although now 'more egalitarian,' it is still 'much narrower' for women politicians than for males and it continues to stress women politicians' personal characteristics (dress, looks, hair style) over the substance of their speeches.

More generally, Robinson advises that 'naming' people by culturally infused gender categories continues to create 'presences and absences, accesses and exclusions, spaces for voices to talk and spaces where as wo/man one has to remain silent.' She adds, 'Gender also creates ways of exchanging and not exchanging information, help, emotional sustenance, ethical enlightenment, and human closeness. Gender does not *cause* communication practice, it *is* communication practice and this practice is structured by deep-seated assumptions about inequality.'[54]

SOME QUESTIONS

This concluding section addresses some issues concerning Professor Robinson's political economy, places her thought within the larger context of foundational Canadian communication thought, and addresses the significance of her writing for the present and future.

Political Economy
Gertrude Robinson is at her best when acknowledging that news discourse employs 'symbolic conventions'[55] that help construct 'world pictures'[56] for readers. Introducing an essay collection on the New World Information Order, for example, she noted that 'all journalistic

reports [are] reconstructions of events which include an inevitable in-terpretive bias.' Purported 'objectivity' in reporting, she continued, is little more than a 'strategic ritual' whose main purpose is to protect the reporter from criticism.[57]

Robinson contended that her 'symbolic approach' to understanding news reports sees through stylistic objectivity, as it assumes from the outset that 'there are no neutral media systems.'[58] Media systems for Robinson, then, more often than not, are like the school and church: they *'reinforce* the general principles and outlooks often called 'ideolo-gies' accepted by the society in which they are embedded.'[59] In doing this they are part and parcel of the power structure.

By making these claims, Gertrude Robinson assuredly qualifies as a political economist. Moreover, as noted above, she has repeatedly drawn attention to power differentials through her analyses of gender, again making 'political economist' appropriate in describing Gertrude Robinson.

But hers is a moderate political economy – at least when compared to that of her mentors, Dallas Smythe, George Gerbner, and Herbert Schiller. 'Reinforce' in connection with media's ideological work is, after all, a much milder term than, say, 'inculcate' (Smythe in fact used the terms 'brainwash' and 'brain rinse' in this regard). To imply, as she does, that principles and outlooks reside already with the public, in other words, is much less disquieting than to avow that dominant groups create, control, and drum into people's hearts and minds false principles and erroneous interpretations that are advantageous to themselves. Robinson always insists that audiences co-construct the meanings of media out-puts and that 'truth' is merely consensual, whereas 'realists' or materi-alists like Smythe declare firmly that there is indeed an objective existence to the material conditions and that audiences can choose only from a narrow range of media offerings, few of which are unduly problematic for hegemonic interests.

In personal correspondence Professor Robinson explained that she began her academic career strictly as a political economist. However, with time, she became convinced that political economy needs to be supplemented, first by interactionist theory, and second (a conclusion she drew still later in her career) by feminist perspectives. She ex-plained: 'The reason for this is that political economy has a very simple notion of "human agency." Human agency involves individual and group factors such as cognitive frames, what we call "passive" knowledges [*sic*] in a social situation, as well as the unique experiences of individuals and groups in a particular social setting.' She added:

> Smythe's assertion that audiences can choose only from a narrow range of
> media offerings to make sense of a social situation is theoretically oversim-
> plified. The following example demonstrates how viewers/readers bring
> to this 'narrow range of media offerings' (a notion with which I agree) *a*
> *range of interpretive skills* which grow out of their passive knowledges [sic]
> of a given social situation ... This might be the president of McGill claim-
> ing that the university has "greatly improved" the working condition of
> women and minority professors; in this situation I might laugh out loud
> and exclaim: "Dream on," an interpretation which makes NO SENSE
> without taking account of the interpretive skills mentioned above.[60]

We might summarize Robinson's break with the political economy of
Smythe/Schiller/Gerbner by noting that the dispute revolves, essentially, upon the questions of whether and to what extent hegemonic
interests can and do homogenize interpretive patterns in audiences,
causing them to interpret messages in the 'preferred way,'[61] and the
extent to which media messages are indeed polysemic. Whereas interpretive control resides with message propagators in the view of Smythe/
Schiller/Gerbner, for Robinson each individual's interpretation depends
primarily upon the group(s) of which she is a member.

There is a further aspect of Robinson's political economy deserving
comment. This has to do with the criterion of truth. With regard to her
analyses of press systems, she stated,'Our symbolic focus is thus not so
much interested in the "truthfulness" or "adequacy" of foreign affairs
portrayals ... as in the social values informing and underlying their
construction. These values indicate what journalists consider important
in the world environment.'[62]

In her recent book on the Quebec referendum she elaborated:

> The quality of interpretations and their generalizability ... is guaranteed
> not by a single set of truth values, but by the *systematic* way in which
> methods are employed and our interpretations fit in with the accounts of
> others. Our interpretations in this study meet this standard. [In the Refer-
> endum book] the additional evidence we used was provided by voting
> statistics, government documents, ... and the accounts of participants, as
> well as the reports of political scientists and sociologists, and of the politi-
> cal actors involved.[63]

In these statements Professor Robinson once again is demonstrating her agreement with the position of Thomas Kuhn and the symbolic-interactionists, and implicitly her rejection of, say, of Karl Popper. The 'truth' of a proposition, Kuhn argued, depends primarily on the 'habits of thought' of the given community; its members consciously or unconsciously perceive selectively, and therefore bring forth only those data that support their 'truth.' For Popper, on the other hand, truth is objectively given and is testable; scientific propositions yield *predictions* that, if and when fulfilled, warrant tentative acceptance of the theory making those predictions.[64] Robinson, therefore, can be interpreted as arguing one pole of the ancient dialectic of idealism versus realism, as typified in our day by the polar positions of symbolic-interactionism and positivistic science.

Robinson's own proposition, however, that 'truth' is group-specific and consensual, itself becomes problematic, it may be pointed out, once that proposition is understood to issue (according to her analysis) from *her* membership of *her* community. Other communities may be equally correct (according to her criterion of truth as mere consensus within a community) in judging truth to be objective and universal; after all, that is *their* consensus.

There is yet a further irony. On the one hand, Robinson berates political economy for downplaying human agency. On the other, however, she judges 'truth' to be group-specific and as being an outcome of symbolic interaction. We may ask, therefore, on what basis an individual can choose *which* symbolic community to be a member of, that is, *whose truth* to accept, if truth is regarded merely as an outcome of membership, not as a criterion for selecting membership. In denying the possibility of recognizing objective truth, then, Professor Robinson would also seem to minimize human agency.

The question of the objectivity versus the artefactual nature of truth arose significantly in her commentary prepared for the edited volume *Information and Communication in Economics,* in which she engaged in a lively exchange with renowned political economist Edward S. Herman. In the original article, Herman compared news coverage by the American press in the early 1990s of Cuba and El Salvador. He noted disparities in tone, language, intensity, and selectivity in the reporting on these two countries, and concluded that policy and ideology 'inject observably profound bias into the news coverage,' and further that 'a political agenda clearly overwhelms professional [news] values.'[65] In her commentary, Professor Robinson did not address directly Herman's comparative content analysis; rather she challenged what she took to be his implicit ontology. She charged that Herman presumed 'there is a reality "out there" which is directly apprehensible by the observer, ... that there is a one-to-one type of correspondence between facts/events and their descriptions'[66] - assumptions totally inconsistent with Robinson's social-constructionist world-view. Given her ontological position that 'truth' is contingent upon the communicative group of which one is a member, it is also evidently unconscionable to be critical of a press system since it is simply and ineluctably selecting and reporting events from the perspective of its own myth or narrative.

Political economy certainly entails comparing texts and relating their content and presentation to the interests and outlook of the organizations originating them. This task Robinson carried out flawlessly in her book on the referendum. But at some stage, one can argue, political economy must also peer at the phenomenal world and compare media coverage to that, for ultimately it is in the material, phenomenal world that people live, eat, work, suffer pain and bereavement, seek shelter, are murdered or 'disappear.' George Gerbner, one of Robinson's mentors, is renowned for comparing the world as it appears on television with social reality revealed through social statistics; he charged, for instance, that mass media make human affairs seem to be more violent than they really are. We also reviewed Dallas Smythe's early content analyses and his contention that television presents a distorted view of reality. This, too, is precisely what commentators such as Noam Chomsky, Edward Herman, and James Winter do by calling attention to the types of international news stories that are systematically underplayed or left unreported by mainline media. According to political economists such as Gerbner, different depictions of reality, while certainly benefiting different interests, *can be judged by how well they accord with or depict the phenomenal world*. This aspect of *judgment* respecting truth value is what ultimately makes Gerbner and like-minded colleagues *critical* theorists in Lazarsfeld's sense of the term, and what makes that appellation less apt in reference to Robinson.

Robinson's approach to the political economy of media studies, nonetheless, is at times proactive, particularly when it comes to representations of women. She argues that women should be treated equally with men, that historically they have not been so treated, and that media (largely controlled by males) represent women as inferior to men. To bring about desirable social change, she maintains, media should take the lead and begin representing women on the basis of equality, her presumption evidently being that *social reality will follow the media's representational lead*. Here Robinson is presenting a much closer correspondence between media depictions and lived realities than she does when addressing aspects of news coverage.

Note again, however, the marked differences between her position and how Gerbner, Smythe, and other political economists see things: these latter commentators argue that social change can be effected only if and when *media depicts reality (i.e., the social conditions) more closely*; otherwise, they argue, we continue to be deluded. In the case of gender relations, they might argue, media depictions of ideal equality would serve principally to obscure a pressing social issue and constitute thereby yet another force for sustaining inequality.

It was possibly John Grierson who came closest to bridging the gap between these dialectically opposed positions. Grierson argued that media should forcefully represent stark reality, but always from an idealist (or value-laden) perspective. Grierson is the common ground between these otherwise dichotomous, non-communicative positions.

ROBINSON AND CANADIAN COMMUNICATION THOUGHT

Robinson's analysis is connected to that of Harold Innis in several ways. First, she is in accord with Innis in claiming that there is 'a dialectical interdependence between human beings and their natural and social environments.'[67] Second, in maintaining that even scientific work is inevitably situated in a particular place and time, she at least recalls Innis's insistence that theory *ought* to be indigenous to each locality. In her studies of gender, moreover, like Innis, she sees bidirectional connectivity between symbolization and the material conditions. Finally, in apparently denying that correspondence to objective reality can be used as a criterion for judging news reports (and indeed scientific/social scientific theories), Robinson may be seen as fulfilling Innis's prediction that in space-bound cultures there will be an erosion of value and meaning: In denying the very *possibility* of congruence between verbal structures and material reality, Professor Robinson, in other words, is thoroughly postmodern and echoes, as we shall see, Northrop Frye.

Robinson's work in some respects is closely aligned to that of C.B. Macpherson. Macpherson's objective, it will be recalled, was to place scholarship in service of the struggle for a political order that blended the freedoms hitherto associated with capitalism and the social justice of socialism. Such also has been a main thrust of Professor Robinson's work and is a major reason why she afforded so much attention during the 1970s to media practices in Yugoslavia, that country then being for her 'a bridge between capitalist and socialist ideas and organization.'[68] In her work on feminism, in particular, she has been a protagonist in a struggle for sexual equality, even as Macpherson's scholarship was intended to promote equality in terms of property. Indeed the central place accorded property in Macpherson's work is paralleled by gender in Robinson's, particularly when she contends, for example, that culturally infused gender categories create 'presences and absences, accesses and exclusions, spaces for voices to talk and spaces where as wo/man one has to remain silent.'

Finally, a brief comparison of Robinson's ontology as it pertains to communication studies with that of George Grant seems warranted. Grant and Robinson were agreed that there are no 'raw data,' that selections are made according to one's predispositions from an infinitely complex material reality, and hence that 'fact' is never separate from 'value.' Knowledge for both these social constructionists is subjective and/or a matter of social convention. Grant maintained, however, that there is Truth, whether that be called Natural Law, Natural Justice, or Perfection; that this constitutes an unchanging ground against which one can appraise socially constructed truths and practices. In Robinson's writings, the ideal against which actual practices and conditions can be appraised was confined largely to that of sexual equality. Furthermore, Robinson appears to believe that societies are much more fragmented in making interpretations than Grant believed. For Grant there have been but two interpretative epochs, the antiquarian and the modern, whereas, for Robinson, modern society is so thoroughly fragmented that consensus between or among social groups is highly problematic.

FOR THE NEW MILLENNIUM

Studying Robinson's work alongside the theorizing and media practices of such figures as Innis, Grierson, Smythe, Gerbner, Herman, and Schiller raises profound questions on the role of media in helping bring about social reform. In our day, after all, media are represented as providing 'simulations' and 'simulacra,' the implication being that people 'live' in mediated worlds of manufactured images that are 'virtually' as real as the material world in which they move about, eat, and breathe. The question arises, therefore, can or do these mediated worlds provide intimations of ideals towards which people can and should strive? Or are they, rather, and must they be, devices that divert attention from real social problems? And exactly *whose* ideals are being depicted and emphasized in hyper-reality, anyway: those of advertisers and politicos, or reformers, as Robinson and Gerbner would recommend? And can we even talk about improvement if we deny that, in principle, we can judge one representation of reality as being more accurate or truthful than another?

As we enter the new millennium, Robinson's work, particularly on the October Crisis and the Quebec referendum, informs us that news reporting is never neutral, that conventions of 'objectivity' and 'balance' notwithstanding the slant of any particular press system is quite predictable, given the economic/political interests of media owners, and that the 'reality' painted by news media affects issues both large and small in everyday life. As well, Robinson's work points to the importance for feminist scholarship of communicative action, the social construction of gender, and how gender, in turn, configures social interaction. These are major contributions indeed.

10

The Communication Thought of
NORTHROP FRYE (1912–1991)

Man lives not directly or nakedly in nature like the animals, but within a mythological universe, a body of assumptions and beliefs developed from his existential concerns.

– The Great Code, xviii

ABOUT NORTHROP FRYE

Author of more than thirty books, literary theorist Northrop Frye remains Canada's most internationally acclaimed scholar.[1] Herman Northrop Frye was born at Sherbrooke, Quebec, on 14 July 1912, to a devout Methodist family. His parents planned a career in the ministry for their son,[2] and as a child Northrop was receptive to the idea. In his youth Northrop Frye read many books, a favourite being *Pilgrim's Progress*.

In 1919, the family hardware business having failed, the Fryes moved to Moncton, New Brunswick. There they lived in a state of 'shabby genteel poverty.'[3] Awkward and bookish, young Northrop felt quite out of place, as he did not relish the sports favoured by most of the city's youth.[4] Years later he recounted that the dissonance he felt then made him 'extremely introverted and drawn in on myself,'[5] even to the point of living 'in an imaginary dream world.'[6] Indeed, by the time he reached maturity, Frye's shyness had become legendary and perhaps helps explain his expansive enthusiasm for art and literature, which, for Frye, became the sole means of escaping the banality, absurdity, and cruelty of everyday life.[7]

Frye's scholarship was shaped also by a series of 'epiphanies.' The first, characterized by his biographer John Ayre as 'a parody of the Methodist conversion experience,'[8] occurred while walking to high school in Moncton. Quite suddenly, he no longer regarded the Bible as being divinely inspired. Moreover, at that instant, God ceased to be for him a transcendent Being. Nor did Frye waver from these deontological principles for the rest of his life.

'There is no divinity in Sky, nature or thought superior to our selves,' he wrote confidently a couple of decades later. 'There is no form of life superior to our own.'[9] Nonetheless, and somewhat paradoxically, Frye retained a keen interest in the Bible, and he continued to study and write about it – more on account of its symbolism and cultural consequences, however, than for its presumed historicity or to attain divine revelation.[10]

As well he continued to think and write about God. Rather than being an 'objective centrality,' however, 'God' became, for Frye, a diffuse ideal: 'the totality of all imagination.'[11] As he once put it, God is just another name for 'human culture' or for 'civilization.'[12] In being creative, Frye proposed, 'we perceive *as* God,'[13] and the more imaginative or creative we are, the more closely we approach transcendence, and *become* God. He wrote: 'Man in his creative acts and perceptions is God, and God is Man.'[14] This unification of 'God' and 'Man,' he insisted, is essential: otherwise, 'you have merely God who is a scarecrow in the sky and merely man who is a psychotic ape,'[15] that is, an animal cursed with the capacity to recognize the absurdity of the human condition but bereft of any means for doing something about it. Frye's belief in the potential divinity of humans and in the humanness of divinity was the main reason he continued to call himself Christian. For him, 'the central form of Christianity is its vision of the humanity of God and the divinity of risen Man.'[16]

After majoring in English and philosophy at Victoria College at the University of Toronto between 1929 and 1933, Frye began studying theology at the same university. Upon graduating in 1936, he was ordained into the United Church of Canada.[17] He had previously decided, however, not to be active in the ministry; his intent, rather, was to become a professor of English literature.

Frye experienced a second epiphany in 1931 while staying in the YMCA in Edmonton. There he discovered *The Decline of the West* by Oswald Spengler.[18] As Frye explained, 'I suddenly got a vision of coherence. That's the only way I can describe it; things began to form patterns and make sense.'[19] Spengler helped form in Frye's mind an 'organic and cyclical conception'[20] of literary history and culture. He showed Frye how 'all the cultural products of a given age, medieval or Baroque or contemporary, form a unity that can be felt or intuited, though not demonstrated, a sense of unity that approximates the feeling that a human culture is a single larger body, a giant immersed in time.'[21]

Later, Frye dismissed Spengler, however, as a 'stupid bastard' with a 'muzzy, right-wing, Teutonic, folkish' mind.[22] Nonetheless, *Decline of the West* wrought its effect, and Frye 'practically slept with Spengler under [his] pillow for several years.'[23]

Besides Spengler, another formative influence was Sir James Frazer (1854–1941), whose *The Golden Bough*[24] was, for Frye, 'a kind of grammar of the human imagination.'[25] Frye first read *The Golden Bough* in 1934–5 and felt 'a whole new world opening out.'[26] According to him, Frazer's book is not really about what people may or may not have done in a remote and savage past; rather, it is an account of 'what the human imagination does when it tries to express itself about the great mysteries, the mysteries of life and death and after-life.'[27] By exploring unconscious symbolism, Frye remarked, *The Golden Bough* parallels works by Freud and Jung, albeit at a social rather than an individual or psychological level. Frye believed that Frazer demonstrated conclusively the importance of myth or story for *all* societies, including our own.[28] As with Spengler, however, Frye became disenchanted with Frazer, complaining that, apart from 'one tremendous intuition ... he had a rather commonplace mind.'[29]

The one of whom Frye was persistently in awe, and to whom he continued to pay much homage, was, of course, the English poet, painter, and engraver William Blake (1757–1832).[30] Frye was wont to ascribe everything he knew to Blake.[31]

Frye first encountered works by Blake while a student at Victoria College, but his most dramatic and seminal encounter was two years later. He was preparing a paper, due the next day, on Blake's *Milton*. According to his recollection, 'it was around three in the morning when suddenly the universe just broke open, and I've never been, as they say, the same since.'[32] At that moment Frye had the sensation

of an enormous number of things making sense that had been scattered and unrelated before. In other words, it was a mythological frame taking hold ... Toward the end, I had the feeling that what united Blake and Milton, for all their differences – one was a Puritan and the other was very

much an eighteenth-century nonconformist – was their common dependence on the Bible and the fact that the Bible had a framework of mythology
that both Milton and Blake had entered into.[33]

In these three flashes of illumination (there were others), we find in
embryo much of Frye's subsequent scholarship: his rejection of biblical
literalism; his quest for symbolic and narrative coherence or unity; his
locating the Bible as the source of that coherence; and his insistence that
we live within a storied or mythological universe. Years later, Frye
remarked that, although the total duration of his times of enlightenment had been less than an hour, they consumed his life.[34]

Frye studied next at Oxford, but his time there was not satisfying. In
1939, degree almost in hand, he was appointed to the permanent staff of
Victoria College. Eventually he rose to be the college's principal, and
then its chancellor. At Victoria College, Frye was a legendary teacher.[35]
Even from the beginning, it was only *after* lecturing that he made notes –
on the ideas that emerged during class time.[36] His aim always was to
teach from within the personality and thought structure of the particular author, whether Dante, Spenser, Blake, or Milton.[37] He always insisted that 'the authority in what you're teaching never comes from
yourself ... it always comes from what you're teaching, and you try to
make yourself a transparent instrument of that.'[38]

In his role as an educator, Frye's goal was, in important respects,
similar to Innis's. Both were at pains to avert closure. Frye maintained
that the teacher's task is to 'liberate' students' minds – 'a militant
activity' that requires increasing students' facility with language. Frye
insisted that, since 'everything we know is formed out of words and
numbers,'[39] real freedom comes 'only from articulateness, the ability to
produce as well as respond to verbal structures ... What we express
badly we do not know.'[40] Nor did Frye believe in cramming information into students' heads, for, he stated, they are already filled with
more information than they can handle as it is. Instead he strove to 're-
create' in students' minds what they already knew, at least potentially,
and thereby break up habits of thought and repressions that inhibited
fuller awareness. Hence, he declared, 'it is the teacher, rather than the
student, who asks most of the questions ... To answer a question ... is to
consolidate the mental level on which the question is asked. Unless
something is kept in reserve, suggesting the possibility of better and
fuller questions, the student's mental advance is blocked.'[41] Frye did
not wish to impose closure on *readers* either. His style, often aphoristic,

is seldom analytical, and, like Innis, he often covers a huge ground in but a few sentences.

Frye received many honours. He became a Fellow of the Royal Society of Canada in 1951. He received the Governor General's Award for Non-Fiction (for *Northrop Frye on Shakespeare*) in 1987. He was appointed a Companion of the Order of Canada in 1972. In 1974 he was made an honorary Fellow of Merton College, Oxford. He lectured at more than 100 universities around the world. By all standards, he was a distinguished and celebrated scholar.

Northrop Frye died at Toronto on 23 January 1991. His final book, *The Double Vision,* appeared a few months later – 'a shorter and more accessible version,' as he described it, of his two longer works on the Bible: *The Great Code* and *Words with Power.* In the preface, Frye made an oblique reference to a favourite book of his childhood, declaring that the thoughts which followed should be interpreted 'as proceeding [not] from a judgment seat of final conviction, but from a rest stop on a pilgrimage, however near the pilgrimage may now be to its close.'[42]

SYNOPSIS

This chapter reviews two major areas of Frye's thought. First is his theory of perception and cognition, which relates closely to his theory of reality. For this we focus particularly on *Fearful Symmetry* (1947), his first book. His discussion there of William Blake's prophetic works evolved into his contrasting of two ontologies – the scientific and the mythopoeic – in subsequent writings. The second focus is Frye's exploration of interactions between these two ontologies, as manifested particularly in the dialectic of literature and society. Major publications in this regard include *The Modern Century* (1967) and *The Critical Path* (1971). There he theorized that literature emerges from society, forms a part of the culture, and helps transform the society. Furthermore, in these books Frye considered the properties and consequences of various means of communication – oral, written, electronic. He maintained that each mode of transmission has distinct effects.

It is worth noting that, although in his later writings Frye explored some political-economic dimensions of myth and literature, he missed the opportunity Blake presented him. Blake, of course, is still renowned as the social critic who attacked the dark satanic mills of the industrial revolution, an autocratic and unfeeling church, an inhumane state, disease-infested streets, child labour, and exploitation of all kinds. The poem '*London*' captures well the materialist realism and radical dissent of William Blake:

> I wander through each charter'd street,
> Near where the charter'd Thames does flow,
> And mark in every face I meet
> Marks of weakness, marks of woe.
>
> In every cry of every Man,
> In every Infant's cry of fear,
> In every voice, in every ban,
> The mind-forg'd manacles I hear.
>
> How the Chimney-sweeper's cry
> Every black'ning Church appalls,
> And the hapless Soldier's sigh
> Runs in blood down Palace walls.
>
> But most thro' midnight streets I hear
> How the youthful Harlot's curse
> Blasts the new-born Infant's tear,
> And blights with plagues the Marriage hearse.[43]

Although references to passages like these are not absent in *Fearful Symmetry*, they are rare. The emphasis is entirely on Blake's *imaginative* vision.

TWO 'COSMOLOGIES'

Fearful Symmetry **versus** *Anatomy of Criticism*
In his preface to the 1969 edition of *Fearful Symmetry*, Frye maintained that people generally accept or dwell in one or other of two 'cosmologies.'[44] One is the 'realist' or objectivist world-view, which conceives the universe as existing independently of the thinker or observer. The task of knowing for those subscribing to this world-view or ontology is to understand the world 'as it is.'[45] For Frye and William Blake, however, this outlook is unduly passive, which is why Blake complained of the 'sleep' of Locke, Newton, and Bacon.[46]

The second 'cosmology' is imaginative, subjectivist, and mythological. This was the lived ontology of Blake and of his disciple, Northrop

Frye. It is much the older of the two and, in *Fearful Symmetry,* said to be much the superior. There are, Frye acknowledged, many imaginative world-views, but every one, he insisted, positions *humans* at the very centre of things. The earth, for example, according to mythopoeic understanding, was created for human enjoyment. As soon as a person accepts that proposition, he added, the environment takes on 'a human shape.'[47]

However, in his next book, *Anatomy of Criticism* (1957), Frye shifted ground. There he championed the scientific world-view, which allows no place of special importance for humans in a universe subject to chance and necessity. In *Anatomy,* Frye even proposed inaugurating a *science* of literary criticism, that is, a body of knowledge concerning literary works that progresses, is empirical, and is value-free![48]

For the remainder of his life, Frye continued to see much merit in objective science, but oscillated between these two, antithetical, 'cosmologies.' In the end, we will argue, he did not achieve a balance or synthesis between them; rather, for him, they cancelled one another out.

Fearful Symmetry and the Two 'Cosmologies'

Typified by Ezikiel's image of God's chariot with its wheels within wheels, Blake's mythological outlook, or 'cosmology,' according to Frye, conceived the universe as being in a state of perpetual flux, 'continuously transformed by applications of the human imagination.'[49] For Blake the human mind indeed can 'make a world from a grain of sand, and heaven of a wildflower.'[50]

Frye's own mythopoeic world-view, derived from Blake and as expressed in *Fearful Symmetry,* can be summarized by a number of axioms linking perception, imagination, the will, experience, knowledge, and truth. These propositions, in fact, are at the core of certain modern schools of communication thought – mentalism, social constructionism, symbolic interactionism, and postmodernism, for example. This subsection sets forth six that can at least be inferred from Frye's book on Blake.

- *Perception as Creation.* The first concerns the unification through mental experience of subject and object, of image and form, of perceiver and perceived,[51] and hence of time and space.[52] 'Mental experience,' Frye proclaimed, 'is a union of a perceiving subject and a perceived object.'[53] But, he added, this union or synthesis is not what it might seem: the senses being organs of the mind means that *'all knowledge comes from mental experience.'* In saying this, Frye in effect dissolved the dialectic of objectivity/subjectivity, or of realism/mentalism, opting rather for the single pole of subjectivity or mentalism. 'Unification,' then, entails dissolving objects into subjects, the known into the knower. According to Frye, unless and until matter in the universe is perceived, it has neither image nor form. He explained, 'If there is such a thing as a key to Blake's thought, it is the fact that these two words [i.e., form and image] mean the same thing to him.'[54]

For many people, of course, *form* denotes an objectively given property of an object, whereas *image* denotes a subjective rendering or perception of a form. For Frye and Blake, however, 'objects' *are* subjective images; forms are imagined. This is the case because the properties of forms are realized (i.e., made real) only when perceived. Frye attested: 'Nothing is real beyond the imaginative patterns *men* make of reality.'[55]

- *Double Vision.* Frye and Blake were certainly dialectical thinkers. In *Fearful Symmetry*, Frye extolled *double vision*, that is, a capacity to see simultaneously the fallen (material/fragmented) world and an unfallen (imaginatively united) one. Fallen or normal vision sees things 'as they are,' complete with antitheses, oppositions, struggles, fragmentations. The imaginative vision, by contrast, creatively reconstructs and makes whole, thereby transcending the absurdity or nihilism of single vision. Blake *could* see both ways, and Frye was fond of quoting these lines as proof:

> For double the vision my Eyes do see,
> And a double vision is always with me.
> With my inward Eye 'tis an Old Man grey;
> With my outward, a Thistle across my way.[56]

Indeed, according to Frye, it was essential that Blake be able to do this. The poet/mystic was sometimes considered mad on account of apparitions.[57] But Blake was not mad, Frye insisted, for he always retained the capacity to see with an 'outward eye,' thereby keeping his visions in check.[58]

Essential though normal vision is, it is through creative vision, that is, through an innate capacity to unify, that humans approach divinity. Transcendence, for Frye, meant being or feeling at one with the cosmos. 'Heaven *is* this world as it appears to the awakened imagination,' Frye declared, and 'Hell ... similarly [is] this world as it appears to the repressed imagination.'[59]

- *Perception, Will, and Learning.* A third principle concerns the centrality of the will and learning to perception. Perception is 'a mental act ... The eye does not see; [it is simply] a lens for the mind to look through.'[60] Every 'acting man' *directs* the senses. Perception, accordingly, is not just a mental act, but also an act of will. Frye declared: 'The wise man *will choose* what he wants to do with his perceptions just as he will choose the books he wants to read.'[61] Being an act of will implies further that perception (or imagination) is learned, not imposed upon the senses, and a person with much learning is experienced in choosing wisely what to pay attention to.[62]

- *'Truth' as Imaginative.* Fourth, according to Frye, people differ markedly in their capacities to imagine: a 'visionary,' he wrote, is one who charges the objects of her perception 'with a new intensity of symbolism.'[63] The 'idiot,' by contrast, possesses paltry imaginative prowess. Most people have imaginative capacities between these extremes, but the point remains that each will tend imaginatively to construct images unique to herself. Indeed, Frye averred, 'there are exactly as many kinds of reality as there are men';[64] but, he added quickly, the visions of the most imaginative are *more* real or more true.[65]

- *Shared Reality.* Despite this, people often do have a sense of shared reality. Shared reality stems in part from the work of theorists ('abstract reasoners'). An abstract reasoner, or analyst, is one who attempts to impose an *independent* existence on what she perceives. To do this, however, she must exercise only a 'normal' or average level of imagination. Frye illustrated this process of normalization by quoting Blake on dichotomous possibilities of perceiving the sun: '"What," it will be Question'd, "When the Sun rises, do you not see a round disk of fire somewhat like a Guinea?" O no, no, I see an innumerable company of the Heavenly host crying, "Holy, Holy, Holy is the Lord God Almighty."'[66]

  The 'guinea-version' of the sun, metaphorically, is the Locke/Newton/Bacon version; it is, in a sense, the way most people can see it without applying much imagination. Blake, too, *could* see it that way, but his imagination was so charged that to do only this was repugnant. For him, the sun was so much more!

  In society, however, there often needs to be a consensus on how the sun, and much else, is perceived or imagined; people have a need to agree, to believe that 'their minds are uniform and their eyes interchangeable.'[67] On the basis of that premise, Frye moved from the contention that reality is a perceptual and imaginative construction on the part of each individual to the notion that, through communication and for purposes of communicating, perceptions are consensual. Frye insisted, however, that consensus exacts a toll: It is not just the 'idiot's' version that is disregarded, but also the vision of the seer.

• *Verum Factum.* Finally, Frye invoked Vico's[68] dictum *Verum Factum,* meaning what is true for us is what we ourselves make; or, as Frye preferred, 'we understand only what we make ourselves.'[69] This sixth axiom follows directly from the first; to reject the first is to deny the sixth also.

SCIENTIFIC VERSUS MYTHIC CONSCIOUSNESS

In *The Critical Path,* a book he wrote in mid-career, Frye continued exploring dichotomous world-views. There, however, he reformulated his position somewhat. On the one hand, scientific objectivity took the place of unimaginative social consensus; on the other, mythic consciousness, also termed 'the potentially created world,' replaced imaginative personal vision. Nonetheless, the basic notion of an all-encompassing dialectic concerning world-views persisted: science, he argued, seeks to negate mythic consciousness, and mythic consciousness seeks to incorporate scientific knowledge into itself by claiming, for instance, that the lawful order detected by science points to a divine mind. In the following subsections, we review Frye's comparisons of these rival ontologies, particularly with regard to their use of language and narrative.

Language

Nowhere are the differences between the two 'cosmologies' more pronounced than in the language used for their expression. Scientific discourse is characterized by logic and fact. It uses the language of mathematics (counting), which, although concrete initially, becomes immensely abstract as the imagination takes hold. Moreover, when non- mathematical symbols *are* used, there is an abundance of nouns and adjectives but fewer metaphors and analogies.[70] Scientific expression concentrates on literal meanings, has specialized vocabularies and is precise. Seeking to detect causes rather than purposes,[71] scientific discourse is unemotional. The language of science, Frye added, offers us a corpus of knowledge that *progresses*, meaning each age 'stands on the shoulders of its predecessors.'

The mythopoeic mode of expression is much different. Narrative and poetry are communicated through 'a mythical language of hope, desire, belief, anxiety, fantasy and construction.'[72] Mythopoeic knowledge functions, not to describe the world 'as it is,' according to Frye, but to make the world seem to be a place in which people can feel they are at home. Without stories, Frye asserted, humans would be adrift in a universe bereft of purpose and devoid of meaning. This natural estrangement is overcome, to a degree, by projecting human concerns onto the cosmos through such tropes as analogy, simile, metaphor, and personification.[73]

Furthermore, unlike scientific knowledge, mythopoeic knowledge does not progress; rather, it *recurs*.[74] By this, Frye meant that stock characters, basic themes, and archetypal symbols populate the worlds of literature and myth. This is in part what he had in mind when, in *Anatomy of Criticism*, he referred to literature as being 'an order of words'; this point is elaborated upon below.

The Myth of Freedom, the Myth of Concern

Scientific knowledge is tested by what Frye called *the truth of correspondence*,[75] that is, by impersonal evidence, prediction, observation, and verification, as well as by the soundness of the argument (logic). The scientific method, in turn, has given rise to the marvels of modern technology, which also are its verification.

So successful indeed has the scientific enterprise been that it has engendered a distinct political philosophy – namely, *liberalism*, which Frye referred to also as 'the myth of freedom.' He defined the myth of freedom as a verbal expression that includes among its social values objectivity, judgment, tolerance, and respect for the individual.[76] (Why he called this the *myth* of freedom will be addressed below.) Since the myth of freedom derives from 'the truths and realities that are studied rather than created, [that is, from truths] provided by nature rather than by a social vision,'[77] Frye saw political and philosophic liberalism as a biproduct or outcome of Western science.

The dialectical opposite of the myth of freedom, for Frye, is 'the myth of concern.' As a culture develops, he explained, its myths become increasingly comprehensive, touching on most or all of society's major concerns. He used the phrase 'myth of concern'[78] to denote 'concern expressing itself in myth.'[79] He insisted that the human condition is inherently one of estrangement: people are condemned to live in a universe bereft of meaning and devoid of purpose. That existential condition, he maintained, weighs heavily upon the psyche and continuously engenders people's quest for identity; that quest, in turn, constitutes the predominant subject matter of humanity's myths, which considered collectively comprise its 'myth of concern.'[80]

Verbal Culture

The term 'myth' was used by Frye in different ways. When employing such terms as the 'myth of freedom,' the 'myth of concern,' and the 'myth of progress,' for example, he was denoting fundamental values, ontological premises, and characteristic modes of perceiving – not individual narratives. At other times, however, myth indeed denoted particularly important stories. We now pursue for a few moments this second meaning of myth.

Every human society, according to Frye, has its distinct verbal culture[81] consisting in part of stories or narratives, the most basic of which are myths.[82] In Frye's view, myths are 'true' – at least, for those holding them. However, 'truthfulness' of a myth is not a question of logic or of correspondence to the phenomenal world, as it is for science; rather, it is a matter of social convention.[83] Truth is what people agree to be true.

Myths often conjoin to form a *mythology*, defined by Frye as 'a large interconnected body of narrative that covers all the religious and historical revelation that [a] society is concerned with';[84] myths, then, are the 'functional units' of a mythology.[85] When a mythology 'crystallizes' at the centre of a culture, he continued, it is as if a 'magic circle' is drawn, because thereafter literature develops always 'within a limited orbit of language, reference, allusion, belief.'[86] As writing develops, in other words, oral myths expand into literature; put another way, 'every literature in effect inherits a mythology.'[87]

So central to each society are its myths, Frye advised, that they are seldom thought of as being products of the imagination at all. Some, the *sacred stories*, are believed to have been divinely inspired. Others, the *secular myths*, are thought to recount accurately real events.[88] Although perhaps based on actual happenings, historical accounts can never fully 'map' them, meaning that every recounting is 'mythic' on account of incompleteness. History is intrinsically mythic, however, for another reason too: it is, after all, a sequential verbal structure or narrative, whereas the events themselves were non-verbal.

Frye was adamant that the core concern of every society is its quest for identity. Key questions include: Who are we? Why are we here? Where are we going? How do we relate to nature, to one another, and to God? Myths propose answers to these questions. In the West, Frye declared, the Bible has been the seminal repository of stories that set out themes of human identity: from Genesis to Revelation, the overriding concern is loss of identity upon expulsion from the Garden of Eden, the quest to regain it, and finally its retrieval upon the arrival of the New Jerusalem. The Bible is also replete with smaller stories, or *mythoi*, which replay that grand theme – the Jews wandering in the desert and finally attaining the promised land, only to lose it again; the parable of the prodigal son; the stories of Ruth and Job; and so on. The premise of lost identity likewise structures many social myths – from the legends of *Ulysses* to *Pilgrim's Progress* and *The Wizard of Oz*.

Frye maintained that it is not just the conventional plots of fiction that echo biblical themes; so, too, does much historical and philosophical thought.[89] He pointed to Gibbon's history of the Roman Empire as a historical work premised on the Fall. Likewise, what he called 'the idea books' – *The Decline of the West, An End to Innocence, Eros and Civilization, The Secular City* – replay biblical themes.[90] One suspects Frye would discern mythic elements in the subtitle of C.B. Macpherson's tome *Democratic Theory: Essays in Retrieval*, as well as in Macpherson's entire discussion of human nature; and certainly also in Marshall McLuhan's epic theory of the media (reviewed in the next chapter).

Frye insisted that identity is not simply an awareness that 'I am myself and not another.' Rather, it is the realization that there is 'one man, one mind, one world.' Identity for Frye, then, as for Blake, meant seeing oneself in relation to the whole.

What Myths of Concern Do

In Frye's view, myths or narratives do a number of things. First, they serve the therapeutic function of *catharsis*.[91] That is, they express, and hence release or alleviate, an individual's or a society's deepest concerns.

Second, they provide comfort or a sense of security through what Frye called 'controlled hallucinations.' Normally people prefer to live within the cloistered protection of their myth of concern because seeing beyond or through myths can be scary: 'A breakdown in illusion,' Frye wrote, 'is often more disturbing than genuine dangers.'[92]

Third, myths help people impose structure on potential chaos.[93] Frye maintained that a principal task of the literary critic is to explain how societal myths unify or make comprehensible the material universe.

Fourth, myths provide the source of authority for rituals. Frye defined a ritual as 'the epiphany of the myth, the manifestation or showing forth of it in action.'[94] There are religious rituals, of course, that re-enact sacred stories. There are also secular rituals, however, such as 1 July celebrations in Canada and 4 July festivities in the United States, which commemorate national or other secular stories.

Fifth, myths lend support to (or, alternatively, oppose) the power structure of society. Frye declared: 'In every structured society the ascendant class attempts to take over the myth of concern and make it, or an essential part of it, a rationalization of its ascendancy ... The authority of concern, in itself, is always the authority of a social establishment.'[95] From this insight we begin to see that there is a *political-economic* dimension to Frye's treatment of myth and literature, the topic explored in the next main section.

Qualifications

Frye admitted there are problems with his reformulation of antithetical world-views that he set out, in particular, in *The Critical Path*. For one thing, science and technology, like literature and mythology, are *human-centred* activities.[96] People pursuing scientific endeavours exercise their *wills*. Scientific knowledge is not thrust upon researchers. Investigators *select* what they want to find out. Scientific knowledge, therefore, is value-laden, or, as Gregory Bateson put it: 'The point of the probe is always the heart of the explorer.'[97]

Moreover, in pursuing scientific knowledge, people are generally intent on securing for themselves or for their sponsoring organizations commercial, military, or other advantage. They desire, in other words, to re-create the material world (or a portion thereof) according to their own concerns. In *The Educated Imagination*, Frye indeed acknowledged that the two 'cosmologies,' which he there referred to simply as *arts* and *science*, converge once scientific knowledge is deployed practically. In areas such as engineering, agriculture, medicine, and architecture, he attested, 'one can never say clearly where the art stops and the science begins or vice versa.'[98]

In addition Frye conceded that scientific knowledge is similar to art, literature, and mythology in so far as it, too, is a mental and verbal construction. Indeed, he acknowledged, the standards of the truth of correspondence (logic, evidence, and the sense of an objective reality) *are themselves mythic*: they are but 'analogies [and ideals] of a model world that may not exist.'[99] Hence, although the myth of concern and the truth of correspondence confront each other dialectically, in the end, according to Frye, *both are myths*, that is, constructs of the human imagination. This is why Frye spoke of 'the *myth* of freedom.'

THE POLITICAL ECONOMY OF MYTH AND LITERATURE

The Dialectic of Literature and Society

In *Anatomy of Criticism*, Frye staked out the non-dialectical position that literature is largely independent of outside factors.[100] 'Nothing is prior in significance to literature itself,' he announced, although he did acknowledge that poets are 'certainly conditioned by their historical and cultural surroundings.' What he meant by his firm statement, though, was that works of literature reflect and refer primarily to one another – through their conventions, genres, images, archetypes, and so forth. Literature is therefore an 'order of words,' a seamless structure: 'The new poem, like the new baby, is born into an already existing order and is typical of the structure of poetry, which is ready to receive it.'[101] Furthermore, Frye contended that *literary criticism* (which he defined as the theory of literature) is likewise a verbal structure, and hence it exists somewhat independently of literature.[102] (Likewise, scientific knowledge, according to Frye, being a verbal structure, to a degree has an autonomous relationship to the 'order of nature' to which it refers.) It was the belief that criticism exists independently of literature that induced Frye to call for the development of a 'science' of literary criticism. In *The Critical Path*, however, Frye departed from those arguments. There he saw the autonomy of literature and of criticism as constituting but one pole of an overarching dialectic. He wrote: 'The critic should see literature as a coherent structure, historically conditioned but shaping its own history, responding to but not determined in its form by an external historical process.'[103] Indeed, Frye now advised that the literary critic must recognize the tension between the autonomy of literature and criticism, on the one hand, and their contingent qualities, on the other:

Criticism will always have two aspects, one turned toward the structure of literature and one turned toward the other cultural phenomena that form the social environment of literature. Together they balance each other: when one is worked on to the exclusion of the other, the critical perspective goes out of focus. If criticism is in proper balance, the tendency of critics to move from critical to larger social issues becomes more intelligible.[104]

Moreover, Frye now maintained not only that literature derives from the culture, but that it forms a component of the culture, and thereby helps give culture its direction. This means that groups in power and those seeking power try to control society's literature and its myths. Citing Plato, Frye declared: 'The story is popular, addresses itself to untutored minds, and so helps to overcome the gap between the rulers who know and the ruled who must believe ... Indoctrination is the real social function of literature.'[105] There is, in other words, an 'authority of concern,' as well as an 'anatomy of criticism.'

Myths as Mediation

Myths and literature, then, according to Frye, *mediate* human relations. Stories are *models* of human comportment, and as such are imitated in everyday life.[106] Our social mythology, in telling us where we come from, where we are going, and how to get there, has immense power implications. In this subsection, we review Frye's understanding of the power dimensions of some sacred Western stories and of the literature they have spawned.[107]

- *Creation Stories.* According to the Judaeo-Christian tradition, humankind was created asexually by a male God. Frye commented that creation stories suggest that intelligence and planning are inherent in the universe, implying 'an authoritarian structure.'[108] He elaborated: 'Everything man has that seems most profoundly himself is thought of as coming to him from outside, descending from the most ancient days in time, coming down from the remotest heights in space. We belong to something before we are anything, and, just as an infant's world has an order of parents already in it, so man's first impulse is to project figures of authority, or precedence in time and space, stretching in an iron chain of command back to

God.'[109] Creation stories can be and have been used to justify hierarchical structures – a 'great chain of being.'

- *Story of the Fall.* Since we live in a world so evidently imperfect, a creation story must be supplemented by 'an alienation myth,' that is, a story of a human 'fall.'[110] An alienation myth, Frye explained, connotes that the identity we have at birth is not our true identity, and to attain or recover that we must search or struggle.

  Myths of origin and fall affect among other things our relations with the environment. The story of Adam and Eve, for instance, remains cogent in our day, according to Frye, because it depicts a humanity alienated from nature,[111] a nature which, we believe, we can refashion through impositions of our will. How different a system of power relations and relationship with nature, he commented, is provided by the myth of Mother Earth whereby the earth is conceived as the womb and tomb of all life.[112]

- *The Myth of Contract.* The contract myth, too, according to Frye, has origins in the distant past. By the biblical account, upon expelling Adam and Eve from the Garden of Eden, God bound himself by contract or 'testament' to humankind.

  In the hands of modern myth-makers, contract theory can be an *apologia* for an oppressive power system. Frye maintained that modern contract theory began with Edmund Burke,[113] who proposed that people are born into a social order they did not create and hence acquire loyalties they did not choose. To reject these givens, according to Burke, would be chaotic.

  Secular or national myths, Frye continued, are often contractarian: 'Because we have been born British or German or French or what not, the constituted authority has a right not only to our unquestioned loyalty but, in time of war, to our lives.'[114] But, Frye commented, the weakness of this inherently conservative myth is that being involuntarily born into a nation is hardly a compelling reason for accepting the platitude 'my country right or wrong.' Being non-voluntary, he judged, this social-contract myth lacks a genuinely ideal dimension. He continued: 'Complete acceptance of the contract, conceived as the existing structure of authority in society, can only end either in resigned cynicism or in the identifying of reality [with] appearance [that is, by assuming a highly naive, or non-critical stance].'[115] It is at this point that Frye's analysis of the public relations industry,[116] or, in his terms, the 'communicating arts,' takes on added significance. (This point is discussed below.) It is also to be noted that Frye differs markedly from George Grant and others who emphasize obligation and the common good: Frye's critique of the 'contract myth' is totally 'liberal' in its thrust since he advocates complete individual autonomy to pick and choose loyalties.

- *Myth of Utopia.* Alongside the conservative contract myth is a radical alternative, also ancient in origin, which Frye termed *the myth of utopia.* The New Testament's fulfilment myth of the City of God, for instance, is utopian.[117] Myths of utopia focus critically on what conservative contract myths take to be given – namely, the existing structure of authority. With myths of utopia, therefore, loyalty is to a social ideal not yet in existence.[118] The utopian myth proposes an *ideal contract*, which the society of the future will restore or manifest. Utopia is the dialectical opposite of the Fall, and what connects the Fall with Utopia is the search or struggle for identity.

  In Frye's judgment, utopians can be even less tolerant of dissent than conservatives since loyalty to a potential society demands a more intense commitment than loyalty to the present order. Hence radical utopians are 'still less critical, even more eager to rationalize, more impatient with dissent, more anxious to suppress the perception of anomalies in itself.'[119]

- *Myth of Progress.* The myth of utopia is not unrelated to another formidable myth – that of, *progress.* Historically, according to Frye, this myth has had devastatingly harmful consequences. Developing out of science and technology, and from Darwinian speculations regarding the origin of species, the myth of progress has been used to 'justify' horrendous acts of enslavement, even the extermination of 'primitive' peoples, by more technologically advanced ones. At times, in addressing the myth of progress, Frye was positively Innisian, as in the following extract: 'According to the myth of progress, history shows a progress from primitive to civilized states, which turns out on investigation to be a progress in technology, though it is often called science. If two cultures collide, the one that gets enslaved or exterminated is the primitive one.'[120] Progressivist myths, Frye continued – bourgeois and Marxist alike – invariably propagate 'a very cruel deception': namely, that future benefits warrant current sufferings. Both produce leaders with 'the abstracted gaze of the car driver, looking away from the immediate community into the imminent.'[121]

  The myth of progress, or at least its out-working in terms of continual technological advance, has in turn given rise to its oppo-

site, *the alienation of progress*, which Frye defined as a type of consciousness that despairs at keeping up in a world given over to
steadily increasing rates of change. The root of this alienation is a
deeply felt sense on the part of individuals that they have lost
control over their future, that they can no longer participate mean-
ingfully in basic decisions. At least part of the reason for widespread passivity in our day, and hence the flight of people to mass
entertainment (what Frye called 'the communicating arts'), stems
from a sense of impotence engendered by unceasing technological
change.[122]

Creative and Communicating Arts

The political economy of literature and myth has other dimensions
also. Realism in the arts, for example, according to Frye, is generally
conservative, since by definition there is little room for imagining alternatives. Stalin adopted a policy of 'socialist realism' in the arts, including literature, to bolster his authoritarian rule.[123] We saw previously
Dallas Smythe's observations concerning 'capitalist realism.'

In Frye's view, ours is probably the first civilization that has tried to
understand itself 'objectively,' to become aware of its own presuppositions.[124] This social self-consciousness, according to Frye, has resulted
in 'a sharp cultural dialectic.'[125] On the one hand, there are those
striving to be informed and wishing to help bring about social change.
On the other, there are those with a passive attitude. Alienated by
progress, members of this latter group learn some things about current
affairs from the mass media, but remain little inclined to make much
effort to attain a deeper understanding. Nor can they imagine alternatives. They are, in a phrase, 'last men.'[126]

Frye maintained that the bifurcation of modern society into active
and passive people has a correlate in the antithesis between the 'creative' and the 'communicating arts.' The *creative arts* are typified by
contemporary fine arts and literature, which not only promote, but
demand active and critical responses from audiences. The *communicating
arts,* in contrast, typified by the mass media, breed passivity. Frye wrote
that the twentieth century 'is pre-eminently the age of the *perce-oreille*,"
the steady inculcation of suggested attitudes and responses.'[127] The
overall thrust of the communicating arts for him is to stifle critical
thought.[128] He remarked,

Wherever we turn, there is the same implacable voice, unctuous, caressing, inhumanly complacent, selling us food, cars, political leaders, ideologies, culture, contemporary issues, and remedies against the migraine we get from listening to it. As I have tried to suggest by this list, it is not only the voice we hear that haunts us, but the voice that goes on echoing in our minds, forming our social attitudes, our habits of speech, our processes of thought.[129]

Advertising and propaganda, according to Frye, have now converged into public relations. So prevalent has public relations become that few now question its necessity – not even those intent on furthering worthwhile or altruistic causes![130] 'The invariable tendency,' Frye warned, 'is to destroy the critical intelligence and its sense of the gap between appearance and reality.'[131] The communicating arts, in other words, inveigh against the truth of correspondence, giving rise to and shoring up new myths of concern.

THE POLITICAL ECONOMY OF MEDIA

Orality and Literacy

Like Innis, Frye proposed that the means of message transmission have a bearing on the nature of the messages transmitted. In oral society, Frye suggested, the chief transmitters of culture are people with poetic and rhetorical skills, particularly the bards, prophets, and religious leaders. Reliant on memory, oral culture uses verse, formulaic units, stock epithets, and metrical phrases.[132] Frye characterized oral and early writing cultures as expressing themselves 'in continuous verse and discontinuous prose.'[133] *Discontinuous prose* consists of a series of disconnected but easily remembered proverbs or aphorisms – the Gospels of the New Testament, for instance.[134] Continuity in verse, on the other hand, is achieved by mnemonic devices such as rhythm and rhyme.

A culture habituated to writing, however, in Frye's view, tends towards 'continuous prose and discontinuous verse.'[135] *Continuous prose* denotes continuity of ideas and logic, a requisite for the development of philosophy and history. *Discontinuous verse* means that poetry makes a break with continuous rhythms and rhymes, and is intended more to be read than heard.[136]

Frye contended that writing helps transform a society's myth of concern – from the language of proscription ('thou shalt not'), and from stories recounting origins ('in the beginning ...'), to a more conceptual and propositional language.[137] People therefore begin to think less in terms of community and common heritage ('common good'), and more in terms of confronting an objectively given world.[138] Indeed, Frye proposed that it was writing that gave rise to *the truth of correspondence*. In part this was because authors and readers in a culture with writing are less reliant on memory since they can turn to documents which can be cross-referenced, stored, and compared. As well, writing allows for greater abstraction and the induction of general principles (laws of nature).

Linear and Sequential Media

Frye noted that his celebrated colleague at the University of Toronto, Marshall McLuhan, proposed that oral communication is 'simultaneous,' whereas written communication is 'linear.' McLuhan further contended that electronic media, in reasserting orality, emphasize simultaneity over sequence. These media therefore contribute to a process McLuhan called 'retribalization,' that is, a retrieval of characteristics of oral cultures – for instance, a decline in linear thought and a rise in lateral thinking; a decline in individualism and specialization, and an increase in communality and general knowledge; the reassertion of feeling over logic; and so on. Frye, however, insisted that McLuhan was quite mistaken. For one thing, Frye rejected McLuhan's idea that electronic media comprise a new, autonomous order to which people must adjust. He proposed, rather, that electronics are subordinate to, or are contained within, literacy – a position, assented to, incidentally, by an eminent student of McLuhan, Walter Ong.[139] Electronics, in other words, could not be sustained in the absence of literacy.

Furthermore, Frye claimed that *all* media – oral, written, and electronic – are both linear *and* simultaneous, albeit in different stages. He wrote, 'The difference between the linear and the simultaneous is not a difference between two kinds of media, but a difference between two mental operations within all media ... There is always a linear response followed by a simultaneous one whatever the medium. For words, the document, the written or printed record, is the technical device that makes *the critical or simultaneous response* possible.'[140]

Simultaneous response for Frye, then, entails comparing the position forwarded by the message sender with other evidence or knowledge, and entails an evaluation. Frye argued further that the *new* 'oral' (i.e., electronic) media, compared with print, actually *increase* the purely linear (or uncritical) response. This result is due in large measure to the fact that electronic media do not allow time for critical reflection: 'Far from encouraging a shift from linear and fragmented to simultaneous and versatile response, the electronic media have intensified the sense of a purely linear experience which can only be repeated or forgotten.'[141]

But here, as in other matters, Frye could be inconsistent, or, as he might prefer, 'dialectical.' He wrote also that media such as film and television reassert properties of the oral tradition and of poetry by 'presenting things in terms of symbol and archetype,'[142] and that they thereby retrieve such non-linear modes of thought as astrology, tarot cards, and the I Ching.[143] This all sounds highly McLuhanesque!

Another result of electric media, Frye remarked, is 'a concerted effort to break down the distinction between art and life, between stage and audience, between drama and event.'[144] There hence appear new forms of social activity that are really improvised symbolic dramas performed before cameras and for the purpose of being reported (i.e., 'pseudo events').[145]

At times Frye could be Innisian, moreover, in comparing old and new media. He remarked that media developed primarily in the twentieth century, such as film, radio, and television, being 'mass media,' follow 'the imperial rhythms of politics and economics more readily than the regionalizing rhythms of culture.'[146] He remarked also that 'the fight for cultural distinctiveness ... is a fight for human dignity itself,'[147] the implication being that, in homogenizing cultures, mass media erode people's sense of uniqueness, and hence of worth.

Privacy and Introversion

Furthermore, Frye maintained that electric media erode privacy and increase introversion. They do this by invading the mind – for Frye, 'the last stand of privacy.' It is worthwhile quoting him at length on this:

> If certain tendencies within our civilization were to proceed unchecked, they would rapidly take us toward a society which, like that of a prison, would be both completely introverted and completely without privacy. The last stand of privacy has always been, traditionally, the inner mind. It is quite possible however for communication media, especially the newer electronic ones, to break down the associative structures of the inner mind and replace them by the prefabricated structures of the media. A society entirely controlled by their slogans and exhortations would be intro-

verted, because nobody would be saying anything: there would only be echo, and Echo was the mistress of Narcissus. It would also be without privacy, because it would frustrate the effort of the healthy mind to develop a view of the world which is private but not introverted, accommodating itself to opposing views.

Whereupon he concluded, again in a manner worthy of Innis, 'the triumph of communication is the death of communication: where communication forms a total environment, there is nothing to be communicated.'[148]

In these remarks, Frye anticipated by several years the more famous formulation of the same thoughts by Michel Foucault![149]

The Dialectic of Technology

The *alienation of progress* can be experienced by rich and poor alike. For the disadvantaged, however, the communicating arts engender a particular type of alienation. Communication through mass media is largely one-way, and hence not merely reflects but exacerbates asymmetries in the distribution of power. This breeds resentment, and people are apt to seize any opportunity, destructive or otherwise, to 'talk back.'[150] More generally, Frye could not abide the optimistic views regarding the electronic media as espoused by McLuhan. He wrote disparagingly of the 'McLuhan cult' and the 'McLuhan rumour.'[151] In Frye's view, technology is at best dialectical, increasing welfare for some, but decreasing it for others.[152]

SYNTHESIS: AN EDUCATED IMAGINATION

Against the undesirable poles of conservative contract myth and the myth of progress/myth of utopia, and also as a desirable synthesis between the myth of freedom and the myth of concern, Frye proposed *the educated imagination*. He also called this 'the critical path.' When attention is cast to the great theorists of contract and of utopia – Plato, More, Locke, Rousseau – we see, Frye claimed, not works centring on contracts or utopias at all, but those focusing on education: 'It is clearly education these four writers at least most cared about.'[153]

An educated person, Frye proclaimed, although perforce living within a complex of social authority arising from the myth of concern, is one who is aware of, and submits to, a different kind of authority – an authority based on rational argument, on accurate measurement, on repeatable experiments, and on 'the compelling imagination.'[154] Frye used the term 'compelling imagination' to emphasize that science (the 'truth of correspondence') must be moderated by mythic narrative; neither science nor the myth of concern alone suffices. Although the myth of freedom is not subject to the same political-economic abuses as myths of concern (after all, the 'authority of reason and evidence and repeatable experiment' differs markedly from the authority of an elite),[155] untempered by the human imagination the truth of correspondence turns people into 'psychotic apes,' knowing not who they are or why they are here. To retain our sanity, in other words, we must never disregard the 'compelling imagination.'

In the concluding section we examine the extent to which Frye succeeded in achieving this necessary synthesis.

SOME QUESTIONS

Frye's dialectic of realism versus imagination, of alienation versus integration, is well captured by Blake's poem 'The Tyger,' from which he derived the title of his first book. Here is an excerpt:

> Tyger! Tyger! burning bright
> In the forests of the night,
> What immortal hand or eye
> Could frame thy fearful symmetry?
> …
> What the hammer? what the chain?
> In what furnace was thy brain?
> What the anvil? what dread grasp
> Dare its deadly terrors clasp?
>
> When the stars threw down their spears,
> And watered heaven with their tears,
> Did he smile his work to see?
> Did he who made the Lamb make thee?

Frye is an author difficult to grasp. His elusiveness, however, stems not from lack of clarity in his prose; to the contrary, he is a consummate writer. It arises, rather, from the nature of his dialectics. Time and again, Frye put forth a position only later to champion its opposite. In fact, a case can be made that at times Frye was not dialectical at all, if by that we mean one who perceives or seeks a balance between, or a synthesis of, opposites. This section, then, addresses critically Frye's dialectics. Furthermore, since Frye explored themes developed by other theorists, it is appropriate to inquire into the similarities and differences between his thought and theirs. Finally, as is the case with all our authors, we inquire into Frye's relevance for the early twenty-first century.

Dialectics versus Nihilism

Northrop Frye continued in the Canadian tradition of dialectical analysis pioneered by Harold Innis. However, Frye's dialectics are different. First, Frye was 'Hegelian' in the sense that he dealt primarily with opposing ideas, whether epistemological or ontological, whereas Innis was more Marxian in that he was concerned also with the clash of opposites in the phenomenal world – European versus indigenous North American cultures, orality versus literacy, fish versus lumber, and so on. Innis, of course, decried what he perceived to be the collapse in the dialectic of space versus time due to the proliferation of space-binding media; Frye, on the other hand, usually maintained that the 'cosmologies' of science versus the arts are locked in perpetual struggle. Certainly, however, Frye's 'truth of correspondence' is subsumed within Innis's space bias, and his mythopoeic narrative bears affinity to Innis's time-bias. On the other hand, at times Frye also seemed to contend that polar opposites, rather than creating tensions within which people must live, or interacting so as to produce syntheses at higher levels, cancel each other out. At one point he set this idea forth as an axiom, declaring that 'no idea is anything more than a half-truth unless it contains its own opposite, and is expanded by its own denial or qualification.'[156]

In *Fearful Symmetry*, for example, Frye argued that 'reality' is entirely imaginative, although even there a 'double vision' is recommended. In *Anatomy of Criticism* and in *The Critical Path*, on the other hand, objectivity and the truth of correspondence are held to be the sole means we have of seeing things as 'they really are,' of piercing, as it were, our narcissistic gaze. Truth of correspondence and scientific knowledge, however, Frye later affirmed in *The Educated Imagination*, are themselves verbal structures originating in the human mind; nor, as a practical matter, is applied science really very far removed from human concern. This sequence of thought represents continuous reversal and negation, not balance, synthesis, or integration.

Another example: In *Anatomy of Criticism*, Frye urged critics to place each literary work within the whole body of literature, and enjoined them not to deem influential anything outside the 'order of words.' In keeping with these injunctions, he dissuaded critics from interpreting literary texts from the perspective of any 'school of thought,' whether Marxist, Freudian, or Thomist; by refraining from doing this, he claimed, critics could establish a 'science' of literary criticism. Subsequently, however, Frye acknowledged that works of literature indeed develop within a social context, that is, within a framework of political, economic, social, and cultural power, and in *The Critical Path* he went so far as to state that 'criticism will always have two aspects,' one turned towards 'the structure of literature' (the position he presented in *Anatomy of Criticism*), and the other 'turned toward the other cultural phenomena that form the social environment of literature.' Frye went on to say that, together, these two perspectives balance each other, and that when only one is present 'the critical perspective goes out of focus.'[157] Finally, however, also in *The Critical Path*, Frye seemingly negated the importance of such efforts by remarking: 'The whole point about literature is that it has no direct connection with belief'; and, again, it is 'the reader himself [who] is responsible for the moral quality of what he reads.'[158] Invoking and assenting to the thesis of the 'active reader' not only attenuates the claim of scientific objectivity for literary criticism but goes a long way towards denying to literature the power to mould society that he had previously ascribed to it.

In *Fearful Symmetry*, Frye distinguished between 'a contrary' and 'a negation.' Contraries, he wrote, are dialectical opposites that nonetheless share certain underlying truths or assumptions, thereby making for fruitful interaction. Frye advised that contraries '*must* clash or we shall never know who is right.' With negation, however, there is no common ground, and hence nothing is to be accomplished even by mutual acknowledgment. Blake *disagreed* with Newton, Bacon, and Locke as they were his contraries, but Hobbes he *ignored*, for Hobbes was his negation.[159]

Sometimes Frye's analysis deals with contraries, and at those times he is a keen dialectical thinker. At other times, however, he deals with negations, and it is then that his analysis could be termed 'nihilistic.'[160]

Frye's Ontology

Frye's penchant for negation is perhaps most apparent when he presents his ontology. From a scientific point of view, he claimed, we understand that the universe is without meaning or purpose. At the close of *The Modern Century*, referencing Blake's poem 'The Tyger,' he wrote: 'The child's vision is far behind us. The world we are in is the world of the tiger, and that world was never created or seen to be good. It is the subhuman world of nature, a world of law and of power, but not of intelligence or design. Things "evolve" in it.'[161] But, by projecting our concerns onto this 'world of the tiger,' we construct a 'home.' The purposes and meanings we construct, however, according to Frye, remain just that – imaginative constructions. They are continually in tension with, and are belied, by the tiger (the 'truth of correspondence').

To say, as Frye does, that meaning and purpose depend ultimately on closing our eyes to what is real or, stated alternatively, imaginatively fabricating stories out of the raw material presented to our senses in order to relieve our existential angst, seems rather bleak, if not altogether nihilistic, making Frye by far the darkest of the thinkers here encountered.[162] It is surprising that Frye – Bible scholar and one so versed in the writings of the poets, and a person who was not bereft of love in his life – should have failed to emphasize that, *through human relations*, people transcend, at least to a degree, the absurdity of an empty universe. Empathy, friendship, common cause, intimations of bliss, all allow the individual to become part of something larger than the self. Frye acknowledged this in *Fearful Symmetry*,[163] but seldom articulated that ontological position in later works;[164] rather, it was mythic stories, not love, that provided the fragile sense of coherence and cohesion for Frye.

Granting, for sake of argument, Frye's position regarding the emptiness of the universe, and assuming also a reluctance on his part, for whatever reason, to invoke human feeling and common cause as means of transcendence, an optimistic synthesis nonetheless was still at hand. Note, for example, the following remarks from Paulo Freire: 'As men relate to the world by responding to the challenges of the environment, they begin to dynamize, to master, and humanize reality. They add to it something of their own making, by giving temporal meaning to geographic space, by creating culture ... As men create, re-create, and decide, historical epochs begin to take shape.'[165] The notion of people actually acting upon the material world, of applying their imaginations to their physical surroundings to render that less alien, is all but absent from Frye's thought. Frye remained all his life a mentalist who paid scant attention to changes people make to their the physical surroundings as they build a *material* home. In an early essay reflective perhaps of his days in Moncton, Frye in fact declared: 'It is in daylight that man is really in the power of darkness, a prey to frustration and weakness; it is in the darkness of nature [i.e., night time, when people dream] that the "libido" or conquering heroic self awakes.'[166]

Frye, it turns out, held a rather dark view of human nature and of people's propensity to create: 'Man is not very good at the creating business,' he pronounced; 'he is much better at destroying, for most of him, like an iceberg, is submerged in a destructive element.'[167]

We may speculate further on Frye's nihilism. It is likely that he believed, or felt, that meaning stems ultimately from God. But, according to his account, God disappeared for him one day on the streets of Moncton, never to return. Thereafter, God could only be 'imagined.' Indeed, for Frye, Imagination became God. Henceforth, meaning was solely what Imagination could conjure up. Although relishing the ostensible freedom to imagine whatever meanings or purposes he chose, Frye was also beset by an existential angst as to the solidity of these meanings or purposes. No wonder he characteristically expressed negation!

Let us examine briefly, however, Frye's major premise, from which evidently he did not waver throughout his mature lifetime – namely, that science or the truth of correspondence points starkly to a universe devoid of intelligence higher than our own. Two statements by eminent scientists may suffice to demonstrate that this belief is far from being universally shared within the scientific community. According to Sir James Jeans, 'today there is a wide measure of agreement, which on the physical side of science approaches almost to unanimity, that the stream of knowledge is heading towards a nonmechanical reality; the universe begins to look more like a great thought than a great machine.'[168] And, from Sir Arthur Eddington, 'The stuff of the world is mind-stuff.'[169] A dialectic formed around the propositions of Jeans and Eddington, on the one hand, versus Frye's myth of concern, on the other, would be markedly different from the dialectic of the truth of correspondence versus the myth of concern, such as Frye proposed.

CONTINUITY AND DIFFERENCES WITH OTHER WRITERS

Frye and Innis
Frye's depiction of scientific knowledge and the scientific mode of discourse is quite consistent with Innis's notion of space-biased com-

munication. Those participating in scientific discourse, according to Frye, presume an objective reality and focus on objects occupying space. Nor is scientific discourse intended to be interpretative: readers are expected to extract from texts the sender's intention, and this again is in accord with Innis's conception of space-biased communication as a concomitant of empire.

Likewise, mythopoeic discourse, by Frye's account, aligns well with Innis's concept of time-binding communication. Time relates to the imagination since objects no longer existing in space can only be recalled or imagined.

Frye and Innis, however, reached remarkably different conclusions concerning the power dimensions of the foregoing. For mythopoeic (or time-bound) societies, both writers envisaged power as residing with an elite that controls the myths. In scientific (space-bound) societies, however, Innis saw an administrative and military autocracy exercising control, whereas Frye conjectured freedom – freedom arising from the authority of the truth of correspondence. (On the other hand, Frye also acknowledged that technological achievements stemming from scientific knowledge can be and are used to diminish freedom: the communicating arts, for instance, carry propaganda and advertising, while rapid technological change gives rise to the alienation of progress.)

Like Innis, Frye commended the Socratic method as a way to encourage independent thought and to throw off the shackles of received wisdom. However, Frye was much less pessimistic than Innis regarding the consequences of book culture. By Frye's account, books liberate, since they allow readers the time to pause and reflect critically upon the contents, whereas electronic media deny this possibility. Nor did Frye accept Innis's contention that print leads readers step by step to the author's pre-formed conclusions, arguing rather that writing opens up a dialogue whereby readers mentally test an author's claims at their leisure.[170] Moreover, for Frye, oral cultures are far from participatory since stories are controlled by an elite, and stock phrases and other mnemonic devices characterize the communication. The most significant difference between them, however, must be Frye's focus on content or stories versus Innis's attention to media. In terms of political economy, Frye exhibited a keener analysis of the power implications of stories, but his analysis of media pales in comparison with that of Innis.

Frye and Smythe
There is surprising affinity in the communication thought of Northrop

Frye and Dallas Smythe. Smythe saw erosion of indigenous cultures as a means for territorial expansion by dominant political-economic interests and so recommended 'cultural screens' to help preserve local independence. Likewise, Frye wrote that 'the creative instinct has a great deal to do with the assertion of territorial rights.'[171] Rather than recommending 'cultural screens,' however, Frye favoured policies that stimulate creative activity, for example, grants through the Canada Council and other sponsoring bodies.

Like Smythe, Frye detected a tension, or dialectic, between culture and political control. According to Smythe's formulation, economic/political forces subvert local culture, whereas indigenous cultural institutions and practices constitute loci of resistance to international homogenization. Smythe undoubtedly favoured the local and regional over the national and international. Frye, however, while expressing similar thoughts, recommended a balance, that is, retaining a tension between these opposing forces, as illustrated by the following oft-quoted statement: 'Identity is local and regional, rooted in the imagination and in works of culture; unity is national in reference, international in perspective, and rooted in a political feeling ... Assimilating identity to unity produces the empty gestures of cultural nationalism; assimilating unity to identity produces the kind of provincial isolation which is now called separatism.'[172]

Smythe and Frye both saw a bifurcation of the arts. Smythe distinguished between the 'fine arts,' which under Monopoly Capitalism tend to elicit mainly aesthetic interpretations, but which nonetheless possess revolutionary potential, and the popular arts, which, he felt, are controlled by the Consciousness Industry, serving therefore to inculcate compliance in audiences. Frye certainly agreed with Smythe regarding the content of the mass media (which he termed 'the communicating arts') but was more hopeful with regard to the higher (or, in his terms, the 'creative') arts; these, he held, demand active and critical responses from audiences.

A major thrust also of Frye's work, however, is that audiences should not be too critical when it comes to art, since its function, after all, *is* to beguile, that is, to lead audiences out of the cold, harsh reality of the truth of correspondence and into the soothing myth of concern. Smythe, one senses, would be quite contemptuous of the magical role Frye set out for the artist, since Smythe's concern was, first and foremost, actually to improve the material conditions, not to beguile people into imaginatively escaping them. Smythe dismissed aestheticism because it neutered the political import of art; he would, I suggest, dismiss Frye's theory of genres and other highly abstract models for precisely the same reason. As remarked by Bruce Powe, Frye continually presented 'theoretical packages ... which offer keys to "stubborn structures," "great codes," "critical paths," and so forth';[173] each work of literature, in Frye's view, is to be understood as devolving from and taking its place within an 'order of words,' trivializing thereby the political-economy thrust of any given work.

Ontologically, Smythe and Frye were at opposite poles. Smythe maintained that reality is in the material conditions and that symbols can either heighten awareness and understanding of these conditions or be used to beguile and deceive. When the Consciousness Industry is at work, people tend to live in a 'false' symbolic environment, one that nonetheless interacts dialectically with the material conditions that continually belie that false system of symbolization. For Frye, in contrast, the symbolic environment is primary; people live in a mythic universe of their own construction, that is, within an 'order of words,' for which 'truth' is not the primary issue (the 'truth of correspondence,' after all, arose late in human history and points to an absence of meaning, that is, to only fragmented truths). Unlike Frye, Smythe never appeared to be in doubt that there is meaning to be had in the material conditions; and, like Macpherson, he appeared to hold fast to an eternal set of values that include equality and justice, whereby the material conditions, as they exist from time to time, can be judged. Indeed, Smythe can be seen as providing a response to Frye's anxiety regarding the human condition; Frye's assertion of an 'empty' universe, Smythe might say, is now obsolete, as it was premised on 'information' and not on 'communication.'

Marked differences notwithstanding, it is also the case that both Smythe and Frye reviled and detested the advertising/public relations complex, Smythe on account of the 'false consciousness' and 'cultural imperialism' aspects, Frye primarily because of the passivity engendered by the 'communicating arts' and the invasion of people's minds by those intent on exploitation.

Frye and Macpherson
The closest parallel that exists in the writings of these two authors concerns the respective roles played in society by political philosophy and myth. Frye, of course, contended that myths mediate human relations, and that they can be used to justify systems of power. Macpherson

accorded the same properties to political philosophy, arguing that it justifies one or other of two dichotomous modes of property.

Likewise, Macpherson's modes of property, including their justificatory philosophies, bear considerable correspondence to Frye's opposing myths. The myth of concern, according to Frye scholar Robert Denham, 'leads man to uphold communal rather than individual values,' whereas the myth of freedom is 'inherently "liberal" helping to develop and honouring such values as objectivity, detachment, suspension of judgment, tolerance and respect for the individual'[174] – and, presumably, private property.

Frye and Grierson

Frye and Grierson held almost dialectically opposite views on the functions of art and education when these are considered separately, but their views converge when art and education are considered together. Grierson maintained that the true function of art (particularly film) is to heighten people's perception of reality, not to facilitate escape into fantasy; Frye, conversely, held that the necessary function of art is to help people escape an otherwise intolerable reality. Regarding education, however, Grierson thought it should touch people's emotions more than their intellects and stir people to action rather than hone their critical faculties; he contended that educators ought to adopt the dramatic, rhetorical, and emotional tactics of the commercial media to accomplish these goals. For Frye, on the other hand, education should heighten awareness and stimulate critical faculties, not impose ideology upon students. What art is to do, in Grierson's opinion, education is, in a sense, to accomplish for Frye; likewise, what education is to accomplish for Grierson, art does for Frye.

Frye and Grant

Grant has been termed the brooding philosopher of modernity because he unflinchingly broached the nihilistic implications of technological change when unbounded by considerations of natural law or the common good. Grant denied being a pessimist, however, claiming, rather, that he derived the courage to think things through from his great hope and belief that beyond time and space there is order. Frye, in contrast, has seldom been termed dark or brooding, possibly because he spent so much time exploring the imaginative worlds of literature and myth. In a sense literature and myth provided for Frye relief from the existential angst that Grant described so poignantly in *Time as History*. In the end, however, literature and myth failed Frye, whereas Grant abided in the comfort of his faith.

On the other hand, both writers were disturbed by conditions as they exist and trends they foresaw. What Frye termed the *alienation of progress*, for instance, was at the root of George Grant's lament. Grant believed that life is meant to be based on sharing and love, not on power relations, and that the 'will to power' therefore is ultimately nihilistic as it wipes this communal purpose of life. Moreover, rapid technological change challenges people's sense of continuity, raising doubts as to whether anything, including notions such as goodness and justice, remain cogent. Frye, too, in addition to recognizing the disruptive consequences of technological change, associated rugged individualism with a 'death wish' – both as a practical matter in terms of the rape of nature, and psychologically. He wrote: 'It was a long time before the philosophers got around to realizing that egocentric consciousness is primarily a consciousness of death, but the poets had always known that.'[175]

There are other interesting comparisons between these writers, particularly with regard to value. Grant claimed we can never properly separate fact from value because what we choose as fact is a question of the will; we choose to know what we value. Frye, too, understood that science results from acts of will, and so ultimately is value-laden. Those similarities notwithstanding, it is also the case that Grant presumed an objective value ('natural law') that can be discerned by humans, whereas Frye, of course, contended that in the end we simply project our existential concerns onto an indifferent universe; there is no objective value according to Frye whereby we can judge ourselves. Grant understood well the perspective adopted by Frye, and he addressed it at length in his discourse on Nietzsche.

Grant's dialectic of antiquarian versus modern conceptions of time is mirrored to some extent in Frye's opposition between the myth of concern and the truth of correspondence. Both agreed that the latter ontologies (namely, time as history and truth of correspondence), although nihilistic in their implications, dominate the Western mind, and both attributed that predominance to rapid technological change.

Moreover, Grant and Frye had remarkably similar things to say about electronic media, advertising, and propaganda. Both recognized and expounded upon political-economic dimensions of communication, education, and media. Grant's approach to literature differed significantly from Frye's, though, as he objected to a stance of 'scientific' detachment, such as endorsed by Frye. Grant wrote: 'But, of course, literature is not an object at our disposal, as the atom may be.'[176]

FRYE'S RELEVANCE FOR TODAY

Mythologizing

When Northrop Frye was a youth and then a young scholar, Bible stories still were part of the curriculum of Canadian public schools, and the Bible remained a central repository of Canadian imagery and mythology. As Rick Salutin notes, everyone in the 1950s knew the basics of the story told in Cecil B. DeMille's *The Ten Commandments*: Moses's birth, his placement in the bullrushes, the flight from the palace, the burning bush, the plagues, the parting of the Red Sea, the breaking the stone tablets, the golden calf. Salutin adds, in a manner worthy of Frye, that when a mythology 'is truly embedded in a culture, it comes at you from all directions, you swim in it, everyone takes it for granted,' and it provides the 'common set of references for believers and non-believers alike.'[177]

Today, biblical narratives are not nearly as well known, and few would claim that the Bible now provides the central mythology for Canadian society. Indeed, the very day Salutin's column appeared in the *Globe and Mail*, another piece reported on a Supreme Court of British Columbia decision ruling that school boards cannot use religion as the framework for decisions regarding textbooks and curriculum; the moral code, rather, must derive from Canada's Charter of Rights and Freedoms, and from the British Columbia Human Rights Code.[178]

But simply because the Bible no longer constitutes, at least directly, the principal storied lens through which the majority interpret and judge current events and social issues is not to say that there is no longer a central mythology in Canadian society. To find out what that is, however, Salutin advises, requires us to think about the set of images *we* take for granted.

Put this way, Frye's analysis of myth retains relevance for what some might term a post-Bible era. First, if Frye is correct, in order to comprehend thoroughly the mythology of the present, we must relate current symbols, archetypes, characters, themes, images, and so forth, to biblical ones. We live, Frye proclaimed, in a symbolic order with direct connections to the past.

Even more basically, Frye's analysis encourages us not to take for granted common-sense explanations, received wisdoms, pious platitudes, and the like, but rather to apply our critical faculties to present-day affairs to infer not only what the contemporary myths *are*, but also their implications for our well-being. Elsewhere,[179] I have proposed that Market, Technology, and Evolution constitute the core of contemporary myths and that, to truly understand our present condition, critical scrutiny must be applied to them. Like Bible stories, myths of Market, Technology, and Evolution have political and economic implications. By positing omnipotent, abstract mechanisms such as the Market, Technology, and Evolution as controlling human affairs, the pursuit of justice is annihilated since the capacity of humans to influence or control affairs is at least implicitly denied.

Frye argued that people of every culture interpret life through stories or myths that gather past and future into an eternal present. The nature of the stories, according to Frye, is all important. Today, much of the responsibility and power for telling stories, and for replaying ancient myths in modern guises, resides with the 'cultural industries,'[180] what Frye referred to derisively as the 'communicating arts,' of which television is probably the most potent. Frye warned of the ever-present danger of the myth of concern being high-jacked by powerful groups who would twist it and make it their own. And hence, through myths such as those of Market, Technology, and Evolution, we witness the continual propagation and celebration in the media of such notions as globalization, deregulation, privatization, consumerism, individualism, the necessity of rapid technological change, and the collapse of social space.

Alienation of Progress

When Frye wrote in the 1960s of the alienation of progress, people were enduring a seemingly endless arms race and were living under continual threat of nuclear annihilation. By the 1990s, those concerns had largely dissipated, at least for the time. Nonetheless, were Frye alive, one suspects he would see little improvement in the sense of people taking charge of their destinies. Governments pronounce that we must be at the 'cutting edge' of technological advance, seemingly irrespective of the dislocations involved. Businesses restructure and downsize with impunity in the name of global competitiveness. Job skills previously expected to last a lifetime are obsolesced, often within a few years.[181] A whole generation is referred to as Generation X. The alienation of progress, in brief, persists.

Frye's most enduring contribution, therefore, may well be his insistence that science and technology (or, perhaps more fundamentally, the price system and markets) need to be counterbalanced by 'concern,' that we must guard against the tendency of the 'truth of correspondence' to obliterate all non-price or non–market value – values that cannot be objectified, mathematized, and empirically verified. Frye likened science and technology to a 'death wish' that needs to be offset by life-giving stories: 'Every "improvement" in communication,' he wrote, 'in railway, highway, or airway, has meant a shorter and straighter path through nature until, with the plane, the sense of moving through nature practically disappears; what does not disappear is the attitude of arrogant ascendancy over nature.'[182] The arrogant ascendancy that accompanies technological change may, in the not so distant future, spell grave consequences for the human race, as ecologists such as David Suzuki have warned.

11

The Communication Thought of
MARSHALL McLUHAN (1911–1980)

I have no theories whatever about anything. I make observations by way of discovering contours, lines of force, and pressures. I satirize at all times, and my hyperboles are as nothing compared to the events to which they refer ... My canvasses are surrealist, and to call them 'theories' is to miss my satirical intent altogether.

– Letter to W. Kuhns, December 1971

A theory of cultural change is impossible without knowledge of the changing sense ratios effected by various externalizations of our senses.

– *The Gutenberg Galaxy*, 42

ABOUT MARSHALL McLUHAN

Herbert Marshall McLuhan was born at Edmonton, Alberta, on 21 July 1911, to Elsie Naomi Hall, a schoolteacher, elocutionist, and stage performer, and to Herbert Ernest McLuhan, a real estate agent/insurance salesman and erstwhile farmer.[1] According to Marshall's younger brother, Maurice, Elsie had an exceedingly strong will: she 'trampled' men she dominated, including her husband,[2] whom she eventually divorced. Marshall stood up for himself, though, and undoubtedly the verbal jousting of his childhood and youth prepared him well to withstand opposition outside the home in later years.[3] Elsie encouraged Marshall to read voraciously, which he did, and evidently he inherited also her flair for performance.

Marshall McLuhan grew up in Winnipeg in the 1920s. This was the time when radio broadcasting was in its infancy. Reflecting his lifelong interests in new media, McLuhan built a crystal set to which he and his brother would listen while drifting off to sleep.[4] In his formative years, Marshall also became very interested in religion, and rarely missed a Baptist Bible class.[5]

In 1928 McLuhan enrolled as an undergraduate in the Faculty of Engineering at the University of Manitoba, but switched to Arts the following year[6] to focus on English, history, and philosophy.[7] He received a BA in 1933 and was awarded an MA in English in 1934. Next he studied at Cambridge, which, despite his having earned two previous degrees, permitted him to enrol only as an undergraduate. Soon he became imbued with the writings of T.S. Eliot ('easily the greatest modern poet'),[8] Ezra Pound, James Joyce ('probably the only man ever to discover that all social changes are the effect of new technologies … on the order of our sensory lives'),[9] and the British author and painter Wyndham Lewis – none of whom had merited a place on the syllabi at Manitoba. McLuhan loved in particular Joyce's wordplay and the manner in which that poet/novelist required readers to tease out meanings from words, often neologisms, by their context and by applying the reader's own insights and experiences. Joyce abandoned linear narrative in favour of a multilayered mode of exposition, and this enthralled McLuhan.

At Cambridge, McLuhan attended lectures by, among others, I.A. Richards, a pioneer of 'practical criticism.' Richards maintained that words derive meanings from context and are best understood in terms of 'effects,' often subliminal, as opposed to their 'content' or dictionary definitions. Richards also discussed at length the theory of metaphors and their relation to contextual meaning.[10] Richards's influence is apparent even in the opening sentence of McLuhan's first scholarly publication, an essay on G.K. Chesterton, in which McLuhan refers to 'the meaning and effect' of that author's work.[11]

In his mature scholarship, McLuhan applied 'practical criticism' to artefacts other than literary works – to the wheel, for example, and the electric light bulb, and to furniture, clothing, and the printing press. He argued that all artefacts have 'effects' on people's psychologies and on their interpretative processes. In endeavouring to discern these effects, McLuhan was inspired also by F.R. Leavis, whom he also heard lecture at Cambridge. In *Culture and Environment*, Leavis applied techniques of literary criticism to the social environment.[12]

It is useful to pause here to consider a point of possible confusion. McLuhan insisted that his concern was for rhetoric, not dialectic. According to the classical trivium,[13] 'rhetoric' concerns the effects of texts on readers, whereas 'dialectic' pertains to the text alone – how the components fit together, how logically sound the text is, and so on. This is, however, a much different rendering of the term 'dialectic' from that advanced by Hegel and adopted in this book. As we will see, McLuhan certainly was dialectical in the Hegelian sense: figure–ground, eye–ear, hot–cool, logical–analogical, phonetic–non-phonetic, print–manuscript, medium–message – these are but a few of the bipolarities that he held in tension to forward his media analysis. McLuhan also emphasized the principle of reversal (he called it 'chiasmus'), whereby each concept or force is held to carry the seed of its opposite.

In 1936, McLuhan was hired as a graduate teaching assistant in the English department at the University of Wisconsin. Immediately he set out to familiarize himself with popular culture – sports, comics, music, advertising, news of the day – to help ingratiate him with students.[14] That research eventually surfaced as *The Mechanical Bride*, McLuhan's first book.

Also at Wisconsin, McLuhan converted formally to Catholicism – on Holy Thursday, 25 March 1937.[15] As a convert, he was devout and attended Mass virtually every day for the rest of his life.

McLuhan recognized, but only occasionally admitted, that religious zeal undergirded his media studies. In an interview with G.E. Stearn, though, he confessed:

> Here perhaps my religious faith has some bearing. I think of human charity as a total responsibility of all, for all. Therefore, my energies are directed at far more than mere political or democratic intent ... The Christian concept of the mystical body – all men as members of the body of Christ – this becomes technologically a fact under electric conditions. However, I would not try to theologize on the basis of my understanding of technology.[16]

The following year he moved to Saint Louis University, a Catholic institution, but returned to Cambridge on a year's leave of absence in 1939 for doctoral studies. He received his PhD in 1943 for a dissertation on Thomas Nash, thereby solidifying his status as a literary scholar of the Elizabethan period.[17]

In 1944, he accepted an appointment at Assumption College, now part of the University of Windsor. Two years later he moved to St Michael's College at the University of Toronto, whereupon he wrote to his friend and former student Walter Ong: 'So Walter, I must regard this move as a permanent one.'[18] And so it proved.

Like most of the Canadian communication theorists considered in this volume, Marshall McLuhan was born an outsider – and remained one. As Liss Jeffrey said in summary,

> he [McLuhan] was born in western Canada to a loving but ineffectual father, and an ambitious mother ... Money was tight; ideas and a life of the mind were encouraged ... As a Canadian at Cambridge, as later in St. Louis, McLuhan felt the outsider, the superior outsider ... His conversion to Catholicism confirmed his identity as a *superior* outsider because he made a conscious choice as to who was 'we' and who was 'they.'[19]

McLuhan maintained that only 'outsiders' *really* understand their culture or environment: 'The poet, the artist, the sleuth – whoever sharpens our perception tends to be antisocial; rarely "well-adjusted", he cannot go along with currents and trends. A strange bond often exists among antisocial types in their power to see environments as they really are. This need to interface, to confront environments with a certain antisocial power, is manifest in the famous story, "The Emperor's New Clothes".'[20] Certainly McLuhan saw himself very much as a poet, artist, and sleuth. And 'superior' is also an apt term for his self-appraisal. In an interview he once remarked: 'The road to understanding media effects begins with arrogant superiority; if one lacked this sense of superiority – this detachment – it would be quite impossible to write about them.'[21]

The Mechanical Bride was published in 1951. The original edition sold but a few hundred copies. Nonetheless, it well exemplifies its author's lifelong scholarly stance. There, McLuhan wrenched artefacts of commercial culture from their normal context and subjected them to critical scrutiny and commentary.

McLuhan's critics sometimes point to a disjuncture between his *The Mechanical Bride* and works that followed,[22] an observation in accord with McLuhan's own position. Whereas the critics suggest pecuniary considerations may have guided McLuhan's later, 'less critical' scholarship, McLuhan's explanation was simply that his first tome had been a misguided attempt to preserve book culture in an electric age.[23]

McLuhan's next milestone, *Explorations,* a journal he co-edited with anthropologist Edmund Carpenter, was published between 1953 and 1959. It, too, attained scant distribution but, according to James Carey, was at the time 'influential among ... a small group of academics.'[24] Subscribers, or at least readers, included Susan Sontag, Jacques Derrida, Claude Lévi-Strauss, and Roland Barthes.[25] The journal proposed that 'revolutions in the packaging and distribution of ideas and feelings modified not only human relations but also sensibilities ... We are largely ignorant of literacy's role in shaping Western man, and equally unaware of the role of electronic media in shaping modern values.'[26] In these two, highly condensed sentences we find McLuhan's basic thesis: that media, whether print or electronic, modify both individuals and cultures by reshaping ideas and perception; that media 'massage' users imperceptibly; and that culture has become a product or commodity. Writing in *Explorations* were such luminaries as Siegfried Giedion, Northrop Frye, David Riesman, Karl Polyani, and Robert Graves.

In 1963 the University of Toronto established the Centre for Culture and Technology to induce McLuhan to stay in Canada. The seminars at the 'coach house,' as the headquarters were often called, were renowned. Guests included John Lennon, Yoko Ono, Buckminster Fuller, Glenn Gould, Pierre Eliott Trudeau, and Edward Albee.[27] Derrick de Kerckhove, today director of McLuhan studies at the revivified McLuhan Program in Culture and Technology, studied under McLuhan in the late 1960s and recalls that, as a teacher, McLuhan endeavoured to equip students to deal in new ways with information they already had. Nor would McLuhan close an argument; his probes and aphorisms were intended to stimulate students into thinking things out for themselves.[28]

McLuhan's most notable scholarly milestones were *The Gutenberg Galaxy* (1962) and, most eventfully, *Understanding Media* (1964). In 1965 the American public relations firm Gossage & Feigen, seeing in McLuhan mass-marketing possibilities, contracted with him and proceeded to make him into a celebrity.[29] In the same year, journalist Tom Wolfe published a highly influential essay, 'What If He Is Right?' in *New York* magazine. McLuhan thereby became media guru, whose writings attracted attention from such commentators as Raymond Williams, Kenneth Burke, Kenneth Boulding, George Steiner, Susan Sontag, and Theodore Roszak. Although many were detractors, that attention further propelled McLuhan into stardom; he appeared on television talk shows, advised politicians on their images, and was quite simply the most famous living academic. Over the next few years some dozen other volumes, many co-authored, appeared, embossed with his signature.

The secondary literature on McLuhan and his work also became substantial, and is still growing. Most notably he is the subject of two

major biographies,[30] a book of reminisces by some seventy acquaint-
ances,[31] and several collections of critical essays.[32] *Wired* magazine named
him its 'Patron Saint.'[33]

When McLuhan burst into public prominence in the mid-1960s, he
was, in Northrop Frye's phrase, 'caught up in the manic-depressive
roller coaster of the news media': 'hysterically celebrated in the sixties,'
he was all but ignored in the seventies and eighties.[34] Indicative of the
obscurity into which he fell is Bruce Powe's reminiscence that in 1978–
9, the last year he taught his once-famous seminar at the coach house at
the University of Toronto, he achieved an enrollment of but six students. Cardboard boxes filled with remaindered copies of *The Executive
as Drop-Out* and *From Cliché to Archetype* littered the classroom.[35]

In the 1990s, however, there began a resurgence of interest in McLuhan,
and at the dawn of the new millennium there is, if anything, greater
scholarly respect for him than ever before. Perhaps electric technology
has penetrated the academic mind sufficiently to make his ideas seem
less outrageous.[36] McLuhan scholar Glenn Wilmott has suggested that
the rise of post-structuralism as an academic stance in the postmodernist
age has sufficiently 'problematized' objectivity, empiricism, rational-
ism, specialized knowledge – the very critical values invoked to dismiss McLuhan – to now make him more academically acceptable.[37]

In 1979 McLuhan suffered a stroke that left him virtually speechless.
His former colleague Edmund Carpenter recounted touchingly,

> I immediately went to see him. He stood before the fireplace, next to [his
> wife] Corrine, looking much the same as when we'd first met, but now no
> words came & his hands flew about in frustration. Corrine took them &
> held them before her. 'Tell me, Marshall. I can understand you. I can tell
> Ted.' She looked into his eyes & he smiled & they both laughed, holding
> hands, and this was communication even more dazzling than that first
> day.[38]

McLuhan died on 31 December 1980.[39] On his tombstone, in a 'digital-
analogue typeface,' is the inscription 'The Truth Shall Make You Free.'[40]

FOUR INFLUENCES

Apart from poets and literary critics such as those noted above, there
were others who had a major influence on McLuhan. One was Lewis

Mumford. His *Technics and Civilization* appeared in 1934, and was one of the first books to emphasize the interplay of technology and culture. Although in subsequent works Mumford dismissed the thesis he had advanced there – namely, that electricity is an organic, egalitarian, decentralizing technology that fosters community and reverses the fragmenting effects of industrial technology, McLuhan embraced it and continued to promote it all of his scholarly days.[41]

Important also was the Swiss historian of architecture, Siegfried Giedion, author of *Space, Time and Architecture* (1954) and of *Mechanization Takes Command* (1948). The latter book's subtitle, *A Contribution to Anonymous History*, captures well Giedion's contention that the meaning of history arises from and is revealed by 'humble objects.'[42] Giedion saw mechanization as an extension, indeed as a supplanting, of the hand.[43] He maintained also that industrialization 'mechanized' consciousness: it split thought from feeling – a most precarious condition for a time when the technological means of doing things have attained such immense power. For civilization to survive, Giedion warned, intellect and emotions must be reintegrated. McLuhan extended Giedion's thought by viewing various media of communication, particularly the printing press, as mechanizing human relations. And, like Giedion, McLuhan argued that mechanical innovations fracture thought from feeling.[44] He also saw the inorganic (i.e., the technological) as melding with the organic so as to utterly transform human nature – creating a 'new' (i.e., prosthetic) man. McLuhan referred often to the myth of Narcissus to emphasize that, in being mesmerized by their technological extensions, people become completely oblivious to the effects that technological extensions have on them.

A third figure to note was classicist Eric Havelock. Born in England in 1903 and educated at Cambridge, Havelock taught at the University of Toronto between 1929 and 1947. As noted in a previous chapter, along with other classicists at the University of Toronto in the 1940s, Havelock is credited with helping to inspire Harold Innis's communication thesis, and indeed Havelock's 1951 tome, *The Crucifixion of Intellectual Man*, is acknowledged in the preface to Innis's last book, *Changing Concepts of Time*. After leaving the University of Toronto, moreover, Havelock developed themes parallel to those of McLuhan. For such reasons he is sometimes regarded as a founding member of the 'Toronto School of Communication.'[45]

On the other hand, Havelock attested that while at Toronto he had little contact with Innis.[46] Moreover, Havelock's most influential book as far as McLuhan was concerned – *Preface to Plato*[47] – was published in 1963, sixteen years after he had left Toronto and one year after the appearance of McLuhan's *The Gutenberg Galaxy*. Nonetheless, McLuhan referred often to *Preface to Plato* and regarded it as being very supportive. For McLuhan, Havelock was the first classicist to have made a careful investigation of how the phonetic alphabet created disequilibrium in the ancient world.

Finally, we must consider Innis. McLuhan often referred to himself as being a 'disciple of Harold Adams Innis.' However, although they were for several years contemporaries at the University of Toronto, Innis and McLuhan hardly knew each other: as late as December 1948, McLuhan still misspelled Innis's name,[48] and not until 1951 did he begin reading anything by that great political economist. Upon learning that Innis had placed *The Mechanical Bride* on his syllabus, however, the future communication guru decided he should learn more about such a person, and turned immediately to 'Minerva's Owl,' and was immediely won over — so much so that McLuhan referred to his *The Gutenberg Galaxy* as being but a 'footnote to the observations of Innis.'[49]

One thing about Innis's work that resonated with McLuhan was its style. McLuhan saw Innis as an artist: 'Without having studied modern art and poetry, he [Innis] yet discovered how to arrange his insights in patterns that nearly resemble the art of our time [the poetry of Baudelaire and the paintings of Cézanne, for instance]. Innis presents his insights in a mosaic structure of seemingly unrelated and disproportioned sentences and aphorisms ... He expects the reader to make discovery after discovery that he himself had missed.'[50] McLuhan added: 'How exciting ... to encounter a writer whose every phrase invited prolonged meditation and exploration.'[51]

McLuhan was also impressed by Innis's method. In his view, Innis did not investigate in detail the *content* of structures – for example, the *types* of books in the ancient libraries or the *nature* of the philosophies, religions, and sciences of antiquity. Rather, it was the *existence* of libraries or the predominance of religious belief per se that Innis deemed important. McLuhan concluded that Innis 'invites us ... to consider the formalities of power exerted by these structures in their mutual interaction.'[52]

Furthermore, McLuhan was enamoured of Innis's scholarly tactic in both his staples and his communication writings, whereby the political economist painstakingly catalogued details from which 'leapt' conclusions based on 'the sudden realization of a pattern';[53] McLuhan thereafter recommended 'pattern recognition' as a means of coping in an era of information overload.

Finally, and most importantly, McLuhan accepted wholeheartedly Innis's main thesis that culture, society, and civilization change in tandem with changes in the media of communication. It has been suggested that McLuhan's famous aphorism and axial principle 'the medium is the message' was formulated while reading Innis's introduction to *Empire and Communications*.[54] That insight alone made McLuhan greatly indebted to Innis, a person, incidentally, towards whom he did not particularly warm on a personal basis.[55] We will see below, however, that McLuhan reworked, indeed inverted, Innis's explanation of the nature of the interaction between media and society; for that reason in particular, McLuhan's collaborator and close friend Edmund Carpenter has suggested that Innis's influence on McLuhan has been overstated.[56]

LITERARY CRITICISM APPROACH TO MEDIA STUDIES

McLuhan's media studies derived from and extended his literary work.[57] He both folded the non-verbal world into literature and myth, much as Northrop Frye did, and applied the techniques and concepts of literary criticism to the non- verbal world. McLuhan justified these procedures with the claim that language often 'evokes' objects and situations which are themselves non-verbal, and by contending that the 'interplay' works both ways. He declared, 'We are taking for granted that there is at all times interplay between these worlds of *percept* and *concept*, verbal and nonverbal. Anything that can be observed about the behavior of linguistic cliché or archetype can be found plentifully in the nonlinguistic world.'[58] The terms 'percept' and 'concept' figure prominently in McLuhan's work. His associate and co-author Barrington Nevitt, interpreting McLuhan, defined *percepts* as 'the raw sensory data of human experience generated by direct encounter with existence.'[59] *Concepts* are 'replays of percepts,' that is, abstractions formed from experiencing similar percepts. Being abstractions, concepts are verbal, whereas percepts are non-verbal.

McLuhan claimed, further, that since language is *a technology* (i.e., an artefact), it can properly be compared with other artefacts or technologies, again justifying his practice of applying the tools of literary criticism to the non-verbal world. In this regard he was fond of invoking lines from the poet William Butler Yeats which emphasize the notion that poets are like inventors in recycling refuse to forge new creations:

Those masterful images because complete [i.e., fulfilled]
Grew in pure mind, but out of what began?
A mound of refuse or the sweepings of a street,
Old kettles, old bottles, and a broken can,
Old iron, old bones, old rags, that raving slut
Who keeps the till. Now that my ladder's gone,
I must lie down where all the ladders start,
In the foul rag-and-bone shop of the heart.[60]

We turn now to some of the ways whereby McLuhan applied techniques and concepts of literary criticism to non-verbal artefacts, bearing in mind that all artefacts for McLuhan, by 'extending' the human organism, are 'media': we are joined by, or meet in, our extensions, which thereby mediate our interactions.

Archetype and Cliché

McLuhan cited approvingly Northrop Frye's definition of 'archetype' as a recurring form in literature that becomes recognizable on account of repetition. Archetype, therefore, is 'a form of cliché.'[61]

Unlike Frye, however, McLuhan applied the literary notions of cliché and archetype to the material or non-verbal environment. Every innovation, he averred, recalls an older form (a former cliché), and in so doing becomes an archetype. He provided several examples: A flagpole flying a flag is a present-day commonplace or cliché, but in recalling ('retrieving') a spear with a banner it becomes an archetype.[62] Likewise an electric circuit is a contemporary cliché, but is an archetype when feeding an electric log fire.[63]

New media for McLuhan are 'new clichés' whose first effect is to liquidate or scrap the clichés (media) of previous cultures and environments. McLuhan noted that there is consequently a tendency for a sense of absurdity or alienation to arise during times of rapid technological change – what Frye had called the 'alienation of progress.' The secondary effect of new media, however, is to retrieve ancient, broken, and fragmented clichés, 'making them transcendental.'[64]

McLuhan believed that artists help re-establish a sense of equanimity in times of rapid change. Poets such as Eliot and Joyce, he claimed, drew upon the fragments of cultures both past and present to construct archetypes as a way of patterning the human condition, thereby restoring for audiences a sense of meaning and stability. McLuhan repeatedly invoked the following line from Eliot's *The Waste Land* to indicate the artists' endeavours in this regard: 'These fragments I have shored against my ruins.' But even here McLuhan was dialectical. For, if archetypes can restore meaning by retrieving past forms, they can also lull audiences into quiescence.[65]

Clichés, too, he saw dialectically. Although normally they are 'dull habituation,' with but slight modification they can function as 'probes'[66] or stimuli, inducing thought and discovery. His revised aphorism 'the medium is the massage,' for example, in recalling but differing slightly from the original, became a probe.

Late in his career, McLuhan amplified his analysis of cliché and archetype to arrive at four 'laws of the media.' He set them out as combined propositions and questions:

- What does the artefact enhance or intensify or make possible or accelerate?
- If some aspect of a situation is enlarged or enhanced, simultaneously the old condition or unenhanced situation is displaced thereby. What is pushed aside or obsolesced by the new 'organ'?
- What recurrence or retrieval of earlier actions and services is brought into play simultaneously by the new form?
- When pushed to the limits ... the new form will tend to reverse what had been its original characteristics. What is the reversal potential of the new form?

McLuhan insisted that this 'tetrad of effects' is simultaneous, not sequential: 'All four aspects are inherent in each artefact [or medium] from the start.'[67]

The automobile, for instance, (i) *enhances* privacy (alone at a drive-in movie; going outside to be alone); (ii) *renders obsolete* the horse and buggy; (iii) *retrieves* the knight in shining armour and the countryside; and (iv) *reverses* into traffic jams, suburbs, and 'corporate privacy.'[68] The telephone *(i) enhances* dialogue; (ii) *renders obsolete* privacy by eroding barriers between physical spaces; (iii) *retrieves* instant access to users, as in a tribal village; and (iv) *reverses* into the mythic world of discarnate, disembodied intelligences ('the sender is sent').[69] Money (i) *enhances* or speeds up transactions; (ii) *renders obsolete* haggle and barter; (iii) *retrieves* the potlach in the form of conspicuous consumption; and (iv) pushed to its limit disappears into credit and the credit card, that is, *reverses* into an absence of (tangible) money.[70]

McLuhan even claimed that 'all our artifacts are in fact words,'[71] although a better rendering would perhaps have been 'signs.' To justify that claim, McLuhan coined a pun: 'All of these things [i.e., artefacts, words] are the outerings and utterings of man.'[72] He noted further that in some traditional societies 'speech and weaving are synonymous,'[73] that is, stories are told through the patterns woven into fabrics. But most profoundly he argued that each 'tetrad,' being the potential inherent action or power of an artefact, is that object's 'word or *logos*':

> Each tetrad is the word or the *logos* of its subject, and all these words are peculiarly human, with *the utterer as the etymology.* They constitute, in opposition to the Shannon–Weaver construct, a right-hemisphere theory, or model, of communication; and, as they provide both exegesis and etymology of a (rhetorical) utterance, they serve to bring up to date the ancient and medieval tradition of grammar-allied-to-rhetoric in a way that is consonant with the forms of awareness imposed on the twentieth century by electronic technology.[74]

Artefacts, indeed, have a logic or grammar when they are combined to make statements. We noted previously R.S. Perinbanayagam's observation that each commodity is a sign in a semiological field that people use to make statements about self-identity and their relations to others.

Metaphors

Another literary convention that McLuhan applied to the world of material artefacts was the *metaphor*. McLuhan joked: 'A man's reach must exceed his grasp or what's a metaphor.'[75] The term comes from the Greek *metapherein*, meaning 'to carry across or transport.'[76] McLuhan remarked that only with the advent of the telegraph did information become separated from material media such as stone, papyrus, and paper; before that time, 'communication' had been closely linked to roads, bridges, sea routes, rivers, canals, and other means of *carrying across*. Hence, McLuhan concluded, for communication media, 'the notion of metaphor was apt.'[77]

In the age of electricity, moreover, McLuhan continued, *media as metaphor* regains cogency, but now what the media translate or carry over are *users*: 'In this electric age we see ourselves being translated more and more into the form of information, moving toward the technological extension of consciousness.'[78] More generally, he declared, 'All media are active metaphors in their power to translate experience into new forms. The spoken word was the first technology by which man was able to let go of his environment in order to grasp it in a new way ... Just as a metaphor transforms and transmits experience, so do the media.'[79] When we use the telephone, *we* are transported, angelically, without bodies, to distant locations. When we use television, *we* are grafted into the logic of the medium that is our prosthesis. It goes almost without saying that McLuhan used metaphors and analogies continuously to explain or illustrate his position.

Symbols

McLuhan maintained that people often confuse objects with symbols, and he took exception, in particular, to Northrop Frye's definition of 'symbol' as 'any unit of any work of literature which can be isolated for critical attention.'[80] McLuhan insisted that, in the Greek, *symballein* meant 'throwing together.'[81] The concept of 'symbol,' therefore, is structural, denoting the juxtaposing of things.[82] He wrote: 'A kettle is not a symbol unless related or juxtaposed with stove, or pot, or food. Things in isolation are not symbols. Symbolism as an art or technique meant precisely the *breaking* of connections.'[83] McLuhan borrowed from the symbolist poets, who intentionally broke commonplace associations and constructed new ones. In his figure/ground analysis, for instance, McLuhan imaginatively wrenched out of normal context *figures* and focused attention on normally taken-for-granted *grounds*.

Myth

Like Frye, Innis, and Grant, McLuhan proposed that there are essentially only two modes of discourse – the linear, logical mode as practised in Western scientific and philosophical thought, and the mythic. *Myth*, he declared, characterizes the thought and expression of preliterate cultures, is narrative in form and encapsulates timeless, as opposed to particularistic human drama. Given information overabundance and speed-up due to electric technology, he contended that people are turning again to mythic modes of understanding: 'When man is overwhelmed by information,' he expounded, 'he resorts to myth; myth is inclusive, time-saving, and fast.'[84] He wrote also: 'Myth is a succinct statement of a complex social process.'[85]

True to his pronouncements, McLuhan spoke and wrote in mythic terms: of King Cadmus and the dragon's teeth, which he likened to letters of the alphabet chewing up oral culture; of Narcissus's self-absorption through a bodily extension, which he saw paralleling our own mesmerization with technological extensions; and, most fundamentally, albeit implicitly, the biblical story of the Fall and the coming of the New Jerusalem. Let us pause, then, and see how that biblical narrative structures McLuhan's media theory.

According to McLuhan, there was once a golden age of manuscript culture when all the senses were in balance. Thought at that time was not divorced from feeling since literate people still participated in oral dialogue. On the other hand, through literacy, people of that era *had* attained a sense of logic and an appreciation of objectivity, and so were able to ward off pre-literate superstition. Upon developing the printing press, however, people became alienated from their now increasingly objectified and fragmented world. (McLuhan's justification for making these assertions is addressed in the next section.) However, the good news is that, through electronics, people are now being reunited and becoming whole once more. In an interview, McLuhan exclaimed: 'The Christian concept of the mystical body – all men as members of the body of Christ – this becomes technologically a fact under electronic conditions.'[86] On the other hand, as previously emphasized, McLuhan definitely had a dialectical cast of mind, and so he also warned that *the global village* (his metaphor for an electronically interconnected world) is a dangerous, undesirable, claustrophobic, and possibly totalitarian place in which to live: 'The more you create village conditions, the more discontinuity and division and diversity. The global village absolutely insures maximal disagreement on all points. It never occurred to me that uniformity and tranquillity were the properties of the global village. It has more spite and envy.'[87] And again: 'There's nothing at all difficult about putting computers in the position where they will be able to conduct carefully orchestrated programming of the sensory life of whole populations ... The computer could program the media to determine the given messages a people should hear in terms of their over-all needs, creating a total media experience absorbed and patterned by the senses.'[88] These warnings respecting the trials and tribulations inhering in the global village can be likened to prophecies concerning the plagues of the Apocalypse, destined to occur prior to the New Jerusalem.

MEDIA AND PERCEPTION

Perception
Whereas the Western scientific world-view, at least until the beginning of the twentieth century, maintained that objects and forces have identi-

ties in and of themselves and that language ought ideally to have the exactitude of 'one word – one meaning' in order properly to represent these things, McLuhan held a different opinion. He contended that words, *like all else*, derive meaning primarily from context.

It follows, therefore, that we cannot expect McLuhan to remain completely consistent in his use of key terms such as 'visual' and 'acoustic.' And, indeed, he was not. At times these terms refer literally to sensory perception by the eye and ear, respectively, but, on other occasions, to generic modes of cognition and ways of processing data. Hence flickering television images, paintings by Seurat, mosaics, symbolist poetry, cartoons, and ideographs, although sensed by the eye, are not 'visual,' according to McLuhan: they lack continuity and detail, and hence require people to experience them *as if* by hearing or touch; in these instances, often unconsciously, viewers add information to what they actually receive visually. McLuhan therefore termed these 'audile–tactile' media.[89] This seemingly outrageous proposition should become less outlandish once we have further reviewed McLuhan's work. For the present, however, it is sufficient to emphasize that, in reading McLuhan, one must always be on guard for shifting meanings, and indeed for multiple layers of meaning.

The Sensorium

McLuhan insisted that each sense interacts with and hence is modified by all the others.[90] Recalling Thomas Aquinas, he proposed the notion of the *sensorium* to denote the five senses in interaction. At any given time, the sensorium will be characterized by a particular ratio or proportion among the various senses. Some individuals or cultures afford greater emphasis to hearing, for example; others, to sight. Ratios among the senses tend to be stable for a given time and place, but, when shifts do occur, 'massive' changes for individuals and for the society result. Parallels to Innis's thought regarding the consequences of shifting to a new staple or the rise of a new medium of inscription are apparent.

Eye and Ear

It is something of an understatement to say that McLuhan drew attention to differences between the eye and the ear as modes of apprehending the world. The eye, he claimed, perceives, or perhaps more accurately creates, *visual space*, which he described as connected, linear, and serial. We look at one thing at a time, in sequence, and think of there being continuity, connectedness, or relatedness among the things we view. Visual space, therefore, is continuous, can be filled up with objects, and is in that sense undifferentiated or homogeneous. In our culture, kilometres, for instance, measure distances irrespective of time (époque), location, or what different spaces may contain.

Furthermore, visual space is infinitely divisible and extensible.[91] When using the eye, therefore, there is a tendency to think of things as comprising parts, giving rise to a propensity for dissection as a mode of inquiry. Objects are always in front of and seemingly detached from the viewer, supporting also to the notion of 'objectivity,' a premise or goal upon which much of Western science has been based.

Nonetheless, and somewhat paradoxically, McLuhan also emphasized that each spectator has a distinct point of view or perspective, helping explain also the rise of individualism and the fragmentation of society into specialties.

The ear, by contrast, according to McLuhan, is attuned to or creates *acoustic space,* which is neither connected nor continuous. Silences, rhythms, and a potpourri of sounds incessantly fragment or differentiate acoustic space. The auditory world therefore can be full of surprises, some calamitous, others serendipitous: 'To the blind all things are sudden,' McLuhan exclaimed.[92]

Furthermore, acoustic space is characterized by simultaneity, as when musical instruments combine symphonically. Audition usually occurs within the context of multiple sounds and other sensory impressions, including visual ones, unlike silent reading, where sight alone is used; in combination, these multiple sensory impressions affect interpretation.

In auditory space, the hearer is always at the centre of things, not in front of them; sound surrounds. Moreover, sounds penetrate and resonate with interiors, whereas vision takes in surface phenomena only. Objectivity, therefore, has little meaning in an acoustic world: indeed, to use acoustic data, positivistic science must first convert it through instrumentation into visual information.

According to McLuhan, part of the explanation for the *apparent* objectivity of sight versus the subjectivity inherent to sound (and touch) is that the gaps or intervals are obvious with touch and sound, but less so with vision. Sometimes, however, gaps in visual space *are* manifest: 'Darkness is to space what silence is to sound, i.e., the interval,' McLuhan pronounced.[93] Darkness encourages people imaginatively to visualize or 'fill in' what might be there. McLuhan attested that mosaics therefore are visual equivalents of sound and touch since their components are separated by darkness, and viewers need to establish connections or patterns.

Epistemology and Ontology of Visual and Acoustic Space

Whereas vision usually gives the sensation of there being no gaps, for McLuhan this is a false impression. He maintained that normally there are neither *logical* nor *causal* connections between or among items in visual space, merely proximities. Advertisers well know that, by carefully arranging objects, connections are created in viewers' minds between the product and the scene, no matter how ludicrous (see figure 11.1).

McLuhan traced distinctions between logic and analogy as modes of thought to differences between the properties of visual and acoustic space. He contended that logic derives from the (illusion of) connectedness of visual space, whereas analogy derives from gaps inherent in audile/tactile space. It is from gaps or intervals, not connections, that knowledge of proportions, and hence analogies, stem. It is worth quoting McLuhan at length on this important insight:

> Perhaps the most precious possession of man is his abiding awareness of the analogy of proper proportionality, the key to all metaphysical insight and perhaps the very condition of consciousness itself. This analogical awareness is constituted of a perpetual play of ratios: A is to B what C is to D, which is to say that the ratio between A and B is proportioned to the ratio between C and D, there being a ratio between these ratios as well. This lively awareness of the most exquisite delicacy depends upon there being no connection whatever between the components. *If A were linked to B, or C to D, mere logic would take the place of analogical perception.*[94]

MEDIA

Theory of Media

McLuhan's media theory stems in large part from his analysis of perception and his concern for effects. Media, he declared, may extend or amplify one or other of the senses, increasing thereby the relative importance of that perceptor in the sensorium.

McLuhan's media analysis, however, was not confined to extensions of the senses. He was concerned also with media that extend other parts of the body. The wheel, for example, extends or amplifies the leg, just as the axe extends the hand, and clothing the skin. Likewise a chair

Figure 11.1   Matinée Cigarette Advertisement (1983). According to McLuhan, *figures* (here the cigarette pack) derive their meaning from context or *ground*. To fully understand situations or texts McLuhan recommended inverting matters – highlighting grounds instead of figures. It that is done in the present instance, outdoor activities, instead of being healthy and life-affirming, take on an aura of danger, stemming perhaps from air pollution.

'outers' the human posterior. According to McLuhan, *all* artefacts extend some aspect of the person, and therefore mediate human relations, making *all artefacts* media of communication: It is through our 'outerings,' as well as our 'utterings,' that we meet.

Moreover, human extensions interact bidirectionally with the environment. On the one hand, the environment 'selects' or favours certain extensions while rendering others obsolete. On the other, the environment comprises, in part, human extensions previously selected. Environments therefore also mediate human relations.

Although McLuhan considered all artefacts to be bodily extensions, and therefore to constitute media, he afforded considerably greater attention to those extending or amplifying the senses. These, he attested, directly affect perception and consciousness. Moreover, he distinguished in particular between media that emphasize the simultaneity of hearing versus those that amplify the sequential logic of the eye. Furthermore, he distinguished between 'hot' and 'cool' media. A *hot* medium like radio and the movies extends a single sense in high definition. High definition is the state of being well filled with data. Hot media, therefore, are low in audience participation. For McLuhan, print is a hot medium *non pareil*. (Recall Innis's complaint that writing leads readers ineluctably, step by step, to the authors' conclusions.) By contrast, a *cool* medium, one low in definition (for example, a voice over the telephone or a cartoon), gives relatively little information, thereby requiring the recipient to fill in or supplement the information.[95] McLuhan's distinction between hot and cool media parallels Frye's dichotomy between the truth of correspondence and mythopoeic consciousness, and more generally between the ontologies of scientific objectivity and social construction.

Tribal cultures, in McLuhan's view, use predominantly cool media. When confronted with hot media, cultures based on cool ones tend to collapse: 'A tribal and feudal hierarchy of a traditional kind collapses quickly when it meets any hot medium of the mechanical, uniform, and repetitive kind. The medium of money or wheel or writing, or any other form of specialist speedup of exchange and information, will serve to fragment a tribal structure.'[96]

A recurring theme of McLuhan's, however, what we might call his principle of inversion or reversal, is that 'every process pushed far enough tends to reverse or flip suddenly; this is the *chiasmus pattern*, perhaps first noted by ancient Chinese sages in *I Ching: The Book of Changes*.'[97] Vision is normally associated with continuity and connectedness, for example, but in the highly visually intensive era combining the phonetic alphabet and the printing press, it fosters logic (rationality), empiricism, dissection, and fragmentation. Vision in high definition encourages division, subdivision, and classification.[98] Furthermore, as noted above, it affords the sighted person a distinct point of view, giving rise to specialist knowledge, another form of fragmentation within society.[99] But when visual information is further speeded up with electronics, in particular, television, chiasmus or reversal occurs again. Information speed-up erodes categories and requires people to interpret meanings and seek out patterns from juxtaposed blocks of information. McLuhan wrote: 'A very much greater speed-up, such as occurs with electricity, may serve to restore a tribal pattern of intense involvement such as took place with the introduction of radio in Europe. ... Specialist technologies detribalize; the nonspecialist electric technology retribalizes.'[100] Likewise, tactility and hearing, which normally are associated with community and interdependence, when pushed to an extreme lead to fragmentation. McLuhan wrote: 'At [the audile–tactile] end of the sensory spectrum, individuality is created by the interval of tactile involvement ... Intense individuality is even more characteristic of the nonliterate population depicted by Dickens or Al Capp than it is of the consciously cultivated individuality of the highly literate.'[101]

Media Analyses

Spoken Language

For McLuhan, language is an amplification of mental processes. He wrote: 'Language does for intelligence what the wheel does for the feet and the body; it enables [people] to move from thing to thing with greater ease and speed and ever less involvement.'[102] He also declared, 'Language is ... man's greatest and most complex artifact.'[103]

McLuhan thought of spoken language as being one of the very first 'mass media.' Citing his associate, Edmund Carpenter, he wrote: 'In the oral tradition, the myth-teller speaks as many-to-many, not as person-to-person. Speech and song are addressed to all.'[104] We see here that McLuhan's conception of orality aligns more closely with that of Frye than Innis. As Carey pointed out, for McLuhan orality 'is deeply informed by a liturgical sense of chant and memory rather than [as in the case of Innis] a political sense of discussion and debate.'[105]

By McLuhan's account, in oral cultures people live in the simultaneous, all-inclusive world of acoustic space. This means, among other things, that pre-literate people apprehend interdependencies readily;[106] they have, in other words, an implicit ecological understanding. On the other hand, simple causality tends to elude them: failure to strike a prey for an ear-oriented person is a sure sign of cosmic displeasure, not poor marksmanship.[107]

However, McLuhan saw a world of difference between spoken and written language. Every word a person utters (and 'outers'), he declared, 'extends or involves all of his sensory life.'[108] By comparison, other media, including written language (but excluding computers), are 'specialist extensions.'

Spoken words fly by through time; they are not materially embedded so as to take up visual space. However, paradoxically, spoken words are more concrete in meaning and 'evoke things directly.'[109] Speech, then, is 'resonant, live, active'; it is, according to McLuhan, a 'natural force.'[110] In oral cultures, speech is always associated with power: The Book of Genesis, for instance, begins with pronouncements that God spoke and things came to be; Adam named the animals and attained power over them.

Writing

Since writing makes the thought world visible, it makes the eye predominant over the ear. Consequently, writing causes cultures to move from acoustic to visual space. This movement has both benefits and costs. On the one hand, predominance of the eye enables the detached, objective, logical, and experimental world-view of science to take hold. Moreover, visual detachment via the written page gives people 'the power of the second look,' permitting them to escape the uncritical, superstitious, and emotionally involved life.[111] On the other hand, by deepening dependence on the eye, literacy causes thought to separate from feeling, alienation being the alter ego of objectivity. Writing causes organic tribal society to fragment into specialties and individualism.

All modes of writing, of course, emphasize the eye, and to that extent have similar effects. McLuhan, however, contrasted ideograms with typography and the phonetic alphabet, claiming that the phonetic alphabet and typography induce much greater visual intensity. We now take a closer look at his analyses of these various modes of inscription.

- *Ideographs versus the Phonetic Alphabet.* McLuhan maintained that ideographs are 'totally different' from the phonetic alphabet because they do not so completely substitute the eye for the ear. Ideographs, he contended, are 'complex Gestalts' that do not separate meaning from sight or sound, and that involve 'all the senses at once.' McLuhan's associate Barrington Nevitt explained, for example, that Chinese ideographic writing entails simultaneity, not merely sequence as does alphabetic writing. The Chinese figure for 'east,' for instance, combines signs for tree and sun (themselves pictograms), indicating that at sunrise the sun is tangled in the tree's branches. For 'red,' Chinese writing combines abbreviated pictures of rose, iron rust, cherry, and flamingo.[112]

Phonetic writing, in contrast, is merely (but powerfully) 'a visual code for speech.' McLuhan maintained that the alphabet not only 'dissociates or abstracts ... sight and sound, but separates all meaning from the sound of the letters.'[113] The letter sequence c-o-w, for instance, derives meaning from linguistic convention only; considered separately, the letters (and their associated sounds) are meaningless.

Moreover, McLuhan saw the alphabet as wiping out non-alphabetic modes of discourse – both indirectly by facilitating the issuance of military orders across vast tracts of space,[114] and directly by folding non-alphabetic languages into itself. Pictographic and ideographic modes of writing require many signs and are quite unwieldy; the phonetic alphabet, in contrast, has few letters and so can easily encompass pictographic languages.[115] The translation of ideographic languages into the phonetic alphabet, therefore, is a one-way street: 'The alphabet cannot be assimilated; it can only liquidate or reduce.'[116]

- *Manuscripts versus Print.* Manuscripts provided only a foretaste of the transformative effects of the printing press and movable type. Although centuries of predominance of manuscripts assuredly did diminish the importance of the ear compared with what it had been in oral culture, manuscripts nonetheless were 'highly tactile'; consequently, there was no separation of vision from the 'audile–tactile complex.'[117]

All that changed in the sixteenth century, however, with Gutenberg's invention: movable type 'split vision and tactility asunder,' the two modes of perception thereafter going 'their divergent ways to set up the rival empires of Art and Science.'[118] Typography for McLuhan caused an utter change of consciousness. In manuscript culture, since readers utilized fully senses other than sight, the notion of a single 'literal meaning' never arose. 'To the oral man,' McLuhan declared, 'the literal is inclusive, contains all possible meanings and levels [for example, allegorical and metaphorical meanings],' whereas for literate people 'literal' refers exclusively to denotative meanings.[119] Indeed, he added, from the sixteenth century on, readers felt 'impelled to separate level from level, and function from function, in a process of specialist exclusion.'[120]

McLuhan made the same distinction by contrasting 'light on' (literal meaning) and 'light through' (allegorical or metaphorical meaning). 'Light through' implies that the spectator is glimpsing a portion of complex reality *through* (or with the aid of) a text, whereas 'light on' presumes the text is all there is to see.[121] In terms of visual arts, the equivalent distinction is between a stained-glass window and a realistic painting.

McLuhan saw other consequences flowing from movable type. The printing press, he speculated, was probably the first instance of a reduction of a handicraft into mechanical terms. Not only was print 'the first mass-produced thing,' it was also the first 'uniform and repeatable "commodity."' He added: the 'assembly line of movable types' foreshadowed and made possible 'a product that was uniform and as repeatable as a scientific experiment; such a character does not belong to the manuscript.'[122]

The linearity of type, moreover, helped ingrain 'lineal, sequential habits.' But, most important, print relegated 'auditory and other sensuous complexity to the background.'[123] 'Objectivity means leaving out all modes of awareness except the visual.'[124] Furthermore, print is associated with changes in the perception of time and space. Time as duration, that is, as something that happens between two points, arose with writing and the clock.[125] Time came to be 'measured not by the uniqueness of private experience but by abstract uniform units.'[126] Likewise typography converted sacred spaces into merely profane ones. 'A "sacred" universe,' he wrote, 'is one dominated by the spoken word and by auditory media; a "profane" universe, on the other hand, is one dominated by the visual sense.'[127] He added: 'For medieval man, as for the native, space was not homogeneous and did not *contain* objects. Each thing made its own space, as it still does for the native (and equally for the modern physicist).'[128]

Electronic Media

For hundreds of thousands of years, from the invention of the wheel to the birth of the electric telegraph, media were 'mechanical' — that is, they extended only a part of the body, and hence induced detachment, fragmentation, objectivity, specialization, detribalization, and individuality. The mechanical era thus was one of 'explosion' and fragmentation.

With electronic circuitry, however, there is a reversal – an 'implosion.' Electronic media merge individuals and environment into an interdependent, simultaneous system whereby the 'globe [becomes] no more than a village.'[129] Individualism is superseded by communitarianism, and an ecological understanding replaces instrumentalism.

Electronic technologies do not simply amplify select body parts, but extend and 'outer' the entire central nervous system. The result is to 'involve us in the whole of mankind and to incorporate the whole of mankind in us.' Through electronics, we approach a state of cosmic consciousness whereby each person is, and knows him- or herself to be, part of everyone else. It is no longer possible to adopt the 'aloof and dissociated role of the literate Westerner.'[130]

Stated otherwise, electronic technologies, some more than others, reassert the primacy and inclusiveness of acoustic space, albeit now on a global scale. Even television, McLuhan claimed, bears the properties of an audile–tactile medium. One basis for this claim was the blurriness of the television image; McLuhan claimed that the TV picture, based on dots and lines, requires viewers to 'fill in' the missing information, just as they do in acoustic space. A second, and more convincing explanation, concerns information speed-up and abundance. With information overload, old strategies for attaining knowledge and making sense of the world – isolating a structure or institution, studying it in detail, and making either logical or causal connections among its parts – no longer suffice. We are required instead to *make* sense of the superfluity of information by detecting patterns, intuiting resonances, and comprehending the pressures that various blocks of information and their originating structures bring to bear on one another, because in principle no connections exist except those we forge. The message recipient, in other words, must adopt once more mythic modes of decoding by becoming an artist – integrating the 'mosaics' formed by unrelated bits.

ART AND ARTISTS

Role of the Artist
By McLuhan's account, people are normally blithely unaware of the media's *massage*, that is, of media effects. Generally, we are too preoccupied with the individual messages that media deliver to notice media's broader ramifications. 'The "content" of a medium,' McLuhan dis-

closed, 'is like the juicy piece of meat carried by the burglar to distract the watchdog of the mind.'[131]

McLuhan contended further that media users are the 'servo-mechanisms' of evolving technology. He wrote that users are the veritable 'sex organs of the technological world,'[132] just as bees are the sex organs of the plant world; 'to behold, use or perceive any extension of ourselves in technological form is necessarily to embrace it.'[133] Citing both William Blake and the Old Testament psalmist, McLuhan proposed that we 'become what we behold.'[134] In another formulation, he charged that users are the real content of a medium, because media not only enfold (contain) users, but, more important, shape them in ways consistent with the media's logic. In the case of the phonetic alphabet and typography, for example, users become logical, linear, fragmented, detached, empirical, and objective; with television, however, they become analogical, intuitive, involved, feeling, communal.

Being a servo-mechanism, of course, is the apotheosis of unfreedom. And it is precisely at this point that McLuhan called upon the artist as saviour. 'The serious artist,' he declared, 'is the only person able to encounter technology with impunity, just because he is an expert aware of the changes in sense perception.'[135] He asserted further:

> The job of the artist is to keep people tuned to the present and if you're going to tune their sensibilities and their perceptions you have constantly to rearrange the focusing of their perceptions. The artists' job is to make it new at all times, not for the sake of novelty but for the sake of relevance ... If you want to tune in on your time and know where it's at, the artists' new rhythms, new images will show you how.[136]

Method of the Artist

Normally, since the environment is background, it is of low intensity or low definition. We tend therefore to pay it little attention. However, a storm in nature or a polluting smoke stack suddenly raises the environment to high intensity and we cannot avoid noticing it. Technological change likewise can push the fabricated environment into high definition, and it is then that a reversal, or *chiasmus*, occurs. When an environment is pushed to high intensity and thereby becomes an object of attention, it becomes in effect 'an antienvironment,' assuming thereby the character of 'an art object'[137] on account of the attention it engenders. 'Anti-environments,' according to McLuhan, are *figures* to environments, and as such they enable people to perceive their *ground*, that is, their accustomed environment, with greater clarity. Intensification of an environment (i.e., turning a portion of the environment into an 'art form') is in McLuhan's opinion the principal strategy used by artists to increase awareness (see figure 11.2).

In *Beyond the Vanishing Point*, McLuhan, with Harley Parker, demonstrated how poets and visual artists through the ages have constructed counter-environments to increase awareness. Through his pointillist technique, Seurat, for instance, painted *light* through 'making paint itself the [apparent] light source';[138] Seurat, according to McLuhan, thereby anticipated the electric age since, in confronting thousands of tiny dots, the spectator is placed as if in acoustic space, where there is no single point of view. Likewise, cubism, which depicts objects simultaneously from many different angles, dropped entirely 'the illusion of perspective in favor of instant sensory awareness of the whole.'[139] In literature, Eliot's *The Waste Land*, Wyndham Lewis's *The Apes of God*, Joyce's *Finnegans Wake*, and the entire Theatre of the Absurd[140] create anti-environments to the accustomed literary forms, again anticipating the electric age.

McLuhan saw himself, of course, as an artist, and he consistently adopted tactics analogous to those of the artist. In the preface of *The Mechanical Bride*, for instance, he announced he would wrench out of the everyday context typical commercial imagery (our accustomed 'ground') to induce concentrated attention.[141] Likewise, in *The Gutenberg Galaxy*, he eschewed the logical, linear mode of presentation, typified by print, in favour of a mosaic style consisting of brief sections headlined by a principal thought; undoubtedly McLuhan intended thereby to represent, through a printed form, information speed-up in an electric environment.

However, McLuhan acknowledged, artists do not always strive to increase critical awareness. In preliterate societies, art was a principal means of socialization; it helped merge individuals into their environment.[142] In contemporary culture, too, art produced by 'fallen' artists is often used for propaganda and for advertising.[143] (We elaborate upon this point below.) On several occasions, McLuhan referred favourably to Jacques Ellul's classic text *Propaganda*,[144] remarking that propaganda is 'the total culture in action,'[145] by implication including artworks.

McLUHAN'S POLITICAL ECONOMY

At times – for instance, when discussing the role of artists and advertisers and the blind spots of liberal economics – McLuhan was seminal in political-economic analyses. At other times, however, his aphorisms

Figure 11.2   Claes Oldenburg, *Clothespin, Philadelphia* (1976). McLuhan claimed artists make audiences aware by wrenching commonplace artefacts from their usual contexts, thereby giving them new meanings and importance. Is the juxtaposing of this mundane (albeit enormous) clothespin with the glass and concrete towers of the urban environment a commentary on the inhuman scale of modern technology, or is it rather an insistence that human basics survive and grow even in the modern megalopolis? (Courtesy Leo Castell. Gallery, New York)

simply denied the existence of asymmetries in the distribution of power and revealed an antipathy to major political-economic concerns. In this section, we explore the paradoxical nature of McLuhan's political economy.

Overt Political Economy

Artists and Advertisers

An incisive insight into political economy emerges from McLuhan's treatment of artists and advertisers. The true artist, he contended, like the inventor, is the 'ultimate enemy' of established power. The artist causes perceptions to change, thereby enabling people to see things as they really are. Similarly inventors create products and processes that, by transforming environments, increase awareness.[146] Awareness, for McLuhan, is always an enemy of established power.

Like Dallas Smythe, however, McLuhan was cognizant that capitalist economies tend to domesticate artists and their works. McLuhan asked: 'If it is true that the artist possesses the means of anticipating and avoiding the consequences of technological trauma, then what are we to think of the world and bureaucracy of "art appreciation"? Would it not seem suddenly to be a conspiracy to make the artist a frill, a fribble, or a Milltown?'[147] Aesthetics, then, for McLuhan, as for Smythe and Grierson, is the antithesis of critical awareness.

McLuhan also recognized that artists who fulfil their function must often pay a high price in terms of forgone wealth. Many artists, therefore, choose to work for advertising agencies and public relations firms. McLuhan was consistent throughout his career in critiquing such 'fallen' artists and their works. In *Understanding Media*, he remarked bitterly: 'Ads are not meant for conscious consumption. They are intended as subliminal pills for the subconscious in order to exercise an hypnotic spell.'[148] In *From Cliché to Archetype*, likewise, he cautioned that, in an age of electricity, much greater power accrues to advertisers than hitherto on account of a reversal between product and information. He wrote:

> As the economy moves more and more into the electrical orbit of programmed information, production is oriented increasingly toward service. Hardware becomes software. This process appears sufficiently in the world of advertising. As the means of advertising have greatly enlarged, the images created by advertising become an ever larger portion of the

needs and satisfactions of the public. Eventually, people could look to the ad image as a world in itself.[149]

McLuhan perceived that the mass media generally have become little more than vehicles for advertisers: 'The film medium,' for instance, is now a 'monster ad for consumer goods. In America this major aspect of film is merely subliminal ... In fact, the movie is a mighty limb of the industrial giant.'[150]

Technological Change

McLuhan also frequently drew attention to power dimensions of technological change. As noted, he ascribed to the innovator a role in democratization by heightening the public's awareness of the environment. He proposed also other political-economic dimensions to technological change. He remarked, for instance, that 'lack of homogeneity in speed of information movement creates diversity of patterns in organization; ... any new means of moving information will alter any power structure whatever.'[151]

That principle, he continued, holds true both within cultures and organizations, and between them. Regarding intra-organizational conflict, technologically based discrepancies can cause collapse;[152] hierarchies, for example, can be rent asunder as the free flow of information increases. Regarding intercultural communication, information speed-up makes porous previously well-defined borders; historically the independence of villages and city-states declined as information movement sped up. McLuhan declared that, as information movement accelerates, new centralist powers invariably take action 'to homogenize as many marginal areas as possible.'[153] Although he acknowledged that the wheel, roads, paper, money, and the mechanical clock were important innovations accelerating transactions, and thereby shifting power,[154] the phonetic alphabet and typography were, for him, of greatest importance: 'The phonetic alphabet has no rival ... as a translator of man out of the closed tribal echo-chamber into the neutral visual world of lineal organization.'[155]

On the other hand, McLuhan proposed that at some point a reversal (*chiasmus*) occurs – a most non-Innisian contention. The electric telegraph and ensuing electronic media have sped up information movement to such an extent that there is now an implosion. Rather than centres of power extending their reach as they did with 'mechanical' media, the trend with electronics is towards the negation of centres of power; as in a pointillist painting, everyone and everything is increasingly understood as being related simultaneously to all else in a complex system of mutual interdependence. It is precisely at this point, then, that McLuhan abandoned the realism of political economy in favour of an idealism devoid of power considerations. Evidently it did not occur to him that, even in an age of electronics, technologies can be associated with a particular ruling class, or, as Innis would put it, with a new monopoly of knowledge.

Critique of Liberal Economics

In *The Mechanical Bride*, McLuhan satirized liberal economists' faith in the price system and the 'invisible hand.'[156] Mainstream economics, he judged, gives short shrift both to conflict and to power. Although eschewing the thoroughly class-based critical analysis typifying Marxism, McLuhan's early and later work is rife with insights on how everyday business practices conflict fundamentally with democratic values and with the broader public interest. Advertising, news, public relations, and 'entertainment,' for McLuhan, are all instruments whereby corporations lull audiences into a somnambulent state or, worse, seduce them into compliance.

Furthermore, McLuhan charged, mainstream economics presumes incorrectly that products merely insert themselves into existing environments. In reality, products create new environments[157] and thereby utterly transform the cultural, social, and psychological fabric of life. Paralleling the political economy of Dallas Smythe, McLuhan even regarded time spent with media as unpaid *work*, a notion far removed indeed from economic orthodoxy. 'Newspaper reading,' he advised, is 'a form of employment ... All media that mix ads with other programming are a form of "paid" learning.'[158]

McLuhan averred that 'work' does not exist in a non-literate world: the primitive hunter or fisher 'worked' no more than does the poet, painter, or thinker of today, because *the whole person* was engaged in the activity. 'Where the whole man is involved,' McLuhan insisted, 'there is no work.' Work for McLuhan, then, is synonymous with the division of labour and the specialization of functions celebrated by Adam Smith as the means for increasing the wealth of nations. Division of labour, for McLuhan, however, is part and parcel of the fragmentation characteristic of visual space. McLuhan's analysis at this point recollects and parallels analyses of Irene Spry and C.B. Macpherson.

However, McLuhan pointed out with enthusiasm, fragmentation ends with the predominance of electric media and the ensuing speed-up of information. In the electronic global village, everyone is once again a hunter/gatherer – albeit now of information rather than of food: 'Today information-gathering resumes the inclusive concept of "culture," exactly as the primitive food-gatherer worked in complete equilibrium with his entire environment.'[159] Becoming 'totally involved in our roles,' we have a renewed dedication and commitment 'as in the tribe.'[160] (Here again McLuhan's inclination towards hyperbole and mythic depiction is evident, even when himself critiquing the hyperbole of the 'invisible hand.')

Anti–Political Economy

Whenever McLuhan rhapsodized about the electronic age of information speed-up, he lost all thought of political economy. Except in those instances where he painted bleak pictures of the global village, political economy, for him, was, in effect, a feature or concern only of the previous mechanical age.

This subsection assembles some brief and highly provocative quotes that demonstrate McLuhan's apparent contention that political economy disappears in the electronic age.

- 'The electric gives powerful voices to the weak and suffering.'[161]
- 'The man who stays on welfare the longest is the welfare bureaucrat. He is now achieving the least with the most. In welfare it is the unemployed who are the employers.'[162]
- 'By electricity, we everywhere resume person-to-person relations as if on the smallest village scale. It is a relation of depth, and without delegation of functions or powers.'[163]
- 'Electricity takes away the old "centre–margin" of visual and written structures of authority. As with the pointillism of Seurat, everywhere is a centre and there are no margins.'[164]
- 'New forms of tribal structures and leadership are developing today in unexpected areas. The terms "consortium" and "conglomerate" refer to business structures and organizations that deal with individual businesses themselves as members of a single family or tribe.'[165]
- 'Today, anyone with $40,000 a year has as much access to the services available to Western man as the billionaire.'[166]

In the next section, we return to the paradoxical nature of McLuhan's political economy.

SOME QUESTIONS

The McLuhan Paradox

The corpus of McLuhan's writing is like a minefield, sown not only with serious, indeed profound, insights, but also with satirical, hyperbolic bombs, making him a difficult author to systematize or summarize. Moreover, McLuhan contended that the content of any text, including his own, is the reader, implying that certain ideas and assertions can be taken seriously by some commentators and be dismissed by others merely as 'probes,' satire, or hyperbole. McLuhan certainly was paradoxical and ironic, and intended his terms, ideas, and claims not to be interpreted 'literally,' but to be construed with multiple levels of meaning – indeed, as forming 'anti-environments,' which presumably means that his statements on occasion were intended to connote the opposite (*chiasmus*) of what they apparently say.

When, then, if at all, can McLuhan be taken at face value, as meaning precisely what he said? Was it when he affirmed his Catholicism and declared that electronics makes imminent on earth the mystical body of Christ? Or was it when he admitted that he was resolutely opposed to all innovation, to all change, and urged people turn off all the buttons and leave things alone for a while? Was it when he claimed to be a value-free scientist,[167] simply observing and describing what was going on? Or when he intimated he was an artist, exploring, making probes, creating anti-environments to shock people into awareness?

Perhaps all of these McLuhans, and others, are equally true – and false. It is a principle of systems theory that, when a researcher changes levels of analysis, everything he or she surveys changes too. (Atoms of hydrogen and oxygen, studied separately, for example, have much different properties than when they combine to form molecules of water, a higher-level system.) McLuhan insisted that he was a systems analyst, addressing the interactions of large structures and how they mutually transform one another. Perhaps in his mind, at the highest level of Being, the contradictions that he displayed and seemed to embody are resolved.

McLuhan's inconsistencies are nowhere more apparent than in his evaluations of television and of the world ushered in by that medium. One side of McLuhan reviled television. As a parent he limited his children to about one hour of viewing a week. As a grandparent he told his son, Eric, that television is 'a vile drug which permeates the nervous system especially in the young.'[168] In an interview with G.E. Stearn, published three years after *Understanding Media*, he announced, 'Most media ... are pure poison – TV, for example, has all the effects of LSD.'[169] On the other hand, McLuhan did not become a media celebrity by castigating the idiot box. To the contrary, he proffered an utopian vision of a 'retribalized' humanity, of universal harmony and the emergence of a 'collective consciousness.'

Yet a further way of understanding the McLuhan paradox is by again invoking the myth of Minerva's owl. In opening *The Gutenberg Galaxy*, McLuhan maintained, we in the modern West 'are experiencing the same confusions and indecisions which [the Elizabethans] had felt.' We, like they, are living 'simultaneously in two contrasted forms of society and experience.'[170] Living in paradoxical times cannot help but result in paradoxical scholarship – and in immense creativity!

According to Isaiah Berlin, 'few new truths have ever won their way against the resistance of established ideas save by being overstated.'[171] Perhaps McLuhan agreed with that proposition. In any event, he practised hyperbole, and in so doing drew attention to his key thesis that modes of communicating affect social organization through shifts in perception.[172]

McLUHAN AND CANADIAN COMMUNICATION THOUGHT

Despite world renown, McLuhan was quintessentially a *Canadian* communication scholar. The terms, methods, and concerns we have here identified with Canadian communication thought abound in McLuhan's writings – the dialectical method, holism, ontological concerns, historical study, critical approaches, mediation, change, and transformation.[173] To attempt to draw out all the parallels and differences with the other theorists surveyed in this volume would require another chapter at least. Here comparisons and contrasts with Innis, Macpherson, and Frye are addressed, but, even given that limitation, the analysis must remain partial.

McLuhan and Innis
McLuhan accepted and elaborated upon Innis's main claim that changes in the means of communication lie at the very heart of civilizational change. Moreover, McLuhan seized upon and developed into a leitmotif Innis's remark that writing causes the eye to substitute for the ear.[174]

To that extent at least, we may say that Innis and McLuhan were of one mind. We noted previously as well an affinity of style and similarity in scope of these eminent scholars.

In important respects, however, McLuhan departed from, even inverted (*chiasmus* again), Innis's work. Whereas Innis arrayed media along a spectrum of time bias–space bias, McLuhan distinguished media as to their relative audile–tactile versus visual properties. Whereas Innis emphasized that media are extensions of message *senders* and analysed the implications of that, particularly with regard to the exercise of power through time or across space, McLuhan drew attention to media as extensions of the sensory apparatus of message *recipients*, and on how media alter perception. Whereas Innis insisted that a medium's effects depend upon context, and even then a medium creates only tendencies, McLuhan frequently was more deterministic, even referring to people as servo-mechanisms of technological change. Innis's approach was inextricably bound up with political economy, but McLuhan's was tied most directly to individual and social psychology; by downplaying the importance of messages and message senders, McLuhan deflected attention from power considerations.

There is also a marked difference between Innis and McLuhan with regard to the linearity of their analyses. Adopting the stance of literary critic, McLuhan applied the rhetorical term *chiasmus* to media to indicate that, at high intensity, there is a reversal in a medium's effects. Innis, to the contrary, never argued that a space-binding medium pushed to the limit becomes time-binding! The divergence between Innis and McLuhan in this regard probably has something to do with their differing religiosities: Innis, the agnostic brought up in a strict Baptist faith, envisaged the collapse of civilization on account of an ever-increasing present-mindedness as a result of a growing imbalance between space-binding and time-binding media; McLuhan, devoutly Catholic but likewise apocalyptic, saw in technology the means of redemption and the possibility, even inevitability, of recovering an idyllic state.[175]

Of course, every medium, by definition, brings sender and recipient into contact (see figure 1.1), and hence each medium is simultaneously an extension of sender *and* recipient. A microphone, for instance, serves to augment the voice of the speaker, but also to intensify the hearing capacity of the listener, as does a hearing aid. The fact that media are simultaneously extensions of both senders and receivers, and serve to bring them together into a communicating system, could indicate that the analyses of Innis and McLuhan are both partial, and that they can profitably be integrated to attain an enlarged, more holistic understanding.

But combining Innis and McLuhan is no easy task. Although their depictions of tribal and literate cultures were consistent, there is a perplexing antithesis regarding electronics. Do electronic media augment and heighten the space-binding properties of print, as Innis suggested, or do they amplify the acoustic–tactile sensibilities associated with time-bound tribalism, as McLuhan claimed? Innisian analysis suggests that, with electronics, there will continue to be increased global hegemony on the part of a shrinking number of power centres, and possibly the collapse of civilization as all sense of permanence and commonalty is destroyed. From McLuhan, on the contrary, we learn that electronics will re-create on a global scale the harmony and balance purported to exist in manuscript society. (However, as noted previously, McLuhan was not consistent in making these predictions, and at other times prognosticated a bleak future, one not inconsistent with Innis's dark vision.)

McLuhan and Macpherson

Macpherson's notion of people as doers, exerters, and developers of capacities and talents finds parallel in McLuhan's depiction of the artist. For McLuhan, the artist is society's innovator, who constructs anti-environments whereby the general populace can come to understand better their condition. Whereas Macpherson's hope was that everyone, given improved property relations, could become an 'artist' in McLuhan's sense, McLuhan proffered no such hope: artists, for him, are seldom well-adjusted people; they are, rather, the tiny enlightened minority functioning on the margins of society, and it was these very characteristics that accounted for their insight and understanding.

Macpherson and McLuhan were alike, however, in maintaining that human nature evolves and is malleable. For Macpherson, though, human nature is affected primarily by the institution of property and by the accompanying philosophical/propaganda discourses 'justifying' the mode of property existing at any given time. McLuhan, in contrast, looked to the 'extensions of man' (of which the mode of property is undoubtedly one, but certainly one among many others) as fixing human nature; McLuhan's analysis, therefore, was much more de-politicized than Macpherson's.

Both scholars thought that at present people in society are alienated from themselves, from their environments, and from each other. Whereas Macpherson attributed this condition to the mode of property and supportive ideologies, McLuhan attributed alienation to the mode of communication, particularly the phonetic alphabet and the printing press. The two theorists were alike in presenting an alternative, more organic vision, founded, in Macpherson's case, on common property, and, in McLuhan's, on the commonality induced by electronic modes of communication. In both cases the organic society entails a 'retrieval' of things lost: the wisdom of the ancients concerning human nature and common property, in the case of Macpherson, and the simultaneous, 'acoustic' space and mythic consciousness in the opinion of McLuhan.

McLuhan and Frye

McLuhan's thought begs comparison with that of Frye. For one thing, both were literary theorists, and were contemporaries at the University of Toronto. Periodically they referred in their writings to each other, usually critically. Most significantly, both centred their communication thought on a theory of perception.

McLuhan and Frye agreed that there are two competing 'cosmologies,' what we can loosely term 'science' and 'arts,' or realism versus the mythopoeic world-view. McLuhan and Frye agreed further that, since knowledge comes from perception, and since sense organs feed information to the mind, knowledge is derived from mental experience. In addition, both Frye and McLuhan insisted that, without application of the human imagination to sensory data, the world is fragmented; stated otherwise, the connections or meanings forged are imaginative products of human construction. Both recommended, finally, a 'double vision.' Single vision for McLuhan was when one sense overpowers the others; for Frye, single vision was scientific, unimaginative, sight-based knowledge.

Where McLuhan and Frye parted company, however, was with regard to what they attributed the ascendancy of one or other of these world-views at any given time or place. For Frye, the mythopoeic world-view marked a necessary and innate attempt by people to make themselves at home in a universe devoid of meaning and purpose; furthermore, he claimed, the mythopoeic world-view is continually challenged in our era by science (the truth of correspondence). For McLuhan, in contrast, the human condition is not a struggle between the reality principle and mythic invention; for him, rather, myth is a high, indeed the highest, form of truth: like scientific theory, McLuhan insisted, myth generalizes recurrences and particulars. For that reason, McLuhan continually invoked ancient myths – of Narcissus and Cadmus, for example – as these are applicable to and help explain our present condition.

In a sense, what myths accomplished in Frye's thought, sensory extensions do for McLuhan. Frye argued that people view the world through stories; that myths and literature affect, or bias, how people experience their environment, and therefore how they act upon it. McLuhan, on the other hand, argued that our sensory extensions bias our perceptions and thereby our understanding, and hence affect our actions. Frye and McLuhan both sought transcendence. For Frye, however, transcendence was a fiction, a delusion, a social construction; by suspending disbelief one can enter for a time mythic worlds where nature has a human face, and existence seems to have meaning – but only for a time, since Frye understood science and technology as standing against and subverting these imaginary worlds with the harsh existential truth that there are, in nature, no connections, no meanings. McLuhan, conversely, ascribed no ultimate tension or conflict between myth and transcendence, on the one hand, and science and technology, on the other; for McLuhan, rather, technology is *the means* of reunification, the way whereby humanity can approach the godhead.

Frye and McLuhan both argued for balance. In Frye's case, the balance was between science and arts, and he referred to this balance as 'the educated imagination.' The balance McLuhan recommended, by contrast, was between eye and ear, which he referred to as 'common sense.' McLuhan's balance was not in order that people might escape reality, but that they might approach it more closely. In that regard he put forward a remarkably different role for the creative artist than did Frye. McLuhan declared that the artists' job is to tune people's sensibilities to the present, to make audiences more aware of their condition, so that we might either adjust to altered circumstances, or counter and attempt to neutralize those conditions. In McLuhan's work, there is no affirmation or approval whatever afforded the notion that the artist should help audiences escape the anxiety of harsh reality, although, when his discussions turn to advertising, he disapprovingly notes that this is often the case. McLuhan viewed advertisers as fallen artists who beguile. Both scholars agreed, however, that critical awareness is a requisite for self-defence against the machinations of advertisers and public relations professionals.

Frye assented to McLuhan's characterizations of oral versus literate cultures, but did not attribute the differences to extensions of the eye or ear. For Frye, rather, it was more a question of information storage, objectification, and abstraction. Being able to store knowledge outside the human mind through writing frees people to create new and more abstract knowledge and engenders the notion that knowledge can be objective. These thoughts are not inconsistent with McLuhan's, but neither are they McLuhanesque.

In the previous chapter, we noted Frye's disputation of McLuhan's distinction between linear and sequential media. Neither did McLuhan refrain from critiquing Frye; indeed, he charged that his famous colleague's theory of genres ignored all media but print. 'In this century,' McLuhan admonished, 'the effect of nonprint media on literature has been as extensive as it has been on psychology and anthropology.' He concluded pointedly that, 'by ignoring the oral tradition of both preliterate and postliterate cultures, Professor Frye sets up a system of classifications that apply [only] to a recent segment of human technology and culture – a segment that is rapidly dissolving.'[176]

Finally, Frye and McLuhan each presented a dialectic of media and society. For Frye, technology empowers even as it alienates; media erode critical consciousness even as they entertain; they inform even as they increase the power of the advertiser and the public relations professional; they decrease privacy and imprison audiences even as they empower them. McLuhan likewise, as we have seen, entertained sharply dichotomous images of the global village.

THE RELEVANCE OF McLUHAN'S THOUGHT FOR THE TWENTY-FIRST CENTURY

In this final subsection, we touch on several areas for which McLuhan's analysis seems to be of greatest relevance for the coming years.

Ecology

McLuhan's mode of media analysis opens the way for a new environmentalism. Consider first his notion of the global village. As ecologists Paul and Anne Ehrlich remark, most people still don't realize that humanity has become 'a truly global force, interfering in a very real and direct way in many of the planet's natural cycles.'[177] McLuhan's key construct, the global village, should, therefore, be helpful in increasing global ecological awareness.

It is not only by emphasizing globalism, however, that McLuhan helps foster environmentalism. He does this implicitly also through his notion of shifting sensory ratios. In this regard we again cite the Ehrlichs:

> People are sight-oriented animals and have relatively poorly developed chemosensory abilities. Toxification of the planet might be much more obvious to dogs, which live in a world shaped to a greater extent by their sense of smell. One can barely imagine how we would perceive changes in our environment if, like some fishes, we oriented to it primarily by detecting distortions in electrical fields, or if we responded primarily to sonar returns as bats do.[178]

McLuhan's insistence that we recognize patterns in a fast-changing world, rather than seeking to understand fragments, is also in accord with ecological understanding. Ecologist David Suzuki, for example, remarks that scientists usually 'focus on parts of nature, attempting to isolate each fragment and control the factors impinging on it,' thereby attaining only a 'fractured mosaic of disconnected bits and pieces, whose parts will never add up to a coherent narrative.'[179] McLuhan and Suzuki are like-minded in recommending that we should supplement fragmented knowledge with holistic knowledge – and as well by mythic narrative! Suzuki, of course, insists that the 'new' narratives or myths encourage ecological balance.[180]

McLuhan was quite aware that his thought had ecological dimensions. He saw people and their artefacts as being in dynamic interaction, and indeed termed his mode of analysis an 'ecological approach.'[181] He affirmed further that 'the electric age is the age of ecology. It is the study and projection of the total environment of organisms and people, because of the instant coherence of all factors, made possible by moving information at electric speeds ... Our ecological approach is paleolithic. It assumes total involvement in process rather than fragmentation and detachment.'[182]

Postmodernism

In some respects, McLuhan was a postmodernist before the term had even been coined. This helps explain both the opprobrium he engendered at the apex of his career on the part of many entrenched scholars, and the renewed interest and heightened favour that his work currently enjoys. His writings have, if not inspired, then at least been 'warmly regarded' by such key postmodern theorists as Jean Baudrillard, Charles Jencks, and Mark Poster.[183] McLuhan's stance on the relativity and subjectivity of meaning, his disregard for scientific absolutes, his insistence that readers actively engage with texts, and his anti-authoritarianism resonate with the postmodern mind.

This is not to say that McLuhan anticipated accurately all elements of our day. Thirty years or so after publication of *Understanding Media*, his prediction concerning the demise of the automobile is yet to be fulfilled.[184] Nor do we notice a rise in communitarian sentiments as a reading of McLuhan would lead us to expect in an electronic information age. It is indeed the failure of this last-mentioned prediction to be fulfilled – if anything, the trend has been in the opposite direction and our era is aptly described as being neo-liberal or neo-conservative – that requires us to inquire again into McLuhan's truncated political economy.

Truncated Political Economy
McLuhan paid more attention to political economy than is commonly recognized. His *The Mechanical Bride* and *Culture Is Our Business*, along with passages in other works, demonstrate a keen understanding that business interests have taken over cultural production and shaped it to their pecuniary ends. He understood also that modern media crush indigenous cultures, and at times he displayed an awareness and concern regarding the totalitarian possibilities of electronic media. McLuhan's contributions to political economy are real and should be celebrated.

Yet, political economy certainly was not McLuhan's forte, his explanation of how viewers, readers, and audiences participate in the construction of meaning being a case in point. As we saw in chapter 1, present-day analysts with a stronger political-economy bent than McLuhan insist that there is a class- or wealth-based dimension to interpretation, that interpretation is a site of struggle between groups with different class interests, but on these matters McLuhan remained largely silent.

Likewise, his insistence that 'the medium is the message' is quite antithetical to political economy. For if it is merely the existence or non-existence of a medium that matters, as McLuhan contended, then media owners and programmers are absolved of responsibility for content. (It is to be recalled that McLuhan did not assume that position in *The Mechanical Bride*; there he set out to combat the influence of advertising messages through an innovative mode of cultural criticism.)

Moreover, McLuhan insisted that television is *not* a visual medium, a contention that is absurd on the surface and one that minimizes certain political-economic aspects of media practice. Compare McLuhan's position with that, say, of environmental writer and media analyst Alison Anderson, who insists that 'television *is* a visual medium' *non pareil*, and hence that 'the availability and quality of pictures is of much … importance.'[185] She continues: 'Certain environmental issues receive more television news coverage than others because of their visual qualities … Environment stories really need good pictures … Global warming is very difficult because you can't actually see global warming.'[186] Activist groups such as Greenpeace have gone to great lengths, some life-forfeiting, to concoct great visuals for the nightly television news.[187] All of this escapes McLuhan on account of his insistence that television is an audile–tactile medium.[188]

Moreover, even the closest reading of McLuhan's texts will not uncover treatment of key political-economic trends and issues linked to proliferating global communications: for example, global divisions of labour and the ever-increasing predominance in world commerce of transnational corporations (TNCs); the decline in national sovereignty; heightening disparities between rich and poor. These trends are dependent upon, or can be explained in part by, proliferating media interconnected globally, but none is captured by the phrase 'the global village.' A much clearer picture of present-day political economy can be attained by reading McLuhan's mentor, Harold Innis, or his contemporary, Dallas Smythe.

On the other hand, it is also to be affirmed that Marshall McLuhan remains the most creative, imaginative scholar that Canada has produced. His immense contribution to Canadian and world communication thought is increasingly recognized, and deservedly so. By juxtaposing his thought with that of others we have studied, we can achieve a truly comprehensive understanding.

12

CONCLUSION

Was it not precisely the discovery of a discrepancy between words, the medium in which we think, and the world of appearances, the medium in which we live, that led to philosophy and metaphysics in the first place? ... It seems only natural that the former will discriminate against appearances and the latter against thought.

– Hannah Arendt, *The Life of the Mind*, 8

Although anyone can stand on the street corner, only the rich can have direct access to our homes through the costly channels of the media.

– A.C. Hutchinson and A. Petter, 'Private Rights/ Public Wrongs,' unpublished paper, Osgoode Hall Law School/University of Victoria

Now it is time to synthesize the communication thought of these distinguished scholars. The discussion is presented under headings that have recurred throughout this book as themes and topics.

BIOGRAPHIES

Chapters of this book have presented the communication thought of ten theorists in the context of their individual biographies on the presumption that a basic relationship is to be found there. From this, a pattern in biography has emerged. For one thing, virtually all of the scholars profiled here experienced intense religious training as children, and they retained profound religious sensibilities for the remainder of their lives. This is true even in the cases of Northrop Frye and Harold Innis, both of whom lost their childhood faith but retained a deep and abiding interest in religion and in the Whole. Religiosity may well help explain why these theorists were so preoccupied with ontological and epistemological questions, and also the high moral standard they applied to social affairs, making them all, in varying degrees, *critical* scholars.

Apart perhaps from Innis, all these writers read voluminously as children, a pastime not necessarily common at that stage of life. For a significant number of the men, their mothers were of greatest influence, an aspect of their upbringing that perhaps dissuaded them from adopting an instrumentalist or more prototypically 'masculine' world-view.[1] In his childhood and youth, likewise, Northrop Frye did not wish to participate in the typical male sports, although this would certainly have been expected of him. This identification with the feminine may be partly at the root of the male analysts' penchant for dialectical modes of analysis, and their 'leftist' (i.e., nurturing, communal) political stance.

Most were 'outsiders,' whether by birth or by disposition. Innis was a farm boy and a 'dirt economist'; McLuhan and Smythe were raised on the prairies; Grierson was born in a poor working-class town; Robinson was raised in an 'American household in fascist Germany' and moved first to the United States and then to Canada; Irene Spry was born in South Africa and raised for a time in what is today Bangladesh, and even when living in England was yanked out of school to study economics by correspondence. Both Northrop Frye and McLuhan experienced the trauma of a family business that failed and moved out of the province of their birth on that account. After a serious illness, Smythe moved from Saskatchewan to California and returned to Canada in middle age after becoming totally disaffected with what to him were America's military and imperial aspirations. Grant and Graham Spry were born into more stable, 'mainstream' households, but Spry became the family's 'rogue' on account of his socialism and could not even secure employment in Canada despite a degree from Oxford, while Grant, a passivist in the midst of war, not only deserted the armed forces but earned antipathy from his fellow philosophers on account of his religiosity. We recall, therefore, McLuhan's dictum, that to understand the world one must stand apart from it.

Another feature common to these ten is that all pursued graduate work abroad, even though, for one, Irene Spry, that meant the Department of Political Economy at the University of Toronto. Study abroad, of course, acquaints students with different points of view. Moreover, a number literally changed disciplines. Innis and Smythe forsook mainstream economics for political economy and media studies. Marshall McLuhan became a media theorist instead of, or in addition to, being a literary critic. Northrop Frye was both a theologian and a literary theorist. Gertrude Robinson left philosophy for sociology, and then turned to media studies. George Grant embarked on a career as a political philosopher after having taken only one formal course in philosophy and having studied law and theology at the graduate level. Grierson studied philosophy before embarking on a media career as both theorist and practitioner. Graham Spry's formal education was as a historian.

DIALECTICS

Common threads in biographies may go some distance to explaining the prominence of dialectics in Canadian communication thought. Radical shifts in perspective and being positioned on the outside, after all, help inculcate a capacity for stereoscopic vision. In addition, however, there was the common experience of living, and choosing to live, in Canada, which is at the margin of a great power. This helps explain not only these analysts' affinity for dialectics, but as well *the common nature of their dialectics*: local culture versus empire in Innis's terms – a theme that, with variations, reverberates throughout the foundations of Canadian communication thought.

Dialectical analysis does not generally characterize Western social science, where the usual goal is to detect linear causes. Linear analysis, however, obscures conflict and contradiction. Nor is dialectical analysis typical of mainstream American thought in the humanities. In part this may be because people at the centre of power are inclined to see things instrumentally, that is, in terms of unidirectional determinisms. This may be the case because they are most interested in achieving results by exercising their power. According to the liberal/pluralist political and economic doctrines of the invisible hand, moreover, analysts *need not* delve into contradiction and conflictual relations because, it is held, each person exercising his or her power contributes automatically to the 'common good.'

People at the margins, however, generally see things differently, that is, dialectically, since, on the one hand, they cannot escape being exposed to dominant perspectives, and, on the other, once enlightened, they understand that the power the centre wields is frequently used *on them*, and not necessarily for their benefit.

Dialectics, however, indeed infuse Canadian communication thought. McLuhan self-consciously borrowed from, and placed himself in dialectical tension to, Innis when he transmuted the dialectic of time/space into that of eye/ear and of thought/feeling. Frye did not necessarily have Innis in mind when he developed his theme of 'double vision,' but his work too is suffused with a tension and opposition between time and space (mythopoeic versus scientific modes of understanding; myth of concern versus truth of correspondence; the creative versus the communicating arts). George Grant's dialectical conception of time and his analysis of technology recall central aspects of both Innis's and Frye's thought while at the same time exploring novel dimensions of that same basic dialectic. The struggle and tension between private property/public property, as developed in particular by Macpherson, the Sprys, and Smythe, represents a further variation on that theme. Smythe, of course, saw virtually *everything* dialectically – art, commodities, institutions, media. Grierson contrasted two ways of knowing and two modes of educating, and these accord well with McLuhan's analysis of media (mechanical versus organic) and information processing. Gertrude Robinson's dialectic of positivism versus symbolic interactionism/social constructionism is yet another variation on the Innisian theme, as is Irene Spry's discourse on the confrontation of indigenous peoples with market-dominated society.

Most of these writers were not 'radical' thinkers. Usually they recommended striving for *a balance* between the poles of the dialectic, opting neither for one pole nor the other.

POLITICAL ECONOMY

Power considerations figure prominently in Canadian communication thought. Innis, of course, focused on monopolies of knowledge, whether through time or over space, and on the power that accrues to those controlling media predominant in a society at any given time. Control of communication for him, as for Dallas Smythe, is the essence of political power. When space-bound cultures contact time-bound ones, at the very least Minerva's owl takes flight; historically, though, as Innis, Grant, Smythe, Irene Spry, and even McLuhan observed, the outcome usually is destruction of the way of life of the time-bound (mythopoeic) culture. McLuhan, of course, put a characteristic spin on Innis's political economy, affording greater emphasis to the technologies themselves than to the controllers. The alphabet, McLuhan argued, particularly as amplified by the printing press, devastates audile–tactile cultures by rendering obsolete ideographic modes of writing. Likewise, he argued, television subverts print cultures. McLuhan nonetheless, like many other theorists we have reviewed, attributed great power to advertisers and to artists, both of whom, he maintained, understand media and use them effectively, either to exploit and control, or to enlighten. Macpherson replayed Innis's political-economic analysis of media in terms of property, as did Irene Spry. Others, such as Dallas Smythe, George Grant, Northrop Frye, and John Grierson, focused more on the power dimensions of media ownership and content. Macpherson investigated closely power implications of schools of political philosophy, and Frye did the same with regard to narrative and myth.

The political-economic dimension is not accorded equal emphasis by all these authors, of course. Frye and McLuhan particularly, both grounded in literary criticism, exhibited a sometimes truncated political economy – Frye because he minimized the role of literature in increasing people's awareness of their real-life conditions (indeed, he championed the opposite function of literature, maintaining that literature serves humanity well by providing a means to escape harsh reality); and McLuhan on account of an apparent technological determinism and a seeming antipathy to equality. Nonetheless, there are jewels of political economy to be found in the works of both theorists. Robinson's symbolic-interactionism likewise weakens her political economy as she questions whether there is 'a reality out there' to be concerned with at all.

ONTOLOGY

Concern for ontological understanding permeates Canadian communication thought, and this finding accords well with Margaret Atwood's contention that the theme of 'survival' permeates Canadian literature. In the opening chapter, it was suggested that Canada's harsh climate and vast empty spaces have had much to do with this concern for ontology.

Three of the important ontological issues that our ten theorists raise are: whether there exists a constancy behind temporal change; whether fact can be separated from value (sometimes referred to as a question of *axiology*); and whether reality is merely an assemblage of individual components or transcends the components. These issues are broached by the theorists within the context of media/mediation/communication.

With regard to the first question, many of the Canadian theorists explicitly distinguish between and contrast two ontologies, and attribute predominance at any given time and place of one or the other to the prevailing modes of communication. Innis, of course, distinguished between time-bound and space-bound cultures, the former based on the premise that there is a constant order of things, the latter tending to deny any permanence. George Grant expounded on a similar theme by comparing two conceptions of time, the antiquarian and modern, the former proposing a fixity in ideals and the latter denying the same. By Northrop Frye's account, what is real for people are their stories and myths, which forge for them imaginative connections with the material universe; what *recurs* for Frye are the themes, symbols, and archetypes within myths and literature. For Dallas Smythe, in contrast, connectivity is not imaginative, but is characteristic of the universe; but connectivity (communication) also implies continual change. Smythe contrasted 'information,' as a proxy for autonomy and permanence, to 'communication,' which points to evolution and interdependence. The information viewpoint, he seemed to argue, is a consequence of capitalism and the Consciousness Industry. In McLuhan's formulation, the ontological divide is between *matching* (the aim of 'objective' science) and *making* (the aim of the artists and poets); McLuhan, like Frye, maintained that 'making' is a human proclivity, but, unlike Frye, he also attested that undergirding these humanly constructed connections is a beneficent, intelligent (and intelligible) order.

The second, and related, ontological question concerns objectivity/subjectivity, and fact versus value. Here the contrast is most marked between Frye and Grant. Frye contended that there is a way of approaching reality that is empirical, objective, value-free; this he termed 'the truth of correspondence.' He also argued that most of the time people do not approach the world that way, but live, rather, in a socially constructed, imaginative, symbolic world of narrative and myth: that is, their 'home.' This implies that much of our knowledge is subjective (projecting human concerns onto an indifferent universe), and that it is value-laden. For Frye, however, whereas humans throughout history have lived in a socially constructed universe, with the invention of writing, and especially the printing press, it became possible to understand nature scientifically, that is, through the truth of correspondence, a mode of understanding that at least makes a pretense of being objective and value-free. George Grant likewise recognized the existence of these two world-views, and attributed the power of the objective, scientific cosmology to the manifestations of science – namely, technology. Grant maintained, however, that ultimately there is not, nor can there be, value-free knowledge. This is the case because the choice of *what* to learn always involves conscious decisions.

The case of C.B. Macpherson is a bit more difficult. Macpherson certainly wrote, however, as if equality were a value *intrinsic* to the order of things, that is, as if it were a value *extrinsic* to human construction, meaning that there is a criterion whereby human knowledge and variable 'human nature' can be judged. John Grierson, too, advocated democratic values, and argued that one must anticipate the implications of mediated messages for democracy. For him, furthermore, there is no neutrality, which is to say that fact cannot be separated from value. Even Innis proposed that values, to be truly authentic, must be eternal. These authors, therefore, qualify as 'critical theorists' in so far as they maintained there exist enduring values whereby events, policies, 'facts,' and conditions can be judged; of the ten theorists, Northrop Frye and Gertrude Robinson would appear to be the chief exceptions in this regard. McLuhan at times claimed to be a 'value-free' scientist probing reality, but was sufficiently inconsistent as to be regarded a critical theorist most of the time.

Which brings us to the third ontological question. None of the theorists considered here based his or her analyses on the presumption that reality is merely a collection of individual parts, as would be the position of a liberal or a libertarian analyst. Every theorist, rather, maintained that reality is more than the sum of the parts. This ontological stance leads to a concern for the common good (Dallas Smythe); for common property (Macpherson, I. Spry); for time-bound media (Innis); for myth, narrative, and symbolic interactionism (Frye, Robinson); for social justice (Grant, Grierson, Smythe); for democracy (Grierson, Macpherson); for public broadcasting (G. Spry, Grant); and for the global village (McLuhan). All of the theorists, in other words, exhibit an *ecological understanding*.

For a number of them, the scope of analysis is the sweep of history, the veritable rise and fall of civilizations. Even for those who generally confine their attention to the modern period, there is very much a concern for social as opposed to individual change; for bidirectional or multidirectional interaction and multiple causations; for interpretation rather than for single, universally shared meanings; and for human agency rather than mechanical determination. McLuhan in that last respect is the closest we come to an exception. At times, as we have seen, his analysis posits a technological determinism, but he also claimed that with the aid of artists people can overcome determinisms and begin to fulfil their potential.

Much more could be said, of course; brief recapitulation cannot do justice to the complexity of these authors' ontological stances. The point remains, however, that irrespective of differences, ontology is an abiding concern in Canadian communication thought, and a dichotomy between time and space, between making and matching, doing and consuming, and a concern for value and the common good permeates the media theories of these scholars.

MEDIATION

As befits communication theorists, each of the ten writers focused on mediation, that is, on what allows people to interact and the consequences of relying upon particular media for those interactions. Moreover, none of the theorists considered mediation to be simply the 'joining' temporarily of message senders and receivers; rather, they maintained, *first*, that the means of communication affects fundamentally the meanings that are transmitted or exchanged, and, *second*, that communicators live within environments that mediate (i.e., affect fundamentally) the nature of people's interactions.

Innis inaugurated inquiries into mediation by maintaining that media 'bias' messages. His concern was for how predominant media 'select' messages for transmission on the basis of whether they are time-binding or space-binding. Innis's 'disciple,' McLuhan, inverted that model by emphasizing reception, and investigating whether media amplify eye or ear. Others, such as Frye and Grierson, addressed themes similar to McLuhan's.

A number of the theorists – in particular, Innis, Grant, Smythe, and McLuhan – regarded technology generally, not just media narrowly construed, as mediating human relations. Smythe and Grant saw technologies as 'teaching machines.' For Smythe, under capitalism, consumers' and producers' goods of all types inculcate values suitable to the expansion of the capitalist order. Grant likewise viewed technological change in the age of progress as inculcating such values as speed, efficiency, change, and growth, while denigrating others – respect for tradition, equality, the common good. McLuhan maintained that industrial technologies, for example, the automobile, fragment the cohesiveness of oral culture by extending only portions of the human being,

leading to specialization; however, he also contended that technological change pushed to an extreme reunites humanity on a global scale.
Innis concentrated on technologies of transportation and staples extraction, which he saw as affecting centre–periphery relations, hierarchy
and centralization/decentralization. For none of these theorists was
technology 'neutral'; at least implicitly, all viewed technology as being
part and parcel of the power structure, although different emphases
were placed by the various writers on this key political-economic aspect of technological change.

For C.B. Macpherson, Northrop Frye, and Gertrude Robinson, the
environment of greatest concern is neither natural nor technological,
but rather ideational, that is, symbolic. People reside within an 'order of
words' that sets the pattern for how they interact. Modes of transmission for Frye, however, do affect that symbolic order: writing, for instance, gave rise to science as well as to literature and written poetry,
and as science became increasingly abstract so too did mathematics.
For George Grant also, the symbolic environment is influenced by
technology, and in particular by the pace of technological change. For
Macpherson, our environment is propertied; on the one hand, there is
a thought structure (political philosophy) that justifies or challenges
property arrangements, and, on the other, a mode of ownership that
fulfils or challenges the thought structure. The mode of property
(*including conceptions of human nature*), structures human relations and
either allows people to fulfil their potential or impedes them from
doing this; property, for Macpherson, is in part symbolic, and hence is
communicatory.

For Grierson, mass-mediated messages, including education, affect
fundamentally who we think we are and how we relate to one another.
If the media denigrate our higher aspirations by telling us insistently
that we are but selfish, acquisitive beings, then how else will we view
ourselves? On the other hand, if the media promote an ethic of human
dignity and the common good, do we then not tend to see ourselves
more selflessly, and act accordingly? All these theorists – McLuhan, the
Sprys, Frye, Innis, Grant, Macpherson, Grierson, and Smythe particularly – understood and emphasized that the present distribution of
power and control hinges vitally upon people conceiving themselves as
infinite desirers and profligate consumers, as this self-perception puts
them on the treadmill whence élite interests derive their power; hence
so much effort and money are spent buttressing that view of human
nature – through media advertising, through the teaching of behav-

ioural psychology and mainstream economics, through the news and
public affairs, through professional sports, through (in Smythe's phrase)
the activities of the Consciousness Industry.

HUMAN NATURE

All of the Canadian communication theorists surveyed here consider
human nature to be variable. That supposition could imply that conditions and conditioners mould people at will, except for another remarkable feature that most of these writers share – namely, a belief that the
human spirit is in principle indomitable. Most of these writers affirm
that humans possess or can attain an intrinsic freedom, a capacity to
overcome (with help, perhaps) the determinisms around and about –
whether these be technological or ideological. Humans, they attest, are
transcendent beings who can at least strive for and approach either
what they wish to be or what they ought to be. Many of our theorists
look to the artist as being of vital assistance in liberating people from
technological and ideological determinisms, and many point to education. Not a few of the theorists consider advertising and public relations
to be unduly influential in moulding people's minds and perpetuating
an inferior human nature. The fact that most of these theorists are able
to contemplate a *superior* human nature, that is, to compare things as
they should be with things as they are, qualifies them as *critical theorists*
in the tradition acknowledged by Lazarsfeld.

TECHNOLOGY AND PROGRESS

At the outset of this book, we noted that, beginning with the Canadian
Pacific Railway, a doctrine (or myth) of technological nationalism seized
the Canadian imagination. How startling, then, that virtually all of
these key communication theorists, including the one who began his
scholarly career with a treatise on the CPR, should be so critical of
technology generally, and of communication media in particular. With
the possible exception of McLuhan, and then only at times, none of the
theorists accepted the proposition, so commonly held today, that technological change *means* human betterment.

In terms of communication thought, the Canadian critique of technology, we may say, began with Innis. He was a founder of dependency
theory – the school of thought that equates control of evolving media
with cultural, economic, and political power. He also foresaw in an

unrelenting growth of space-binding media the imminent collapse of Western civilization. In the closing essay of *The Bias of Communication*, he wrote starkly: 'The conditions of freedom of thought are in danger of being destroyed by science, technology, and the mechanization of knowledge, and with them, Western civilization.'[2] Most of the other theorists have expressed somewhat similar concerns, albeit perhaps in different terms.

For Dallas Smythe, for instance, the very term 'technology' is rife with misapprehension and intended deception; for him 'technology' is one of the twentieth century's great mythic cover-ups, masking intended domination and exploitation through the guise of inevitability, progress, and the order of things. Smythe linked electronic communication to the entire capitalist order and viewed 'technologies' generally, not just mass media, as 'teaching machines' that inculcate capitalist values. He also saw them as congealed power relations, which at once derive from, reflect, and entrench inequality. Smythe was very concerned, as was Innis, at how quickly and thoroughly modern technologies can crush modes of organization founded on love, kinship, tradition, wholeness, and empathy. Technological advance, in Smythe's framework, is retrogressive in so far as, and to the extent that, it is used to overcome non-commodified relations and turn them into relations of commodity exchange.

George Grant's analysis of technology bears close affinity to that both of Innis and Smythe. Like Innis, he saw technological change effacing non-technologically derived values from human consciousness, and therefore as being ultimately nihilistic. Like both Innis and Smythe, he recognized technology as being part and parcel of an increasingly global capitalist economic order, homogenizing modes of human interaction and increasing disparities between rich and poor. Like Smythe, he saw technologies as teaching machines, subliminally inculcating values in unsuspecting citizens, that, unless countered by concerted efforts to remember the wisdom of the ancients, strip people of freedom, dignity, and power.

Northrop Frye's analysis of modern media was equally disturbing. He saw the media as imprisoning users in two senses. First, media are used to invade and take control of the mind, for Frye the last refuge of privacy. Second, media lead to introversion as people forsake person-to-person communication in favour of largely one-way, point-to-point mass communication.

Others of our theorists emphasized the potential good of technological change, even while castigating the uses to which media technologies are largely put within the prevailing system of power. C.B. Macpherson maintained that technological change possesses the potential to liberate people to pursue self-development, although he also remarked that at present media are used primarily to persuade people that they ought to consume more, entrenching yet more firmly the doctrine of possessive individualism, and, thereby, capitalist power relations. John Grierson likewise, although recognizing that media are controlled largely by advertisers and other anti-democratic forces, maintained that they *could* be used to increase democracy and to achieve a higher, more egalitarian civilization. Graham Spry, too, recognized the anti-nationalist, anti-communitarian uses to which media are put when in commercial, private hands, but Spry also held out the prospect of improvement if and when citizens take control of the media of mass communication, a position echoed by Dallas Smythe.

And then, of course, there is McLuhan. In moments of candour, it would seem, McLuhan acknowledged that electronic media are totalitarian; at other times, however, he professed enchantment with the communitarian potential of electronics.

IMPLICATIONS

Having detected and summarized key themes and concerns that permeate Canadian communication thought, let us conclude by addressing implications of media trends for environment, community, human rights, democracy, and peace.

The writers treated here are virtually univocal in their condemnation of the market as the chief means of organizing human activity, and, by implication, of subordinating communication systems to commercial concerns. In the view of these theorists, markets cause people to be unduly individualistic in their actions, whereas human existence is radically contingent upon the actions of others. The price system and concerns for power and speed tend to wipe out both an ethic of community and the ecological understanding vital for survival on a finite planet. Media trends that emphasize pay-as-you-go and home entertainment, furthermore, can be erosive of democracy, and hence of human rights, as people passively consume the virtual realities presented for their amusement and persuasion by advertisers and spin doctors. All of the theorists ask us to consider critically the communication environment in which we are immersed, and thereby begin to free ourselves from media practices not designed to promote the common good. In combination, our theorists issue a clarion call to resist, and thereby to become more free.

Studying the communication thought of these ten acclaimed scholars increases awareness of questions we should continue to ask, and provides some answers that may fit the circumstances in which we find ourselves, and thereby help open further possibilities for the pursuit of freedom, equality, peace, and justice in the early decades of the twenty-first century.

Finally, it is worth remarking that a quite different field of questions is raised by the seminal and foundational Canadian communication theorists than by those often taken to be the founders of American communication thought (Lazarsfeld, Lasswell, Lewin, Hovland, Schramm). It is likely more than merely coincidental that raising important ontological questions, adopting a critical stance, and employing holistic modes of analysis detract from the lustre both of technological achievement and of the free flow of information – mainstays of American thought and policy.

NOTES

1: Introduction

1 Freire writes: 'The world of human beings is a world of communication' (Paulo Freire, *Education for Critical Consciousness*, 137).

2 See *Encyclopaedia Britannica* (1967), vol. 6, 203.

3 James W. Carey, 'A Cultural Approach to Communication.' See also Mary Douglas, *Natural Symbols: Explorations in Cosmology*.

4 Harold Lasswell, 'The Structure and Function of Communication in Society,' 84. See also William Leiss, 'On the Validity of Our Discipline – New Applications of Communications Theory.'

5 Lewis Mumford, *Technics and Civilization*, 14–15.

6 W. Terrence Gordon, *McLuhan for Beginners*, 43.

7 Marshall McLuhan, *Understanding Media: The Extensions of Man*, 8.

8 Claude Shannon and Warren Weaver, *The Mathematical Theory of Communication*.

9 See, for example, Stuart Hall, 'The Rediscovery of "Ideology": The Return of the Repressed in Media Studies.'

10 Barrington Nevitt, *The Communication Ecology: Re-presentation versus Replica*.

11 This subsection in particular has benefited much from discussions with Dwayne Winseck.

12 Mark Poster, 'Databases as Discourse; or Electronic Appellations,' 176.

13 R.S. Perinbanayagam, *Discursive Acts*, 20.

14 Frank Webster, *Theories of the Information Society*, 165.

15 Cf. Stephen Littlejohn, *Theories of Human Communication*, 30–3.

16 This statement itself, however, can be seen as being paradoxical: 'people facing different material conditions interpret phenomena differently' is

itself a generalization belying the particularistic thrust of the statement. The paradox is addressed in the concluding section of chapter 3.

17 George Grant,'What Is Philosophy?', 34.

18 However, in this, as in other matters, McLuhan was paradoxical, if not to say inconsistent. He insisted that his 'four laws of the media' were 'scientific,' in the sense of having predictive power, and hence were subject to refutation.

19 This proposition, incidentally, has been formalized as Heisenberg's Uncertainty Principle, and in the twentieth century has been increasingly accepted by Western science, blurring thereby the distinctions between arts and sciences as set out in this section.

20 Such essentially is the position of Thomas Kuhn in his landmark publication *The Structure of Scientific Revolutions*. Kuhn argued that scientific activity, like all other human activity, is undertaken in the context of social groupings, and hence the particular nature of the social grouping has an important bearing on the activity. When this argument is applied to scientific activity, the implication is that the knowledge attained is not absolute truth, but rather a social construction that will change as the characteristics of the group undertaking the activity change.

21 Percy Bysshe Shelley, 'A Defense of Poetry.' Philosopher and historian of science Jacob Bronowski agreed wholeheartedly with this assessment, although framing the argument in precisely the opposite terms: all great *scientific* discoveries, Bronowski advanced, originate with an artistic imagination since scientific discovery entails recognition of *likeness* where previously only differences had been seen. Bronowski gave as an instance Newton's perceiving likeness between the thrown ball and the moon sailing majestically in the sky: see Jacob Bronowski, *The Origins of Knowledge and Imagination*, 60–1.

22 Bronowski,*The Origins of Knowledge and Imagination*.

23 That is, predictive powers. See Karl Popper, *Conjectures and Refutations: The Growth of Scientific Knowledge*, 33–65.

24 Everett Rogers, *A History of Communication Study: A Biographical Approach*, 100; emphasis added. Rogers comments that this may be a case of research methods determining acceptance of theories, rather than the methods being applied to test the theories. He writes: 'Individualistic research methodologies (centering on quantitative techniques) in which communication scholars are mostly trained are unsatisfactory tools for studying relational behavior. Again we see a lack of fit between rich theoretical concepts and the available methodologies for testing them': ibid., 91.

25 Shannon and Weaver, *The Mathematical Theory of Communication*. See also

Colin Cherry, *On Human Communication: A Review, a Survey, and a Criticism.*

26 For a critique of this approach, see, *inter alia,* my *Communication and the Transformation of Economics.*

27 Shannon and Weaver, *The Mathematical Theory of Communication*, 8.

28 Paul Felix Lazarsfeld, 'Remarks on Administrative and Critical Research.' The term 'critical' was actually coined in 1937 by Max Horkheimer in an article entitled 'Traditionelle und Kritische Theorie'; see Rogers, *A History of Communication Study*, 110.

29 Dallas W. Smythe and Tran Van Dinh,'On Critical and Administrative Research: A New Critical Analysis.'

30 Lazarsfeld, 'Remarks on Administrative and Critical Research.'

31 Ibid., 159.

32 Smythe and Van Dinh,'On Critical and Administrative Research,' 118.

33 See, for example, Vincent Mosco, *The Political Economy of Communication: Rethinking and Renewal*; also Mosco, *The Pay-Per Society: Computers and Communication in the Information Age.*

34 For example, Armand Mattelart, *Mapping World Communication: War, Progress, Culture*, and G.J. Mulgan, *Communication and Control: Networks and the New Economics of Communication.*

35 See, for example, Herbert I. Schiller, *Culture Inc.: The Corporate Takeover of Cultural Expression.*

36 Ibid., 160.

37 Lazarsfeld, 'Remarks on Administrative and Critical Research.' 161. It is important to note that Lazarsfeld was himself an administrative researcher *par excellence.* He founded research institutes and served clients such as CBS. He determined the size of radio audiences, their composition, and the 'gratifications' listeners derived from media use. He even helped construct the so-called minimum-effects model of media, which claims that media content is essentially insignificant in terms of personal and social effects, a panacea to media organizations if ever there was one. Nonetheless, despite his marked administrative bent, Lazarsfeld not only acknowledged the vital importance of critical research to the proper functioning of a humane, democratic society, but also gave practical expression to this belief by making space available, albeit not without serious disagreement, to critical researchers Max Horkheimer and Theodor Adorno: see Hanno Hardt, *Critical Communication Studies: Communication History and Theory in America*, 106–14.

38 Smythe and Van Dinh, 'On Critical and Administrative Research,'118.

39 See, for example, Hall, 'The Rediscovery of "Ideology."'

40 This section has benefited from discussions with Sheehan Carter.

41 Stuart Ewen, *PR! A Social History of Spin*, 406.

42 See, for example, Hall, 'The Rediscovery of "Ideology"'; also Robert Hackett, *News and Dissent: The Press and the Politics of Peace in Canada*, and James Winter, *Common Cents: Media Portrayal of the Gulf War and Other Events*.

43 Kevin Robins and Frank Webster, 'The Communications Revolution: New Media, Old Problems.'

44 For example, Daniel J. Czitrom, *Media and the American Mind*, 91–121; Jesse Delia, 'Communication Research: A History'; Rogers, *A History of Communication Study*; and James W. Carey, 'The Chicago School of Communication Research.'

45 John Dewey, *Democracy and Education*, 4.

46 Thorstein Veblen, *The Theory of the Leisure Class*.

47 Thorstein Veblen,'Mr Cummings's Strictures on "The Theory of the Leisure Class,"' 22.

48 Ursula Franklin, *The Real World of Technology*, 15.

49 Czitrom, *Media and the American Mind*, 112.

50 Rogers, *A History of Communication Study*.

51 Hardt, *Critical Communications Studies*.

52 John Peter, 'Democracy and American Communication Theory: Dewey, Lippmann, Lazarsfeld,' cited in Rogers, *A History of Communication Study*, 159; emphasis added.

53 Rogers, *A History of Communication Study*, 11–13.

54 Seymour Martin Lipset, *North-American Cultures: Values and Institutions in Canada and the United States*, 2.

55 Ibid.

56 Ibid., 4.

57 Ibid.

58 Ibid.

59 Harold A.Innis, 'Reflections on Russia,' 74.

60 Northrop Frye, 'Sharing the Continent,' 66.

61 Lipset, *North-American Cultures*, 7. Here Lipset is quoting Frye, 'National Consciousness in Canadian Life,' 46.

62 George Grant, *Lament for a Nation*.

63 Gad Horowitz, 'Tories, Socialists, and the Demise of Canada,' 2, cited in Lipset, *North-American Cultures*, 5.

64 Northrop Frye, *The Bush Garden: Essays in the Canadian Imagination*, 142.

65 R. Bruce Elder, *Image and Identity: Reflections on Canadian Film and Culture*, 25.

66 Frye wrote: 'Small and isolated communities surrounded with a physical or psychological "frontier," separated from one another and from their American and British cultural sources: communities that provide all that their members have in the way of distinctively human values, and that are compelled to feel a great respect for the law and order that holds them together, yet confronted with a huge, unthinking, menacing, and formidable physical setting — such communities are bound to develop what we may provisionally call a garrison mentality': Frye, 'Conclusion to a *Literary History of Canada*,' 73.

67 Margaret Atwood, *Survival: A Thematic Guide to Canadian Literature*.

68 Northrop Frye, 'Sharing the Continent,' 68.

69 Frye, 'National Consciousness in Canadian Life,' 49.

70 'Highway 17,' a modern folk song by Tamarack, lyrics by James Gordon.

71 Harry J. Boyle, 'The Canadian Broadcasting System,' 8.

72 Northrop Frye, 'Culture as Interpenetration,'17.

73 Herschel Hardin, *A Nation Unaware: The Canadian Economic Culture*, 13.

74 Ibid., 12.

75 Ibid., 55.

76 Leslie Armour, *The Idea of Canada and the Crisis of Community*, 43. These thoughts are confirmed by David Staines, who describes Canada as existing in 'a dialectic of regional and ethnic tensions.' Staines continues: 'The tension of the French and the English, the two founding peoples of the country, is at the center of this dialectic, and such tensions, always dynamic and demanding, have given Canada its uniqueness. And the mosaic pattern becomes a further element operating against national unity. Canadian history follows a pattern of attempts to impose order and political unity, but not cultural homogeneity, on the whole country': see Staines, 'Introduction,' 3.

77 Over the last decade, many of these venerable Crown corporations have been privatized by neo-liberal governments.

78 Armour, *The Idea of Canada and the Crisis of Community*, 109.

79 Canada, *House of Commons Debates, Official Report*, 8580–1; quoted in Lipset, *North-American Cultures*, 28.

80 Arthur Kroker, *Technology and the Canadian Mind: Innis/McLuhan/Grant*, 8.

81 The allusion here is to a memorable phrase from Northrop Frye, which he derived from the poet Blake.

82 Ibid., 8.

83 Robin Mathews, *Canadian Identity: Major Forces Shaping the Life of a People*, 1.

84 Ibid.

85 Henry A. Giroux, *Ideology, Culture, and the Process of Schooling*, 114.

86 Ibid., 120.

87 Ibid., 114.

88 Kenneth E. Boulding, *A Primer on Social Dynamics: History as Dialectics and Development*, 53.

89 Giroux, *Ideology, Culture, and the Process of Schooling*, 116.

90 Sandra Braman, 'Commentary,' 101.

91 Atwood, *Survival*.

92 Maurice Charland, 'Technological Nationalism.'

93 Kroker, *Technology and the Canadian Mind*.

94 See Robert E. Babe, *Telecommunications in Canada: Technology, Industry, and Government*.

95 Heather Menzies, *The Railroad's Not Enough: Canada Now*, 68–9.

96 See generally Herbert I. Schiller, *Mass Communications and American Empire*. See also Alan Smith, *American–Canadian Public Policy: Canadian Culture, the Canadian State, and the New Continentalism*.

97 Heather Menzies, *Whose Brave New World? The Information Highway and the New Economy*, 137.

98 Dwayne Winseck, *Reconvergence: A Political Economy of Telecommunications in Canada*, and Babe, *Telecommunications in Canada*, 91–101.

99 Roger de la Garde, 'Mr Innis, Is There Life after the "American Empire?",' 10.

100 Gaetan Tremblay, 'Some Reflections on the Theoretical Discourse on Communications in Quebec and Canada,' 15.

101 Michael Dorland and Arthur Kroker, 'Culture Critique and New Quebec Sociology,' 28. Tremblay actually makes a similar point in remarking that Quebec 'is situated at the crossroads of the great English and French intellectual traditions': Tremblay, 'Some Reflections,' 18.

102 See, for example, John F. Conway, 'Reflections on Canada in the Year 1997–98.' Conway writes: 'The old National Policy, the core economic strategy of Canada as a nation, is finished. But we have developed no new National Policy, no new core economic strategy but free trade, free markets and globalization. It goes without saying that an economic strategy singularly characterized by free trade and free markets amounts to no economic strategy at all' (p. 21).

2: The Communication Thought of Graham Spry (1900–1983)

1 For example: 'A Case for Nationalized Broadcasting'; 'The Canadian Broadcasting Corporation, 1936–1961'; 'The Decline and Fall of Canadian

Broadcasting'; 'The Costs of Canadian Broadcasting'; 'Culture and Entropy: A Lay View of Broadcasting'; 'Public Policy and Private Pressures:
The Canadian Radio League 1930–6 and Countervailing Power.'

2 For example: 'The Fall of Constantinople – 1453'; 'Canada, The United
Nations Emergency Force, and the Commonwealth'; 'A Canadian Looks at
the Commonwealth'; 'India and Self-Government'; 'Economic Changes in
the Canadian Prairie Provinces'; 'Canada: Notes on Two Ideas of Nation in
Confrontation'; 'One Nation, Two Cultures'; and 'French Canada and
Canadian Federation.'

3 Rose Potvin, ed., *Passion and Conviction: The Letters of Graham Spry*, 8.

4 Graham Spry, letter to Arnold Heeney, winter 1923, reprinted in ibid., 37.

5 Potvin, ed., *Passion and Conviction*, 65.

6 Michael Nolan, *Foundations: Alan Plaunt and the Early Days of CBC Radio.*

7 From a press release announcing the founding of the Canadian Radio
League, quoted in Potvin, ed., *Passion and Conviction*, 72.

8 Graham Spry, 'A Case for Nationalized Broadcasting,' 169.

9 Ibid., 151–69.

10 Presentation by the Canadian Radio League before Parliamentary Committee on Radio Broadcasting, 18 April 1932, as quoted in Potvin, ed.,
Passion and Conviction, 81.

11 For instance, Robert W. McChesney, 'Graham Spry and the Future of
Public Broadcasting'; Frank Peers, *The Politics of Canadian Broadcasting,
1920–1951*; E. Austin Weir, *The Struggle for National Broadcasting in Canada*;
and Marc Raboy, *Missed Opportunities: The Story of Canada's Broadcasting
Policy.*

12 Potvin, ed., *Passion and Conviction*, 2.

13 Alan Plaunt, *The Canadian Radio League: Objects, Information, National
Support.*

14 In his presentation to the Royal Commission on Railways and Transportation on 14 January 1932, Graham Spry described membership of the
League in these terms: 'The Canadian Radio League is a voluntary association with the chief aim of securing the operation of Canadian broadcasting
as a national enterprise. It consists of a national council, representing
business, financial, educational, and women's interests, as set out in the
pamphlet submitted. It has the support of women's organizations with a
total membership of 683,800, of national associations, and of farm and
labour organizations with a membership of 279,000, of the heads of the
Anglican, Roman Catholic, United, Baptist, and Presbyterian churches, of
sixteen university presidents and eight provincial superintendents of
education.'

15 Margaret Prang,'The Origins of Public Broadcasting,' 30.
16 Quoted in Potvin, ed., *Passion and Conviction*, 93.
17 Ibid., 111.
18 Quoted in ibid., 118.
19 Ibid., 1.
20 Irene Spry related that he learned Russian the same way, and that he even translated some children's stories by Dostoevsky for their son, Robin. Spry never completed the final chapter of his 'History of Russia.'
21 The first meeting was held on 23 January 1966 by the Ralegh Club at Oxford, with R.D.E. Spry, President, as chair; the second was on 26 January by the Atlantic Group and the United Kingdom Council of the European Movement, London, meeting chaired by the Right Hon. Lord Tweedsmuir. Spry notes: 'Both meetings were private.'
22 Graham Spry, 'One Nation, Two Cultures,' 14.
23 Graham Spry, 'Canada: Notes on Two Ideas of Nation in Confrontation,' 173.
24 Spry, 'One Nation, Two Cultures,' 18.
25 Spry, 'Canada,' 196.
26 Personal reminiscence of the author.
27 Graham Spry, 'Culture and Entropy,' 89–101.
28 Ibid., 91.
29 Ibid.
30 Ibid.
31 Ibid., 91–2.
32 Once produced, information can be shared virtually without limit, with little if any increased costs; cost per users, therefore, declines as the number of users increases.
33 See Bruce Cummings,*War and Television*; also Hamid Mowlana, George Gerbner, and Herbert I. Schiller, *The Triumph of the Image: The Media's War in the Persian Gulf.*
34 Spry, 'Culture and Entropy,' 96, 98.
35 Ibid., 90.

3: The Communication Thought of Harold Adams Innis (1894–1952)

1 Donald Creighton, *Harold Adams Innis: Portrait of a Scholar*, 72.
2 As can be seen readily by scanning Innis's entries in his 'idea file.' See Harold Adams Innis, *The Idea File of Harold Adams Innis.*
3 Creighton, *Harold Adams Innis*, 19. See also Robin Neill, *A New Theory of Value: The Canadian Economics of H.A. Innis*, 18.
4 She used a part of her small legacy to attend De Mille Ladies College at Whitby for one year.

5 Creighton, *Harold Adams Innis*, 9.

6 Harold A. Innis, *The Bias of Communication*, xvii.

7 He remarked to his sister at the time, 'If I had no faith in Christianity, I don't think I would go': quoted in Creighton, *Harold Adams Innis*, 31.

8 Neill, *A New Theory of Value*, 12.

9 On Park's influence, see particularly Marshall McLuhan, 'Introduction' to Innis's *The Bias of Communication*. On the Chicago School of communication generally, see *inter alia*, Daniel J. Czitrom, *Media and the American Mind: From Morse to McLuhan*, ch. 4; also Everett M. Rogers, *A History of Communication Study: A Biographical Approach*, ch. 5. James Carey makes connection between Innis and the Chicago School in his essay 'Space, Time, and Communications: A Tribute to Harold Innis.'

10 Whereas standard economics teaches, for instance, that 'capital' is wealth or equipment deployed by people to generate incomes, Clark asked whether *people* might not just as easily be thought of as instruments in the service of capital. See Judith Stamps, *Unthinking Modernity: Innis, McLuhan, and the Frankfurt School*, 54.

11 See, for instance, Fletcher Baragar, 'Influence of Veblen on Harold Innis'; also William Christian, 'Preface,' xi. In 1929, Innis wrote an appreciative interpretation of Veblen's work, presaging his own method, for the *Southwestern Political and Social Science Quarterly* and republished as 'The Work of Thorstein Veblen.'

12 See 'The Communication Theory of Thorstein Veblen,' in Robert E. Babe, *Communication and the Transformation of Economics*, 141–58. See also Max Lerner, 'Editor's Introduction.'

13 Smith wrote: 'As by means of water-carriage a more extensive market is opened to every sort of industry than what land-carriage alone can afford it, so it is upon the sea-coast, and along the banks of navigable rivers that industry of every kind naturally begins to subdivide and improve itself, and it is frequently not till a long time after that those improvements extend themselves to the inland parts of the country: Adam Smith, *An Inquiry Into the Nature and Causes of The Wealth of Nations*, 18.

14 Adam Smith, *The Theory of Moral Sentiments*.

15 For a thorough discussion of the 'market plus framework' perspective of the classical political economists, see Warren J. Samuels, *The Classical Theory of Economic Policy*.

16 See generally, Ian Drummond, with William Kaplan, *Political Economy at the University of Toronto: A History of the Department 1888–1982*, particularly 81–107.

17 Interview with Art Ferri, at the University of Ottawa, on 9 November 1998. Innis also stated, however, that oral dialectic, although important 'in the

discovery of new truth [, is] of very little value in disseminating it': Harold A. Innis, 'A Critical Review,' 191.

18 Eric Havelock, *Harold A. Innis: A Memoir*, 25.

19 Neill, *A New Theory of Value*, 18.

20 Havelock, *Harold A. Innis: A Memoir*, 22.

21 Creighton, *Harold Adams Innis*, 82. In his 1933 essay 'Government Owner-ship and the Canadian Scene,' for instance, Innis cautioned about the 'dangers of inadequate planning,' contending that 'planning leads inevita-bly to more planning,' and that 'interdependence in modern economic life necessitates the extension of planning once it has been started': see Innis, *Essays in Canadian Economic History*, 78– 84.

22 Harold A. Innis, 'Adult Education and Universities,' 474, 472.

23 Arthur Lower wrote that Innis was physically awkward. Aboard Lower's yacht, his friend related, Innis could be counted on 'to cast off the wrong rope, or put the tiller round the wrong way … How he got through those long northern trips of his, when he was tracking the fur trade to its lair, I cannot understand': Arthur Lower, 'Harold Adams Innis as I Remember Him,' 8.

24 Creighton, *Harold Adams Innis*, 63.

25 Ibid.

26 Christian, 'Preface,' in Harold A. Innis, *Innis on Russia: The Russian Diary and Other Writings*, 10.

27 Harold A. Innis, 'The Strategy of Culture,' 19–20.

28 Rick Salutin, 'Last Call from Harold Innis,' 246.

29 Innis, *The Bias of Communication*, 190.

30 Innis, *Innis on Russia*, 47.

31 *The Idea File of Harold Adams Innis*, 39. Innis's wit is particularly evident in his public addresses, for example, 'Government Ownership and the Canadian Scene' (1933) and 'Economic Trends in Canadian–American Relations' (1938), both printed in Innis, *Essays in Canadian Economic His-tory*, 78–96 and 233–41.

32 Lower, 'Harold Innis as I Remember Him,' 4.

33 Personal communication with author.

34 Creighton, *Harold Adams Innis*, 101.

35 Northrop Frye, 'Across the River and Out of the Trees,' 36.

36 Robin W. Winks, 'Foreword,' viii.

37 E.R. Adair, 'Review Article.'

38 In his 'Introduction' to *The Bias of Communication*, McLuhan wrote further: 'How exciting it was to encounter a writer whose every phrase invited prolonged meditation and exploration … He includes a small library on

each page, and often incorporates a small library of references on the same page in addition. If the business of the teacher is to save the student's time, Innis is one of the greatest teachers on record' (p. ix).

39 Marshall McLuhan, *The Gutenberg Galaxy*, 216.

40 Andrew Wernick, 'The Post-Innisian Significance of Innis,' 130.

41 Harold A. Innis, 'The Church in Canada,' 387. Wernick, who quotes these lines from Innis, adds: 'A non-conformist in the prophetic tradition of speaking truth to power, Innis can hardly be accused of kowtowing to elites': see Wernick, 'The Post-Innisian Significance of Innis,' 130. In fact, A. John Watson maintains that the central dialectic running through Innis's work was not space versus time or centre versus margin, but power versus intelligence, in which case the above-quoted self-effacement takes on increased irony. See A. John Watson, 'Harold Innis and Classical Scholarship,' 58.

42 Christian, 'Preface,' to *The Idea File of Harold Innis*, vii.

43 Ibid. And again: 'The writing of books necessitates presenting a case as the final argument. As a result books contribute powerfully to the closing of minds, particularly of writers, as they have strong vested interests in positions which they have elaborated': *The Idea File of Harold Innis*, 157, quoted in Ronald Keast, '"It Is Written – But I Say Unto You": Innis on Religion,' 14.

44 Harold A. Innis, *Empire and Communications*, xiii; emphasis added. He adds, '"It is written but I say unto you," is a powerful directive to Western civilization': ibid., xiii.

45 Ibid., 56–7.

46 Ibid., 57.

47 Ibid.

48 A. John Watson, author of a doctoral dissertation on Innis entitled 'Marginal Man,' related in an interview with David Cayley of the CBC's *Ideas* the rather eccentric, if not indeed bizarre, manner whereby Innis prepared his communication manuscripts: 'The method of composition that Innis used was to have a room set up in his house, where he would spread out the books like waves and read books jumbled together. He might have twelve or twenty books on the go, make copious notes, photocopy the notes – and we're talking about very primitive photocopying technology back then – and then he would cut and paste. He would take the précised notes from these books he had read, he would cut them up, jumble them together, add bridges, and *voila!* you had the communication work': CBC *Ideas*, 'The Legacy of Harold Innis,' 14.

49 William H. Melody, 'Introduction,' *Culture, Communication, and Dependency: The Tradition H.A. Innis*, 7.

50 Harold A. Innis, *A History of the Canadian Pacific Railway*.

51 A. John Watson argues that distinctions between the 'early' and 'late' Innis can be overdrawn. According to Watson, throughout his academic life Innis 'was essentially a colonial intellectual who continually struggled against the dominant and myopic paradigms in research set by metropolitan institutions and intellectuals': Watson, 'Harold Innis and Classical Scholarship,' 45. William Christian is another who minimizes the demarcation between the second and third periods; Christian even denies that Innis's books from the latter phase were really about communication at all: 'Innis's real interest lay in the underlying political and cultural issues, and the studies in communication were to a considerable degree a device for getting at more important questions': Christian, 'Preface,'xi. In any event, whether Christian is correct or not regarding Innis's intention, communication media loom large enough in these later works to comprise a new theory of media as underlying social change.

52 Northrop Frye, 'Harold Innis: The Strategy of Culture,' 157.

53 Ibid., 156.

54 Cf. Barrington Nevitt, *The Communication Ecology: Re-presentation versus Replica*, 100–4.

55 See, for instance, my essay 'The Place of Information in Economics.' On Innis's position, see his classic essay 'The Penetrative Powers of the Price System.' Seminal articles by neoclassicists on money as a medium of communication include: F.A. von Hayek, 'The Use of Knowledge in Society'; R.H. Coase, 'The Nature of the Firm'; and G. Stigler, 'The Economics of Information.'

56 Harold A. Innis, 'Minerva's Owl,' 3–4.

57 Rogers, *A History of Communication Study*, 499; and Czitrom, *Media and the American Mind*, 148.

58 See, for instance, Stamps, *Unthinking Modernity*.

59 Edward Comor, 'Harold Innis's Dialectical Triad.' I acknowledge gratefully helpful comments by Professor Comor regarding Innis and technological determinism.

60 Paul Heyer, *Communications and History: Theories of Media, Knowledge, and Civilization*, 115. See also Angus, *A Border Within*, 65.

61 Innis, *The Bias of Communication*, 192.

62 Innis, *A History of the Canadian Pacific Railway*, 292.

63 Ibid., 287; emphasis added.

64 Keast, '"It Is Written — But I say Unto You,"' 13.

65 As noted by William Kuhns, Innis appears to have used the term 'monopolies of knowledge' in at least three distinct, albeit related senses: (1) the

constriction of communication primarily to one medium; (2) limitation to a
certain type of knowledge; and (3) fairly tight control over a medium or a
knowledge system by an élite: see Kuhns, *The Post-industrial Prophets:
Interpretations of Technology*, 154–5.

66　Neill, *A New Theory of Value*, 29.

67　Innis wrote: 'An interest in this subject has followed from a study on the
Canadian Pacific Railway. A sense of the incompleteness of that volume
and of all volumes which have centred on that subject and on the subject
of Canadian confederation is the occasion for this work': Innis, *The Fur
Trade in Canada*, ix. Likewise in his unpublished autobiography he confessed, 'My immediate task [in *The Fur Trade in Canada*] was offsetting the
limitations of my thesis by attempting to show the inherent unity of
Canada as it developed before the railroad in relations to lakes and rivers':
quoted in Neill, *A New Theory of Value*, 36.

68　Innis, *The Fur Trade in Canada*, 393.

69　As Innis was later to note, in interacting with other staples such as timber,
the landscape produced pressures for assimilation by the United States.

70　Ibid.

71　Harold A. Innis, 'The Teaching of Economic History in Canada,' 3.

72　See, for example, Bernard Dasah, 'Application of Neoclassical Economics
to African Development: A Curse in Disguise.' Also John Cavanagh,
Daphney Wysham, and Marcos Arruda, eds., *Beyond Bretton Woods: Alternatives to the Global Economic Order*.

73　Harold A. Innis, "On the Economic Significance of Culture,' cited in Neill,
A New Theory of Value, 43.

74　They can also lead to the stifling of new technologies, as when the Hudson's Bay Company attempted to thwart Western penetration of the
telegraph in order to protect its lands for the fur staple: see Innis, *A History
of the Canadian Pacific Railway*, 38–42.

75　Irene M. Spry, 'Overhead Costs, Rigidities of Productive Capacity, and the
Price System,' 156.

76　Innis, *Empire and Communications*, 5–6.

77　Creighton, *Harold Adams Innis: Portrait of a Scholar*, 96.

78　Innis, *The Fur Trade in Canada*, 15.

79　Ibid., 383–4.

80　Ibid., 383.

81　Ibid., 385.

82　Ibid., 391.

83　Ibid.

84　Ibid.

85 Ibid., 110.
86 As Innis put it, 'The persistent and increasing demand for European commodities led to the more rapid extermination of the beaver, to increased hostilities, especially between Indian middlemen such as the Huron and Iroquois, to the westward flight of the Indians, to the spread of new cultural traits, and to further expansion of the trade. The pressure of tribes on the territory of the Indians to the interior was an additional and important cause of renewed Indian wars and destruction. Wars between tribes, which with bows and arrows had not been strenuous, conducted with guns were disastrous': ibid., 20.
87 Ibid., 388.
88 Harold A. Innis, *The Cod Fisheries: The History of an International Economy*, 56, 87.
89 Ibid., 484.
90 Ibid., 504.
91 Ibid., 494.
92 Ibid., 144, 317.
93 Ibid., 321.
94 Ibid., 387.
95 Ibid., 463.
96 Ibid., 495.
97 Ibid., 501.
98 Ibid., 502.
99 See, in particular, H.A. Innis, 'The Pulp and Paper Industry'; 'The Lumber Trade in Canada'; 'The Newspaper in Economic Development'; and Harold Innis, *The Press: A Neglected Factor in the Economic History of the Twentieth Century.* Also, 'Paper and the Printing Press' and 'Technology and Public Opinion in the United States.' According to Robin Neill, Innis began a book on pulp and paper in the 1930s but became distracted by his concerns regarding economic cycles and the role of technology: Neill, *A New Theory of Value,* 42.
100 Harold A. Innis, 'The Strategy of Culture,' 1. Gresham's Law states that inferior specie drives out the superior; Say's Law is that supply creates its own demand.
101 Innis, 'The Lumber Trade in Canada,' 242.
102 Ibid., 243.
103 Ibid., 242.
104 Ibid., 243.
105 Ibid., 246.
106 Harold A. Innis, 'The Canadian Economy and the Depression,; in *Essays in Canadian Economic History*, 136–7; first published in 1934.

107 Ibid., 127.
108 Harold A. Innis, 'The Newspaper in Economic Development,' 27.
109 Innis, *The Bias of Communication*, 167–8.
110 Ibid., 186.
111 Ibid., 188.
112 Watson, 'Harold Innis and Classical Scholarship,' 45.
113 Ibid., 46 ff.
114 Innis, Minerva's Owl,' 3.
115 Ibid.
116 Ibid., 5.
117 Innis, *The Idea File of Harold Adams Innis*, 6.
118 According to Robin Neill, Innis inaugurated his writing on communication when U.S. hegemony was coming to the fore, and his 'intense nationalism was aroused' as a result. If Gibbon wrote *The Decline and Fall of the Roman Empire* about Britain and not about Rome, as Innis said he had, then, Neill declares, Innis in the same sense wrote his history of communications 'about Canada and not about Egypt, Greece, and Europe': Neill, *A New Theory of Value*, 17.
119 Kroker, *Technology and the Canadian Mind*, 98.
120 James W. Carey, 'Culture, Geography and Communications: The Work of Harold Innis in an American Context,' 80.
121 McLuhan, 'Introduction,' to Innis, *The Bias of Communication*, xv.
122 Innis, Minerva's Owl,' 4; emphasis added.
123 Ibid., 6.
124 Ibid., 18.
125 Ibid., 20.
126 Ibid., 11. And again: 'Pervasiveness of language becomes a powerful factor in the mobilization of force particularly as a vehicle for the diffusion of opinion among all classes. Language exposed to major incursions became more flexible, facilitated movement between classes, favoured the diffusion of technology and made for rapid adjustment': ibid.
127 Cf. James W. Carey, 'Harold Adams Innis and Marshall McLuhan,' and Havelock, *Harold A. Innis: A Memoir*, 29–38.
128 Innis quotes approvingly Plato's dictum that the invention of writing will 'create forgetfulness in the learner's souls, because they will not use their memories; they will trust to the external written characters and not remember of themselves': Innis, *Political Economy in the Modern State*, vii. In Innis's view, anticipating McLuhan, each new invention, although enhancing power in one direction, weakens power in other directions.
129 Innis wrote, for instance, 'The skyscraper has become the modern cathedral; long-term credit is the new basis of modern belief': Innis, 'The

Penetrative Powers of the Price System,' 270. And again: 'The accountant has penetrated the holy of holies ... economics have displaced creeds': Innis, 'The Passing of Political Economy,' 441.

130 Cf. David Harvey, *The Condition of Postmodernity*, 238.
131 Harold Innis, 'A Plea for Time,' 72.
132 Ibid., 67; here Innis is quoting W.A. Irwin.
133 Ibid., 66.
134 David Harvey, *The Condition of Postmodernity*, 232.
135 Harold A. Innis, 'Problem of Space,' 105.
136 Ibid.
137 Innis, *Empire and Communications*, 44.
138 Ibid., 10.
139 Ibid.
140 Ibid.
141 Ibid., 127.
142 Although, as Raymond Williams has noted, advertising often makes use of myth: see Williams, 'Advertising: The Magic System.'
143 Innis, 'The Bias of Communication.'
144 Innis, 'Minerva's Owl,' 26.
145 Innis, 'The Bias of Communication,' 34.
146 Innis, *Empire and Communications*, 116.
147 Ibid., 138.
148 Innis, 'The Bias of Communication,' 48–9.
149 Ibid., 47.
150 Ibid., 48.
151 Ibid., 49.
152 Ibid., 50.
153 Ibid., 52.
154 Innis reports that in 1470 a printed Bible cost about one-fifth that of a manuscript Bible: Innis, *Empire and Communications*, 141.
155 Ibid., 148.
156 Innis, 'The Bias of Communication,' 55.
157 Innis, 'The Press,' 82.
158 Innis, 'The Strategy of Culture,' 17.
159 Ibid., 15.
160 Ibid.
161 Innis, 'The Bias of Communication,' 60.
162 Ibid., 87.
163 Innis, 'The Problem of Space,' 111.
164 Innis, 'A Plea for Time,' 64.

165 Innis, 'A Critical Review,' 191.

166 Innis, 'Industrialism and Cultural Values,' 132.

167 Innis, 'A Plea fo Time,' 76.

168 Ibid., 89.

169 Ibid.

170 J. Herbert Altschull, *From Milton to McLuhan: The Ideas Behind American Journalism*, 345; James R. Beniger, *The Control Revolution: Technological and Economic Origins of the Information Society*; Ronald J. Deibert, *Parchment, Printing, and Hypermedia: Communication in World Order Transformation*; Elizabeth Eisenstein, *The Printing Press as an Agent of Change*; Walter J. Ong, *Orality and Literacy: The Technologizing of the Word*; David Crowley and Paul Heyer, eds., *Communication in History: Technology, Culture, and Society*.

171 Herbert I. Schiller, *Communication and Cultural Domination,* 1. See also Richard J. Barnet and Ronald E. Müller, *Global Reach: The Power of the Multinational Corporations*; Richard J. Barnet and John Cavanagh, *Global Dreams: Imperial Corporations and the New World Order*; G.J. Mulgan, *Communication and Control: Networks and the New Economies of Communication*; Jill Hills, 'Communication, Information, and Transnational Enterprise.'

172 Innis, *The Bias of Communication,* 82.

173 Jean Baudrillard, *For a Critique of the Political Economy of the Sign.* Theme parks for postmodernists are more 'real' than what they supposedly refer back to; 'society becomes a collage of theme parks which one enters at will (and for a price),' writes Mark Poster in 'The Mode of Information and Postmodernity,' 179.

174 Many postmodernists agree that the overabundance of messages, often contradictory, diminishes the value of each one, and on that account they urge that we abandon all search for truth and rather celebrate *difference*. To abandon the hope or goal of forming consensus, however, is to edge ever closer to the abyss of nihilism, a theme explored at great length by other theorists, Grant and Frye in particular, considered in this volume.

175 Innis, *Political Economy in the Modern State,* vii.

176 Book 1, Chapter 2.

177 Innis, *Empire and Communications,* 3.

178 See, for instance, Dwayne Winseck, *Reconvergence: A Political Economy of Telecommunications in Canada.*

179 Schiller, *Information Inequality.*

180 See, for example, Herbert I. Schiller, 'Is There a United States Information Policy?' Also Colleen Roach, 'Dallas Smythe and the New World Information and Communication Order.'

181 Joseph Nye, Jr, and William Owens, 'America's Information Edge,' 29. See also Schiller, "Is There a United States Information Policy?'

182 For example, Armand Mattelart, *Mapping World Communication: War, Progress, Culture*, 3–121.

183 A draft PhD thesis by Michael Strangelove, although referring neither to Innis nor to the dialectic of space versus time, was very suggestive in forming these arguments: Michael Strangelove, 'Collective Memory and the Social Control of Thought: Mass Media, Cyberspace and the Globalization of Symbols.'

184 Mark Poster, 'Databases as Discourse; or Electronic Interpellations.'

185 Oscar Gandy, Jr, *The Panoptic Sort: A Political Economy of Personal Information*.

186 Robert E. Babe, 'Understanding the Cultural Ecology Model.'

187 Ibid.

188 Innis, 'A Plea for Time,' 82.

189 William Birdsall, 'The Ideology of Information Technology.'

190 Organization for Economic Cooperation and Development, *Information Networks and New Technologies: Opportunities and Policy Implications for the 1990s*, 23; excerpted in Birdsall, 'The Ideology of Information Technology,' 288.

191 Robert Chodos, Rae Murphy, and Eric Hamovitch, *Lost in Cyberspace? Canada and the Information Revolution*, 78.

192 Babe, *Communication and the Transformation of Economics*.

4: The Communication Thought of John Grierson (1898–1972)

1 Forsyth Hardy, *John Grierson: A Documentary Biography*, 11–12.

2 James Beveridge, *John Grierson: Film Master*, 4. Also Jack C. Ellis, *John Grierson: A Guide to References and Resources*, 1.

3 Hardy, *John Grierson*, 19.

4 Quoted in ibid., 29.

5 According to Hardy, Grierson's subject originally was 'Immigration and Its Effects on the Social Problems of the United States," later modified to include "Public Opinion, Social Psychology and Newspaper Psychology.': ibid., 31.

6 Ibid., 34.

7 See, for example, Grierson's essay 'Propaganda and Education.'

8 Forsyth Hardy, 'Introduction,' 9.

9 Beveridge, *John Grierson: Film Master*, 23.

10 John Grierson, 'The Course of Realism,' 74.

11 Quoted in Beveridge, *John Grierson: Film Master,* vii.
12 Hardy, 'Introduction,' 11.
13 John Grierson, 'First Principles of Documentary,' 35.
14 John Grierson, 'Battle for Authenticity,' 83.
15 Grierson, 'First Principles of Documentary,' 37.
16 Grierson, 'The Course of Realism,' 79.
17 Hardy, 'Introduction,' 12.
18 Grierson, 'The Course of Realism,' 76.
19 Joyce Nelson, *The Colonized Eye: Rethinking the Grierson Legend*, 35.
20 Grierson remarked that 'if a film-maker is working for a national agency, he must be a loyal civil servant and work within the framework of government information policy; he is not making films for himself, but for the government; he can't do anything he damn well pleases.' Grierson went on to say, however, that this fact does not absolve the documentary film-maker of moral responsibility; to the contrary, Grierson admonished: 'The day a government information service runs only for the interests of the party in power, I would have nothing to do with it, nor would any information man worth his salt': quoted in Donald F. Theall and Joan B. Theall, 117.
21 Grierson once remarked: 'For a short time, I heard people in one great London theatre applaud the faces of the British working class. Then I knew that I had really done something. Besides making a picture I had made the audience applaud themselves': quoted in ibid., 118.
22 Grierson, 'The Course of Realism,' 77.
23 Quoted in Hardy, 'Introduction,' 13.
24 Interview with Basil Wright, in Beveridge, *John Grierson: Film Master,* 73.
25 Grierson, 'First Principles of Documentary,' 41.
26 Grierson, 'The Course of Realism,' 81.
27 Ellis, *John Grierson: A Guide to References and Resources*, 5.
28 John Grierson, 'The Film at War,' 86.
29 Rick Salutin, 'The NFB Red Scare.'
30 Grierson, 'The Film at War,' 86.
31 John Grierson, 'Summary and Survey 1935,' 64.
32 Nelson, *The Colonized Eye*, 63.
33 Grierson, 'The Film at War,' 87–8.
34 Salutin, 'The NFB Red Scare,' 17.
35 Kirwan Cox, 'The Grierson Files,' 16.
36 Ibid., 21.
37 Gary Evans, *John Grierson and the National Film Board: The Politics of Wartime Propaganda*, 14.

38 CRTC transcript of interviews with Grierson 1969–71, 75–6; excerpted in Cox, 'The Grierson Files,' 23.
39 Hardy, 'Introduction,' 16.
40 National Film Board of Canada, *Grierson*.
41 Martin Knelman, *This Is Where We Came In: The Career and Character of Canadian Film*, 12.
42 Interview with Harry Watt, published in Beveridge, *John Grierson: Film Master*, 90.
43 Theall and Theall, 'John Grierson on Media, Film and History,' 113.
44 Donald Theall, 'Communication Theory and Marginal Culture: The Socio-Aesthetic Dimensions of Communication Study,' 8–9.
45 Grierson, *Eyes of Democracy*, 5.
46 Gabriel Marcel, *Man against Mass Society*, 51; emphasis in original.
47 Jacques Ellul, *Propaganda: The Formation of Men's Attitudes*, xi, 6; emphasis in original.
48 Grierson, 'Education and the New Order,' 130. The 'qualification' referred to was Grierson's insistence that 'public guidance [must never become] a matter of one-way traffic.' He explained: 'The government has as much information and guidance to get from the people as the people from the government:' ibid., 129.
49 Quoted in *John Grierson: Master Film Maker*.
50 In addition to the Joyce Nelson reference cited earlier, see Peter Morris, 'Rethinking Grierson: The Ideology of John Grierson.'
51 Walter Lippmann, *Public Opinion*, 163.
52 Ibid., 144.
53 As pointed out by Noam Chomsky, however, even the classical theorists of democracy, such as Thomas Jefferson and John Locke, would confine the franchise to a 'worthy' class of individuals. See Noam Chomsky, 'Force and Opinion.' See also chapter 6, on C.B. Macpherson, in the present volume.
54 Raymond Williams,'Democracy, Old and New.'
55 The phrase is from Reinhold Niebuhr, and forms the title of one of Noam Chomsky's treatises on the antidemocratic nature of mass media: See Noam Chomsky, *Necessary Illusions: Thought Control in Democratic Societies*, 17.
56 Grierson, *The Eyes of Democracy*, 27.
57 Ibid., 28.
58 Ibid., 26.
59 Grierson, 'Searchlight on Democracy,' 91.
60 Conversation with Gary Evans, 10 September 1998. Evans is author of two

books on the NFB and was a doctoral candidate under Grierson's supervision.

61 Grierson, *The Eyes of Democracy*, 28.
62 Grierson, 'Searchlight on Democracy,' 95.
63 John Grierson, 'Education and Total Effort,' 135.
64 John Grierson, 'The Library in the International World,' 157.
65 Ibid.
66 Ibid.
67 Grierson, 'Education and Total Effort,' 134.
68 Grierson, 'The Nature of Propaganda,' 109.
69 Grierson, 'Searchlight on Democracy,' 96.
70 Grierson, 'Propaganda and Education,' 150.
71 Ibid., 151.
72 Grierson, 'Searchlight on Democracy,' 91.
73 Grierson, 'Education and Total Effort,' 139.
74 Ibid., 140.
75 Grierson, 'The Challenge of Peace,' 176.
76 Grierson insisted: 'You may not tell lies to the public. Your duty to the public is more important than your duty to your wife and children, not to say your bloody conscience before God. You can tell private lies. That's O.K. That we do in fictional movies. But public lies may not be told': quoted in Theall and Theall, 'John Grierson on Media, Film and History,' 117.
77 John Grierson, 'The Documentary Idea: 1942,' 113.
78 Cited in Beveridge, *John Grierson: Master Film Maker*, 98.
79 Grierson, *Eyes of Democracy*, 74.
80 Grierson, 'Searchlight on Democracy,' 90.
81 Ibid.; emphasis added.
82 Ibid., 90–1.
83 Grierson, 'The Nature of Propaganda,' 109.
84 Donald and Joan Theall quote Grierson as follows: 'The active verb which changes things, represents a dramatic pattern which turns the report into a story, which in fact [the yellow press] was doing because people were talking about stories ... And so the whole theory of the dramatic film came as a theory of newspapers, the theory of newspaper reporting': 'John Grierson on Media, Film and History,' 115.
85 John Grierson, 'Revolution in the Arts,' 28–9.
86 Grierson, 'Propaganda and Education,' 148.
87 John Grierson, 'Learning from Television,' 218.
88 Interview with Grierson, National Film Board, *Grierson*.

89 Gary Evans, personal communication to author, undated.
90 John Grierson, 'Of Whistler and a Light That Failed,' *Chicago Evening Post* (*c.* 1925), extracted in Hardy, *John Grierson*, 35.
91 Grierson, quoted in ibid., 118.
92 John Grierson, quoted in Theall and Theall, 'John Grierson on Media, Film and History,' 125.
93 John Grierson, quoted in ibid.
94 John Grierson, quoted in ibid.
95 John Grierson, quoted in ibid., 122–3.
96 See, for example, Len Masterman, *Teaching the Media*.
97 Paulo Freire, *Education for Critical Consciousness*, 32.
98 Ibid., 114.
99 Paulo Freire, *Pedagogy of the Oppressed*, 52.
100 Richard Shaull, 'Foreword,' 13.
101 Grierson, 'Searchlight on Democracy,' 96.
102 Grierson, *Eyes of Democracy*, 66.
103 Ibid.
104 Quoted in George Myerson and Yvonne Rydin, *The Language of Environment: A New Rhetoric*, 16.
105 Freire, *Education for Critical Consciousness*, 36, 96.
106 John Grierson, quoted in Theall and Theall, 'John Grierson on Media, Film and History,' 122.
107 Grierson, 'The Challenge of Peace,' 171.
108 Grierson, *Eyes of Democracy*, 93–4.
109 For example, Noam Chomsky, *Necessary Illusions*; Tony Clarke, *Silent Coup: Confronting the Big Business Takeover of Canada*; and Robert D. Kaplan, 'Was Democracy Just a Moment?'
110 A noteworthy instance being media coverage of the Gulf War, which included a story, invented by a public-relations firm, of babies being torn from incubators by Iraqi soldiers and of course an all-out vilification of the Iraqi president, as well as extraordinary measures to contain news pools reporting on the war itself.
111 Giles Gherson, 'Marchi Lashes Out at Critics of MAI.'
112 Quoted in James Winter, *Common Cents: Media Portrayal of the Gulf War and Other Events*, 83.
113 See generally Tony Clarke and Maude Barlow, *MAI: The Multilateral Agreement on Investment and the Threat to Canadian Sovereignty*. Also, Andrew Jackson and Matthew Sanger, eds., *Dismantling Democracy: The Multilateral Agreement on Investment (MAI) and Its Impact*. In the winter term of 1998 I required all sixty of my students in Public Opinion at the

University of Ottawa to analyse press coverage of the MAI between January and April; the unanimous response was surprise bordering on incredulity at the paucity of coverage of such an immensely important issue.

114 Madelaine Drohan, 'How the Net Killed the MAI.'
115 Ibid.
116 For her own account, see Maude Barlow, *The Fight of My Life: Confessions of an Unrepentant Canadian*, 208–29.

5: The Communication Thought of Dallas W. Smythe (1907–1992)

1 John A. Lent, 'Interview with Dallas W. Smythe, 4 December, in John A. Lent, *A Different Road Taken: Profiles in Critical Communication*, 21. Unless noted otherwise, material in this section is derived from pp. 21–30 of this source or from unpublished sections of Smythe's autobiography.
2 Dallas W. Smythe, *Dependency Road: Communications, Capitalism, Consciousness, and Canada*, viii.
3 In an unpublished passage of his autobiography, Smythe wrote: 'My own radicalization ... came from the reality of Marxism and not at all from the academics whose only effect on my relation to Marx was to give me a feeling of frustration about reading him.'
4 Federal Communications Commission, *Public Service Responsibility of Broadcast Licensees*, 7 March 1946, reprinted in Frank J. Kahn, ed., *Documents of American Broadcasting*, 125–206.
5 Dallas W. Smythe, 'Excerpt from Autobiography, Chapter 4, Mature Immaturity: The Urbana Years, 1948–1963,' in Dallas W. Smythe, *Counterclockwise: Perspectives on Communication*, 39. There were other reasons also: The House Un-American Activities Committee opposed Smythe's appointment since he had hired the first Black secretary in the history of the commission, for instance.
6 Smythe, 'Autobiography,' 42. In his interview with Lent Smythe stated: 'About 1979 I obtained my FBI file under the Freedom of Information Act. In it there appears that in the summer and fall of 1948, Schramm was in the role of informer to the FBI. A check with *Who's Who* revealed that Schramm had been consultant and adviser to the intelligence agencies of the U.S. military, the OSS, and the CIA over the period from 1942 on': Lent, 'Interview With Dallas W. Smythe,' 32.
7 Smythe, 'Autobiography,' 38.
8 Lent, 'Interview with Dallas W. Smythe,' 43.
9 Spectrum management for Smythe was 'no sterile, neutral process.' 'It is,'

he insisted, 'political in every sense of the word … The radio spectrum is to telecommunications as is water to fish, soil to plants': Dallas W. Smythe, 'Clear across Australia,' 439.

10 See, in particular, Dallas W. Smythe, *The Structure and Policy of Electronic Communication.*

11 Smythe, *Dependency Road*, xi, xii; emphasis in original.

12 Dallas W. Smythe, 'Reality as Presented by Television.'

13 Canada, Royal Commission on Broadcasting, *Report.*

14 Smythe, 'Autobiography,' p. 47.

15 Ibid., 57.

16 Ibid.

17 Janet Wasko, Vincent Mosco, and Manjunath Pendaleur, eds., *Illuminating the Blindspots: Essays Honoring Dallas W. Smythe.*

18 Thomas Guback, 'Eulogy,' in Smythe, *Counterclockwise*, 333.

19 Smythe, 'Reality as Presented by Television,' 66.

20 Ibid., 61–74.

21 Ibid., 70.

22 Ibid., 61.

23 Smythe, *Dependency Road*, xii.

24 Quoted by Thomas Guback, in Smythe, *Counterclockwise*, 60.

25 In later years Smythe was at pains to place quotation marks about this word, although at the time the manuscript in question was written the term seems to have been unproblematic enough for him. Towards the end of his life, however, he would write that 'technology,' although with very material constituents, 'is a myth.' He explained: 'One part [of 'technology'] is pyramidal bureaucracy which follows orders in both the private and public sectors. A second part is science, which has been taken over increasingly by the third part, capital. Another part is tools and machines created by engineers. The fifth part is ideology, which provides the images with which the sixth part, propaganda, seeks to mould public opinion to accept the myth. In reality, "technology" is just a cover story for modern industrialism in motion': Dallas W. Smythe, 'Review Article: One Canadian Perspective: *Clear across Australia*,' 432.

26 Here Smythe is quoting Harry M. Trebing, 'Common Carrier Regulation – The Silent Crisis,' *Law and Contemporary Problems* 34/20 (Spring, 1969): 327: Smythe, *The Relevance of the United States*, 2–7.

27 Like Macpherson, Smythe defined capitalism as 'a system based on private property in the means of production and consumption and on the appropriation of the surplus product of labor by the owners of capital; it is a worldwide system of interrelated markets for commodities': Smythe, *Dependency Road*, 2.

28 Ibid., xii.
29 Ibid., 13.
30 Dallas W. Smythe, 'Culture, Communication "Technology" and Canadian Policy,' 2.
31 Ibid., 17.
32 Smythe, 'Communications: Blindspot of Economics,' 112.
33 Smythe, 'Culture, Communication, "Technology" and Canadian Policy,' 8.
34 Smythe, *Dependency Road*, xiii.
35 Ibid., 223.
36 Dallas W. Smythe, 'After Bicycles, What?,' 231.
37 Smythe, *Dependency Road*, 240.
38 Smythe, 'Culture, Communication "Technology" and Canadian Policy,' 4.
39 Ibid., 9.
40 Smythe, 'Communications: Blindspot of Economics,' 123.
41 Ibid., 112.
42 Smythe, *Dependency Road*, 23.
43 Dallas W. Smythe and Tran Van Dinh, 'On Critical and Administrative Research: A New Critical Analysis.'
44 Smythe, 'Culture, Communication, "Technology" and Canadian Policy,' 4.
45 Ibid., 5.
46 Ibid., 21
47 Smythe and Van Dinh, 'On Critical and Administrative Research.'
48 Smythe, *Dependency Road*, 20.
49 Ibid., 299.
50 Ibid., 20.
51 Ibid., 299.
52 Ibid., 22.
53 Ibid., 232.
54 Ibid.
55 Myles Alexander Ruggles, *The Audience Reflected in the Medium of Law: A Critique of the Political Economy of Speech Rights in the United States*, x.
56 Smythe, *Dependency Road*, 235.
57 Ibid., 190.
58 Ibid., 199.
59 Ibid., 201.
60 Ibid., 211.
61 Ibid., 216.
62 Ibid., 217.
63 Consider, for example, the definitions of *technology* provided by Emmanuel Mesthene and Jacques Ellul. For the former, technology is 'the organization of knowledge for the achievement of practical purposes': see

Mesthene, *Technologial Change*, 25. For Ellul, technology is 'the one best way of doing things': see Jacques Ellul, *The Technological Society*, 79.

64 Smythe did not always possess this awareness of the ideological function and power of the term 'technology.' The opening pages of his 1957 monograph, *The Structure and Policy of Electronic Communication*, makes repeated and uncritical reference to the 'technological imperative.' Intimations of technological imperative are evident as well in his otherwise masterful 1971 report to the Canadian Department of Communications, *The Relevance of United States Legislative–Regulatory Experience to the Canadian Telecommunications Situation*; for example,5–7, 25.

65 Smythe, *Counterclockwise*, 228.

66 Dallas W. Smythe, 'Foreword,' in Robert E. Babe, *Cable Television and Telecommunications in Canada*, xvii–xxi.

67 Serious objections have been raised with regard to this 'law,' of which but three are recalled here. First, as noted by Herman Daly and John Cobb, in an era of relatively free capital flows, comparative advantage turns into absolute advantage, meaning that some regions become absolutely disadvantaged in the context of specialization and free trade. Second, specialization rips apart communities previously bound together by indigenous production and self-sufficiency. Third, information being a public good, albeit copyright-protected, means that countries specializing in its production give up nothing when entering commodity exchanges with resource-based economies: see Herman Daly and John Cobb, *For the Common Good: Redirecting the Economy toward Community, the Environment, and a Sustainable Future*, 209–35.

68 In large measure, this book addresses that myth in detail. The writings of Harold Innis were among the earliest opposing the myth of technological neutrality in the field of communication.

69 This again is a position consistently refuted by the theorists in this book. Briefly, information is not and cannot be 'commodity alone' both because of its 'public good' quality, and the fact that it continues to circulate and have consequences through time; there is no final consumption, as with normal commodities.

70 In practice, of course, marketplace competition in the realm of ideas aggrandizes the position of the most powerful and tends to silence others. Canadian-content quotas for broadcasting, for example, expand the range of choice of viewers and employment opportunities of creative personnel; they cause productions to be undertaken that otherwise would not be if markets alone had full sway.

71 By this principle, General Motors and Dallas Smythe are equal in so far as

both are 'persons' with a constitutional 'right' to purchase advertising time on network television or take out full-page newspaper advertisements. One recalls in this context the dictum of Anatole France: The King treats everyone equally under the law by forbidding rich and poor alike from sleeping under bridges.

72 Smythe, *Dependency Road*, 93–4.

73 Dallas W. Smythe, 'Theory about Communication and Information,' unpublished draft manuscript dated 1 May 1992. Unless otherwise noted, all quotations in this section are from this document.

74 Smythe remarked, 'I chose "marks" over symbols, as being less encumbered with connotations from the vast literature on symbols.'

75 Smythe, *Dependency Road*, x.

76 Ibid.

77 Smythe, 'Culture, Communication "Technology" and Canadian Policy,' 13.

78 Smythe, 'Communication: Blindspot of Economics,' 112.

79 John Grierson, 'Searchlight on Democracy,' 91.

80 Smythe, 'One Canadian Perspective,' 433.

81 Ibid., 451.

6: The Communication Thought of C.B. Macpherson (1911–1987)

1 See Warren J. Samuels, ed., *Economics as Discourse: An Analysis of the Rhetoric of Economists*. The classic text is Donald McCloskey, *The Rhetoric of Economics*.

2 Canadian Broadcasting Corporation, 'C.B. Macpherson: A Retrospective,' 3.

3 Interview by the author with Kay Macpherson, at her Toronto home, 18 February 1998.

4 Quoted in William Leiss, *C.B. Macpherson: Dilemmas of Liberalism and Socialism*, 29

5 C.B. Macpherson, *The Life and Times of Liberal Democracy*, 69.

6 Macpherson chose a chapter of this book for inclusion in his edited volume *Property: Mainstream and Critical Positions* (133–51).

7 R.H. Tawney, *Religion and the Rise of Capitalism: A Historical Study*, 191.

8 Macpherson, quoted by Leiss, *C.B. Macpherson: Dilemmas of Liberalism and Socialism*, 28.

9 Leiss explains that, during the time Macpherson attended University of London, PhDs in the social sciences were rarely awarded. Macpherson actually earned his doctorate twenty years later by submitting some sixteen published papers: ibid., 30.

10 Ibid., 29.
11 Ed Broadbent, 'C.B. Macpherson: A Tribute,' 24.
12 Macpherson, *The Life and Times,* 4.
13 CBC, 'C.B. Macpherson: A Retrospective,' 4.
14 Daniel Drache and Arthur Kroker, 'C.B. Macpherson, 1911–1987,' 99.
15 Broadbent, 'C.B. Macpherson: A Tribute,' 24.
16 Leiss, *C.B. Macpherson*, 30.
17 C.B. Macpherson, *Democracy in Alberta: Social Credit and the Party System,* 239.
18 Macpherson summarized: 'There is no doubt that in everything he [Burke] wrote and did, he venerated the traditional order. But his traditional order was already a capitalist order': C.B. Macpherson, *Burke,* 5.
19 Victor Svacek, 'Crawford Brough Macpherson: A Bibliography.'
20 Macpherson, *Democratic Theory,* 51.
21 Ibid.
22 Macpherson, 'The Meaning of Property,' 4.
23 Macpherson, *Democratic Theory,* 121; also Macpherson, "The Meaning of Property,' 1.
24 Macpherson, *Democratic Theory,* 121.
25 Macpherson, 'The Meaning of Property,' 1.
26 Ibid.
27 C.B. Macpherson, 'Liberal-Democracy and Property,' in *Property,* 202
28 Macpherson, *The Life and Times,* 102.
29 C.B. Macpherson, 'The Meaning of Property,' in *Property,* 3, 4.
30 Ibid., 3.
31 Ibid., 4.
32 Ibid.
33 Ibid., 5.
34 Ibid., 10. See also 'Human Rights as Property,' in *The Rise and Fall of Economic Justice,* 78–85.
35 C.B. Macpherson, 'Property as Means or End,' 3.
36 Ibid.
37 Ibid. Cf. Karl Polyani, *The Great Transformation: The Political and Economic Origins of Our Time.*
38 Macpherson, 'The Meaning of Property,' 11–12; emphasis added.
39 Macpherson, *The Life and Times,* 11.
40 Macpherson, *The Political Theory of Possessive Individualism: Hobbes to Locke,* 3.
41 Ibid., 39.
42 Ibid., 221.

43 The state, according to Macpherson, does not exist to enforce non-property-tied relations, except in so far as there is an element of power existing in them. Macpherson declared that it is only relations of power that fall within the jurisdiction of the state, because only relations of power need the state to enforce them. 'It is only power that needs power, only relations involving power that need a superior power to keep them in order; and all power relations between individuals do need the power of the state to enforce them.' Moreover, relations of commodity exchange epitomize power relations, as far as Macpherson was concerned, particularly in the market for work: see Macpherson, *The Real World of Democracy*, 40.

44 Macpherson, *The Political Theory of Possessive Individualism*, 33.

45 According to Bentham, people are *governed* by 'two sovereign masters, pain and pleasure,' which alone point out what people ought to do, and 'determine what we shall do.' Bentham further maintained that these opposing forces have several dimensions, each of which is measurable. In principle, he advised, all human conduct is determined by implicit maximizing calculations (the 'felicific calculus') pertaining to these quantifiable factors: see Jeremy Bentham, 'An Introduction to the Principles of Morals and Legislation,' extracts from which appear in Wesley C. Mitchell, *Types of Economic Theory: From Mercantilism to Institutionalism*, 203, 206.

46 Behavioural psychology is premised on the notion that people seek pleasure and avoid pain, that they, in effect, become 'conditioned' to stimuli on account of their anticipated pleasure or pain: B.F. Skinner, *Beyond Freedom and Dignity*.

47 Neoclassical economics is premised on the notion of utility maximization, that 'rational' beings seek to optimize their individual welfare.

48 Macpherson, *The Political Theory*, 275.

49 Ibid., 85; emphasis added.

50 Ibid., 54.

51 Macpherson, *Democratic Theory*, 9.

52 Macpherson, *The Political Theory of Possessive Individualism*, 223–4, and 238.

53 See, for example, Robert E. Babe, 'The Communication Theory of Thomas Robert Malthus,' in *Communication and the Transformation of Economics*.

54 John Locke, 'Some Considerations of the Consequences of the Lowering of Interest and Raising the Value of Money,' in *Works* (1759), vol. 2, quoted in Macpherson, *The Political Theory of Possessive Individualism*, 225.

55 Ibid.

56 See, for example, Jane Jacobs, *Systems of Survival: A Dialogue on the Moral Foundations of Commerce and Politics*.

57 Macpherson, *Democratic Theory*, 13.

58 See, in particular, E.F. Schumacher, *Small Is Beautiful: Economics as if People Mattered*. Also E.F. Schumacher, *Good Work*.

59 Even economists who accept as a principle the notion that human wants are unlimited sometimes admit that the 'law of diminishing marginal utility' points to the desirability of wealth transfers from rich to poor, since the law would imply that the rich get less enjoyment from an additional dollar of income than the poor; this eminently reasonable conclusion is denied by some, however, on the grounds that one cannot make 'interpersonal' utility comparisons. Irrespective of that debate, there also remain environmental concerns, and these again contradict the purported desirability of an unfettered right to accumulate, even given the premise of infinite wants.

60 Macpherson, *The Life and Times*, 99.

61 Macpherson, *Democratic Theory*, 36.

62 Ibid., 37.

63 Ibid., 62.

64 Ibid., 24.

65 Ibid., 51.

66 Macpherson, *Democratic Theory*, 38.

67 William Wordsworth, 'The World Is Too Much with Us' (1807).

68 Macpherson, *Democratic Theory*, 29.

69 Ibid.

70 Ibid., 34.

71 Macpherson, *Burke*, 69.

72 Macpherson, *The Life and Times*, 47; emphasis added.

73 Macpherson, *Democratic Theory*, 37. In another essay in the same book, however, Macpherson did write of 'the *false image* of man as infinite consumer and infinite appropriator': Macpherson, 'A Political Theory of Property,' in *Democratic Theory*, 122; emphasis added.

74 Macpherson, *Democratic Theory*, 37.

75 Ibid.

76 Ibid., 34.

77 Ibid., 4.

78 Ibid., 5.

79 Kenneth Boulding, *A Primer on Social Dynamics: History as Dialectics and Development*, 27. Also Kenneth Boulding, *The Economy of Love and Fear: A Preface to the Grants Economy*.

80 Lewis Hyde, *The Gift: Imagination and the Erotic Life of Property*, 56.

81 Ibid., 67.

82 Ibid., 68.

83 Macpherson, *Democratic Theory*, 4.

84 Macpherson, *The Real World of Democracy*, 38.
85 Macpherson, *Democratic Theory*, 4.
86 Macpherson, *The Rise and Fall of Economic Justice*, 83.
87 Herbert I. Schiller, *Information Inequality*.
88 Tibor Scitovsky, *The Joyless Economy: An Inquiry Into Human Satisfaction and Consumer Dissatisfaction*.
89 See, for instance, ibid.
90 Macpherson, *Democratic Theory*, 76. See also Macpherson, *The Rise and Fall of Economic Justice*, 34, 102.
91 See Babe, 'Understanding the Cultural Ecology Model.'
92 Interview with C.B, Macpherson, 'C.B. Macpherson on Marx,' in Frank Cunningham, *The Real World of Democracy Revisited and Other Essays on Democracy and Socialism*, 19.
93 Macpherson, *Democratic Theory*, 65.
94 James Winter, *Democracy's Oxygen: How Corporations Control the News*, 23.
95 Ibid., 36.
96 Maude Barlow and James Winter, *The Big Black Book: The Essential Views of Conrad and Barbara Amiel Black*, 25.
97 Graham Murdock and Peter Golding, 'Information Poverty and Political Inequality: Citizenship in the Age of Privatized Communications,' 183.
98 Ruggles, *The Audience Reflected in the Medium of Law*, xi, x.
99 Ibid., 17.

7: The Communication Thought of Irene Spry (1907–1998)

1 Author's interview with Irene M. Spry, at her home in Rockcliffe (Ottawa), 29 January 1998.
2 Quoted in Doug Fischer, '"Extraordinary" Life, Indeed.'
3 Gerald Friesen, 'Irene M. Spry: A Biographical Note,' 322.
4 Author's interview with Irene M. Spry, 28 January 1998.
5 Ibid.
6 Ibid.
7 *Wisdom and Wit: Irene Mary Spry*, video; International Tele-film, 1996.
8 Irene M. Biss, 'Overhead Costs, Time Problems, and Prices.' Rigidities, capacity, and overhead costs were themes that continued to concern Professor Spry; see in particular Irene M. Spry, 'Overhead Costs, Rigidities of Productive Capacity and the Price System.'
9 John Stuart Batts, '"Down North" in 1935: A Diary of Irene M. Spry (née Biss),' 270. See also Irene M. Spry, 'A Journey "Down North" to Great Bear Lake and the Yukon in 1935.'
10 Batts, '"Down North,"' 278.

11 Innis attributed 'the weakness of the social sciences' to an 'obsession with national statistics.' He quoted Gibbon approvingly: 'As soon as I understood the principles I relinquished forever the pursuit of mathematics': Harold A. Innis, *The Press: A Neglected Factor in the Economic History of the Twentieth Century*, 42, 45.

12 Interview with Irene Spry, 29 January 1998.

13 Irene Biss, 'The Contracts of the Hydro-Electric Power Commission of Ontario'; Irene Biss, 'Recent Power Legislation in Quebec'; Irene Spry, 'Hydro-Electric Power'; Irene Spry, 'Power Commissions, Provincial'; and Irene Spry, 'Water Power.'The encyclopaedia entries are revisions of articles appearing originally in *The Encyclopedia of Canada* (1937).

14 Irene M. Spry, 'The "Private Adventurers" of Rupert's Land,' 50.

15 Interview with Irene Spry, 29 January 1998.

16 Irene M. Spry, 'Introduction,' lxii.

17 Irene M. Spry, *The Palliser Expedition: An Account of John Palliser's British North American Expedition, 1857–1960.*

18 Irene M. Spry, ed., *The Papers of the Palliser Expedition, 1857–1860.*

19 Ibid., xxiv.

20 Irene M. Spry, 'The Great Transformation: The Disappearance of the Commons in Western Canada.'

21 Interview with Irene Spry, CBC, 'C.B. Macpherson: A Retrospective,' 3.

22 *Wisdom and Wit: Irene Mary Spry.*

23 Fischer, '"Extraordinary" Life, Indeed.'

24 Spry, 'Introduction,' lxxii.

25 Ibid., xc.

26 Ibid., lvii.

27 Ibid., lix.

28 Ibid., lx.

29 Ibid., c.

30 Ibid., cxxiv.

31 Ibid., cxxv.

32 Ibid., cxvi.

33 Ibid.

34 Ibid., cxvii.

35 Ibid.

36 Quoted in ibid.

37 Ibid., cxviii.

38 Ibid., cxviii–cxix.

39 Ibid., cxxi.

40 The phrase, borrowed by Irene M. Spry, is from the seminal book of the

same title by Karl Polyani, *The Great Transformation: The Political and Economic Origins of Our Time.*

41 Spry, 'The Great Transformation,' 21.
42 Ibid.
43 Ibid., 23.
44 Ibid.
45 J.G. Nelson,*The Last Refuge* (Montreal, 1973), 189; quoted in Spry, 'The Great Transformation,' 24.
46 Spry, 'The Great Transformation,' 25.
47 Ibid., 26.
48 Ibid., 28–9.
49 Ibid., 29.
50 Ibid., 36.
51 Ibid., 31.
52 Ibid., 41.
53 Irene Spry, 'Non-Renewable Resources.'
54 Ibid., 13.
55 Irene Spry, 'The Prospects for Leisure in a Conserver Society.'
56 Ibid., 141.
57 Ibid.
58 Ibid., 144.
59 Ibid., 143.
60 Ibid.
61 Ibid., 144.
62 Ibid.
63 Ibid., 145.
64 Ibid.
65 Ibid.
66 Ibid., 147.
67 Ibid.; emphasis added.
68 Ibid.
69 Ibid., 148.
70 Ibid., 150.
71 Ibid., 152.
72 Spry, 'Water Power,' 273.

8: The Communication Thought of George Grant (1918–1988)

1 Charles Taylor, *Radical Tories: The Conservative Tradition in Canada*, 135.
2 William Christian, *George Grant: A Biography*, 11.

3 Ibid., 12.

4 Ibid.

5 Ibid., 26.

6 Ibid., 43.

7 Ibid., 55.

8 Letter to George Grant's mother, undated, quoted in ibid., 70.

9 Letter to mother, undated, printed in George Grant, *Selected Letters*, 75.

10 Christian, *George Grant: A Biography*, 103.

11 Grant, quoted in ibid., 104.

12 Quoted in ibid., 72.

13 George Grant, quoted in David Cayley, ed., *George Grant in Conversation*, 49.

14 Taylor, *Radical Tories*, 79.

15 George Grant, in Larry Schmidt, ed., *George Grant in Process: Essays and Conversations*, 63.

16 Christian, *George Grant: A Biography*, 163.

17 Grant, quoted in Cayley, ed., *George Grant in Conversation*, 54.

18 Grant, quoted in ibid., 186.

19 George Grant, *Lament for a Nation*, 67.

20 Ibid., 64.

21 Christian, *George Grant: A Biography*, 96. In 1958, just prior to publication of his first book, *Philosophy in the Mass Age*, Grant inaugurated *University of the Air* on CBC radio; the program eventually became *Ideas*. According to David Cayley, Grant's 'contributions to the CBC probably exceeded those of any other Canadian thinker of his generation, except perhaps Northrop Frye': Cayley, ed., *George Grant in Conversation*, vi–vii.

22 Grant related: 'I have lived in a department of religion in which much work was done to summons the Bible before the researchers to give them its reasons': George Grant, *Technology and Justice*, 37.

23 Quoted in Cayley, ed., *George Grant in Conversation*, 52–3. Grant also singled out A.D. Lindsay, who had translated Plato's *Republic*.

24 Ellul's *The Technological Society* appeared in English in 1964. Grant built upon definitions of technology originally formulated by Ellul: 'the one best way of doing things'; and 'the totality of methods rationally arrived at and having absolute efficiency (for a given stage of development) in every field of human activity': see Grant, *Philosophy in the Mass Age*, 117. Later, Grant accepted as desirable the ambiguity of the word 'technology,' connoting, on the one hand, the *means* for doing things and, on the other, the *study* of these means; this ambiguity or duality, Grant wrote, accidentally shows how immersed in technique we have become since our very

way of understanding is derived from the things we try to understand: see George Grant, 'Thinking about Technology.'

25 See, for example, Peter C. Emberley, 'Preface.'

26 Grant, *Philosophy in the Mass Age*, 7.

27 Introduction, reprinted in ibid., 117–22. Many years later, Grant also stated that the Marxian notion that good ends can be achieved by bad means was 'already in Hegel': Cayley, ed., *George Grant in Conversation*, 68.

28 Taylor, *Radical Tories*, 129.

29 A bibliography of Grant's work appears in Christian, *George Grant: A Biography*, 450–60.

30 Taylor, *Radical Tories*, 125.

31 See, for instance, Barry Cooper, 'George Grant and the Revival of Political Philosophy.'

32 Alex Colville, 'A Tribute to Professor George P. Grant,' 8.

33 George Grant, 'Philosophy,' 119.

34 Christian, *George Grant: A Biography*, 155. Later in the article, Grant stated explicitly his position that philosophy needed to be guided by faith: Grant, 'Philosophy,' 122 ff.

35 'What do such [philosophic] positions [as pragmatism and positivism] mean,' Grant asked pointedly, 'but that ideas are true insofar as they help men manipulate their natural environment?' That being the case, he continued, 'Canadian philosophers indeed have [… made] philosophy the servant rather than the judge of men's scientific abilities': ibid.

36 George Grant, *Technology and Empire*, 28.

37 Judy Steed, 'Noted Canadian Philosopher Lamented Technology Growth – Obituary.'

38 In addition to the biography, the collection of his letters, and the interview with David Cayley, all referenced above, see also Arthur Davis, ed., *George Grant and the Subversion of Modernity* ; Joan E. O'Donovan, *George Grant and the Twilight of Justice*; and Larry Schmidt, ed., *George Grant in Process*. See also the posthumously published *The George Grant Reader,* edited by William Christian and Sheila Grant.

39 For example, Yusuf Umar, ed., *George Grant and the Future of Canada*; Eugene Combs, ed., *Modernity and Responsibility: Essays for George Grant*; and Emberley, ed., *By Loving Our Own*.

40 Cayley, *George Grant in Conversation*, ix.

41 Grant, *Philosophy in the Mass Age*, 7.

42 Ibid., 21.

43 Ibid., 15.

44 Grant used the dialectic of antiquity and modernity to explain key differ-

ences between Sigmund Freud and Carl Jung. Freud, Grant argued, was a modernist, steeped in Western science. What was ultimately real for Freud was 'the individual and his instincts.' Freud maintained that the road to mental health consists of coming to terms with one's own instincts, and effecting a balance (*ego*) between the pleasure principle (*id*) and the demands and restraints imposed by society (*super ego*). Jung, on the other hand, spoke of a 'collective unconscious,' a 'spiritual inheritance of human development, reborn in every individual.' Jung claimed the content of the collective unconscious was ordered by 'archetypes,' or universal figures, which, when raised to consciousness, are tantamount to partaking of the eternal. For Jung, neglect of these timeless, universal symbols is the essential source of all neuroses and psychotic disorders. Indeed, rationality, science, and technology, in cutting Western people off from their psychic roots, makes us subject increasingly to outward violence and inward meaninglessness. For Jung, the study of ancient myths and world religions was immensely important, as they give vent to the archetypes contained in the collective unconscious, and thereby can help restore meaning to the miasma of our lives: George Grant, 'Carl Gustav Jung,' 63–74, particularly 67–70.

45 George Grant, 'The Computer Does Not Impose on Us the Ways It Should Be Used,' in Christian and Sheila Grant, eds., *The George Grant Reader*, 430.

46 Grant, *Philosophy in the Mass Age*, 41; italics added.

47 And here there is a great divide, some arguing that perfection exists solely in the human imagination as a social construction and hence varies according to time and place; others, that the ideals of perfection are intrinsic to the universe and hence exist apart from human knowers, making them invariable through time and space.

48 George Grant, *Time as History*, 47.

49 Grant, in Cayley, ed., *George Grant in Conversation*, 76.

50 Grant, *Philosophy in the Mass Age*, 19–20; emphasis added. Grant's epitaph bears the words 'Out of the shadows and imaginings into the truth,' recollecting not only the death (and life) of Socrates, but as well the definition of philosophy put forth by St Augustine: see Christian, *George Grant: A Biography*, 372; and Grant, *Philosophy in the Mass Age*, 112.

51 George Grant, *English-Speaking Justice*, 87.

52 Ibid.

53 Grant, *Philosophy in the Mass Age*, 19.

54 Grant, *Technology and Justice*, 59.

55 Ibid., 24.

56 Grant, *English-Speaking Justice*, 34.

57 Ibid., 24. Rawls's theory on contractarianism recalls Thomas Hobbes's speculations on the origins of the Leviathan state, a topic addressed above in chapter 6, on Macpherson.
58 Grant, *English-Speaking Justice*, 44.
59 Ibid., 41.
60 See, for example, Mortimer J. Adler, *Six Great Ideas: Truth, Goodness, Beauty, Liberty, Equality, Justice*, 197–205; and C.S. Lewis, *The Abolition of Man*.
61 George Grant, with Sheila Grant, 'Abortion and Rights,' 126. Cf. Adler, *Six Great Ideas*, 197–205.
62 George Grant, 'The Case against Abortion,' 13; quoted in Christian, *George Grant: A Biography*, 345.
63 Grant, *Philosophy in the Mass Age*, 70. Likewise, in *English-Speaking Justice* (p.77), Grant wrote: 'What is given about the whole in technological science cannot be thought together with what is given us concerning justice and truth, reverence and beauty, from our tradition.' In his essay 'Faith and the Multiversity,' he reformulated essentially the same dilemma as an inconsistency between faith and (scientific) reason. It was in this regard that Simon Weil's declaration that 'faith is the experience that the intelligence is enlightened by love' resonated so deeply in Grant. 'Love,' in this context, meant 'consent to the fact that there is authentic othernesss': Grant, *Technology and Justice*, 38.
64 Grant, *Philosophy in the Mass Age*, 70.
65 Ibid., 71. Later in that book (p. 91), he reformulated essentially the same paradox or contradiction in these terms: 'The question is, then, how can we think an absolute morality that does not deny human freedom and the hope that evil will be overcome? ... It is indeed the failure to resolve this contradiction, to see together the unchangeableness of God with the idea of a God who works in history, which finally makes me unable to accept any of the traditional theologies as adequate.'
66 Ibid., 41. Cf. Mircea Eliade, *The Myth of the Eternal Return*.
67 Cf. Alfred North Whitehead, *Science and the Modern World*, chap. 1. There are interesting parallels to be noted in the thought of Innis and Grant in this regard. Innis distinguished classical or pre-Augustinian thought from post-Augustinian writing:'A society dominated by Augustine will produce a fundamentally different type of historian, who approaches his problem from the standpoint of change and progress, from classicism with its emphasis on cyclical change and the tendency to equilibrium': Harold A. Innis, 'Charles Norris Cochrane, 1889–1945,' 96.
68 George Grant, 'In Defence of North America,' 15.
69 George Grant, 'Introduction to the 1966 Edition,' 118.

70 Grant, *Time as History*, 13, 14.

71 Grant, 'Thinking about Technology,' 16.

72 Grant, *Time as History*, 18.

73 Grant, *English-Speaking Justice*, 29.

74 Ibid., 17; emphasis added.

75 Ibid., 80.

76 Grant, *Technology and Justice*, 50–1.

77 Ibid., 16.

78 Ibid., 64.

79 Ibid., 16, 24.

80 Ibid., 8.

81 Ibid.

82 Ibid.

83 Cf. Jacques Ellul, 'The Power of Technique and the Ethics of Non-Power.'

84 Although Heidegger was undoubtedly influential, Grant was ambivalent towards him. David Cayley relates that Grant periodically turned a small photograph of that German existentialist to the wall, depending on how he happened to feel about 'the old bastard' that day: *George Grant in Conversation*, 26.

85 Grant defined science as 'a particular set of procedures by which men come to understand the world and so have mastery over it': Grant, 'Carl Gustav Jung,' 63.

86 Cf. Thomas Kuhn, *The Structure of Scientific Revolutions*.

87 Cf. Michael Polanyi, *Personal Knowledge: Towards a Post-Critical Philosophy*.

88 Grant, 'Jean-Paul Sartre,' 66.

89 George Grant, 'Faith and the Multiversity,' 38–41.

90 Of the five conceptions of freedom noted by Mortimer J. Adler, Grant is implicitly here acknowledging 'natural freedom of self-determination.' All persons, according to this conception of freedom, have the power to decide what he or she wishes to become: Adler. *The Idea of Freedom, Volume II*, 7.

91 Ibid., 67.

92 His complete statement was: 'The idea of limit to me is the idea of God. I don't have any conception of what God could mean except an imposition that is not tyrannical, an imposition that one imposes on oneself, that there are certain things that one can know in advance should never be done': Grant, quoted in Cayley, ed., *George Grant in Conversation*, 68.

93 Grant, *Time as History*, 24.

94 Grant, quoted in Cayley, ed., *George Grant in Conversation*, 74.

95 Grant, *Philosophy in the Mass Age*, 5–8.

96 Ibid., 5.

 97 George Grant, 'Introduction to the Carleton Library Edition,' vii.
 98 Grant, *Philosophy in the Mass Age*, 9.
 99 George Grant, 'An Ethic of Community,' 10.
100 Ibid., 6.
101 Ibid., 11.
102 Grant, 'Carl Gustav Jung,' 63.
103 Grant, 'An Ethic of Community,' 9–10.
104 Grant, 'Art and Propaganda,' 6–7.
105 Grant, *Philosophy in the Mass Age*, 9.
106 Ibid.
107 George Grant, 'Fyodor Dostoevsky,' 71
108 Ibid., 76–8.
109 Grant, 'Philosophy,' 120.
110 Grant, *Technology and Justice*, 22.
111 Grant, 'An Ethic of Community,' 15.
112 Grant, *Technology and Justice*, 69.
113 George Grant, 'Canadian Fate and Imperialism,' 68.
114 Adam Smith, *An Inquiry into the Nature and Causes of the Wealth of Nations*,
    423. In his essay 'An Ethic of Community' (p. 15), Grant set out some
    reasons for his disdain of Smith's/Rawls's libertarian, individualistic
    world-view:

    The ideal [of profit] tends to encourage ruthlessness as the very mark of
    the manly. But such ruthlessness is the mainspring of that division of
    person from person which is the cause of all social disruption. It is the
    very denial of our membership one with another.
       A society is not likely to be a place of healthy loyalties and ordered
    cohesion if its members are taught to pursue first and foremost their
    economic self-interest and if its leaders are chosen from those who pursue
    that self-interest more ruthlessly.

115 Grant, 'Introduction to the Carleton Library Edition,' x.
116 Grant, 'An Ethic of Community,' 26.
117 Ibid., 59.
118 Ibid., 69.
119 Ibid., 18.
120 Ibid., 2.
121 John Donne, 'Meditation XVII' (1624).
122 Quoted in Christian, *George Grant: A Biography*, 144.
123 Grant moaned, 'Health, entertainment, information, order, beauty and
    truth, are all commodities which individuals purvey at a profit and can

only be socially justified [in our economic order] if they can be "sold" at a profit': Grant, 'An Ethic of Community,' 14.

124 See Robert E. Babe, *Communication and the Transformation of Economics*, 87–122.

125 See, for example, Herman Daly and John Cobb, *For the Common Good: Redirecting the Economy Toward Community, the Environment, and a Sustainable Future.*

126 Grant, *English-Speaking Justice*, 70.

127 Grant, *Lament for a Nation*, 47.

128 On Cochrane's influence on Grant, see O'Donovan, *George Grant and the Twilight of Justice*, 18–19.

129 Grant, 'Philosophy.'

130 See, for example, Grant's review of Frye's *The Great Code*, published originally in the *Globe and Mail*, 27 February 1982, E17, and reprinted in Christian and Sheila Grant, eds, *The George Grant Reader*, 357–61.

131 Book review by Grant of *The Idea File of Harold Innis*, appearing in the *Globe and Mail*, 31 May, 1980, E12; reprinted in Christian and Sheila Grant, eds., *The George Grant Reader*, 356.

132 Quoted in Schmidt, ed., *George Grant in Process*, 61.

133 Grant, Review of *The Idea File of Harold Innis*, in Christian and Sheila Grant, eds, *The George Grant Reader*, 356–7.

134 Harold Innis, 'A Plea for Time,' 89.

135 George Grant, 'Introduction to Plato,' 208.

136 Cayley, ed., *George Grant in Conversation*, 58.

137 Ibid., 171.

138 Ibid., 49.

139 Ibid., 174–8.

140 In the words of Simone Weil, which amount to the same thing, 'Necessity is … that order which God must cross to love God': ibid. See also O'Donovan, *George Grant and the Twilight of Justice*, 25; and Christian, *George Grant: A Biography*, 352–5.

141 Grant, *Time as History*, 68–9.

9: The Communication Thought of Gertrude Joch Robinson (b. 1927)

1 Biographical information has been derived from documents supplied by Professor Robinson and an interview with her in Montreal, 1 July 1998.

2 George Gerbner's interest was in Hungary, and Wayne Vuchinic's in the Soviet Union. Robinson relates that they were unique in the U.S. academy at the time.

3 Gertrude J. Robinson, 'Monopolies of Knowledge in Canadian Communi-cation Studies: The Case of Feminist Approaches,' 66.

4 In our interview she used the phrase 'insider–outsider' repeatedly in refer-ring to herself; she also used it in self-reference in her article 'Monopolies of Knowledge in Canadian Communication Studies,' 66.

5 Gertrude Joch Robinson and Donald F. Theall, eds., *Studies in Canadian Communication*; Marianne Grewe-Partsch and Gertrude J. Robinson, eds., *Women, Communication, and Careers*; Gertrude Joch Robinson and Dieta Sixt, eds., *Women and Power: Canadian and German Experiences*.

6 Stephen Littlejohn, *Theories of Human Communication*, 177.

7 In their famous book, Peter Berger and Thomas Luckman proposed a continuous three-stage process whereby physical reality and mental interpretations infuse and transform one another: (1) An idea is conceived in a person's mind; (2) the person acts on that idea, which is thereby externalized; (3) that manifestation is then perceived and interpreted by others, and is thereby internalized into the human mind: see Peter Berger and Thomas Luckman, *The Social Construction of Reality*.

8 Gertrude Joch Robinson, 'Epilogue: The Papers in Retrospect.'

9 Gertrude Joch Robinson, 'The New Yugoslav Writer: A Socio-Political Portrait,' 186.

10 Ibid.

11 Ibid.

12 Ibid., 186.

13 Personal correspondence, 12 July 1999.

14 Gertrude J. Robinson, *Constructing the Quebec Referendum: French and English Media Voices*, 15.

15 Gertrude Joch Robinson, 'Constructing a Historiography for North Ameri-can Communication Studies,' 164.

16 Gertrude Joch Robinson, 'Paul Felix Lazarsfeld's Contribution to the Development of US Communication Studies,' 89. See also, for example, Gertrude J. Robinson, 'Remembering Our Past: Reconstructing the Field of Canadian Communication Studies,' Southam Lecture, delivered to the annual meetings of the Canadian Communication Association, Sher-brooke, Quebec, June 1999.

17 Gertrude Joch Robinson, 'The Politics of Information and Culture during Canada's October Crisis,' 141.

18 Ibid., 142.

19 Ibid., 146.

20 Ibid., 157.

21 Gertrude Joch Robinson, 'Mass Media and Ethnic Strife in Multinational Yugoslavia,' 490.

22 Ibid., 490–1; emphasis in original.

23 Ibid., 491.

24 Gertrude Joch Robinson, 'Writers as Fighters: The Effects of the Cultural "Thaw" on Yugoslavia's Mass Media,' 16.

25 Robinson, *Constructing the Quebec Referendum*, 18.

26 Quotation from the Beige Paper, as printed in ibid., 114.

27 Ibid., 36.

28 In her analyses of Yugoslavia's national press agency, for example, Robinson noted that Tanjug used only 3 to 18 per cent of the wire copy sent out by the world's five principal international news agencies, and that the copy used was 'most severely edited.' According to Robinson, the Yugoslav news agency made its selections for 'purely journalistic reasons.' 'Journalistic reasons' included the desire to eliminate overlapping material, many human-interest stories, and 'strident propaganda.' She remarked, 'Though selection patterns are different from the American, they too show a concern for objectivity not usually attributed to national news agencies,' and concluded that Tanjug and the Associated Press 'are similar in the types of subject matter covered as well as geographical areas emphasized,' substantiating her conclusion regarding the importance of 'journalistic factors': Gertrude Joch Robinson, 'Tanjug's Complementary Role in International Communications,' 18–27.

29 Robinson quoted a study that found that 79 per cent of francophone journalists voted for the Parti Québécois in the 1976 election, and that 66 per cent had declared themselves sovereignists: Robinson, *Constructing the Quebec Referendum*, 187.

30 Ibid., 186.

31 Ibid., 48.

32 Ibid., 214.

33 Ibid., 139–42.

34 Ibid., 118.

35 Ibid., 153.

36 Ibid., 123.

37 Ibid.

38 Ibid., 187.

39 Ibid., 90.

40 Ibid., 98–9.

41 Ibid., 129, 128.

42 Ibid., 15.

43 Ibid., 8.

44 Gertrude Joch Robinson, 'The Feminist Paradigm in Historical Perspective,' 117.

45 Ibid., 122.
46 Gertrude Joch Robinson, 'Some Thoughts on the Role of Gender in Media Analysis,' 237.
47 Robinson, 'The Feminist Paradigm in Historical Perspective,' 125.
48 Ibid.
49 Robinson, 'Monopolies of Knowledge in Canadian Communication Studies,' 68.
50 Robinson, 'The Feminist Paradigm in Historical Perspective,' 125.
51 Ibid., 127.
52 Gertrude J. Robinson and Armande Saint-Jean, 'Canadian Women Journalists: The "Other Half" of the Equation.'
53 Gertrude J. Robinson and Armande Saint-Jean, 'From Flora to Kim: Thirty Years of Representation of Canadian Women Politicians,' 26.
54 Robinson, 'Monopolies of Knowledge in Canadian Communication Studies,' 66–7.
55 Robinson, 'Binational News,' 149.
56 Ibid.
57 Gertrude Joch Robinson, 'Introduction: The New World Information Order Debate in Perspective,' 5, 6.
58 Robinson, 'Binational News,' 149.
59 Ibid.; emphasis added.
60 Personal correspondence, 12 July 1999; emphasis in original.
61 See, in particular, Stuart Hall, 'The Rediscovery of "Ideology": The Return of the Repressed in Media Studies.'
62 Robinson, 'Binational News,' 149–50.
63 Robinson, Constructing the Quebec Referendum, 15.
64 Karl Popper, Conjectures and Refutations: The Growth of Scientific Knowledge.
65 Edward S. Herman, 'All the Editorials Fit to Print: The Politics of "Newsworthiness,"' 194–5.
66 Gertrude Joch Robinson, 'Notes on the Political Economy of News Production and Communications Research,' 202–3.
67 Robinson, 'Epilogue: The Papers in Retrospect.'
68 Robinson, 'The New Yugoslav Writer,' 185.

10: The Communication Thought of Northrop Frye (1912–1991)

1 In the 1970s, of writers in the arts and humanities born in the twentieth century, Frye was the third most frequently cited: see Robert D. Denham, 'Frye's International Presence,' xxx.
2 John Ayre, Northrop Frye: A Biography, 60.
3 David Cayley, ed., Northrop Frye in Conversation, 43.

4 Ayre, *Northrop Frye: A Biography*, 1.

5 Cayley, ed., *Northrop Frye in Conversation*, 42.

6 Ibid., 43.

7 Paintings, literature, and music, Frye wrote, exist 'in a perpetual state of innocence,' even when produced in or depicting cultures of immense cruelty': Northrop Frye, *Creation and Recreation*, 13.

8 Ibid., 44.

9 Northrop Frye, *Fearful Symmetry: A Study of William Blake*, 39, 32.

10 In a 1986 interview, Frye recounted: 'I thought I was an agnostic for a while, then I realized that if I started revolting against my background, I would just make a long detour and come back to where I started from; so I tried to find a more open way of looking at what I'd been brought up to': Robert D. Denham, ed., *A World in a Grain of Sand: Twenty-two Interviews with Northrop Frye*, 329.

11 Frye, *Fearful Symmetry*, 43.

12 Ibid., 89.

13 Ibid.; emphasis added.

14 Ibid., 30.

15 Quoted in Cayley, ed., *Northrop Frye in Conversation*, 53.

16 Frye, *Fearful Symmetry*, 120. Years later, Frye remarked: 'The only thing that God can possibly mean [today] is what he really does mean in Christianity, that is to say a suffering man ... The only role that God can have in human life is that of a man who cares enough about society to go even to the extent of a hideous death for man's salvation, and I think it is the conception of God as the power that recreates man rather than God as the Creator of the order of nature that is the really vital element in Christianity': Interview published in Denham, ed., *A World in a Grain of Sand*, 96.

17 The United Church of Canada, widely considered to be the most liberal of the country's mainline denominations, was formed in 1925 as an amalgamation of the Presbyterian, Methodist, and Congregational churches; a few Congregational churches and about one-third of the Presbyterian churches remained out of the union.

18 Published originally in German in 1918; first published in English in two volumes in 1926 and 1928 by Alfred A. Knopf, Inc.

19 Cayley, ed., *Northrop Frye in Conversation*, 48.

20 Joseph Adamson, *Northrop Frye: A Visionary Life*, 32.

21 Quoted in ibid., 32. The phrase 'giants immersed in time' is Proust's: see Northrop Frye, *Anatomy of Criticism: Four Essays*, 122.

22 Cayley, ed., *Northrop Frye in Conversation*, 61.

23 Northrop Frye, 'Oswald Spengler,' 86.

24 Published originally in 1890 in two volumes as *The Golden Bough: A Study in Comparative Religions*.
25 Northrop Frye, 'Sir James Frazer,' 27.
26 Quoted in Adamson, *Northrop Frye: A Visionary Life*, 33.
27 Frye, 'Sir James Frazer,' 28.
28 Ibid., 29.
29 Ibid., 29–30.
30 As noted by Marshall McLuhan, 'Blake, the craftsman, fought industrial specialism and fragmentation, by writing, designing and engraving his own works': Marshall McLuhan and Harley Parker, *Through the Vanishing Point: Space in Poetry and Painting*, 141.
31 Cayley, 'Introduction,' in *Northrop Frye in Conversation*, 5.
32 Cayley, ed., *Northrop Frye in Conversation*, 47.
33 Ibid., 48.
34 Ibid., 7.
35 Ayre, *Northrop Frye: A Biography*, 164–5. Frye always claimed his primary vocation was being a teacher, that without his teaching, particularly of undergraduates, most of his writing would have been impossible. Frye's editor Robert Denham notes that at least ten of Frye's books were originally lectures, and adds that 'the large majority of the essays in his nine collections began as public addresses': Denham, 'Introduction,' in *A World in a Grain of Sand*, 1.
36 Extract from a 1968 interview with Frye, published in Denham, ed., *A World in a Grain of Sand*, 42.
37 Cayley, 'Introduction,' in *Northrop Frye in Conversation*, 1.
38 Interview with Frye, 1986, printed in Denham, ed., *A World in a Grain of Sand*, 335.
39 Northrop Frye,'Teaching the Humanities Today,' 99.
40 Ibid., 98.
41 Northrop Frye, *The Great Code: The Bible and Literature*, xv.
42 Northrop Frye, *The Double Vision: Language and Meaning in Religion*, xvii–xviii.
43 William Blake, "London." This aspect of Blake was acknowledged by Frye in *Fearful Symmetry*, particularly 236–7.
44 Frye, 'Preface' to the 1969 edition of *Fearful Symmetry*.
45 Below we will note how Frye inverted this position in criticizing Marx's maxim that the point is to change the world, not just to study it.
46 Blake wrote: 'And twofold Always. May God keep / From Single vision & Newton's sleep!' Frye explained that single vision is the incapacity to see an unfallen world: Frye, *Fearful Symmetry*, 50.

47 Preface in *Symmetry*.

48 A brief overview of the position adopted in *Anatomy* is to be found in his essay 'The Archetypes of Literature,' written in 1951, prior to *Anatomy*, and republished in *Fables of Identity: Studies in Poetic Mythology*.

49 Frye, *Fearful Symmetry*, 50.

50 William Blake, *Auguries of Innocence*.

51 Of fact and value, in George Grant's terms.

52 Frye, *Fearful Symmetry*, 17. Frye wrote that people 'exist in time and perceive in space': ibid., 45.

53 Ibid., 85.

54 Frye, *Fearful Symmetry*, 15. Even in the materialist poem 'London,' one can argue, Blake emphasized the perceiving subject ('[I]mark'; 'I hear'), and the images that the streets summoned up *for him*.

55 Ibid., 19. This claim was then supported by invoking Blake: 'Mental Things are alone Real; what is call'd Corporeal, Nobody Knows of its Dwelling Place: it is in Fallacy, & its Existence an Imposture. Where is the Existence Out of Mind or Thought? Where is it but in the Mind of a Fool?':William Blake, 'A Vision of the Last Judgment,' extracted in Frye, *Fearful Symmetry*, 14–15.

56 Blake, extracted in ibid., 77.

57 Ibid., 4. Blake's biographer, Peter Ackroyd, writes that Blake 'saw spirits,' for example, while in Westminster Abbey: 'The aisles and galleries of the old cathedral suddenly filled with a great procession of monks and priests, choristers and censer-bearers, and his entranced ear heard the chant of plain-song and chorale, while the vaulted roof trembled to the sound of organ music': Peter Ackroyd, *Blake*, 55.

58 Frye remarked: 'Spirits of all kinds appeared to Blake, but only as unpaid models; they were forced to stand around and pose, open their mouths to display their teeth better, and were not allowed to depart before he had finished with them on any such thin excuse as the necessity of getting away at cockcrow': Frye, *Fearful Symmetry*, 78.

59 Ibid., 83; emphasis in original.

60 Ibid., 19.

61 Ibid., 24; emphasis added.

62 Years later Frye wrote that humans are unique not because of consciousness or self-consciousness, but because their consciousness is directed by 'an autonomous will.' He elaborated: 'Machines extended human capacities in all directions including mental ones, but no machine has yet appeared that has any will of its own to exert its power, that is independent of being plugged in or turned on': Frye, 'Literary and Mechanical Models,' 19.

63 Frye, *Fearful Symmetry*, 8.

64 Ibid., 19.

65 Frye wrote: 'If existence is in perception the tree is *more* real to the wise man than it is to the fool. Similarly it is more real to the man who throws his entire imagination behind his perception than to the man who cautiously tries to prune away different characteristics from that imagination and isolate one. The more unified the perception, the more real the existence': Frye, *Fearful Symmetry*, 21.

66 Blake, 'A Vision of the Last Judgment,' extracted in ibid.

67 Frye, *Fearful Symmetry*, 22.

68 Giamattista Vico (1668–1744), an Italian philosopher and jurist, called for a science of history in much the same way that Frye called for a science of literary criticism. In *Scienza nuova (The New Science)*, Vico proposed a stage theory of history, each stage having correspondingly distinct laws, modes of governance, belief system, and so forth.

69 Frye, *Creation and Recreation*, 6.

70 On this point, however, philosopher of science Jacob Bronowski would certainly disagree. He argued persuasively that scientific discoveries result from the imagination, whereby likenesses are seen that had never been seen before. He gives the example of Newton making an analogy between the falling apple and the moon sailing majestically in the sky, and then wondering why the moon, too, does not fall: see Jacob Bronowski, *The Sources of Knowledge and Imagination*.

71 Causation explains present conditions by past occurrences; purpose explains present conditions by anticipated or desired future states.

72 Frye, *The Critical Path*, 57. See also Frye, *The Educated Imagination*, 1–11.

73 Frye, *The Critical Path*, 84.

74 Ibid., 83.

75 Ibid., 44.

76 Ibid.

77 Ibid.

78 Ibid., 36.

79 Cayley, ed., *Northrop Frye in Conversation*, 114.

80 Northrop Frye, *Fables of Identity: Studies in Poetic Mythology*.

81 Frye, *The Secular Scripture*, 6.

82 Frye, *The Critical Path*, 34.

83 Ibid., 36.

84 Frye, *The Secular Scripture*, 9.

85 Frye, *The Modern Century*, 105.

86 Frye, *The Critical Path*, 35.

87 Interview of 1969 with Frye, printed in Denham, ed., *A World in a Grain of Sand*, 70.

88 Frye, *The Secular Scripture*, 8.

89 Frye, *The Modern Century*, 106.

90 Ibid., 113.

91 Northrop Frye, 'Literature as Therapy,' 28–31.

92 Frye, *The Modern Century*, 78.

93 Frye, *The Secular Scripture*, 31.

94 Ibid., 95.

95 Frye, *The Critical Path*, 49, 131.

96 Frye argued that science must always begin 'by accepting the facts and the evidence about the outside world without trying to alter them. Only at a later stage can people develop the "applied arts and sciences" with which to refashion their material environment': Northrop Frye, 3, 5.

97 Gregory Bateson, *Mind and Nature: A Necessary Unity*. Indeed, there are many parallels between the thought of Bateson and the early Frye. Bateson writes, for example: 'all experience is subjective; … our brains make the images that we think we "perceive."' Moreover, Bateson extolled Blake's 'double vision': Asking what is gained by comparing the data collected by one eye with the data collected by the other, Bateson responded, 'The *difference* between the information provided by the one retina and that provided by the other is itself information of a *different logical type*. From this new information, the seer adds an extra *dimension* to seeing … In principle, extra "depth" in some metaphoric sense is to be expected whenever the information for the two descriptions is differently collected or differently coded': ibid., 31, 69– 70; emphasis in original.

98 Frye, *The Educated Imagination*, 5.

99 Ibid., 118–19.

100 Frye, *Anatomy of Criticism*, 17.

101 Northrop Frye, 'The Language of Poetry,' 44.

102 Frye, *Anatomy of Criticism*, 5.

103 Frye, *The Critical Path*, 24.

104 Ibid., 24–5.

105 Frye, *The Secular Scripture*, 19.

106 Frye, *Creation and Recreation*, 29.

107 Before beginning, however, it is worthwhile noting that although Frye was quick to spot authoritarian implications of biblical narratives, he was less inclined to remark on their overarching egalitarianism. Frye's reticence may perhaps be due to the fact that historically Church and State have made much of the authoritarian possibilities of biblical narratives.

Or perhaps it may simply have been that Frye had a blind spot as far as an ethic of equality in the Bible is concerned. Surely his case that worldly power endeavours to 'capture' narratives and make them its own would have been strengthened had he emphasized that, despite the Bible's concern for social justice, the rich and powerful historically have twisted biblical narratives to advance their own power positions; we quoted Locke on this very point in the chapter on Macpherson.

108 Frye, *Creation and Recreation*, 53.
109 Frye, *The Secular Scripture*, 182.
110 Ibid., 33. For Frye, 'what Christianity calls the fall of man was the discovery of the knowledge of good and evil, that is, discovering that good and evil are interpenetrating and that moral good depends on moral evil, that there is no moral good except what is salvaged from an antecedent and prior evil': extract from a 1960s interview with Frye and printed in Denham, ed., *A World in a Grain of Sand*, 90.
111 Ibid., 30.
112 Frye, *Creation and Recreation*, 52–3.
113 Ibid.
114 Ibid., 159.
115 Ibid., 160.
116 See, for example, Stuart Ewen, *PR! A Social History of Spin*; also Daniel Boorstin, *The Image: A Guide to Pseudo-Events in America*.
117 Frye, *The Critical Path*, 158.
118 Ibid.
119 Ibid.; emphasis added.
120 Ibid., 85.
121 Ibid., 88.
122 Frye, *The Modern Century*, 31.
123 Frye, *The Secular Scripture*, 164.
124 Frye, *The Modern Century*, 18.
125 Ibid., 19.
126 Grant, *Time as History*.
127 Frye, *The Critical Path*, 147.
128 Frye, *The Modern Century*, 19.
129 Frye, *The Critical Path*, 147.
130 See, for example, Stephen Dale, *McLuhan's Children: The Greenpeace Message and the Media*.
131 Frye, *The Critical Path*, 117.
132 Ibid., 39.
133 Ibid., 41.

134 McLuhan, in Frye's view, was an 'oracular prose writer,' whose style 'exploited the sense of extra profundity that comes from leaving more time and space and less sequential connection at the end of a sentence': ibid., 42.

135 Ibid.

136 Ibid.

137 Ibid., 43.

138 Ibid.

139 Walter Ong, *Orality and Literacy: The Technologizing of the Word*, 11. Ong spoke of *secondary orality* as it exists in our present-day, high-technology culture. This 'new orality' is sustained by telephones, radio, television, and other electronic devices, that 'depend for their existence and functioning on writing and print.'

140 Frye, *The Critical Path*, 43; emphasis added. Likewise, in *Words with Power*, Frye declared: 'The act of reading, or its equivalent, consists of two operations that succeed one another in time. We first follow the narrative, from the first page or line to the last: once this pursuit of narrative through time is complete, we make a second act of response, a kind of *Gestalt* of simultaneous understanding, where we try to take in the entire significance of what we have read or listened to. The first response is conventionally one of the listening ear, even if we are reading a written text. The association of the second response with visual metaphors is almost inevitable': Frye, *Words with Power*, 69.

141 Frye *The Critical Path*, 43.

142 Ibid., 145. Elsewhere he remarked that film 'is a literary art in itself, and it has a power of expressing symbolism that I think is unmatched by any other form in the history of mankind … because of the combination of the visual and audible symbol': interview from 1968, printed in Denham, ed., *The World in a Grain of Sand*, 47.

143 Ibid., 145.

144 Ibid., 146.

145 See Daniel J. Boorstin, *The Image: A Guide to Pseudo-Events in America*.

146 Frye, 'Across the River,' 38.

147 Northrop Frye, 'National Consciousness in Canadian Culture,' 43.

148 Frye, *The Modern Century*, 38.

149 Michel Foucault, *Discipline and Punish: The Birth of the Prison*.

150 Frye, *The Critical Path*, 149.

151 Frye, *The Modern Century*, 39.

152 Frye, *The Critical Path*, 89.

153 Ibid., 162.

154 Ibid.; emphasis added.
155 Ibid., 131.
156 Frye, *The Modern Century*, 116. Elsewhere, in a similar vein, he wrote: 'Truth precipitates error, and in every culture great imaginative work is done in the face of a consolidating tyranny': Frye, *Fearful Symmetry*, 132.
157 Frye, *The Critical Path*, 25.
158 Ibid., 128, 125. To quote Frye completely on this: 'Of all the things that Milton says about censorship in the *Areopagitica*, the most far-reaching in its implications seems to me to be his remark that a wise man will make a better use of an idle pamphlet than a fool would of Holy Scripture. That is, the reader himself is responsible for the moral quality of what he reads': ibid., 125.
159 Frye, *Fearful Symmetry*, 188–9. Blake's *Songs of Innocence* and *Songs of Experience* were 'contraries,' for they spoke to and enriched each other. Frye wrote: 'The *Songs of Experience* are satires, but one of the things they satirize is the state of innocence. They show us the butcher's knife which is waiting for the unconscious lamb. Conversely, the *Songs of Innocence* satirize the state of experience, as the contrast which they present to it makes its hypocrisies more obviously shameful ... The same imaginative deadlock occurs whenever what may be called the ideal and the actual are brought into conflict. The actual makes the ideal look helpless and the ideal makes the actual look absurd': Frye, *Fearful Symmetry*, 237.
160 Frye seemed to agree that his stance can be regarded as nihilistic. In a 1966 interview with Gregory Baum he commented: 'There is a sense in which salvation is a quest, the quest being the discovery of what gradually becomes more and more negative as you keep discovering it. First of all, you think of it as something sinful or as something wrong. Then eventually it becomes nothingness, just something that isn't there': interview published in Denham, ed., *The World in a Grain of Sand*, 36–7.
161 Frye, *The Modern Century*, 121. In the context of 'The Tyger,' the 'child's vision' is undoubtedly that of 'The Lamb':

> Little Lamb, who made thee?
>   Dost thou know who made thee?
> Gave thee life, & bid thee feed
> By the stream & o'er the mead;
> Gave thee clothing of delight,
> Softest clothing, woolly, bright;
> Gave thee such a tender voice,
> Making all the vales rejoice?

Little Lamb, who made thee?
Dost thou know who made thee?
Little Lamb, I'll tell thee,
Little Lamb, I'll tell thee:
He is called by thy name,
For he calls himself a Lamb.
He is meek, & he is mild;
He became a little child.
I a child, & thou a lamb,
We are called by his name.
Little Lamb, God bless thee!
Little Lamb, God bless thee!

162 But even this does not quite do justice to Frye's dialectical cast of mind,
     for he also hinted that the human mind may be imprinted with a sense of
     eternal good. In an interview he remarked that a martyr is one whose
     'vision of a better form of human life and society is so strong that he lives
     in the light of that vision and acts according to what it suggests.' Asked
     'what is the source of that light?' Frye responded: 'I am not sure what the
     source of it is. It is implanted in the human mind at a depth that makes
     one think there is some point in the destiny of man that we have perhaps
     never really grasped': interview with Frye, February 1970, printed in
     Denham, ed., *A World in a Grain of Sand*, 96.
163 There he defines love as 'the transformation of the objective into the
     beloved,' and art as 'the transformation of the objective into the created,'
     and states that 'these are two activities pursued on this earth to repair the
     damage of the Fall': Frye, *Fearful Symmetry*, 126.
164 In an interview with theologian Gregory Baum, Frye intimated that the
     human condition normally is characterized by 'a sense of loneliness or
     abandonment which is only relieved in certain crucial moments of con-
     flict or tension, which are very often moments of rejection by society': see
     Denham, ed., *A World in a Grain of Sand*, 35.
165 Paulo Freire, *Education for Critical Consciousness*, 5.
166 Frye, 'The Archetypes of Literature,' 18.
167 Frye, *The Modern Century*, 121.
168 Quoted in Arthur Koestler, *The Roots of Coincidence*, 58.
169 Quoted in ibid., 59. There are, of course, a spate of books on the 'new
     physics,' supportive of the claims of Jeans and Eddington; for example,
     Paul Davies, *Other Worlds*.
170 In a 1969 interview with Eli Mandel, Frye affirmed: 'It looks as though a
     book written entirely by one person is a dictatorial or authoritarian kind

of monologue, where the writer is simply holding your buttonhole and not letting you go until he's finished. But actually the written, sequential treatise is a very democratic form of dialogue with the reader. The author is putting all his cards on the table in front of you. He has made his response to the subject with which he has been in dialogue': see Denham, ed., *A World in a Grain of Sand*, 7.

171 Quoted in Linda Hutcheon, 'Introduction: The Field Notes of a Public Critic,' in Northrop Frye, *The Bush Garden: Essays on the Canadian Imagination*, xiv.

172 Ibid., xxii.

173 B.W. Powe, *A Climate Charged*, 48.

174 Denham, *Northrop Frye and the Critical Mind*, 187.

175 Northrop Frye, 'Sharing the Continent,' 69.

176 George Grant, Review of *The Great Code*, published in the *Globe and Mail*, 27 February 1982, E17; republished in *The George Grant Reader*, 358.

177 Rick Salutin, 'We've Come A Long Way since Heston Played Moses,' *Globe and Mail*, 17 December 1998, A18.

178 Jane Armstrong, 'B.C. Court Rejects Ban on Book Depicting Same-Sex Couples,' *Globe and Mail*, 17 December 1998, A3.

179 Robert E. Babe, 'On Political Economy,' *Communication and the Transformation of Economics*, 69–85; also *Telecommunications in Canada*, 247–58.

180 The term 'culture industry' was probably coined by Theodor Adorno and Max Horkheimer in 1941. See *Dialectic of Enlightenment*. Also Theodor Adorno, *The Culture Industry*.

181 See, for example, Heather Menzies, *Whose Brave New World? The Information Highway and the New Economy*.

182 Northrop Frye, 'Culture as Interpenetration,' 20.

11: The Communication Thought of Marshall McLuhan (1911–1980)

1 Philip Marchand, *Marshall McLuhan: The Medium and the Messenger*, 1–5.

2 Interview with Maurice McLuhan, CBC, 'Marshall McLuhan, What If He Is Right?' *Ideas* series, written by Derrick de Kerckhove, 17 November 1980.

3 Marchand, *Marshall McLuhan*, 13.

4 CBC, 'Marshall McLuhan, What If He Is Right?' Regardless of origins of this thought, Marshall McLuhan certainly believed that it is to the artist we must look to understand changing times: 'Though the artistic intentions of the primitive artist and the Renaissance artist may be poles apart, the artistic *effect* under all conditions is a situation that serves to heighten perception. All the arts might be considered to act as counterenviron-

ments or countergradients': Marshall McLuhan and Harley Parker, *Through the Vanishing Point: Space in Poetry and Painting*, 2.

5 W. Terrence Gordon, *Marshall McLuhan: Escape into Understanding*, 25.

6 Marchand writes that McLuhan was dissuaded from a career in engineering when he was bullied one summer on a survey crew; his co-workers 'took a dislike to the lanky young man reading books in his tent while they went off on drinking sprees': Marchand, *Marshall McLuhan*, 17.

7 Gordon, *Marshall McLuhan*, 15.

8 Marshall McLuhan, letter to Elsie, Herbert and Maurice McLuhan, 6 December 1934, in Matie Molinaro, Corrine McLuhan, and William Toye, eds., *Letters of Marshall McLuhan*, 41.

9 Marshall McLuhan and Quentin Fiore, *War and Peace in the Global Village*, 4.

10 Don Theall, *The Medium Is the Rear View Mirror: Understanding McLuhan*, 12.

11 Marshall McLuhan, 'G.K. Chesterton: A Practical Mystic,' 455; emphasis added. McLuhan himself might be thought of as 'a practical mystic.' Like the Catholic mystic Teilhard de Chardin, who thought of evolutionary/ technological processes as creating a 'noosphere,' McLuhan talked and wrote about 'a collective consciousness,' 'a global village,' and the trans formation of human nature through the melding of organic bodies with new technologies: see Tom Wolfe, *The Video McLuhan*, vol. 1: *1958–1964*. As an undergraduate in Manitoba, McLuhan chanced upon G.K. Chesterton's *What's Wrong with the World*, setting him on the road to Catholicism. He was later to remark that Chesterton and St Thomas Aquinas were the two biggest influences on his life.

12 Marchand, *Marshall McLuhan*, 35.

13 The trivium in medieval studies comprised grammar, logic (or 'dialectic'), and rhetoric.

14 CBC, 'Marshall McLuhan, What If He Is Right?' Also, interview with McLuhan by Gerald Emanuel Stearn, published in Gerald Emanuel Stearn, ed., *McLuhan: Hot and Cool*, 262.

15 Gordon, *Marshall McLuhan*, 74.

16 McLuhan interview with G.E. Stearn, 261.

17 At Saint Louis one of his students was the Jesuit Walter Ong, who became a truly eminent scholar in his own right and pursued themes that McLuhan later also explored.

18 Quoted in Gordon, *Marshall McLuhan*, 135.

19 Liss Jeffrey, 'The Heat and the Light: Towards a Reassessment of the Contribution of H. Marshall McLuhan,' 7– 8; emphasis added.

20 Marshall McLuhan and Quentin Fiore, *The Medium Is the Massage*, 88.

21 McLuhan interview with G.E. Stearn, 284.

22 James P. Winter and Irving Goldman, 'Comparing the Early and Late McLuhan to Innis's Political Discourse'; also Dennis Duffy, *Marshall McLuhan*, 11–12.

23 In the interview with G. E. Stearn, McLuhan declared: '*Mechanical Bride* is a good example of a book that was completely negated by TV. All the mechanical assumptions of American life have been shifted since TV; it's become an organic culture': *McLuhan: Hot and Cool*, 261.Dennis Duffy quotes McLuhan as repudiating his *The Mechanical Bride* as follows: 'I did not realize that I was attempting a defence of book-culture against the new media. I can now see that I was trying to bring some of the critical aware- ness fostered by literary training to bear on the new media of sight and sound. My strategy was wrong, because my obsession with literary values blinded me to much that was happening for good and ill': Duffy, *Marshall McLuhan*, 11.

24 James W. Carey, 'Marshall McLuhan: Genealogy and Legacy,' 296.

25 Edmund Carpenter, 'That Not-So-Silent Sea.'

26 Marshall McLuhan, 'Introduction,' *Explorations in Communication*, ix.

27 CBC, 'Marshall McLuhan, What If He Is Right?'

28 Another of McLuhan's students, Bruce Powe, records McLuhan as ex- claiming: 'A good teacher won't just offer his students a package, but a do- it-yourself kit. He will put himself into a point of awareness. He will force him out of his previous modes of thinking. A good teacher saves you time': quoted in B.W. Powe, *A Climate Charged*, 28.

29 Carpenter, 'That Not-So-Silent Sea.'

30 Marchand, *Marshall McLuhan*, and Gordon, *Marshall McLuhan*.

31 Barrington Nevitt and Maurice McLuhan, *Who Was Marshall McLuhan?*

32 For example, Raymond Rosenthal, ed., *McLuhan: Pro and Con*, and Gerald Emanuel Stearn, *McLuhan: Hot and Cool*.

33 *Wired* magazine, January 1996.

34 Northrop Frye, 'Across the River,' 37.

35 Powe, *A Climate Charged*, 19–20.

36 For a brief survey of the influence of McLuhan on postmodernists, his status among communication historians, and the respect he has been afforded by neo-Marxists, see Paul Grosswiler, *Method Is the Message: Rethinking McLuhan Through Critical Theory*, 4–6.

37 Glenn Willmott, *McLuhan, Or Modernism in Reverse*, xii.

38 Carpenter, 'That Not-So-Silent Sea.'

39 Matie Armstrong Molinaro, 'Marshalling McLuhan,' 92–5.

40 W. Terrence Gordon, *McLuhan for Beginners*, 134.

41 See, *inter alia*, Grosswiler, *Method Is the Message*, 9–10. See also James W.
    Carey, 'The Roots of Modern Media Analysis: Lewis Mumford and
    Marshall McLuhan'; James W. Carey, 'Marshall McLuhan: Genealogy
    and Legacy,' 297; and Willmott, *McLuhan, Or Modernism in Reverse*,
    92–100.

42 Siegfried Giedion, *Mechanization Takes Command: A Contribution to Anony-
    mous History*, v. A useful summary of Giedion's thought is to be found in
    William Kuhns, *The Post-Industrial Prophets: Interpretations of Technology*,
    65–81.

43 Giedion, *Mechanization Takes Command*, 5–6.

44 These thoughts are present in Innis too; Innis claimed that mechanized
    communication 'divided reason and emotion'; he had in mind such mani-
    festations as the sensational stories of the Yellow Press. Harold A. Innis,
    'Minerva's Owl,' 30.

45 Derrick de Kerckhove, 'McLuhan and the "Toronto School of Communica-
    tion."'

46 Donald Theall remarks that Innis made reference to Havelock's *The Cruci-
    fixion of Intellectual Man* (1951) in his final volume, *Changing Concepts of
    Time* (1952); however, this hardly makes Havelock a major influence on
    Innis; indeed, the thrust of that volume is much closer to the thought of
    Northrop Frye: see Donald Theall, 'Explorations in Communications since
    Innis,' 230; and E.A. Havelock, 'Foreword to the Original Edition,'ix. See
    also Graeme Patterson, *History and Communications: Harold Innis, Marshall
    McLuhan, The Interpretation of History*, 63–9. Indeed, Havelock wrote that,
    while he was at the University of Toronto, he was 'only on the edge of
    [Innis's] acquaintance, not one of the close circle of his friends': Eric
    Havelock (1982), *Harold A. Innis: A Memoir*, 13.

47 Eric Havelock, *Preface to Plato*.

48 Letter from Marshall McLuhan to Lewis Mumford, 5 December 1948, in
    Molinaro, McLuhan, and Toye, eds., *Letters of Marshall McLuhan*, 208.

49 Marshall McLuhan, 'Introduction,' in Innis, *The Bias of Communication*, ix.
    Innis's main thesis, as we saw in chapter 2, was that the means of inscrip-
    tion 'bias' messages as to time or space. Nonetheless, there are references
    sprinkled in Innis's work of eye and ear substituting for each other as the
    means of communication change, causing a transformation in perception.
    Consider, for example, the following passage from Innis's essay 'The Bias
    of Communication' (p. 41), in which he makes, however, a proposition that
    is antithetical to McLuhan's main thesis: 'Introduction of the alphabet
    meant a concern with sound rather than with sight or with the ear rather
    than the eye. Empires had been built up on communication based on sight

in contrast with Greek political organization which emphasized oral discussion.'

50 McLuhan, 'Introduction,' vii. Also Marshall McLuhan, 'Foreword,' in Innis, *Empire and Communications*, v–xii.

51 McLuhan, 'Introduction,' ix.

52 Ibid., ix–x.

53 A. John Watson, 'Harold Innis and Classical Scholarship,' 46.

54 Innis wrote: 'The significance of a basic medium to its civilization is difficult to appraise since the means of appraisal are influenced by the media, and indeed the fact of appraisal appears to be peculiar to certain types of media. A change in the type of medium implies a change in the type of appraisal and hence makes it difficult for one civilization to understand another one': quoted in editors' introduction to letter of Marshall McLuhan to Harold Innis, 14 March 1951, in Molinaro, McLuhan, and Toye, eds., *Letters of Marshall McLuhan*, 219–20.

55 Innis and McLuhan were introduced by Professor Tom Easterbrook, a boyhood chum of McLuhan's and a colleague of Innis's in the Department of Political Economy. At their first meeting, somehow they got on to the topic of the Church in Spain during the Inquisition – Innis the hard-boiled agnostic and McLuhan the zealous Catholic convert. Years later, Easterbrook reflected, 'It could have been a good friendship': interview with Tom Easterbrook, CBC, 'Marshall McLuhan, What If He Is Right?'

56 Carpenter, "That Not-So-Silent Sea."

57 McLuhan interview with G.E. Stearn, in Stearn, ed., *McLuhan: Hot and Cool*, 261.

58 Marshall McLuhan, with Wilfred Watson, *From Cliché to Archetype*, 20.

59 Barrington Nevitt, *The Communication Ecology*, 176.

60 William Butler Yeats, 'The Circus Animals' Desertion,' quoted in McLuhan, with Watson, *From Cliché to Archetype*, 20.

61 McLuhan, with Watson, *From Cliché to Archetype*, 118.

62 Marshall McLuhan and Bruce R. Powers, *The Global Village: Transformations in World Life and Media in the 21st Century*, 16.

63 McLuhan, with Watson, *From Cliché to Archetype*, 21.

64 Ibid., 118.

65 Ibid., 16.

66 Ibid., 121.

67 Marshall McLuhan and Eric McLuhan, *Laws of the Media: The New Science*, 98–9.

68 Ibid., 148.

69 Ibid., 153.

70 Ibid., 99, 106, 107.
71 McLuhan and Powers, *The Global Village*, 7.
72 Ibid.
73 Ibid.
74 Ibid.; emphasis added.
75 McLuhan, *Understanding Media*, 64.
76 Ibid., 91.
77 Ibid.
78 Ibid., 64–5.
79 Ibid., 64, 66.
80 Quoted in McLuhan, with Watson, *From Cliché to Archetype*, 36.
81 Ibid., 36.
82 Ibid.
83 Ibid.
84 McLuhan interview with G.E. Stearn, in Stearn, ed., *McLuhan: Hot and Cool*, 273.
85 Marshall McLuhan, *The Gutenberg Galaxy*, 25.
86 McLuhan interview with G.E. Stearn, in Stearn, ed., *McLuhan: Hot and Cool*, 261. And again: ' The computer thus holds out the promise of a technologically engendered state of universal understanding and unity, a state of absorption in the logos that could knit mankind into one family and create a perpetuity of collective harmony and peace … In a Christian sense, this is merely a new interpretation of the mystical body of Christ; and Christ, after all, is the ultimate extension of man': ibid.
87 McLuhan, interview with Eric Norden, 131. McLuhan interview with G.E. Stearn, in Stearn, ed., *McLuhan: Hot and Cool*, 272.
88 McLuhan, interview with Eric Norden, 132.
89 Note, for instance, McLuhan's comments on Eliot's *The Waste Land:* that poem, he wrote, 'relinquished conventional visual and traditional space in favor of the Braille like world of touch and the auditory spaces of resonating allusion … The poem presents a disconnected space, psychically and socially': McLuhan and Parker, *Through the Vanishing Point*, 235.
90 Marshall McLuhan, *Counterblast*, 60.
91 See Nevitt, *The Communication Ecology*, 149–53.
92 For example, McLuhan, *Counterblast*, 41.
93 McLuhan and Parker, *Through the Vanishing Point*, 97.
94 Ibid., 240; emphasis added.
95 McLuhan, *Understanding Media*, 36.
96 Ibid., 38.
97 Marshall McLuhan and Barrington Nevitt, *Take Today*, 3–4. Chiasmus was

also expounded upon by Heraclitus, whom novelist Roberston Davies characterized for that very reason as 'that curmudgeonly Greek sage': Robertson Davies, *Murther & Walking Spirits*, 118.

98 McLuhan and Parker, *Through the Vanishing Point*, 222.
99 Ibid.
100 Ibid.
101 Ibid.
102 McLuhan and Nevitt, *Take Today*, 83.
103 McLuhan, with Watson, *From Cliché to Archetype*, 55–6.
104 E.S. Carpenter, *Explorations,* no. 9 (1960), 66–7, extracted in McLuhan, *The Gutenberg Galaxy*, 66.
105 Carey, 'Marshall McLuhan: Genealogy and Legacy,' 294.
106 McLuhan, *The Gutenberg Galaxy*, 63.
107 Dennis Duffy, *Marshall McLuhan*, 23.
108 Ibid.
109 McLuhan, *Counterblast*, 79.
110 McLuhan, *The Gutenberg Galaxy*, 19.
111 McLuhan and Nevitt, *Take Today*, 39–40.
112 Nevitt, *The Communication Ecology*, 59.
113 McLuhan, *The Gutenberg Galaxy*, 47.
114 McLuhan declared: 'The letters of the alphabet are an extremely aggressive extension of the body. Only teeth, in their uniformity and linearity, are comparable to the nature of alphabetic letters. These uniform letters, when committed to parchment or paper, permitted the organization of force at a distance, namely mobile, military bureaucracies. These mobile structures by-passed the old priestly bureaucracies of Egypt and Babylon': McLuhan and Nevitt, *Take Today*, 39–40.
115 McLuhan, *Understanding Media*, 90.
116 McLuhan, *The Gutenberg Galaxy*, 50.
117 Ibid., 56.
118 Ibid., 81.
119 Ibid., 111.
120 Ibid.
121 Ibid., 106.
122 Ibid., 125.
123 Ibid.
124 McLuhan and Nevitt, *Take Today*, 141.
125 McLuhan, *Understanding Media*, 134.
126 Ibid., 135–6.
127 Ibid., 144.

128 Ibid., 149.
129 Ibid., 20.
130 Ibid.
131 Ibid., 32–3. And again: 'A poem or a painting is in every sense a teaching machine for the training of perception and judgment. The artist is a person who is especially aware of the challenge and dangers of new environments presented to human sensibility ... The artist studies the distortion of sensory life produced by new environmental programming and tends to create artistic situations that correct the sensory bias and derangement brought about by the new form': McLuhan and Parker, *Through the Vanishing Point*, 247.
132 Ibid., 196.
133 Ibid., 55.
134 Ibid., 32–3.
135 Ibid.
136 CBC, 'Marshall McLuhan, What If He Is Right?'
137 Marshall McLuhan and Harley Parker (1968), *Beyond the Vanishing Point*, p. 247.
138 McLuhan and Parker, *Through the Vanishing Point*, 181.
139 McLuhan, *Understanding Media*, 28.
140 McLuhan, with Watson, *From Cliché to Archetype*, 152.
141 McLuhan, *The Mechanical Bride*, v–vi.
142 Ibid., 177.
143 McLuhan and Parker, *Through the Vanishing Point*, 243–4.
144 McLuhan and Nevitt, *Take Today*, 177.
145 McLuhan, with Watson, *From Cliché to Archetype*, 77.
146 McLuhan and Nevitt, *Take Today*, 95.
147 McLuhan, *Understanding Media*, 71.
148 Ibid., 202–3.
149 McLuhan, with Watson, *From Cliché to Archetype*, 201. See also *Understanding Media*, 201.
150 McLuhan, *Understanding Media*, 257.
151 Ibid., 92.
152 Ibid.
153 Ibid., 93.
154 For example: 'The point of the matter of speed-up by wheel, road, and paper is the extension of power in an ever more homogenous and uniform space': ibid.
155 Ibid.

156 McLuhan,*The Mechanical Bride*, 139–40.
157 McLuhan and Nevitt, *Take Today*, 59. One is surprised that Innis was not mentioned as an exception here.
158 McLuhan, *Understanding Media*, 185.
159 Ibid., 130.
160 Ibid., 129.
161 Ibid.. 223.
162 McLuhan and Nevitt, *Take Today*, 213.
163 McLuhan, *Understanding Media*, 225.
164 Ibid., 225, 219.
165 McLuhan and Nevitt, *Take Today*, 193.
166 Ibid., 277.
167 As when, for instance, he declared: 'Since … this new cultural gradient is the world, the *milieu* in which I must live and which prepares the students I must teach, I have every motive to understand its constituents, its components, and its operations. I move around through these elements as I hope any scientist would through a world of disease and stress and misery. If a doctor, surgeon or scientist were to become personally agitated about any phenomenon whatever, he would be finished as an explorer or observer. The need to retain an attitude of complete clinical detachment is necessary for survival in this kind of world': McLuhan interview with G.E. Stearn, in Stearn, ed., *McLuhan: Hot and Cool*, 280.
168 Marchand, *Marshall McLuhan*, 61.
169 McLuhan interview with G.E. Stearn, in Stearn, ed., *McLuhan: Hot and Cool*, 286.
170 McLuhan, *The Gutenberg Galaxy*, 1.
171 Quoted in Paul Heyer, *Communications and History*, 125.
172 Ibid., 134.
173 He once declared that Canada is a propitious location from which to understand communication: 'Canada is a land of multiple boderlines, psychic, social, and geographic … A frontier, or borderline, is the space between two worlds, constituting a kind of double plot or action that the poet W. B. Yeats discovered to be the archetypal formula for producing the "emotion of multitude" or the sense of universality': Marshall McLuhan, 'Canada: The Borderline Case,' 244, 247.
174 For example, Innis, 'The Bias of Communication,' 41, and 'A Plea for Time,' 81.
175 See, for example, David F. Noble, *The Religion of Technology: A Divinity of Man and the Spirit of Invention*.

176 McLuhan, with Watson, *From Cliché to Archetype*, 87.
177 Paul R. Ehrlich and Anne H. Ehrlich, *Betrayal of Science and Reason: How Anti-Environmental Rhetoric Threatens Our Future*, 14.
178 Ibid., 43.
179 David Suzuki, with Amanda McConnell, *The Sacred Balance: Rediscovering Our Place in Nature*, 15.
180 Ibid., 28.
181 McLuhan, *Counterblast*, 33.
182 Ibid., 36, 33.
183 Grosswiler, *Method Is the Message*, 4.
184 Ehrlich and Ehrlich, *Betrayal of Science and Reason*, 48.
185 Alison Anderson, *Media, Culture and the Environment*, 121.
186 Ibid., 121–2.
187 Stephen Dale, *McLuhan's Children: The Greenpeace Message and the Media*.
188 See also David L. Altheide, *An Ecology of Communication: Cultural Formats of Control*.

12: Conclusion

1 Citing Russell Brown, Seymour Lipset remarks that Canadian fiction differs from American fiction with regard to the treatment of father–son relations, and this difference may reflect differences in national origins. American novels, Brown proposed, are 'Oedipal' in the sense that they depict the rejection of fathers by their sons in the same way that Americans rejected the British king. Canadian novels, by contrast, are 'Telemachian,' which is to say that the son searches for the absent father; in support of this thesis, Brown cites various Canadian novels, including Hugh MacLennan's *Each Man's Son*, Robert Kroetsch's *Badlands*, and Margaret Laurence's *The Diviners*.

  We can speculate, then, that the secondary role played by fathers in the upbringing of several of these Canadian communication theorists resonates with the myth of Telemachus, which is embedded (according to Brown) in the Canadian psyche: see Seymour Lipset, *North American Cultures*, 9, where Lipset refers to Russell M. Brown, 'Telemachus and Oedipus: Images and Authority in Canadian and American Fiction,' unpublished paper, University of Toronto, n.d.

2 Harold A. Innis, 'A Critical Review,' 190.

BIBLIOGRAPHY

Ackroyd, Peter. *Blake.* London: Sinclair Stevenson, 1995

Adair, E.R. 'Review Article.' *Canadian Historical Review* 33 (1952): 393–4

Adamson, Joseph. *Northrop Frye: A Visionary Life.* Toronto: ECW Press, 1993

Adler, Mortimer J. *The Idea of Freedom.* Vol. II: *A Dialectical Examination of the Controversies about Freedom.* Garden City, NY: Doubleday, 1961

– *Six Great Ideas.* New York: Macmillan, 1981

Adorno, Theodor. *The Culture Industry.* Edited by J.M. Bernstein. London: Routledge, 1991

Adorno, Theodor, and Max Horkheimer. *Dialectic of Enlightenment.* New York: Continuum, 1941

Altschull, J. Herbert. *From Milton to McLuhan: The Ideas behind American Journalism.* New York: Longman, 1990

Altheide, David L. *An Ecology of Communication: Cultural Formats of Control.* New York: Aldine De Gruyter, 1995

Anderson, Alison. *Media, Culture and the Environment.* New Brunswick, NJ: Rutgers University Press, 1997

Angus, Ian. *A Border Within: National Identity, Cultural Plurality, and Wilderness.* Montreal and Kingston: McGill-Queen's University Press, 1997

Arendt, Hannah. *The Life of the Mind,* one-volume ed. New York: Harcourt Brace Jovanovich, 1978

Armour, Leslie. *The Idea of Canada and the Crisis of Community.* Ottawa: Steel Rail, 1981

Armstrong, Jane. 'B.C. Court Rejects Ban on Book Depicting Same-Sex Couples.' *Globe and Mail,* 17 December 1998, A3

Atwood, Margaret. *Survival: A Thematic Guide to Canadian Literature.* Toronto: House of Anansi, 1972

Ayre, John. *Northrop Frye: A Biography.* Toronto: Vintage, 1990

Babe, Robert E.*Communication and the Transformation of Economics.* Boulder,
    CO: Westview, 1995
– 'T.R. Malthus and the Origins of Communication in Economics.' In *Commu-
    nication and the Transformation of Economics,* 124–40. Boulder, CO: Westview,
    1995
– 'The Communication Theory of Thorstein Veblen.' In *Communication and the
    Transformation of Economics,* 141–58. Boulder, CO: Westview, 1995
– 'The Place of Information in Economics. In *Information and Communication in
    Economics,* ed.Robert E. Babe, 41–67. Boston: Kluwer Academic, 1994
– *Telecommunications in Canada: Technology, Industry and Government.* Toronto:
    University of Toronto Press, 1990
– 'Understanding the Cultural Ecology Model.' In *Cultural Ecology: The Chang-
    ing Dynamics of Communication,* ed. Danielle Cliche, 1–23. London: Interna-
    tional Institute of Communications, 1997
Baragar, Fletcher. 'Influence of Veblen on Harold Innis.' *Journal of Economic
    Issues* 30 (September 1996): 667–83
Barlow, Maude. *The Fight of My Life: Confessions of an Unrepentant Canadian.*
    Toronto: HarperCollins Canada, 1998
Barlow, Maude, and James Winter. *The Big Black Book: The Essential Views of
    Conrad Black and Barbara Amiel Black.* Toronto: Stoddart, 1997
Barnet, Richard J. and John Cavanagh. *Global Dreams: Imperial Corporations and
    the New World Order.* New York: Simon and Schuster, 1994
Barnet, Richard J., and Ronald E. Müller. *Global Reach: The Power of the Multi-
    national Corporations.* New York: Simon and Schuster, 1974
Bateson, Gregory. *Mind and Nature: A Necessary Unity.* New York: Dutton, 1979
Batts, John Stuart. '"Down North" in 1935: A Diary of Irene M. Spry (née
    Biss).' In *Explorations in Canadian Economic History: Essays in Honour of Irene
    M. Spry,* ed. Duncan Cameron, 269–80. Ottawa: University of Ottawa Press,
    1985
Baudrillard, Jean. *For a Critique of the Political Economy of the Sign.* St Louis:
    Telos, 1981
Bell, Daniel. 'The Social Framework of the Information Society.' In *The Compu-
    ter Age: A Twenty-Year View,* ed. Michael Dertouzos and Joel Moses,
    163–211. Cambridge, MA: MIT Press, 1979
Beniger, James R. *The Control Revolution: Technological and Economic Origins of
    the Information Society.* Cambridge, MA: Harvard University Press, 1986
Berger, Peter, and Thomas Luckman. *The Social Construction of Reality.*
    Harmondsworth: Penguin, 1966
Beveridge, James. *John Grierson: Film Master,* New York: Macmillan, 1978
Birdsall, William. 'The Ideology of Information Technology.' *Queen's Quarterly*
    104/2 (Summer 1997): 287–99

Biss, Irene. 'The Contracts of the Hydro-Electric Power Commission of Ontario.' *The Economic Journal* 46 (1936): 549–54

– 'Overhead Costs, Time Problems, and Prices.' In *Essays in Political Economy in Honour of E.J. Urwick,* ed. H.A. Innis, 11–26. Toronto: University of Toronto Press, 1938

– 'Recent Power Legislation in Quebec.' *Canadian Journal of Economics and Political Science* 3/4 (1937): 550–8

Boorstin, Daniel J. *The Image: A Guide to Pseudo-Events in America.* New York: Atheneum, 1978

Boulding, Kenneth E. *The Economy of Love and Fear: A Preface to the Grants Economy.* Belmont, CA: Wadsworth, 1973

– *A Primer on Social Dynamics: History as Dialectics and Development.* New York: The Free Press, 1970

Boyle, Harry J. 'The Canadian Broadcasting System.' Speech delivered to the Canadian Section of the Association for Professional Broadcasting Education Seminar, Washington, DC, 6 November 1970 (mimeo)

Braman, Sandra. 'Commentary.' In *Information and Communication in Economics,* ed. Robert E. Babe, 92–103. Boston: Kluwer Academic, 1994

Broadbent, Ed. 'C.B. Macpherson: A Tribute.' *This Magazine* 21/6 (1987), 24.

Bronowski, Jacob. *The Origins of Knowledge and Imagination,* New Haven, CT: Yale University Press, 1978

Canada. *House of Commons Debates, Official Report,* vol. 8 (13 September–19 October 1971). Ottawa: Queen's Printer, 1971

– Royal Commission on Broadcasting. *Report.* Ottawa: Queen's Printer, 1957

– Special Joint Committee of the Senate and House of Commons Reviewing Canadian Foreign Policy. *Canada's Foreign Policy: Principles and Priorities for the Future,* Ottawa: Publications Service, Parliamentary Publications Directorate. 1994

Canadian Broadcasting Corporation. 'The Moving Image of Eternity.' *Ideas,* 27 January, 3 February, and 10 February 1986 (Transcripts). Montreal: Canadian Broadcasting Corporation, 1986

– 'C.B. Macpherson: A Retrospective.' *Ideas,* 23, 24 May 1988 (Transcripts). Toronto: Canadian Broadcasting Corporation, 1988

– 'The Legacy of Harold Innis.' *Ideas,* 6, 13, 20 December 1994 (Transcripts). Toronto: Canadian Broadcasting Corporation, 1994

Carey, James.'Canadian Communication Theory: Extensions and Interpretations of Harold Innis.' In *Studies in Canadian Communications,* ed. Gertrude Joch Robinson and Donald Theall, 27–59. Montreal: McGill Studies in Communication, 1975

– 'The Chicago School of Communication Research.' First published in *Ameri-*

can Communication Research: The Remembered History, ed. Everette E. Denis and Ellen Wartella. Chicago: Lea, 1996; reprinted in *James Carey: A Critical Reader*, ed. Eve Munson and Catherine Warren, 14–53. Minneapolis: University of Minnesota Press, 1997

– 'A Cultural Approach to Communication.' First published in *Communications* 2/2 (1975); reprinted in *Communication as Culture: Essays on Media and Society*, 13–36. Boston: Unwin Hyman, 1989

– 'Culture, Geography and Communications: The Work of Harold Innis in an American Context.' In *Culture, Communications, and Dependency: The Tradition of H. A. Innis*, ed. William H Melody, Liora Salter, and Paul Heyer, 73–91. Norwood, NJ: Ablex, 1981

– 'Harold Adams Innis and Marshall McLuhan.' First published in *The Antioch Review* 67/1 (Spring 1967): 5–31; reprinted in *McLuhan: Pro and Con*, ed. Raymond Rosenthal, 270–308. Harmondsworth: Pelican, 1969

– 'Marshall McLuhan: Genealogy and Legacy.' *Canadian Journal of Communication* 23/3 (Summer 1998): 293–306

– 'Mass Communication and Cultural Studies.' In *Communication as Culture: Essays on Media and Society*, 37–68. Boston: Unwin Hyman, 1989

– 'The Roots of Modern Media Analysis: Lewis Mumford and Marshall McLuhan.' First published in *Journal of Communication* (Spring 1980): 162–78; reprinted in *James Carey: A Critical Reader*, ed. Eve Stryker Munson and Catherine A. Warren, 34–59. Minneapolis: University of Minnesota Press, 1997

– 'Space, Time, and Communications: A Tribute to Harold Innis.' In *Communication as Culture: Essays on Media and Society*, 142–72. Boston: Unwin Hyman, 1989.

Carpenter, Emund. 'That Not-So-Silent Sea.' Portions of the paper appear in *Canadian Notes & Queries* 46 (Spring 1992): 3–14

Cavanagh, John, Daphney Wysham, and Marcos Arruda, eds. *Beyond Bretton Woods: Alternatives to the Global Economic Order*. London: Pluto, 1994

Cayley, David, ed. *George Grant in Conversation*. Toronto: House of Anansi, 1995

– *Northrop Frye in Conversation*. Toronto: House of Anansi, 1992

Charland, Maurice. 'Technological Nationalism.' *Canadian Journal of Political and Social Theory* 10/1, 2 (1986): 196–220

Cherry, Colin. *On Human Communication: A Review, a Survey, and a Criticism.* 1957. Reprint, Cambridge, MA: MIT Press, 1980

Chodos, Robert, Rae Murphy, and Eric Hamovitch. *Lost in Cyberspace? Canada and the Information Revolution*. Toronto: James Lorimer, 1997

Chomsky, Noam. 'Force and Opinion.' *Z Magazine,* July/August 1991, 10–24

– *Necessary Illusions: Thought Control in Democratic Societies.* Toronto: CBC Enterprises, 1989

Christian, William. *George Grant: A Biography.* Toronto: University of Toronto Press, 1993

– 'Preface.' In *The Idea File of Harold Innis,* introduced and edited by William Christian, vii–xvi. Toronto: University of Toronto Press, 1980

Christian, William, and Sheila Grant, eds. *The George Grant Reader.* Toronto: University of Toronto Press, 1998

Clarke, Tony. *Silent Coup: Confronting the Big Business Takeover of Canada.* Toronto: James Lorimer, 1997

Clarke, Tony, and Maude Barlow. *MAI: The Multilateral Agreement on Investment and the Threat to Canadian Sovereignty.* Toronto: Stoddart, 1997

Coase, R.H. 'The Nature of the Firm.' *Economica* 4 (1952): 386–405

Colville, Alex. 'A Tribute to Professor George P. Grant.' In *By Loving Our Own: George Grant and the Legacy of 'Lament for a Nation',* ed. Peter C. Emberley, 3–10. Ottawa: Carleton University Press, 1990

Combs, Eugene, ed. *Modernity and Responsibility: Essays for George Grant.* Toronto: University of Toronto Press, 1983

Comor, Edward. 'Harold Innis's Dialectical Triad.' *Journal of Canadian Studies* 29/2 (Summer 1994): 111–27

Conway, John F. 'Reflections on Canada in the Year 1997–98.' In *Images of Canadianness: Visions on Canada's Politics, Culture, Economics,* ed. Leen d'Haenens, 1–28. Ottawa: University of Ottawa Press, 1998

Cooper, Barry. 'George Grant and the Revival of Political Philosophy.' In *By Loving Our Own: George Grant and the Legacy of 'Lament for a Nation',* ed. Peter C. Emberley, 97–121. Ottawa: Carleton University Press, 1990

Cox, Kirwan. 'The Grierson Files.' *Cinema Canada* 56, June/July 1979, 16–24

Creighton, Donald. *Harold Adams Innis: Portrait of a Scholar.* 1957. Reprint, Toronto: University of Toronto Press, 1978

Crowley, David, and Paul Heyer, eds. *Communication in History: Technology, Culture, and Society.* New York: Longmans, 1991

Cummings, Bruce. *War and Television.* London: Verso, 1992

Cunningham, Frank. 'C.B. Macpherson on Marx." In *The Real World of Democracy Revisited and Other Essays on Democracy and Socialism,* 14–21. Atlantic Highlands, NJ: Humanities Press, 1994

– *The Real World of Democracy Revisited and Other Essays on Democracy and Socialism.* Atlantic Highlands, NJ: Humanities Press, 1994

Czitrom, Daniel J. *Media and the American Mind: From Morse to McLuhan.* Chapel Hill: University of North Carolina Press, 1982

Dale, Stephen. *McLuhan's Children: The Greenpeace Message and the Media.* Toronto: Between the Lines, 1996

Daly, Herman, and John Cobb. *For the Common Good: Redirecting the Economy toward Community, the Environment, and a Sustainable Future.* Boston: Beacon, 1989

Dasah, Bernard. 'Application of Neoclassical Economics to African Development: A Curse in Disguise.' In *Information and Communication in Economics,* ed. Robert E. Babe, 281–92. Boston: Kluwer Academic, 1994

Davies, Paul. *Other Worlds.* New York: Simon and Schuster, 1980

Davies, Robertson. *Murther & Walking Spirit.* Toronto: McClelland and Stewart, 1991

Davis, Arthur, ed. *George Grant and the Subversion of Modernity.* Toronto: University of Toronto Press, 1996

Deibert, Ronald J. *Parchment, Printing, and Hypermedia: Communication in World Order Transformation.* New York: Columbia University Press, 1997

De Kerckhove, Derrick. 'Marshall McLuhan, What If He Is Right?" CBC *Ideas* series, 17 November 1980 (Transcript)

– 'McLuhan and the "Toronto School of Communication."' *Canadian Journal of Communication,* 14/4 & 5, special issue, December 1989: 73–9

De la Garde, Roger. (1987), 'Mr. Innis, Is There Life after the "American Empire"? The 1987 Southam Lecture.' *Canadian Journal of Communication,* special issue, December 1987: 7–21

Delia, Jesse. 'Communication Research: A History.' In *Handbook of Communication Science,* ed. Charles R. Berger and Steven Chaffee, 20–98. Newbury Park, CA: Sage, 1987

Denham, Robert D. 'Frye's International Presence.' In *The Legacy of Northrop Frye,* ed. Alvin A. Lee and Robert D. Denham, xxvii–xxxii. Toronto: University of Toronto Press, 1994

– *Northrop Frye and the Critical Mind.* University Park: Pennsylvania State University Press. 1978

– ed. *A World in a Grain of Sand: Twenty-two Interviews with Northrop Frye.* New York: Peter Lang, 1991

Dewey, John. *Democracy and Education.* New York: Macmillan, 1915

Dorland, Michael, and Arthur Kroker. 'Culture Critique and New Quebec Sociology.' In *Culture Critique: Fernand Dumont and New Quebec Sociology,* ed. Michael A. Weinstein, 7–37. Montreal: New World Perspectives, 1985

Douglas, Mary. *Natural Symbols: Explorations in Cosmology.* 1970. Reprint, New York: Routledge, 1996

Drache, Daniel. 'Celebrating Innis: The Man, the Legacy, and Our Future.' In

Harold A. Innis, *Staples, Markets and Cultural Change*. Edited by Daniel Drache, xiii–lvix. Montreal and Kingston: McGill-Queen's University Press, 1995

Drache, Daniel, and Arthur Kroker. 'C.B. Macpherson, 1911–1987.' *Canadian Journal of Political and Social Theory* 11/3 (1987): 99– 105

Drohan, Madelaine. 'How the Net Killed the MAI.' *Globe and Mail,* 29 April 1998, A1

Drummond, Ian, with William Kaplan. *Political Economy at the University of Toronto: A History of the Department, 1888–1982*. Toronto: Faculty of Arts and Science, University of Toronto, 1983

Duffy, Dennis. *Marshall McLuhan*. Toronto: McClelland and Stewart, 1969

Ehrlich, Paul R., and Anne H. Ehrlich. *Betrayal of Science and Reason: How Anti-Environmental Rhetoric Threatens Our Future*. Washington, DC: Island Press, 1996

Eisenstein, Elizabeth. *The Printing Press as an Agent of Change*. Cambridge: Cambridge University Press, 1979

Elder, R. Bruce. *Image and Identity: Reflections on Canadian Film and Culture*. Waterloo, ON: Wilfrid Laurier University Press, 1989

Eliade, Mircea. *The Myth of the Eternal Return*. Princeton, NJ: Princeton University Press, 1954

Ellis, Jack C. *John Grierson: A Guide to References and Resources*. Boston: G.K. Hall, 1986

Ellul, Jacques. 'The Power of Technique and The Ethics of Non-Power.' In *The Myths of Information: Technology and Postindustrial Society,* ed. Kathleen Woodward, 242–7. Madison, WO: Coda, 1980

– *Propaganda: The Formation of Men's Attitudes*. 1965. Reprint, New York: Vintage, 1973

– *The Technological Society*. 1954. Reprint, New York: Vintage, 1964

Emberley, Peter C. 'Preface.' In *By Loving Our Own: George Grant and the Legacy of Lament for a Nation,* ed. Peter C. Emberley, xi–xxvi. Ottawa: Carleton University Press, 1990

Evans, Gary. *John Grierson and the National Film Board: The Politics of Wartime Propaganda*. Toronto: University of Toronto Press, 1984

Ewen, Stuart. *PR! A Social History of Spin,* New York: Basic, 1996

Fischer, Doug. '"Extraordinary" Life, Indeed. Obituary, Irene Spry.' *Ottawa Citizen,* 19 December 1998, A6

Foucault, Michel. *Discipline and Punish: The Birth of the Prison*. Harmondsworth: Penguin, 1979

Franklin, Ursula. *The Real World of Technology*. CBC Massey Lectures Series. Toronto: CBC Enterprises, 1990

Freire, Paulo. *Education for Critical Consciousness.* New York: Continuum, 1980
- *Pedagogy of the Oppressed.* New York: Continuum, 1970; rpt. 1992
Friesen, Gerald. 'Irene M. Spry: A Biographical Note.' In *Explorations in Canadian Economic History: Essays in Honour of Irene M. Spry,* ed. Duncan Cameron, 319–26. Ottawa: University of Ottawa Press, 1985
Frye, Northrop. 'Across the River and Out of the Trees.' In *Divisions on a Ground: Essays on Canadian Culture.* Edited with a preface by James Polk, 26–40. Toronto: House of Anansi, 1982
- *Anatomy of Criticism: Four Essays.* 1957. Reprint, Princeton, NJ: Princeton University Press, 1971
- 'The Archetypes of Literature.' *The Kenyan Review* 13 (1951); reprinted in Northrop Frye, *Fables of Identity: Studies in Poetic Mythology,* 7–20. New York: Harcourt, Brace & World, 1963
- *The Bush Garden: Essays in the Canadian Imagination.* Toronto: House of Anansi, 1971
- 'Conclusion to a *Literary History of Canada.*' First published in Carl F. Klinck, general editor, *Literary History of Canada.* Toronto: University of Toronto Press, 1965; reprinted in Northrop Frye, *Mythologizing Canada: Essays on the Canadian Literary Imagination.* Edited by Branko Gorjup, 63–111. Ottawa: Legas, 1997
- 'Conclusion to a *Literary History of Canada,* Second Edition.' First published in Carl F. Klinck, general editor, *Literary History of Canada,* 2d ed. Toronto: University of Toronto Press, 1976; reprinted in *Divisions on a Ground: Essays on Canadian Culture.* Edited with a preface by James Polk, 71–88. Toronto: House of Anansi, 1982
- *Creation and Recreation.* Toronto: University of Toronto Press, 1980
- *The Critical Path: An Essay on the Social Context of Literary Criticism.* Bloomington: Indiana University Press, 1971
- 'Culture as Interpenetration.' In *Divisions on a Ground: Essays on Canadian Culture.* Edited with a preface by James Polk, 15–25. Toronto: House of Anansi, 1982
- *The Double Vision: Language and Meaning in Religion.* Toronto: University of Toronto Press, 1991
- *The Educated Imagination.* Massey Lectures, 2d series. Toronto: CBC Enterprises, 1963
- *Fables of Identity: Studies in Poetic Mythology.* New York: Harcourt, Brace & World, 1963
- *Fearful Symmetry: A Study of William Blake.* 1948. Reprint, Princeton: Princeton University Press, 1969
- *The Great Code: The Bible and Literature.* Toronto: Academic, 1982

– 'Harold Innis: The Strategy of Culture.' In *The Eternal Act of Creation: Essays, 1979–1990,* ed. Robert D. Denham 154–67. Bloomington and Indianapolis: Indiana University Press, 1993

– 'Humanities in a New World.' In *Divisions on a Ground: Essays on Canadian Culture.* Edited with a preface by James Polk, 102–17. Toronto: House of Anansi, 1982

– 'The Language of Poetry.' Excerpt from *Anatomy of Criticism,* in *Explorations in Communication,* ed. Edmund Carpenter and Marshall McLuhan, 43–53. Boston: Beacon, 1960

– 'Literary and Mechanical Models.' An address presented at the Conference on Computers and the Humanities, Toronto, 6 June 1989; published in *The Eternal Act of Creation,* ed. Robert D. Denham, 9–20. Bloomington and Indianapolis: Indiana University Press, 1993

– 'Literature as Therapy.' An address presented at Mount Sinai Hospital, Toronto, 23 November 1989; published in *The Eternal Act of Creation,* ed. Robert D. Denham, 21–34. Bloomington and Indianapolis: Indiana University Press, 1993

– *The Modern Century.* Toronto: Oxford University Press, 1967

– 'National Consciousness in Canadian Culture.' In *Divisions on a Ground: Essays on Canadian Culture.* Edited with a preface by James Polk, 41–55. Toronto: House of Anansi, 1982

– 'Oswald Spengler.' *Architects of Modern Thought,* 83–90. Toronto: Canadian Broadcasting Corporation, 1955

– 'Preface.' In *Fearful Symmetry: A Study of William Blake.* Princeton, NJ: Princeton University Press, 1969

– *The Secular Scripture: A Study of the Structure of Romance.* Cambridge, MA: Harvard University Press, 1976

– 'Sharing the Continent.' In *Divisions on a Ground: Essays on Canadian Culture.* Edited with a preface by James Polk, 57–70. Toronto: House of Anansi, 1982

– 'Sir James Frazer.' *Architects of Modern Thought,* 3d and 4th series, 22–32. Toronto: Canadian Broadcasting Corporation, 1957

– *The Stubborn Structure: Essays on Criticism.* Ithaca, NY: Cornell University Press, 1970

– 'Teaching the Humanities Today.' In *Divisions on a Ground: Essays on Canadian Culture.* Edited with a preface by James Polk, 91–101. Toronto: House of Anansi, 1982

– *Words with Power.* Toronto: Penguin, 1990

Fukuyama, Francis. *The End of History and the Last Man.* New York: The Free Press, 1992

Gandy, Oscar Jr. *The Panoptic Sort: A Political Economy of Personal Information.*
   Boulder, CO: Westview, 1993

Georgescu-Roegen, Nicholas. *The Entropy Law and the Economic Process.*
   Cambridge, MA: Harvard University Press, 1971

Gherson, Giles. 'Marchi Lashes Out at Critics of MAI.' *Ottawa Citizen,*
   14 February 1998, E3

Giedion, Siegfried. *Mechanization Takes Command: A Contribution to Anonymous History.* New York: Oxford University Press, 1948

Gillespie, Michael Allen. 'George Grant and the Tradition of Political
   Economy.' In *By Loving Our Own: George Grant and the Legacy of 'Lament for a
   Nation',* ed. Peter C. Emberley, 123–31. Ottawa: Carleton University Press,
   1990

Ginsberg, Benjamin. *The Captive Public: How Mass Opinion Promotes State
   Power.* New York: Basic, 1986

Giroux, Henry A. *Ideology, Culture, and the Process of Schooling.* Philadelphia:
   Temple University Press, 1981

Gordon, W. Terrence. *Marshall McLuhan: Escape into Understanding.* Toronto:
   Stoddart, 1997

– *McLuhan for Beginners.* Illustrated by Susan Willmarth. New York: Writers
   and Readers, 1997

Grant, George. 'Art and Propaganda.' *Queen's University Journal,* Literary
   Supplement, March 1938: 6–7

– 'Book review of *The Idea File of Harold Innis.*' *Globe and Mail,* 31 May 1980,
   E12; reprinted in *The George Grant Reader,* ed. William Christian and Sheila
   Grant, 354–7. Toronto: University of Toronto Press, 1998

– 'Canadian Fate and Imperialism.' In *Technology and Empire,* 61–78. Toronto:
   House of Anansi, 1969

– 'Carl Gustav Jung.' In *Architects of Modern Thought,* 5th and 6th series, 63–74.
   Toronto: Canadian Broadcasting Corporation, 1962

– 'The Case against Abortion.' *Today Magazine,* 3 October 1981, 12–13

– 'The Computer Does Not Impose on Us the Ways It Should Be Used.' First
   published in *Beyond Industrial Growth,* ed. Abraham Rotstein. Toronto:
   University of Toronto Press, 1975; reprinted in *The George Grant Reader,* ed.
   William Christian and Sheila Grant, 418–34. Toronto: University of Toronto
   Press, 1998

– *English-Speaking Justice.* 1974. Reprint, Toronto: House of Anansi, 1985

– 'An Ethic of Community.' In *Social Purpose for Canada,* ed. Michael Oliver,
   3–26. Toronto: University of Toronto Press, 1961

– 'Faith and the Multiversity.' In *Technology and Justice,* 35–77. Toronto: House
   of Anansi, 1986

– 'Fyodor Dostoevsky.' *Architects of Modern Thought*, 4th series, 71–83. Toronto: Canadian Broadcasting Corporation, 1959
– 'In Defence of North America.' In *Technology and Empire*, 13–40. Toronto: House of Anansi, 1969
– 'Introduction to the Carleton Library Edition.' *Lament for a Nation: The Defeat of Canadian Nationalism*, 9–14. Ottawa: Carleton University Press, 1982
– 'Introduction to Plato.' 1973. Reprinted in *The George Grant Reader*, ed. William Christian and Sheila Grant, 207–13. Toronto: University of Toronto Press, 1998
– 'Jean-Paul Sartre.' *Architects of Modern Thought*, 65–74. Toronto: Canadian Broadcasting Corporation, 1955
– *Lament for a Nation.* 1965. Reprint, Ottawa: Carleton University Press, 1982
– 'Philosophy.' In *Royal Commission Studies: A Selection of Essays Prepared for the Royal Commission on National Development in the Arts, Letters and Sciences*, 119–33. Ottawa: King's Printer, 1951
– *Philosophy in the Mass Age.* 1959. Reprint edited with an introduction by William Christian. Toronto: University of Toronto Press, 1995
– 'Review of Frye's *The Great Code.*' 1982. Reprinted in *The George Grant Reader*, ed. William Christian and Sheila Grant, 357–61. Toronto: University of Toronto Press, 1998
– *Selected Letters.* Edited with an introduction by William Christian. Toronto: University of Toronto Press, 1996
– *Technology and Empire.* Toronto: House of Anansi, 1969
– *Technology and Justice.* Toronto: House of Anansi, 1986
– 'Thinking about Technology.' In *Technology and Justice*, 11–34. Toronto: House of Anansi, 1986
– *Time as History.* Toronto: CBC Learning Systems, 1969
– 'What Is Philosophy?' Written in 1954; published in *The George Grant Reader*, ed. William Christian and Sheila Grant, 33–9. Toronto: University of Toronto Press, 1998
Grant, George, with Sheila Grant. 'Abortion and Rights.' In *Technology and Justice*, 117–30. Toronto: House of Anansi, 1986
Grewe-Partsch, Marianne, and Gertrude J. Robinson, eds. *Women, Communication, and Careers.* New York: K.G. Saur, 1980
Grierson, John. 'Battle for Authenticity.' First published in *World Film News*, November 1938; reprinted in *Grierson on Documentary*; edited and with an introduction by Forsyth Hardy, 83–5. London: Faber and Faber, 1979
– 'The Challenge of Peace.' An address presented to the Conference of the Arts, Sciences, and Professions in the Post-War World, New York, June 1945;

published in *Grierson on Documentary*, edited and with an introduction by Forsyth Hardy, 167–78. London: Faber and Faber, 1979

– 'The Course of Realism.' First published in *Footnotes to the Film*. London: Peter Davies, 1937; reprinted in *Grierson on Documentary*, edited and with an introduction by Forsyth Hardy, 70–82. London: Faber and Faber, 1979

– 'The Documentary Idea: 1942.' Originally published in *Documentary News Letter*, 1942; reprinted in *Grierson on Documentary*, edited and with an introduction by Forsyth Hardy, 111–21. London: Faber and Faber, 1979

– 'Education and the New Order.' First published as 'Democracy and Citizenship' pamphlet no. 7. Ottawa: Canadian Association of Adult Education, 1941; reprinted in *Grierson on Documentary*, edited and with an introduction by Forsyth Hardy, 122–32. London: Faber and Faber, 1979

– 'Education and Total Effort.' Originally an address given in Winnipeg in 1941; reprinted in *Grierson on Documentary*, edited and with an introduction by Forsyth Hardy, 133–40. London: Faber and Faber, 1979

– *The Eyes of Democracy*. Edited by Ian Lockerbie. Newcastle upon Tyne: University of Stirling, 1990

– 'The Film at War.' Originally a broadcast from Ottawa, 30 November 1940; reprinted in *Grierson on Documentary*, edited and with an introduction by Forsyth Hardy, 86–9. London: Faber and Faber, 1979

– 'First Principles of Documentary.' First published in *Cinema Quarterly*, Spring 1932; reprinted in *Grierson on Documentary*, edited and with an introduction by Forsyth Hardy, 35–46. London: Faber and Faber, 1979

– 'Learning from Television.' First published in *Contrast*, Summer 1963; reprinted in *Grierson on Documentary*, edited and with an introduction by Forsyth Hardy, 210–19. London: Faber and Faber, 1979

– 'The Library in the International World.' An address presented to the American Library Association, Buffalo, NY, June 1946; published in *Grierson on Documentary*, edited and with an introduction by Forsyth Hardy, 156–66. London: Faber and Faber, 1979

– 'The Nature of Propaganda.' First published in *Documentary News Letter*, 1939; reprinted in *Grierson on Documentary*, edited and with an introduction by Forsyth Hardy, 101–10. London: Faber and Faber, 1979

– 'Propaganda and Education.' In *Grierson on Documentary*, edited and with an introduction by Forsyth Hardy, 141–55. London: Faber and Faber, 1979

– 'Report from America.' First published in *Theatre Arts Monthly*, December 1946; reprinted in *Grierson on Documentary*, edited and with an introduction by Forsyth Hardy, 179–86. London: Faber and Faber, 1979

– 'Revolution in the Arts.' Originally an address at the University of North

Carolina, 1962; reprinted in *John Grierson: Film Master*, ed. James Beveridge, 26–34. New York: Macmillan, 1978

– 'Searchlight on Democracy.' First published in *Documentary News Letter*, 1939; reprinted in *Grierson on Documentary*; edited and with an introduction by Forsyth Hardy, 90–100. London: Faber and Faber, 1979

– 'Summary and Survey 1935.' First published in *The Arts Today*, London, 1935; reprinted in *Grierson on Documentary*, edited and with an introduction by Forsyth Hardy, 52–69. London: Faber and Faber, 1979

Grosswiler, Paul. *Method Is the Message: Rethinking McLuhan through Critical Theory.* Montreal: Black Rose, 1998

Guback, Thomas. '*Counterclockwise*: Dallas Smythe's Contribution to Communication Policy and Research.' Smythe Memorial Lecture, Occasional Paper Number 1, Institute of Communications Research, College of Communications, University of Illinois at Urbana-Champaign, 1995

– 'Eulogy.' In Dallas W. Smythe, *Counterclockwise: Perspectives on Communication*. Edited by Thomas Guback, 331–3. Boulder, CO: Westview, 1994.

– ed. *Counterclockwise: Perspectives on Communication*, by Dallas W. Smythe. Boulder, CO: Westview, 1994

Hackett, Robert. *News and Dissent: The Press and the Politics of Peace in Canada*, Norwood, NJ: Ablex, 1991

Hall, Stuart.'Encoding/Decoding.' In *Culture, Media, Language*, ed. S. Hall, D. Hobson, and A. Lowe, 128–38. University of Birmingham: Hutchinson, 1980

– 'The Rediscovery of "Ideology": The Return of the Repressed in Media Studies.' In *Culture, Society and the Media*, ed. M. Gurevitch, T. Bennett, J. Curan, and S. Woollacott, 30–55. London: Methuen, 1982

Hardin, Herschel. *A Nation Unaware: The Canadian Economic Culture.* Vancouver: J.J. Douglas, 1974

Hardt, Hanno. *Critical Communication Studies: Communication, History and Theory in America.* London/New York: Routledge, 1992

Hardy, Forsyth. 'Introduction.' In *Grierson on the Movies*, edited with an introduction by Forsyth Hardy. London: Faber and Faber, 1981

– *John Grierson: A Documentary Biography.* London: Faber and Faber, 1979

Harvey, David. *The Condition of Postmodernity.* Oxford: Blackwell, 1990

Havelock, E.A. 'Foreword to the Original Edition.' *Prometheus, with a Translation of Aeschylus' Prometheus Bound.* 1951. Reprint, Seattle: University of Washington Press, 1968

– *Harold A. Innis: A Memoir.* Two lectures sponsored by the Harold Innis

Foundation, given at Innis College in the University of Toronto on 14 October 1978. Reprint, Toronto: Harold Innis Foundation, 1982

– *Preface to Plato*. Cambridge, MA: Harvard University Press, 1963

Hayek, F.A. von. 'The Use of Knowledge in Society.' *American Economic Review* 35/4 (1945): 519–30

Herman, Edward S. 'All the Editorials Fit to Print: The Politics of "Newsworthiness."' In *Information and Communication in Economics*, ed. Robert E. Babe, 177–99. Boston: Kluwer Academic, 1994

– '"Reburial" of Ideology.' In *Information and Communication in Economics*, ed. Robert E. Babe, 208–9. Boston: Kluwer Academic, 1994

Heyer, Paul. *Communications and History: Theories of Media, Knowledge, and Civilization*. New York: Greenwood, 1988

Hills, Jill. 'Communication, Information, and Transnational Enterprise.' In *Information and Communication in Economics*, ed. Robert E. Babe, 293–320. Boston: Kluwer Academic, 1994

Horowitz, Gad. 'Tories, Socialists and the Demise of Canada.' *Canadian Dimension* 2/4 (May/June 1965): 12–15

Hutchinson, A.C., and A. Petter. 'Private Rights? Public Wrongs.' Osgoode Hall Law School/ University of Victoria, unpublished paper, 1985

Hyde, Lewis. *The Gift: Imagination and the Erotic Life of Property*. New York: Vintage, 1983

Innis, Harold A. 'Adult Education and Universities.' 1951. Reprinted in *Markets, and Cultural Change*, ed. Daniel Drache, 471–81. Montreal and Kingston: McGill-Queen's University Press, 1995

– *The Bias of Communication*. 1951. Reprinted with an introduction by Marshall McLuhan. Toronto: University of Toronto Press, 1971

– 'The Canadian Economy and the Depression.' First published in *The Canadian Economy and Its Problems*, ed. H.A. Innis and A.F.W. Plumtre. Ottawa: Canadian Institute of International Affairs, 1934; reprinted in Harold A. Innis, *Essays in Canadian Economic History*. Edited by Mary Q. Innis, 123–40. Toronto: University of Toronto Press, 1956

– 'Charles Norris Cochrane, 1889–1945.' *Canadian Journal of Economics and Political Science* 12 (1946): 95–7

– 'The Church in Canada.' First published in *In Time of Healing*, Twenty-second Annual Report of the Board of Evangelism and Social Service of the United Church of Canada, Toronto: United Church of Canada, 1947; reprinted in Harold A. Innis, *Essays in Canadian Economic History*. Edited by Mary Q. Innis, 383–93. Toronto: University of Toronto Press, 1956

– *The Cod Fisheries: The History of an International Economy*, 1940; rev. ed., Toronto: University of Toronto Press, 1954

– 'A Critical Review.' 1951. Reprinted in *The Bias of Communication*, 190–5.
Toronto: University of Toronto Press, 1971

– *Empire and Communications*. 1950. Revised edition edited by Mary Q. Innis.
Toronto: University of Toronto Press, 1972

– *Essays in Canadian Economic History*. Edited by Mary Q. Innis, Toronto:
University of Toronto Press, 1956

– *The Fur Trade in Canada: An Introduction to Canadian Economic History*. 1930.
Reprint based on the revised edition, prepared by S.D. Clark and W.T.
Easterbrook, with a foreword by Robin W. Winks, Toronto: University of
Toronto Press, 1962

– *A History of the Canadian Pacific Railway*. 1923. Reprint. Toronto: University
of Toronto Press, 1971

– *The Idea File of Harold Adams Innis*. Edited and with an introduction by
William Christian. Toronto: University of Toronto Press, 1980

– 'Industrialism and Cultural Values.' Paper read at the Meetings of the American Economics Association, Chicago, 30 December 1951; published in *The Bias
of Communication*, 132–41. Toronto: University of Toronto Press, 1971

– 'The Lumber Trade in Canada.' First published as 'Editor's Preface' in
A.R.M. Lower, *The North American Assault on the Canadian Forest*, vii–xviii.
Toronto: Ryerson, 1938; reprinted in H.A. Innis, *Essays in Canadian Economic
History*. Edited by Mary Q. Innis, 242–51. Toronto: University of Toronto
Press, 1956

– 'Minerva's Owl.' Presidential Address to the Royal Society of Canada, 1947;
published in Harold A. Innis, *The Bias of Communication*, rprt. Toronto:
University of Toronto Press, 1971, pp. 3–32

– 'The Newspaper in Economic Development.' In *Political Economy in the
Modern State*, 1–34. Toronto: Ryerson, 1946

– 'On the Economic Significance of Cultural Factors.' First published in
Political Economy and the Modern State. Toronto: Ryerson, 1946; reprinted in
Harold A. Innis, *Staples, Markets and Cultural Change*. Edited by Daniel Drache,
297–315. Montreal and Kingston: McGill-Queen's University Press, 1995

– 'The Passing of Political Economy.' First published in *Commerce Journal*,
1938; reprinted in *Staples, Markets, and Cultural Change*, ed. Daniel Drache,
438–42. Montreal and Kingston: McGill-Queen's University Press, 1995

– 'The Penetrative Powers of the Price System.' First published in *Canadian
Journal of Economics and Political Science* 4 (1938): 299–319; reprinted in
Harold A. Innis, *Essays in Canadian Economic History*. Edited by Mary Q.
Innis, 252–72. Toronto: University of Toronto Press, 1956

– 'A Plea for Time.' 1951. Reprinted in *The Bias of Communication*, 61–91.
Toronto: University of Toronto Press, 1971

– *Political Economy in the Modern State*. Toronto: Ryerson, 1946
– *The Press: A Neglected Factor in the Economic History of the Twentieth Century*. Stamp Memorial Lecture, University of London. London: Oxford University Press, 1949
– 'Problem of Space.' 1951. Reprinted in *The Bias of Communication*, 92–131. Toronto: University of Toronto Press, 1971
– 'The Pulp and Paper Industry.' In *The Encyclopedia of Canada*, ed. W. Stewart Wallace, 176–85. Toronto: University Associates of Canada, 1937
– 'Reflections on Russia.' First published in Harold A. Innis, *Political Economy in the Modern State*. Toronto: Ryerson, 1946; reprinted in Harold A. Innis, *Innis on Russia: The Russian Diary and Other Writings*. Edited with a preface by William Christian, 73–85. Toronto: Harold Innis Foundation, 1981
– *Staples, Markets and Cultural Change*. Edited by Daniel Drache. Montreal and Kingston: McGill-Queen's University Press, 1995
– 'The Strategy of Culture.' In *Changing Concepts of Time*, 1–20. Toronto: University of Toronto Press, 1952
– 'The Teaching of Economic History in Canada.' First published in *Contributions to Canadian Economics* 2. Toronto: University of Toronto Press, 1929; reprinted in Harold A. Innis, *Essays in Canadian Economic History*. Edited by Mary Q. Innis, 3–16. Toronto: University of Toronto Press, 1956
– 'Technology and Public Opinion in the United States.' 1949. Reprinted in *The Bias of Communication*, 156–189. Toronto: University of Toronto Press, 1971
– 'The Work of Thorstein Veblen.' In *Essays in Canadian Economic History*. Edited by Mary Q. Innis, 17–26. Toronto: University of Toronto Press, 1956
Kackson, Andrew, and Matthew Sanger, eds. *Dismantling Democracy: The Multilateral Agreement on Investment (MAI) and Its Impact*. Toronto: Lorimer, 1998
Jacobs, Jane. *Systems of Survival: A Dialogue on the Moral Foundations of Commerce and Politics*. New York: Vintage, 1992
Jeffrey, Liss. 'The Heat and the Light: Towards a Reassessment of the Contribution of H. Marshall McLuhan.' *Canadian Journal of Communication*, 15/4 & 5, special issue, December 1989: 1–29
Kahn, Frank J. *Documents of American Broadcasting*. New York: Appleton-Century-Crofts, 1968
Kaplan, Robert D. 'Was Democracy Just a Moment?' *The Atlantic Monthly*, December 1997, 55–80
Keast, Ronald. '"It Is Written – But I Say Unto You": Innis on Religion.' *Journal of Canadian Studies* 20/4 (1986): 12–25
Knelman, Martin. *This Is Where We Came In: The Career and Character of Canadian Film*. Toronto: McClelland and Stewart, 1977

Koestler, Arthur. *The Roots of Coincidence*. London: Pan, 1972

Kroker, Arthur. *Technology and the Canadian Mind: Innis/McLuhan/Grant*. Montreal: New World Perspectives, 1984

Kuhn, Thomas. *The Structure of Scientific Revolutions*, 2d ed., Chicago: University of Chicago Press, 1970

Kuhns, William. *The Post-Industrial Prophets: Interpretations of Technology*, 1971; rprt. New York: Harper and Row, 1973

Lasswell, Harold. 'The Structure and Function of Communication in Society,' 1948. Reprinted in *The Process and Effects of Mass Communication*, ed. Wilbur Schramm and Donald F. Roberts, 84–99. Urbana: University of Illinois Press, 1971

Lazarsfeld, Paul Felix. 'Remarks on Administrative and Critical Research.' First published in *Studies in Philosophy and Social Sciences* 9/1 (1941); reprinted as 'Administrative and Critical Research,' in *Qualitative Analysis: Historical and Critical Essays*, 157–67. Boston: Allyn and Bacon, 1972

Leiss, William. *C.B. Macpherson: Dilemmas of Liberalism and Socialism*. Montreal: New World Perspectives, 1988

– 'On the Validity of Our Discipline – New Applications of Communications Theory. The 1990 Southam Lecture.' *Canadian Journal of Communication* 16/2 (1991): 291–305

Lent, John A. *A Different Road Taken: Profiles in Critical Communication*. Boulder, CO: Westview, 1994

Lerner, Max. 'Editor's Introduction.' In *The Portable Veblen*, ed. Max Lerner, 1–49. New York: Viking, 1948

Lewis, C.S. *The Abolition of Man*. Glasgow: William Collins & Sons, 1943

Lippmann, Walter. *Public Opinion*. 1922. Reprint, New York: The Free Press, 1965

Lipset, Seymour Martin. *North-American Cultures: Values and Institutions in Canada and the United States*, Orono, ME: Borderlands Project, the Canadian-American Center, University of Maine, 1990

Littlejohn, Stephen. *Theories of Human Communication*, 4th ed. Belmont, CA: Wadsworth, 1992

– *Theories of Human Communication*, 6th ed. Belmont, CA: Wadsworth, 1998

Lower, Arthur. (1986), 'Harold Innis as I Remember Him.' *Journal of Canadian Studies*, 20/4 (1986): 3–11

Macpherson, C.B. *Burke*. New York: Oxford University Press, 1980

– *Democracy in Alberta: Social Credit and the Party System*. 1953. Reprint, Toronto: University of Toronto Press, 1962

– *Democratic Theory: Essays in Retrieval*. Oxford: Clarendon Press, 1973

– 'Do We Need a Theory of the State?' First published in *European Journal of*

Sociology 18 (1977); reprinted in C.B. Macpherson, *The Rise and Fall of Economic Justice*, Oxford: Oxford University Press, 1985

– 'Human Rights as Property Rights.' In *The Rise and Fall of Economic Justice*, 76–85. Oxford: Oxford University Press, 1985

– *The Life and Times of Liberal Democracy.* Oxford: Oxford University Press, 1977

– 'The Meaning of Property.' In *Property: Mainstream and Critical Positions*, 1–13. Toronto: University of Toronto Press, 1978

– *The Political Theory of Possessive Individualism: Hobbes to Locke.* Oxford: Oxford University Press, 1962

– 'Property as Means or End.' In *Theories of Property: Aristotle to the Present*, ed. Anthony Parel and Thomas Flanagan, 3–9. Waterloo: Wilfrid Laurier University Press, 1979

– ed. *Property: Mainstream and Critical Positions.* Toronto: University of Toronto Press, 1978

– *The Real World of Democracy.* The Massey Lectures, 4th series. Toronto: Canadian Broadcasting Corporation, 1965

– *The Rise and Fall of Economic Justice.* Oxford: Oxford University Press, 1985

Marcel, Gabriel. *Man against Mass Society.* Translated from French by G.S. Fraser. South Bend, IN: Gateway, 1978

Marchand, Philip. *Marshall McLuhan: The Medium and the Messenger.* Toronto: Random House, 1989

Masterman, Len. *Teaching the Media.* London: Comedia, 1985

Mathews, Robin. *Canadian Identity: Major Forces Shaping the Life of a People.* Ottawa: Steel Rail, 1988

Mattelart, Armand. *Mapping World Communication: War, Progress, Culture.* Translated by Susan Emanuel and James A. Cohen. Minneapolis: University of Minnesota Press, 1994

McChesney, Robert W. 'Graham Spry and the Future of Public Broadcasting. The 1997 Graham Spry Memorial Lecture.' *Canadian Journal of Communication* 24/1 (1999): 25–47

McCloskey, Donald. *The Rhetoric of Economics.* Madison: University of Wisconsin Press, 1985

McLuhan, Marshall. 'Canada: The Borderline Case.' In *The Canadian Imagination: Dimensions of a Literary Culture.* Edited with an introduction by David Staines, 226–48. Cambridge, MA: Harvard University Press, 1977

– 'G.K. Chesterton: A Practical Mystic.' *The Dalhousie Review* 14/4 (January 1936): 455–64

– *Counterblast.* Toronto: McClelland and Stewart, 1969

– 'Foreword.' In Harold A. Innis, *Empire and Communications*, revised by Mary Q. Innis, v–xii. Toronto: University of Toronto Press, 1972

- *The Gutenberg Galaxy: The Making of Typographical Man.* Toronto: University of Toronto Press, 1962
- 'Introduction.' In *Explorations in Communication: An Anthology,* ed. Edmund Carpenter and Marshall McLuhan, ix–xii. Boston: Beacon, 1960
- 'Introduction.' In Harold A. Innis, *The Bias of Communication,* vii–xvi. Toronto: University of Toronto Press, 1971
- *The Mechanical Bride: Folklore of Industrial Man.* 1951. Reprint, Boston: Beacon, 1967.
- *Understanding Media: The Extensions of Man.* New York: Mentor, 1964
- Interview with Eric Norden. Originally published in *Playboy,* 1969; reprinted in *Canadian Journal of Communication* 14/4 & 5, special issue, December 1989: 101–37

McLuhan, Marshall, and Quentin Fiore. *The Medium Is the Massage.* New York: Bantam, 1967
- *War and Peace in the Global Village,* New York: Bantam, 1968

McLuhan, Marshall, and Eric McLuhan. *Laws of the Media: The New Science.* Toronto: University of Toronto Press, 1988

McLuhan, Marshall, and Barrington Nevitt. *Take Today: The Executive as Dropout.* Don Mills, ON: Longman Canada, 1972

McLuhan, Marshall, and Harley Parker. *Through the Vanishing Point: Space in Poetry and Painting.* World Perspectives Vol. 37, planned and edited by Ruth Nanda Anshen. New York: Harper and Row, 1968

McLuhan, Marshall, and Bruce R. Powers. *The Global Village: Transformations in World Life and Media in the 21st Century.* New York: Oxford University Press, 1989

McLuhan, Marshall, with Wilfred Watson. *From Cliché to Archetype.* 1970. Reprint, New York: Pocket, 1971

Melody, William H. 'Introduction.' In *Culture, Communication, and Dependency: The Tradition H.A. Innis,* ed. William H. Melody, Liora Salter, and Paul Heyer, 3–11. Norwood, NJ: Ablex, 1981
- 'Dallas Smythe: Pioneer in the Political Economy of Communications.' In Dallas W. Smythe, *Counterclockwise: Perspectives on Communication.* Edited by Thomas Guback, 1–6. Boulder, CO: Westview, 1994

Menzies, Heather. *The Railroad's Not Enough: Canada Now.* Toronto: Clarke, Irwin, 1978
- *Whose Brave New World? The Information Highway and the New Economy.* Toronto: Between the Lines, 1996

Mesthene, Emmanuel G. *Technological Change: Its Impact on Man and Society.* New York: New American Library, 1970

Mitchell, Wesley C. *Types of Economic Theory: From Mercantilism to Institutionalism.* New York: Augustus M. Kelley, 1967

Molinaro, Matie. 'Marshalling McLuhan.' *The Antagonish Review*, no. 74-75, special McLuhan issue (1988): 88–95

Molinaro, Matie, Corrine McLuhan, and William Toye, eds. *Letters of Marshall McLuhan.* Toronto: Oxford University Press, 1987

Morris, Peter. 'Rethinking Grierson: The Ideology of John Grierson.' In *Dialogue: Canadian and Quebec Cinema,* ed. Pierre Véronneau, Michael Dorland, and Seth Feldman. Montreal: Mediatexte, 1987

Mosco, Vincent. *The Pay-Per Society: Computers and Communication in the Information Age.* Toronto: Garamond, 1989

– *The Political Economy of Communication: Rethinking and Renewal.* London: Sage, 1996

Mowlana, Hamid, George Gerbner, and Herbert I. Schiller. *The Triumph of the Image: The Media's War in the Persian Gulf.* Boulder, CO: Westview, 1992

Mulgan, G.J. *Communication and Control: Networks and the New Economics of Communication.* New York: Guilford, 1991

Mumford, Lewis. *Technics and Civilization.* 1934. Reprint, New York: Harcourt, Brace and World, 1963

Murdock, Graham, and Peter Golding. 'Information Poverty and Political Inequality: Citizenship in the Age of Privatized Communications.' *Journal of Communication* 39/3 (Summer 1989): 180–94

Myerson, George, and Yvonne Rydin. *The Language of Environment: A New Rhetoric.* London: UCL Press, 1996

National Film Board of Canada. *Grierson.* A documentary film directed by Roger Blais, produced by Roger Blais; executive producer David Bairstow. 1979

Neill, Robin. *A New Theory of Value: The Canadian Economics of H.A. Innis.* Toronto: University of Toronto Press, 1972

Nelson, Joyce. *The Colonized Eye: Rethinking the Grierson Legend.* Toronto: Between the Lines, 1988

Nevitt, Barrington. *The Communication Ecology: Re-presentation versus Replica.* Toronto: Butterworths, 1982

Nevitt, Barrington, and Maurice McLuhan. *Who Was Marshall McLuhan?* Toronto: Stoddart, 1994

Noble, David F. *The Religion of Technology: A Divinity of Man and the Spirit of Invention.* New York: Penguin, 1997

Nolan, Michael. *Foundations: Alan Plaunt and the Early Days of CBC Radio.* Montreal: CBC Enterprises, 1986

Nye, Joseph Jr., and William Owens. 'America's Information Edge.' *Foreign Affairs*, March/April 1996, 20–36

O'Donovan, Joan E. *George Grant and the Twilight of Justice.* Toronto: University of Toronto Press, 1984

Ong, Walter J. *Orality and Literacy: The Technologizing of the Word.* New York: Methuen, 1982
– *The Presence of the Word.* New Haven, CT: Yale University Press, 1967
Organization for Economic Cooperation and Development. *Information Networks and New Technologies: Opportunities and Policy Implications for the 1990s.* Paris: OECD, 1992
Patterson, Graeme. *History and Communications: Harold Innis, Marshall McLuhan, The Interpretation of History.* Toronto: University of Toronto Press, 1990
Peers, Frank. *The Politics of Canadian Broadcasting, 1920–1951.* Toronto: University of Toronto Press, 1969
Perinabanayagam, R.S. *Discursive Acts.* New York: Aldine de Gruyter, 1991
Peter, John. 'Democracy and American Communication Theory: Dewey, Lippmann, Lazarsfeld.' *Communication* 11 (1989): 199–220
Philip, Margaret. 'UN Committee Lambastes Canada on Human Rights.' *Globe and Mail*, 5 December 1998, A5
Plaunt, Alan. *The Canadian Radio League: Objects, Information, National Support.* Ottawa: Canadian Radio League, 1931
Polyani, Karl. *The Great Transformation: The Political and Economic Origins of Our Time.* 1944. Reprint, Boston: Beacon, 1957
Polanyi, Michael. *Personal Knowledge: Towards a Post-Critical Philosophy.* Chicago: University of Chicago Press, 1958
Popper, Karl. *Conjectures and Refutations: The Growth of Scientific Knowledge.* New York: Harper and Row, 1963
Poster, Mark. 'Databases as Discourse; or Electronic Interpellations.' In *Computers, Surveillance and Privacy*, ed. David Lyon and Elia Zureik, 175–92. Minneapolis: University of Minnesota Press, 1996
– 'The Mode of Information and Postmodernity.' In *Communication Theory Today*, ed. David Crowley and David Mitchell, 171–92. Stanford, CT: Stanford University Press, 1994
Potvin, Rose, ed. *Passion and Conviction: The Letters of Graham Spry.* Regina: Canadian Plains Research Centre, University of Regina, 1992
Powe, B.W. *A Climate Charged.* Oakville, ON: Mosaic, 1984
Prang, Margaret. 'The Origins of Public Broadcasting.' *Canadian Historical Review* 46/1 (March 1965): 1–31
Preston, William Jr, Edward S. Herman, and Herbert I. Schiller. *Hope and Folly: The United States and UNESCO, 1945–1985.* Minneapolis: University of Minnesota Press, 1989
Raboy, Marc. *Missed Opportunities: The Story of Canada's Broadcasting Policy.* Montreal and Kingston: McGill-Queen's University Press, 1990
Roach, Colleen. 'Dallas Smythe and the New World Information and Commu-

nication Order. In *Illuminating the Blindspots: Essays Honoring Dallas W. Smythe*, ed. Janet Wasko, Vincent Mosco, and Manjunath Pendakur, 274–301. Norwood, NJ: Ablex, 1993

Robins, Kevin, and Frank Webster.'The Communications Revolution: New Media, Old Problems.' *Communication* 10/1 (1987): 71–89

Robinson, Gertrude Joch. 'Binational News: The Social Construction of World Affairs Reporting in the French and English Canadian Press.' *News Agencies and World News in Canada, the United States and Yugoslavia: Methods and Data*, 149–87. Fribourg, Switzerland: University Press of Fribourg, 1981

– 'Constructing a Historiography for North American Communication Studies.' In *American Communication Research – The Remembered History*, ed. Everette E. Dennis and Ellen Wartella, 157–68. Mahwah, NJ: Lawrence Erlbaum Associates, 1996

– *Constructing the Quebec Referendum: French and English Media Voices*. Toronto: University of Toronto Press, 1998

– 'East Germany.' In *Glasnost and After: Media and Change in Central and Eastern Europe*, ed. David L. Paletz, Katrol Jukobowicz, and Pavao Novosel, 173–97. Cresskill, NJ: Hampton, 1995

– 'Epilogue: The Papers in Retrospect.' In *News Agencies and World News in Canada, the United States and Yugoslavia: Methods and Data*, 215–25. Fribourg, Switzerland: University Press of Fribourg, 1981

– 'The Feminist Paradigm in Historical Perspective.' *Medie/Kultur* 4 (November 1986): 113–23

– 'Foreign News Selection Is Non-Linear in Yugoslavia's Tanjug Agency.' First published in *Journalism Quarterly* 47/2 (Summer 1970): 340–51; reprinted in Gertrude Joch Robinson, *News Agencies and World News in Canada, the United States and Yugoslavia: Methods and Data*, 39–55. Fribourg, Switzerland: University Press of Fribourg, 1981

– 'Introduction: The New World Information Order Debate in Perspective.' In *Assessing the New World Information Order Debate: Evidence and Proposals*, ed. Gertrude Joch Robinson, 1–8. Columbia, SC: International Communication Division, Association for Education in Journalism, 1981

– 'Paul Felix Lazarsfeld's Contribution to the Development of US Communication Studies.' In *Paul F. Lazarsfeld*, ed. Wolfgang Laugenbucher, 89–111. Munich: Verlag Olschläger, 1990

– 'Mass Media and Ethnic Strife in Multinational Yugoslavia.' *Journalism Quarterly* 51/3 (Autumn 1974): 490–7

– 'The "Meaning" Characteristics of International News Flow.' In *News Agencies and World News in Canada, the United States and Yugoslavia: Methods and Data*, 103–19. Fribourg, Switzerland: University Press of Fribourg, 1981

– 'Monopolies of Knowledge in Canadian Communication Studies: The Case of Feminist Approaches.' *Canadian Journal of Communication* 23/1 (Winter 1998): 65–72
– *News Agencies and World News in Canada, the United States and Yugoslavia: Methods and Data.* Fribourg, Switzerland: University Press of Fribourg, 1981
– 'The New Yugoslav Writer: A Socio-Political Portrait.' *Mosaic* 6/4 (Fall 1973): 185–97
– 'Notes on the Political Economy of News Production and Communications Research.' In *Information and Communication in Economics*, ed. Robert E. Babe, 200–7. Boston: Kluwer Academic, 1994
– 'The Politics of Information and Culture during Canada's October Crisis.' In *Studies in Canadian Communications*, ed. Gertrude Joch Robinson and Donald F. Theall, 141–61. Montreal: McGill University Graduate Program in Communications, 1975
– 'Remembering Our Past: Reconstructing the Field of Canadian Communication Studies.' 1999 Southam Lecture, delivered at the annual meetings of the Canadian Communication Association, Sherbrooke, Quebec, June 1999
– 'Social Stratification in International News Flow.' Paper presented at the American Sociological Association Convention, Montreal, 26–9 August 1974; published in Gertrude Joch Robinson, *News Agencies and World News in Canada, the United States and Yugoslavia: Methods and Data*, 99–119. Fribourg, Switzerland: University Press of Fribourg, 1981
– 'Some Hypotheses about Canadian–U.S. News Values.' Paper presented at the Binational Conference on Mass Media News Flow between Canada and the United States, Syracuse University, 25–6 September 1976; published in Gertrude Joch Robinson, *News Agencies and World News in Canada, the United States and Yugoslavia: Methods and Data*, 120–7. Fribourg, Switzerland: University Press of Fribourg, 1981
– 'Some Thoughts on the Role of Gender in Media Analysis.' In *Valeriana: Essays on Human Communication*, ed. Miedzy Ludzmi, 237–43. Krakow: Jagiellan University Press, 1996
– 'Tanjug's Complementary Role in International Communications.' Paper read at the UNESCO Symposium on Mass Media and International Understanding, Ljubljana, Yugoslavia, 3–4 September 1968; published in Gertrude Joch Robinson, *News Agencies and World News in Canada, the United States and Yugoslavia: Methods and Data*, 13–38. Fribourg, Switzerland: University Press of Fribourg, 1981
– 'Twenty-five Years of "Gatekeeper" Research: A Critical Review and Evaluation.' In Gertrude Joch Robinson, *News Agencies and World News in Canada,*

the United States and Yugoslavia: Methods and Data, 89–98. Fribourg, Switzer-
land: University Press of Fribourg, 1981
– 'Writers as Fighters: The Effects of the Cultural "Thaw" on Yugoslavia's
Mass Media.' *Cave* 5 (May 1974): 16–29
Robinson, Gertrude J., and Armande Saint-Jean. 'Canadian Women Journal-
ists: The "Other Half" of the Equation.' In *The Global Journalist: News People
around the World*, ed. David H. Weaver, 351–78. Cresskill, NJ: Hampton,
1997
– 'From Flora to Kim: Thirty Years of Representation of Canadian Women
Politicians.' In *Seeing Ourselves: Media Power and Policy in Canada*, ed. Helen
Holmes and David Taras, 23–36. Toronto: Harcourt Brace, 1996
Robinson, Gertrude Joch, and Dieta Sixt. *Women and Power: Canadian and
German Experiences.* Montreal: McGill Studies in Communication/Goethe
Institute, 1990
Robinson, Gertrude Joch, with Vernone Sparkes. 'International News in the
Canadian and American Press: A Comparative News Flow Study.' First
published in *Gazette*, Spring 1977; reprinted in Gertrude Joch Robinson,
*News Agencies and World News in Canada, the United States and Yugoslavia:
Methods and Data*, 128–45. Fribourg, Switzerland: University Press of
Fribourg, 1981
Robinson, Gertrude Joch, and Donald F. Theall, eds. *Studies in Canadian
Communication.* Montreal: McGill Graduate Program in Communications,
1975
Rogers, Everett M. *A History of Communication Study: A Biographical Approach.*
New York: The Free Press, 1994
Rosenthal, Raymond, ed. *McLuhan: Pro and Con.* Baltimore: Pelican, 1969
Ruggles, Myles Alexander. *The Audience Reflected in the Medium of Law: A
Critique of the Political Economy of Speech Rights in the United States.*
Norwood, NJ: Ablex, 1994
Salutin, Rick. 'Last Call from Harold Innis.' Harold Innis Memorial Lecture,
presented at Innis College, Toronto, 5 November 1996; published in *Queen's
Quarterly* 104/2 (Summer 1997), 244–54
– 'The NFB Red Scare.' *Weekend Magazine,* 23 September 1978, 17
– 'We've Come a Long Way Since Heston Played Moses.' *Globe and Mail,*
17 December 1998, A18
Samuels, Warren J. *The Classical Theory of Economic Policy,* Cleveland: World
Publishing, 1966
– ed. *Economics as Discourse: An Analysis of the Rhetoric of Economists.* Boston:
Kluwer Academic, 1990
Schelling, T.C. (1968), 'The Life You Save May Be Your Own.' In *Problems in*

Public Expenditure Analysis, ed. Samuel B. Chase, Jr, 127–76. Washington, DC: Brookings Institute, 1968

Schiller, Dan. *Theorizing Communication: A History.* New York: Oxford University Press, 1996

Schiller, Herbert I. *Communication and Cultural Domination*, New York: M.E. Sharpe, 1976

– *Culture Inc. The Corporate Takeover of Cultural Expression.* New York: Oxford University Press, 1989

– *Information Inequality.* New York: Routledge, 1996

– 'Is There a United States Information Policy?' In *Hope and Folly: The United States and UNESCO, 1945–1985*, ed. William Preston, Jr, Edward S. Herman, and Herbert I. Schiller, 285–311. Minneapolis: University of Minnesota Press, 1989

– *Mass Communications and American Empire.* New York: Augustus M. Kelley, 1969

Schmidt, Larry, ed. *George Grant in Process: Essays and Conversations.* Toronto: House of Anansi, 1978

Schramm, Wilbur. *The Beginnings of Communication Study in America: A Personal Memoir.* Edited by Steven Chaffee and Everett Rogers. Thousand Oaks, CA: Sage, 1997

– 'Human Communication as a Field of Behavioral Science: Jack Hilgard and His Committee.' In *Human Communication as a Field of Study: Selected Contemporary Views*, ed. Sarah Sanderson King, 13–26. Albany: State University of New York Press, 1989

Schumacher, E.F. *Good Work.* New York: Harper & Row, 1979

– *Small Is Beautiful: Economics as if People Mattered.* New York: Harper & Row, 1973

Scitovsky, Tibor. *The Joyless Economy: An Inquiry into Human Satisfaction and Consumer Dissatisfaction.* New York: Oxford University Press, 1976

Serafini, Shirley, and Michel Andrieu. *The Information Revolution and Its Implications for Canada.* Ottawa: Ministry Supply and Services, 1981

Shannon, Claude, and Warren Weaver. *The Mathematical Theory of Communication.* 1949. Reprint, Urbana, IL: University of Illinois Press, 1963

Shaull, Richard. 'Foreword.' In Paulo Freire, *Pedagogy of the Oppressed.* New York: Continuum, 1992

Shelley, Percy Bysshe. 'A Defense of Poetry.' 1821. Reprinted in *The Norton Anthology of English Literature: Major Authors Edition*, M.H. Abrams, General Editor, 1349–62. New York: W.W. Norton, 1962

Skinner, B.F. *Beyond Freedom and Dignity.* New York: Bantam/Vintage, 1972

Smith, Adam. *An Inquiry into the Nature and Causes of the Wealth of Na-*

tions. 1776. Reprint edited with an introduction by Edwin Cannan, and with
  an introduction by Max Lerner. New York: The Modern Library, 1937
- *The Theory of Moral Sentiments.* 1759. Reprint, New York: Augustus M.
  Kelley, 1966
Smith, Alan. *American–Canadian Public Policy: Canadian Culture, the Canadian
  State, and the New Continentalism.* Orono, ME: The Canadian–American
  Center, University of Maine, 1990
Smythe, Dallas W. 'After Bicycles, What?' Written in 1973; published in *Coun-
  terclockwise: Perspectives on Communication*, ed. Thomas Guback,
  230–44. Boulder, CO: Westview, 1994
- 'Autobiography.' Unpublished manuscript, n.d. Portions published in
  Counterclockwise: Perspectives on Communication, ed. Thomas Guback, 13–58.
  Boulder, CO: Westview, 1994
- 'Communications: Blindspot of Economics.' In *Culture, Communication, and
  Dependency: The Tradition of H.A. Innis*, ed. William H. Melody, Liora Salter,
  and Paul Heyer, 111–25. Norwood, NJ: Ablex, 1981
- *Counterclockwise: Perspectives on Communication.* Edited by Thomas Guback.
  Boulder, CO: Westview, 1994
- 'Culture, Communication "Technology" and Canadian Policy. The 1986
  Southam Lecture.' *Canadian Journal of Communication* 12/2 (1986): 1–20
- *Dependency Road: Communications, Capitalism, Consciousness, and Canada.*
  Norwood, NJ: Ablex, 1981
- 'Foreword.' In Robert E. Babe, *Cable Television and Telecommuniclations in
  Canada.* East Lansing, MI: Bureau of Business and Economic Research,
  Michigan State University, 1975
- 'Reality as Presented by Television.' First published in *The Public Opinion
  Quarterly* 18/2 (Summer 1954): 143–56; reprinted in *Counterclockwise: Per-
  spectives on Communication*, ed. Thomas Guback, 61–74. Boulder, CO:
  Westview, 1994
- *The Relevance of United States Legislative-Regulatory Experience to the Canadian
  Telecommunications Situation, a Study for the Telecommission, Department of
  Communications.* Ottawa: Information Canada, 1971
- 'Review Article, One Canadian Perspective: *Clear Across Australia.*'
  Prometheus 3/2 (December 1985): 431–53.
- *The Structure and Policy of Electronic Communication.* Urbana: University of
  Illinois, 1957
- 'Theory about Communication and Information.' Unpublished draft manu-
  script, dated 1 May 1991
Smythe, Dallas W., and Tran Van Dinh. 'On Critical and Administrative

Research: A New Critical Analysis.' *Journal of Communication* 33/3 (Fall 1983): 117–27

Spry, Graham. 'Canada: Notes on Two Ideas of Nation in Confrontation.' *Journal of Contemporary History* 6/2 (July 1971): 173–96

– 'Canada, the United Nations Emergency Force, and the Commonwealth.' *International Affairs* 33/3 (July 1957): 289–300

– 'The Canadian Broadcasting Corpopration, 1936–1961.' *Canadian Communications* 2/1 (Autumn 1961): 1–13

– 'A Canadian Looks at the Commonwealth.' *CORONA* 12/8 (August 1960): 293–5

– 'A Case for Nationalized Broadcasting.' *Queen's Quarterly* 37/4 (Winter 1931): 151–69

– 'The Costs of Canadian Broadcasting.' *Queen's Quarterly* 68/4 (Winter 1961): 503–13

– 'Culture and Entropy: A Lay View of Broadcasting.' Paper presented to the Royal Society of Canada, Ottawa, Ontario, March 1972; published in *Studies in Canadian Communications*, ed. Gertrude Joch Robinson and Donald F. Theall, 89–112, Montreal: McGill University Graduate Program in Communications, 1974

– 'The Decline and Fall of Canadian Broadcasting.' *Queen's Quarterly* 68/2 (1961): 213–25

– 'Economic Changes in the Canadian Prairie Provinces.' *International Affairs* 29/3 (1953): 309–15

– 'The Fall of Constantinople – 1453.' *Middle Eastern Affairs* 4/6, 7 (June/July 1953): 201–17

– 'French Canada and Canadian Federation.' Privately circulated, 1966

– 'India and Self-Government.' In *The United Nations: Today and Tomorrow,* Proceedings from the Canadian Institute of Public Affairs Conference, Lake Couchiching, Ontario, 21–8 August, 1943, ed. Violet Anderson, 68–82. 1943

– 'One Nation, Two Cultures.' In *The Canadian Nation*, 14–23. Ottawa: Association of Canadian Clubs, 1929

– 'Public Policy and Private Pressures: The Canadian Radio League, 1930–1936, and Countervailing Power.' In *On Canada: Essays in Honour of Frank Underhill*, 24–36. Toronto: University of Toronto Press, 1971

Spry, Irene. 'The Great Transformation: The Disappearance of the Commons in Western Canada.' In *Man and Nature on the Prairies*, ed. Richard Allen, 21–45. Regina: Canadian Plains Research Centre, 1976; revised as 'The Tragedy of the Loss of the Commons in Western Canada.' In *As Long as the*

Sun Shines and Water Flows, ed. Ian A.L. Getty and Antoine S. Lussier, 203–28. Vancouver: University of British Columbia Press, 1983

– 'Hydro-Electric Power.'In *Encyclopedia Canadiana*, vol. 5, 211–22. Toronto: Grolier Society of Canada, 1958

– 'Introduction.' In *The Papers of the Palliser Expedition, 1857–1860*, ed. Irene M. Spry, xv–cxxxviii. Toronto: The Champlain Society, 1968

– 'A Journey "Down North" to Great Bear Lake and the Yukon in 1935.' *The Musk-Ox* 31 (1982): 73–8

– 'Non-Renewable Resources.' In *Physical and Technological Constraints*. Volume 2 of *The Conserver Society Project*, Kimon Valiskakis, General Editor, 1–76. Montreal: Gamma, 1976

– 'Overhead Costs, Rigidities of Productive Capacity and the Price System.' In *Culture, Communication and Dependency: The Tradition of H.A. Innis*, ed. W.H. Melody, Liora Salter, and Paul Heyer 155–66. Norwood, NJ: Ablex, 1981

– *The Palliser Expedition: An Account of John Palliser's British North American Expedition, 1857–1960*. Toronto: Macmillan, 1963

– ed. *The Papers of The Palliser Expedition, 1857–1860*. Toronto: The Champlain Society, 1968

– 'Power Commissions, Provincial.' *Encyclopedia Canadiana*, vol. 8, 288–92. Toronto: Grolier Society of Canada, 1958

– 'The "Private Adventurers" of Rupert's Land.' In *Developing West*, ed. John E. Foster, 49–70. Edmonton: University of Alberta Press, 1983

– 'The Prospects for Leisure in a Conserver Society.' In *Recreation and Leisure: Issues in an Era of Change*, ed. Thomas L. Goodale and Peter A. Will, 141–53. Philadelphia: Venture, 1980

– 'Water Power.' *Encyclopedia Canadiana*, vol. 10, 273–90. Toronto: Grolier Society of Canada, 1958

Staines, David. 'Introduction.' In *The Canadian Imagination: Dimensions of a Literary Culture*, ed. David Staines, 1–21. Cambridge, MA: Harvard University Press, 1977

Stamps, Judith. *Unthinking Modernity: Innis, McLuhan and the Frankfurt School*. Montreal and Kingston: McGill-Queen's University Press, 1995

Stearn, Gerald Emanuel, ed. *McLuhan: Hot and Cool*. 1967. Reprint, New York: Signet, 1969.

Steed, Judy. 'Noted Canadian Philosopher Lamented Technology Growth – Obituary.' *Globe and Mail*, 28 September 1988, A11

Stigler, George. 'The Economics of Information.' *Journal of Political Economy* 69/3 (1968); reprinted in *The Organization of Industry*, 171–90. Homewood, IL: Irwin, 1960

– 'Information in the Labor Market.' *Journal of Political Economy* 70/5 (October

1962); reprinted in *The Organization of Industry*, 191–207. Homewood, IL: Irwin, 1960

Stigler, George, and Gary Becker. 'De Gustibus Non Est Disputandum.' *American Economic Review* 67/2 (1977): 75–90

Strangelove, Michael. 'Collective Memory and the Social Control of Thought: Mass Media, Cyberspace and the Globalization of Symbols.' PhD dissertation, University of Ottawa, 1997

Suzuki, David, with Amanda McConnell. *The Sacred Balance: Rediscovering Our Place in Nature.* Vancouver: Douglas and McIntyre, 1997

Svacek, Victor. 'Crawford Brough Macpherson: A Bibliography.' In *Powers Possession and Freedom: Essays in Honour of C.B. Macpherson*, ed. Alkis Kontos, 167–78. Toronto: University of Toronto Press, 1979

Tawney, R.H. *Religion and the Rise of Capitalism: A Historical Study.* 1926. Reprint, New York: Mentor, 1954

Taylor, Charles. *Radical Tories: The Conservative Tradition in Canada.* Toronto: House of Anansi, 1982

Theall, Donald. 'Communication Theory and Marginal Culture: The Socio-Aesthetic Dimensions of Communication Study.' In *Studies in Canadian Communications*, ed. Gertrude Joch Robinson and Donald F. Theall, 7–26. Montreal: Graduate Program in Communications, McGill University, 1975

– 'Explorations in Communications Since Innis.' In *Culture, Communication and Dependency: The Tradition of H.A. Innis*, ed. William Melody, Liora Salter, and Paul Heyer, 225–34. Norwood, NJ: Ablex, 1981

– *The Medium Is the Rear View Mirror: Understanding McLuhan.* Montreal and Kingston: McGill-Queen's University Press, 1971

Theall, Donald F., and Joan B. Theall. 'John Grierson on Media, Film and History.' In *Studies in Canadian Communications*, ed. Gertrude Joch Robinson and Donald F. Theall, 113–29. Montreal: Graduate Program in Communications, McGill University, 1975

Toffler, Alvin. *The Third Wave.* New York: Bantam, 1981

Tremblay, Gaetan.'Some Reflections on the Theoretical Discourse on Communications in Quebec and Canada.' *Canadian Journal of Communication* 8/1 (1981): 14–23

Umar, Yusuf, ed. *George Grant and the Future of Canada.* Calgary: University of Calgary Press, 1992

United States. Federal Communications Commission. *Public Service Responsibility of Broadcast Licensees.* First published 7 March 1946; reprinted in *Documents of American Broadcasting*, ed. Frank J. Kahn, 125–206. New York: Appleton-Century-Crofts, 1968

Veblen, Thorstein. 'Mr. Cummings's Strictures on "The Theory of the Leisure

Class."' First published in *Journal of Political Economy* 8 (December 1899);
reprinted in *Essays on Our Changing Order*, 16–31. New York: Augustus M.
Kelley, 1964

– *The Theory of the Leisure Class*. 1899. Reprint, New York: New American
Library, 1953

Wasko, Janet, Vincent Mosco, and Manjanath Pendakur, eds. *Illuminating the
Blindspots: Essays Honoring Dallas W. Smythe*. Norwood, NJ: Ablex, 1993

Watson, A. John. 'Harold Innis and Classical Scholarship.' *Journal of Canadian
Studies* 12/5 (Winter 1977): 45–61

Webster, Frank. *Theories of the Information Society*. London: Routledge, 1995

Weir, E. Austin. *The Struggle for National Broadcasting in Canada*. Toronto:
McClelland and Stewart, 1965

Wernick, Andrew. 'The Post-Innisian Significance of Innis.' *Journal of Political
and Social Theory* 10/ 1–2 (1986): 128–50

Westfall, William. 'The Ambivalent Verdict: Harold Innis and Canadian
History.' In *Culture, Communication, and Dependency: The Tradition of H.A.
Innis*, ed. William H. Melody, Liora Salter, and Paul Heyer, 37–51. Norwood,
NJ: Ablex, 1981

Whitehead, Alfred North. *Science and the Modern World*. New York: Macmillan,
1926

Williams, Raymond. 'Advertising: The Magic System.' In *Problems in Materialism and Culture*, 170–95. London: Verso, 1980

– *Communications*. 1962. Reprint, Harmondsworth: Penguin, 1971

– 'Culture and Technology. 'In *The Year 2000*, 128–52. New York: Pantheon,
1983

– 'Democracy, Old and New.' In *The Year 2000*, 102–27. New York: Pantheon,
1983

– *Technology and Cultural Form*. Glasgow: William Collins Sons, 1974

Willmott, Glenn. *McLuhan, Or Modernism in Reverse*, Toronto: University of
Toronto Press, 1996

Winks, Robin W. 'Foreword.' In Harold A. Innis, *The Fur Trade in Canada*,
based on the Revised Edition prepared by S.D. Clark and W.T. Easterbrook,
vii–xv. Toronto: University of Toronto Press, 1962

Winner, Langdon. *Autonomous Technology: Technics-out-of-Control as a Theme in
Political Thought*. Cambridge, MA: MIT Press, 1977

Winseck, Dwayne. *Reconvergence: A Political Economy of Telecommunications in
Canada*. Cresskill, NJ: Hampton, 1998

Winter, James. *Common Cents: Media Portrayal of the Gulf War and Other Events*.
Montreal: Black Rose, 1992

– *Democracy's Oxygen: How Corporations Control the News.* Montreal: Black Rose, 1997

Winter, James P., and Irving Goldman, 1989), 'Comparing the Early and Late McLuhan to Innis's Political Discourse.' *Canadian Journal of Communication,* 14/4 & 5, special issue (December 1989): 92–100

Wolfe, Tom. *The Video McLuhan.* Vol. 1: *1958–1964. produced by Stephanie McLuhan. VH03765, 1996*

INDEX